MODERN
POLITICAL
IDEOLOGIES

To students past and present who have argued and
disagreed

MODERN POLITICAL IDEOLOGIES

Andrew Vincent

BLACKWELL
Oxford UK & Cambridge USA

First published 1992
Reprinted 1993

Blackwell Publishers
108 Cowley Road
Oxford OX4 1JF
UK

238 Main Street
Suite 501
Cambridge
MA 02142
USA

British Library Cataloguing-in-Publication Data
A CIP catalogue record for this book is available from the British Library.

Library of Congress Cataloging-in-Publication Data
A CIP catalogue record for this book is available from the Library of Congress.
ISBNs: 0 631 16451 0 (hbk.); 0 631 16452 9 (pbk.).

Typeset in 10 on 11½ pt Sabon
by Setrite Typesetters Ltd.
Printed in Great Britain by T.J. Press (Padstow) Ltd., Padstow, Cornwall

This book is printed on acid-free paper.

I have come to believe that the whole world is an enigma, a harmless enigma that is made terrible by our own mad attempt to interpret it as though it had an underlying truth.
Umberto Eco, *Foucault's Pendulum*

CONTENTS

PREFACE

This book has arisen from a long-standing undergraduate course on ideologies. Generations of students have contributed, wittingly or unwittingly, enriching many hours of discussion with moments of critical insight and humour. In fact, if there is one useful qualification for studying ideologies it is humour and, possibly, a sense of the absurd. In constructing the final text I have drawn unmercifully upon the goodwill, time, patience and expertise of my academic friends and colleagues. In an increasingly fraught academic environment I realize that my debt to them is very great indeed. I would particularly like to thank Gino Bedani who has been a great help and given generously of his time and clear judgement. I would also like to thank Lewis Allan, Robin Attfield, Andrew Belsey, Stefan Berger, David Boucher, Andy Dobson, Mark Donovan, Graeme Duncan, Diana Coole, Sara Delamont, Andrew Edgar, Ian Forbes, Michael George, Bruce Haddock, David Hanley, David Jackson, Roy Jones and Barry Jones, for their reading and commentary upon chapters. They have enabled me to avoid many errors and have also helped to improve the text. Thanks are also due to my wife Mary and to my daughters Lisa and Rachael for help with indexing and proofreading. The final responsibility for the structure and arguments of the book is, of course, mine alone.

While this book has been designed to work *with* a course on ideologies, it is in no way a substitute for doing the reading. It provides some introductory material on the nature of ideologies and engages in comparative discussion of ideas, texts and thinkers. If the student tries to read at least some of the works mentioned in the course of the discussion, then this book should act as a complementary foil for thinking about ideologies.

Despite its more overt commitment to courses on ideologies, there are also a number of arguments which run through the book. These arguments widen the scope of the study and offer a slightly broader interpretation of the nature of ideologies themselves. It is therefore intended that *Modern Political Ideologies* could be read and used on a number of levels.

Andrew Vincent
University of Wales, Cardiff

1
THE NATURE OF IDEOLOGY

This first chapter deals with three issues: first, a short historical sketch of the concept of ideology; second, my own particular use of the concept of ideology is outlined; finally, and briefly, a synopsis of the structure of the book will be given.

This is not a book about the concept of ideology in its own right. It is a book about ideologies. However, it is impossible simply to leap into this task without saying something about the concept of ideology, partly because there is so much controversy here. The history of the concept of ideology is comparatively short — approximately two hundred years old — but complex. Like most substantive 'ideologies', the word 'ideology' dates from the French Revolution era of the 1790s. For the sake of brevity and clarity, the history will be broken down into a number of stages which have given rise to different senses. The discussion will begin with the inception of the word by the French philosopher Antoine Destutt de Tracy in the 1790s. It will move to Marx's usage in the 1840s and the ambiguous Marxist legacy into this century, then turn to the uses of the term in the 'end of ideology' movement of the 1950s. Finally, some of the more recent discussions of the term will be summarized.

The term ideology was first coined between 1796 and 1798 by Antoine Destutt de Tracy in papers read in instalments to the National Institute in Paris under the title *Mémoire sur la faculté de penser*. His book entitled *The Elements of Ideology* was published later (1800–15). To some extent it is true that Tracy would probably now be a fairly obscure figure but for his association with the word 'ideology'. Oddly, there is no one unequivocal sense of the concept deriving from Tracy. In fact, four uses of the term can be discerned. First, there was Tracy's original explicit use to designate a new empirical science of ideas; second, the term came to denote an affiliation to a form of secular liberal republicanism; third, it took on a pejorative connotation implying intellectual and practical sterility as well as dangerous radicalism; finally, and most tenuously, it came in a limited sphere to denote 'political doctrine' in general. All these four senses moved into political currency between 1800 and 1830.

The word 'ideology' was a neologism compounded from the Greek terms *eidos* and *logos*. It can be defined as a 'science of ideas'.[1] Tracy wanted a new term for a new science. He rejected the terms *métaphysique* and *psychologie* as inadequate. For Tracy, the discipline of 'metaphysics' was misleading and discredited; 'psychology' also implied a science or knowledge of the soul, which could give a false, almost religious, impression. Tracy was both deeply anti-clerical and a materialist. Through the 1790s and early 1800s Tracy was involved in bitter infighting with the Catholic Church, particularly over the control of education. Thus any term to describe his science had to be distinct from any taint of religion. It is also worth noting that the term ideology more or less coincides with the early use of the term 'social science' (*la science sociale*). The latter term assumed, like ideology, an Enlightenment optimism in grasping and controlling, by reason, the laws governing social life for the greater happiness and improvement of human life.

Like many of the French Enlightenment *philosophes* and Encyclopaedist thinkers, Tracy believed that all areas of human experience, many of which had previously been examined in terms of theology, should now be examined by reason. The science of ideas was to investigate the natural origin of ideas. It proposed a precise knowledge of the causes of the generation of ideas from sensations. Innate ideas were rejected: ideas were all modified sensations. Tracy described ideology as a branch of zoology, indicating that the human intellect had a physiological basis. In the same rigorous empiricist vein as Bacon, Descartes, Newton, Lavoisier and Condillac, Tracy proposed that the contents of such analyses should be carefully tabulated and detailed in terms of scientific procedures. Newton was particularly esteemed by Tracy. As one writer remarked, 'According to Tracy, Newton was the great theoretical systematizer of previous empirical research, the man who was able to demonstrate that all facts now and in the future, followed the patterns specified by a few simple laws'.[2] Tracy's examination of the way in which ideas were generated, conceived and related to each other (in sum, the 'science of ideas') might now be described as empirical psychology. In fact, one Tracy scholar remarks that he was a 'methodological precursor of behaviouralist approaches to the human sciences'.[3] For Tracy, ideology was *la théorie des théories*. It was the queen of the sciences since it necessarily preceded all other sciences which of necessity utilized 'ideas'.

Tracy, and those who admired his work, believed that such a science of ideas could have an immense impact, on education particularly. If the origin of ideas was understood, then it could be used with great benefit in enlightened education. It could diagnose the roots of human ignorance. It was potentially the foundation for a rational progressive society. Tracy and others thus advocated vigorously the social, political and educative uses of ideology. Between 1799 and 1800, under the Directory, Tracy was appointed Councillor of Public Instruction and issued circulars to schools stressing the role of 'ideology' in the curriculum.[4] There was also the attempt, as in Bentham, to establish a 'science of legislation'. In pursuing these objectives Tracy and the other *idéologues* became associated with a secular republican liberalism, stressing representative government by an enlightened elite. In this sense, ideology became, in the public perception, not so much an 'empirical science' as the political doctrine of a group of propertied liberal intellectuals.[5] Hence, subtly, a second sense of ideology became prevalent – ideology became associated with a political doctrine, although of a very specific form.

Another lasting sense of the term ideology derived from the political associations of Tracy and his compatriots. One of the early and brief honorary members of the *idéologues* was Napoleon Bonaparte. He appears to have had a stormy and ultimately deeply hostile relation to the *idéologues*, later, when in power and pursuing his own autocratic ambitions, accusing them of fomenting political unrest. Bonaparte referred to them as individuals who wished to reform the world simply in their heads, armchair metaphysicians with little or no political acumen. He denounced them before the Council of State in February 1801 as 'windbags', who none the less were trying to undermine political authority. Once Bonaparte had re-established his credibility with the Catholic Church in a Concordat of 1802, he also predictably denounced the *idéologues* as a 'College of Atheists'. Madame de Staël remarked at this time that Bonaparte seemed to suffer from 'ideophobia'.[6] This pejorative use of ideology – indicating intellectual sterility, practical ineptitude, and, more particularly, dangerous political sentiments – tended to stick. The conservative, restoration and royalist circles in France focused critically on the *idéologues* in the latter use, denouncing the republication of Tracy's *Elements* in 1829 as part of the attempt to overthrow 'the ancient confraternity of throne and altar'.[7] One final sense of the term began to glimmer through here. If ideology was partially divorced from the 'science of ideas' of Tracy, Condillac and the sensationalist school, and became associated, more importantly, with a political doctrine (secular liberal republicanism initially), it was but a short step to identifying the royalist critics as espousing another political doctrine, which could equally be described as an 'ideology'. Ideology thus became, in a limited sphere in France, equivalent to 'a political doctrine'. The other senses of ideology co-existed with this latter view.

It remains perennially puzzling as to why Marx chose to use the term ideology. In his early writings he alluded to Tracy in two senses. First, he noted, as a simple historical observation, the existence of a group of thinkers, namely, the *idéologues*. Tracy, as a key member of this group, is mentioned as a minor vulgar bourgeois liberal political economist. In consequence, there are passing references to the fourth volume of Tracy's *Elements*, the *Traité d'économie politique*. Second, Marx employed the concept in the title of his early work, *The German Ideology* – unpublished during his lifetime – as a more pejorative label referring to those (particularly the young Hegelian group) who 'interpret' the world philosophically, but do not appear to be able change it. Marx might also have found some parallels between the young Hegelians and Tracy, given the emphasis in both on 'ideas'. Put loosely, Tracy's thinking contained some suggestions of 'idealist' philosophy.

Marx was obviously aware of something of the initial use of the term ideology, indicating a science of ideas. However, he paid scant attention to this. The only sense he utilized, at first, was Bonaparte's pejorative use. Crudely, he too considered the young Hegelians as 'windbags' and armchair metaphysicians. In addition, he regarded both the *idéologues* and Hegelians as vulgar bourgeois liberals. This idea moves quite definitely away from the initial French royalist sense where the liberalism of the *idéologues* was regarded as a dangerous reforming radicalism.

Marx adds, though, in an unsystematic way, further dimensions to the meaning of the term, which take it into a different realm. In Marx's work, ideology denotes not only practical ineffectiveness but also illusion and loss of reality. More importantly, it becomes associated with the division of labour in society, with collective groups called classes, and most significantly with the domination and power of certain classes. Some aspects of this extension, specifically the illusory aspect, were implicit in Bonaparte's pejorative use of the term, but it was not made fully explicit until Marx. Paradoxically, something of the *idéologues*' use remains in Marx, namely, the belief that societies can be rationally and scientifically interpreted and that humanity is progressing towards some form of rational social, economic and political enlightenment. To grasp Marx's use it is necessary to unpack briefly the materialist theory in which it is couched.

Although it is an ambiguous truism, Marx is essentially a materialist thinker of a particular type. What is of primary importance to humans is their need to subsist. To do so they need to labour and produce. Thought is involved in this process, but it is practice-orientated and therefore of secondary import. The material human needs are primary: thought and consciousness in general enable them to be satisfied. When humans produce, they develop complex social and exchange relations with each other. Humans also produce more effectively in groups; tasks initially become separated to enable people to work more productively. Here we see the earliest forms of the division of labour.

Without outlining the whole theory, it is important to grasp that what is primary is our social and economic being. Marx has a materialist ontology.

Our consciousness is by and large explained through that ontology. Thought can both reflect and misunderstand this process. Much of the problem of the earliest 'division of labour' is that mental labour, by priests and intellectuals, was distinguished from physical labour. Intellectuals and priests tended to serve their own interests by regarding their work as superior to physical labour. They also sought the protection and patronage of the major possessing classes, those who, at a particular stage in the development of society, dominate and control the means of production, distribution and exchange. Directly, or most often indirectly, in exchange for patronage, such mental labourers gave wide-ranging intellectual justifications of an existing order, placing their intellectual benediction (in the nineteenth century) upon capitalism and the bourgeois state. They also provided solace for those who suffered from the social and economic arrangements. Such mental labourers are in essence the ideologists of a political and economic order. Yet much of their production is illusion and a distortion of reality.

It is necessary to realize that the original philosophical source of this materialist ontology (and Marx's conception of ideology) was premised on a critique of religion. The German romantic and, particularly, Hegelian understanding is important to note here. The German tradition, from Kant, Fichte and Hegel, had placed considerable emphasis on the human capacity for self-constitution. In simple terms, the human mind is involved in the structuring of the world and circumstances. It is not merely receiving sensations passively, as Tracy would have argued. In Hegel especially, this self-moulding or self-constituting activity is viewed within a historical framework. Consciousness not only constitutes much of what we call reality, it does so in a slowly changing historical process. Consciousness changes and constitutes reality differently over historical time. The young Hegelians, particularly Ludwig Feuerbach, accused Hegel of dwelling too much upon mind in general, on consciousness or on some notion of spirit in history. It is not 'general mind' or spirit which constitutes itself, but rather it is the individual sensuous human being with physical needs who constitutes reality.

As Feuerbach noted in a famous phrase, 'all theology is anthropology'. Humans create God, spirit or history in their own image. Marx adapted this argument to his own ends. It is labouring productive humans, in particular economic classes, at particular stages of history (determined by economic needs and modes of production), who constitute the world. However, this constitution can be a distorted image. Throughout history, intellectuals have produced a multitude of such distortions which obscure the basic domination and exploitation of one class by another. In one reading, given a particular stage of society, mode of production and configuration of classes, it might be the most accurate account that could be given, yet it is still a distortion. The centrality of economic activity to this process meant that Marx subtly combined Germanic philosophical concerns with both British political economy and French materialism.

Subsequently Marxism, almost before the end of the nineteenth century, came under certain pressures and diverse interpretations on the subject of ideology. A number of questions arose. In his early writings Marx appeared to be contrasting ideology (as an illusion) to reality as practice – a form of philosophical materialist ontology. Liberal capitalism was in an equivalent position to religion as a distortion of the human essence. Later this contrast became ideology (as distortion) as against science (as truth or knowledge). Alienation in Marx's early writings became, in the later writings, expropriation of surplus value and economic exploitation. However, it was not clear whether Marx was using science in the sense of 'natural science' or in the older German sense of *Wissenschaft* (a connected body of systematic knowledge). Some Marxists this century refer to the change that marked these two dimensions as the 'epistemological break' in Marx, differentiating the young from the mature Marx. Even within these two dimensions it is not clear as to what comes under the rubric of ideology. In some writings, Marx suggested that 'consciousness in general', including every aspect of human endeavour, namely art and natural science, are ideology. In others, it appears as though he was thinking only of social, political and economic ideas which uphold and distort a political and economic structure. In addition, the early reference that Marx made in *The German Ideology* to the *camera obscura* image was not particularly helpful. Marx writes of ideology's view of human consciousness being like the *camera obscura*, where the world appears inverted. The image is deeply mechanistic, rigid, and presents a very misleading conception, which Marx himself did not really accept.

Marx also did not make clear the precise relation between ideas (often referred to as superstructure) and the economic base. At some points this appears as a case of a clear 'one-way' determinism, namely, the base determines the superstructure. Yet again, Marx never clarifies what he means by the word 'determine'. For example, it is not obvious whether 'determine' means that A causes B, affects B, or sets parameters to B. At other points, this relation changes into symbiotic or mutually affective relations between ideology and the economic base. Many qualifying letters from Engels are usually discussed at this point to justify this latter view.[8]

The subsequent fate of the Marxist notion of ideology breaks down into a number of contradictory components. The Second International, dominated by the German SPD and under the tutelage of Engels, took up the crude distinction between Marxist science and bourgeois ideology. Engels in particular coined the now notorious term 'false-consciousness' for ideology, something that Marx did not do with any awareness. The idea of true and false consciousness appears as too stark for Marx, at least in his more sensitive moments.[9]

Lenin introduced another confusing dimension into ideology in works like *What Is to Be Done?*. The pejorative connotations are suddenly stripped away and spin into the void. Lenin speaks confidently of socialism *being* an ideology, combating, in the general class struggle, bourgeois ideology. Lenin saw socialist ideology as a weapon of class struggle. This use comes close to that in France in the 1830s, and also to some contemporary usage, namely, in seeing all political doctrines *per se* as ideology. It certainly bears little resemblance to Engel's notion of 'false-consciousness' or the laboured distinction of Marxist science against ideology.

The problem of ideology in Marxism is further complicated when we move into the twentieth century. With writers like Lukács, dialectical materialism was accepted as an ideology, though it was seen, casuistically, as more scientific than bourgeois ideology. Also, for Lukács, ideology was more deeply embedded in social, economic and political life than Lenin had appreciated. In Antonio Gramsci we see the most sophisticated, if equivocal, treatment of ideology. For Gramsci, domination under capitalism is not simply achieved by coercion, but subtly through the hegemony of ideas. The ideology of the ruling class becomes vulgarized into the common sense of the average citizen. Power is not just crude legal or physical coercion but domination of language, morality, culture and common sense. The masses are quelled and co-opted by their internalization of ideational domination. The hegemonic ideas become, in fact, the actual experiences of the subordinate classes. Traditional intellectuals construct this complex hegemonic apparatus. Bourgeois hegemony moulds the personal convictions, norms and aspirations of the proletariat. Gramsci thus called for a struggle at the level of ideology. Organic intellectuals situated within the proletariat should combat this by constructing a counter-hegemony to traditional intellectuals upholding bourgeois hegemony.

In Gramsci we find refinements and qualifications to the Marxist science and ideology thesis (a science which Gramsci dismissed with the curt term 'economism'); dialectical materialism; simple-minded determinism; the false-consciousness thesis and, finally, the idea of socialist ideology. In Gramsci, ideology appears to be more generally applicable to political doctrine, although it is deeply embedded in all language and culture. Despite the subtlety of Gramsci's approach it still asserted, behind complex and elusive argumentation, the 'truth' of Marxism as against other approaches. In this sense, the old distinctions might be said to be reappearing, but in a transformed apparel. Subsequently these apparels have altered quite markedly, whether in the *Ideologiekritik* of the Frankfurt Marxists or in the structuralism of Louis Althusser. One prevailing theme has remained, however: the intricate connection between ideology, power and domination.

One of Lukács' students, who utilized the Marxian terminology from within, but completely transformed its intellectual status, was Karl Mannheim. Mannheim's *Ideology and Utopia* (1929) can be used to take the discussion on to later phases of the concept of ideology. Mannheim's theory will not be discussed here, but one important question in Mannheim needs consideration. Paul Ricoeur calls it 'Mannheim's paradox'. Ricoeur formulates this paradox in the following question: 'What is the epistemological status of discourse about ideology if all discourse is ideological?'.[10] The question is asking Marx to justify his own thought in relation to his suppositions concerning ideology. The effect of following through the logic of the question is devastating on one level.

In the course of trying to extend Marx's insights, Mannheim tried to formulate a comprehensive theory of ideology. There are six main components to it. The first element need not detain us, despite its intrinsic interest. Mannheim examined both ideologies and utopias. Ideologies, in the main, act to defend a particular established order, although they can in some circumstances be made subversive. Utopias (which, unlike Marx, Mannheim suggests are equally as important for social life as ideologies) tend to be forward-looking and a challenge to existing social reality, suggesting wide-scale change.

Mannheim's notion of ideology distinguished between *particular* and *total* conceptions. The particular conception approached an 'individual', examining their psychology and personal interests, often in a polemical manner, in order to show the weakness of an opponent's position. The total idea approached ideology in terms of the assumptions of a complete 'world-view' of a collective culture and, possibly, an historical epoch. In other words, it dealt with a total structure of thought. In Mannheim's view, Marx had, comparative to much previous social theory, fused these two elements and shown that the expressions of individuals needed unmasking in order to unpack the total ideology of a culture. It was precisely at this point that Mannheim asked Marx to justify his own ideas in Marxist terms, something that Marx would have found difficult to do. As Mannheim remarked:

> it is hardly possible to avoid this general formulation of the total conception of ideology, according to which the thought of all parties in all epochs is of an ideological character. There is scarcely a single intellectual position, and Marxism furnishes no exception to this rule, which has not changed through history ... It should not be too difficult for a Marxist to recognize their social basis.[11]

This question led Mannheim on to the third element of his theory. If Marxism imploded in this inquiry, then we still should not abandon its insights into ideology. Rather, we should become self-conscious concerning our own ideological beliefs, life-expressions and their historical situation so preserving Marx's insights within a disciplined academic frame. Mannheim called this new academic frame the 'sociology of knowledge' − examining knowledge and every 'knower' in a particular social and historical context. As he remarked on the Marxist notion of ideology: 'What was once the intellectual armament of a party is transformed into a method of research in social and intellectual history'.[12]

Mannheim claimed, fourthly, that his theory was not relativistic. Relativism was drawn distinct from what he called relationism. Many commentators suggest that this distinction does not really work.[13] Mannheim suggested that whereas relativism was linked with a static, ahistorical notion of truth, relationism 'takes account of the relational as distinct from the merely relative character of all historical knowledge'.[14] In relationism, knowledge and epistemology were not separated from an historical or social context (as appears to be the suppressed premise of relativism). Fifth, Mannheim makes further elaborate additions to the above theory, distinguishing, under the rubric of a 'relational total conception of ideology', non-evaluative and evaluative approaches. For Mannheim, the latter 'evaluative' approach took a full self-conscious account of the situation of both the object studied and of the observer, and was thus the most appropriate method for the sociology of knowledge. Finally, and probably most controversially, Mannheim suggested that this new discipline could only properly be studied by relatively classless individuals, who were both intelligent and capable of such self-analysis. He calls these, following the terminology of Alfred Weber, the *freischwebende Intelligenz* (the socially-unattached intelligentsia).[15]

Mannheim has met with a very mixed, usually very critical response, some totally dismissive of it, others at least appreciating his courage in facing the problematic issues of historical thought. His separation of relativism and relationism is not really adequately explained. In addition, the role of the intelligentsia is presented in only a very sketchy format. Finally, there are unexplained elements in his theory: was he suggesting that all thought, including science and mathematics, was socially and historically relative? This remains unclear. Also, by using the highly academic title 'sociology of knowledge', was he trying, despite the general thrust of the theory, to smuggle in a more objectivist 'social scientific' account, with all its subtle implications of a neutral observation language? There is a sense in which this latter criticism is partially valid and appears to turn the circle fully on Mannheim. We find him paying court to the very paradigm of truth which he has gone out his way to reject.

In another, rather oblique sense Mannheim paves the way for the next phase of the concept which appears in the post-1945 era, often titled the 'end of ideology'.[16] The gradual assimilation of active political ideology into the sanitized academic discipline of sociology not only means the loss of earthy, emotive ideological debate, but also the potential loss of utopias or forward-looking values. Political life becomes absorbed into a closely reasoned social science, conducted by expert intellectuals.

The 'end of ideology' school was a product and phase largely of the

1950s and the Cold War era, although the basic premises of the movement would still be upheld by many who regard themselves as social and political scientists. Recently, some have been somewhat precipitate in anticipating its triumphant vindication in the turbulent late 1980s with the collapse of Eastern European communism and the turn to liberal market economies.[17] This particular debate appeared first in the regions of the American social science establishment, although it was not without relation to certain developments in European thought. It has parallels not only with the 'death of political theory' movement and 'Butskellism' in Britain, but also with the more sinister McCarthyite anti-communist purges in the USA.

It is worth noting that this argument coincided with a number of different but resonant intellectual positions of the time. We have already encountered the movement in philosophy (specifically that influenced by logical positivism) which claimed that classical political theory (or ideology in some minds) was dead. Sceptical conceptual analysis and logic remained supreme. Ideology was equivalent, in some perceptions, to morality or aesthetics in premising itself on 'values'. In the initial crude stages of the argument such values, as distinct from facts, were seen as simply expressions of subjective emotion with no rational substance.

In a very different philosophical format the influential theorist Michael Oakeshott, in books like *Rationalism in Politics*, drew a distinction between a traditionalist and ideological stance in politics. The philosophical roots to this distinction need not concern us. The basic point was that ideology represented a simplification, abstraction, and what Oakeshott calls an 'abridgement' of social reality. Ideologists selected, and consequently distorted, a much more complex social reality. Unsurprisingly (given the casuistical character of much twentieth-century ideological discussion) the approach which is portrayed as non-ideological, philosophical and more academic, and which also appreciates the subtle complexity of the totality of social reality, is a form of conservatism.[18] Oakeshott's basic distinction appears, with some qualifications, in the work of a number of more recent writers in the 1980s.[19]

Another important argument which resonated with the 'end of ideology' was the assertion that 'politics' was distinct from ideology. Ideology denoted a totalitarian mentality which prevented all political discussion other than on its own content. Ideology is distinct from a pluralist, free, tolerant and rational society, where 'politics' takes place. Writers as diverse as Ralph Dahrendorf, J. L. Talmon, Bernard Crick, Hannah Arendt, Karl Popper and Raymond Aron, in their different ways, all spoke of 'totalizing ideology' and closed societies (fascism and communism), as distinct from tolerant civil politics and open societies. Ideology, in this reading, becomes an intolerant, unfree and limited perspective in comparison to forms of non-ideological, open and tolerant politics.

Ken Minogue's *Alien Powers: The Pure Theory of Ideology* (1986), reflects in some ways both the above tendencies. The book still slays Cold War totalitarian ideological dragons in the name of a more open society, but also to some degree in the name of philosophical and academic subtlety, maintaining that the ideologist 'abridges' and constricts the complexities and intricacies of the Oakeshottian social world into an ideological straitjacket. Minogue's basic argument is that ideology is a comparatively new form of thought, originating in the nineteenth century. Ideologies (by which he appears to mean all else apart from liberalism, conservatism and social democracy) exist in a closed world where evil is identified as distinct from human nature. The evil is the dehumanizer. Each ideology has its external evil (capitalism, totalitarianism or patriarchalism). These are the 'alien powers' which have to be slain by the ideologist. Liberation and perfection will come through revolution against the alien power. Ideologists, for Minogue, intrinsically dislike individualism, pluralism and the liberal society; in short, they have a distaste for modernity. They are part of a peculiar self-loathing of Western civilization that is characteristic of some intellectuals. Again, unsurprisingly, Minogue's argument turns on the supposition (which is slightly different to Oakeshott's) that the sophisticated and non-ideological stance is a form of updated classical liberalism.

The initial impetus to the mainly American form of the 'end of ideology' derived from three main sources. First, there was clear belief in the 1950s among a generation that had lived through the 1930s and 1940s – with the wars, Gulags, show trials, Nazism, Jewish pogroms, Stalinism – that ideological politics was a set of dangerous delusions. These apparent delusions focused on Marxism-Leninism in the Cold War period. It was thus accepted that ideological politics was at the root of much of the mass of pain, misery and warfare of the mid-twentieth century. Some of the writers of the 1950s were in fact Jewish intellectuals who reflected with deep uneasiness on the fate of the Jews under ideological dogmas in the 1930s and 1940s. Active ideology appeals to the Don Quixote of politics, tilting at imaginary evil giants.

Second, in spite of the fact that ideologies serve a function in developing immature societies, it was held that in industrialized democratic societies they no longer served anything more than a decorative role. Consensus on basic aims was agreed. Most of the major parties in industrialized societies had achieved, in the welfare, mixed economy structure, the majority of their reformist aims. The Left had accepted the dangers of excessive state power and the Right had accepted the necessity of the welfare state and the rights of working people. Consensus and convergence of political aims were seen in many industrialized countries. As Seymour Martin Lipset remarked, 'This very triumph of the democratic social revolution of the West ends domestic politics for those intellectuals who must have ideologies or utopias to motivate them to political action'.[20] Basic agreement on political values had been achieved. Politics was about more peripheral pragmatic adjustment, gross national products, prices, wages, the public-sector borrowing requirement and the like. All else was gesture and froth. As Lipset commented, 'The democratic struggle will continue, but it will be a fight without ideologies, without red flags, without May Day parades.'[21]

In addition to this, the 1950s saw sustained productivity and growth in the GNPs of Britain and America. In one sense, this whole 'end of ideology' episode was a partial reflection of the improvements and growth of the Western economies in the 1950s.[22] Living standards rose and greater affluence was experienced by a larger number of citizens in America and Britain. Economic and social divisions in society were no longer seen as so pivotal. In Britain, the studies of Butler and Stokes illustrated the decline of the relevance of social class in voting behaviour. Economic prosperity, combined with the growth of the welfare state, was diminishing social, economic and political differences.[23]

Third, the 'end of ideology' coincided with the heroic age of sociology. American sociology in particular, 'offered the world the prospect of freedom from ideology, for it offered a "science" of society, in place of superstition'.[24] In some ways this was a partial return to Tracy, although the terminology had changed. In Tracy, ideology was the science to unravel superstitions. In the social sciences of the 1950s, ideology *was* the superstition which needed unravelling. Despite the altered terminology the impetus to both was remarkably similar, namely, contrasting rational scientific endeavour with superstition and intellectual flummery. The development of empirical social science demanded a value-free rigour, scepticism, empirical verification or falsification, unsullied by the emotional appeals of ideological or even normative political theory. A neo-positivism rigidly separating facts and values lurked behind these judgements.

In this total context it was therefore argued that ideology had literally ended in advanced industrialized democratic societies. Ideology was contrasted with sceptical, empirically-based social science. The latter was the path to political knowledge, the former connoted illusion. As Edward Shils commented: 'Science is not and never has been part of an ideological culture. Indeed the spirit in which science works is alien to ideology.'[25] In this case the ideological illusion was primarily Marxism itself.

There were a number of problems with the 'end of ideology' perspective. It can be contended that it was a temporary phase in industrialized societies reacting against the extremes of the war years. Populations identified themselves with material affluence, consumption and economic growth after the austerity of the inter-war years. Ideology was linked in complex ways with the memories of austerity. However, on a more general theoretical level, as Alisdair McIntyre has perceptively commented, the 'end of ideology' theorists 'failed to entertain one crucial alternative possibility:

namely, that the end-of-ideology, far from marking the end-of-ideology, was itself a key expression of the ideology of the time and place where it arose'.[26] The views propounded by the 'end of ideology' school contain certain evaluative assumptions about human nature, how rationality ought to function, the value of consensus, and details on the characteristics of a tolerant, pragmatic civil society which ought be cultivated. To try to claim that these views are premised simply on a social scientific perspective and that all else is ideology is either blindness or intellectual chicanery. The 'end of ideology' was an ideological position committed to a form of pragmatic liberalism. There was a clear failure, which permeated the 'end of ideology' perspective, to analyse liberalism as ideology.

Despite the sudden resurgence of interest in the thesis in the late 1980s, the 'end of ideology' movement is now regarded with a little more scepticism, as a phase in the development of the concept of ideology. Yet the assumptions behind the 'end of ideology' movement still, almost unconsciously, pervade much discussion and writing in the social science establishment.

The present status of ideology is immensely complex and reflects all the phases that have so far been discussed. The most pervasive theme is still the fierce contrast between 'truth and ideology'. Many who discuss ideology would claim for themselves a non-ideological neutrality. The usual claimants for such neutrality or impartiality are commonly the natural and social sciences, philosophy and political theory. The complexity is intensified when we realize that many liberals, conservatives, feminists, Marxists and so on, would claim to be on the side of science or philosophy as against ideology.

It has been particularly characteristic of the Anglo-American approach to try to maintain a distinction between science and ideology. This is the deeply entrenched attitude which came to full self-consciousness in the social sciences in the 'end of ideology' movement, although it is also implicit in the whole Enlightenment perspective. A fairly recent synoptic and very comprehensive article on the nature of ideology complains that if the notion of ideology is linked with 'belief systems' in general, then 'such a definition simply fails to discriminate between different kinds of ideas ... It fails to discriminate between science and ideology.'[27] The basic position is that for social or natural science to work, there must be some ultimate, and persistent, and objective foundation to our knowledge. This foundation is the yardstick for truth. It can be confirmed and acts as a final court of appeal. It is unaffected by our values and beliefs. The truth of our beliefs – that which enables us to characterize them as knowledge – is that they correspond as nearly as possible to this objective foundation. Rationality is also usually seen as possessing agreed and consensual universal standards, enabling us to establish correspondences. In social science, particularly, this scientific foundationalism must be kept distinct from the more subjective, emotive values and beliefs characterizing ideology. There is no external foundation to which ideologies correspond. Ideologies remain tied to 'theories'; their logic is therefore circular and cannot be tested against the world. Science, on the other hand, has a specific direction since the theory can be falsified by external foundational facts.

The problem with this view of science is that it is a very outdated and much contested one. The complex debates within the philosophy of science cannot be dealt with here. However, the work of philosophers of science like Thomas Kuhn, Paul Feyerabend, Imre Lakatos and Mary Hesse, among many others, has moved the whole discussion of the nature of science beyond the above views.[29] Science, for Kuhn, does not progress by accretion and empirical confirmation; rather, 'dominant paradigms' are seen to take over, via gestalt switches or quasi-religious conversions. Paradigms determine the nature of the puzzles to be solved and what is, or is not, regarded as good or normal science. Once a paradigm is established, the scientific community works within it for a time. One paradigm does not 'fit' better than another; instead, a different paradigm creates different criteria and a different sense of reality. The history of science is not, therefore, a slow, progressive growth but rather a series of periodic paradigm-changes which alter the whole nature of science and its perception of reality. Feyerabend, on the other hand, describes claims of the impartiality and independence of natural science as a 'fairy tale' promulgated by the scientific community, often for the social and economic benefits which accrue to such claims. He contends that every standard of scientific method, whether it be rationality, verification or falsification, has been violated in the course of major discoveries in science. There are therefore no necessary or sufficient conditions to authenticate scientific behaviour and theory choice.

Many philosophers would now contend that, in fact, scientific theories are also to a large degree circular. The theory determines the character of reality. The facts are constituted by the theories. There is, in other words, no one clear foundational external objective reality to which all theories correspond. The crucial point is that both the meaning and fruitfulness of the scientific theory are measured by its internal coherence and social acceptance by a scientific community. These developments in science throw a very confused light on the supposedly hard-and-fast distinctions still sometimes drawn in the social sciences between science and ideology, partly because the manner in which much science is now discussed resonates with the way in which ideology has been traditionally discussed.

The situation becomes even more fraught in the realms of political theory and philosophy. The question turns on the nature of philosophy itself. The relation of philosophy (and political theory) to ideology is largely determined by the understanding of philosophy. If one approaches the subject from the complex compounds of analytic, linguistic, deconstructionist or hermeneutics philosophies, the interpretation of the relation of philosophy to ideology changes markedly in each case. There is no space to deal with all of these philosophies, thus some selective examples will have to suffice.

It is hazardous to generalize on broad and intricate philosophical movements. It would not, however, be too contentious to assert that analytic philosophy has traditionally associated the path of philosophy with a more second-order function of solving identifiable problems, usually arising out of the pre-eminent areas of knowledge in the natural sciences (judged in more traditional sense). Philosophy works via ethically neutral, rigorous, logical, conceptual analysis. It analyses the nature of necessarily true propositions about the world. The key assumption here is that it is only in the pure natural sciences that we find such knowledge. Ideology, like morality, aesthetics or religion, was another non-scientific, value-orientated mode of theorizing. Ideology asserted and prescribed, it did not argue. It exhorted actions and persuaded emotively rather than critically analysing. As a very recent text argues, when dealing with questions of philosophy and ideology we should not confuse the 'method of analysis' with 'that which is analysed'. In other words, philosophy as a method of neutral conceptual analysis of ideology should not be confused with the ideology which is being analysed.[29]

This particular conception of philosophy has come under two pressures which make it more difficult to fashion such a clear distinction between the analysis and the analysed. First, the conception of science, as assumed above, has been changing so markedly that it is no longer feasible to speak of it in the manner that early analytic philosophers did. More recent conceptions, as argued, have moved away from stricter empiricism towards a more interpretative model. Second, the advent of 'ordinary language' and linguistic philosophy, stemming particularly from the later writings of Wittgenstein, have altered our perspective on the nature of language, truth and knowledge, reminding us of their social dimension. To formulate a concept implies having a speaker who knows how to use a language. Languages are not discovered but are socially created. The words embodied in languages do not hook on to things in the world but are subject to a prodigious diversity of uses within 'language games' or forms of life. Learning a concept is not grasping its essence or mastering a mental image but understanding its various uses in a publicly available language. Concepts do not, therefore, correspond with precise things in the world. In fact, the nature of most of the concepts we encounter is their essential contestability. Meaning becomes more a matter of the rules governing use within particular language games. One effect of this trend is to bring ideologies back into circulation as 'forms of life' or 'language games'. Ideology is not a distorted image of the world, but rather is part of the world of language and action. More problematically for some analytic philosophers, science potentially becomes just another language game. This conception, although it has not abandoned the method of rigour and analysis, is distinctly hampered in making a clear distinction between ideology and philosophy.

Other important strands of contemporary philosophy, like deconstruction and hermeneutics, have from their very different perspectives also doubted, with much greater vigour and commitment than late analytic philosophy, both the supposed autonomy of science and the artificial distinction of philosophy from ideological concerns. Writers like Foucault, Derrida, Habermas, Ricoeur and Gadamer have cast serious doubts on the comfortable distinctions concerning ideology which have pervaded the social sciences.

The present position of ideology remains contested. The concept appears now to be at another important crossroads. Most, though not all, of the meanings that we have considered are still canvassed. No longer would anyone use the term for a 'science of ideas', not that the aspiration to have such a science is not still present, under different names, in some areas of psychology and neuro-psychology. In addition, the term would not be used in the French royalist sense, to denote a dangerous atheistical republicanism. Ideology is still used pejoratively, meaning a limited perspective or value bias or, most commonly, illusion. Furthermore, ideology can denote an individual's political perspective: a specific set of views which tries to legitimate political power or all such political views.[30] Ideology can also denote the ideas of a political party, a total metaphysical world-view or human consciousness in general, encompassing all beliefs, including art and science. The latter might imply the politicization of all ideas or simply that interpretative concerns permeate all our claims to knowledge. The permutations here are extremely diverse.[31]

CAUTIONARY POINTS

In my own view ideologies are bodies of concepts, values and symbols which incorporate conceptions of human nature and thus indicate what is possible or impossible for humans to achieve; critical reflections on the nature of human interaction; the values which humans ought either to reject or aspire to; and the correct technical arrangements for social, economic and political life which will meet the needs and interests of human beings. Ideologies thus claim both to *describe* and to *prescribe* for humans. The two tendencies are intermingled in ideology. Ideologies are also intended both to legitimate certain activities or arrangements and to integrate individuals, enabling them to cohere around certain aims. The ideologies that are dealt with in this book pursue the themes listed above quite consciously.

There are a number of critical points on ideology which need to be unpacked. Primarily, one of the criticisms that is made of ideologies is that they are far more simplistic and action-orientated, and far less self-critical and rigorous, than philosophy. Occasionally some ideology looks like crude phrasemongering or propaganda. This is only a half-truth, though. Many philosophical and scientific ideas have functioned within ideologies, in fact many philosophers and natural scientists have allowed their ideas to be used in an ideological manner and have contributed willingly to ideological promotion. My contention is that ideology can be found in phrasemongering as well as in the most abstract philosophical or scientific thought. Some ideological writing can be immensely sophisticated theorizing, yet the same basic ideas can be expressed in the crudest form of sloganizing and propaganda. Also, whereas some ideology remains at a sophisticated theoretical level, some practical philosophy claims a strong action-orientated role. The theme of Plato's philosopher-kings has been echoed throughout the history of philosophy to the present. It is therefore difficult to make a clear distinction between ideology, philosophy and propaganda, except on grounds of the sophistication, edifying nature and self-consciousness of the theory. Ideological ideas can be vapid or profoundly urbane. A related point is that we should not, in consequence of the above, always expect to approach ideologies as coherent constructs. As stated, ideological themes can be found on a continuum from the most banal jumbled rhetoric up to the most astute theorizing. It is at the latter end of the continuum that we could expect to find such coherence. In addition, at all levels of ideology we are dealing with many different thinkers in varying contexts. We search for coherence but we cannot always expect to find it.

Another related concern is the level at which ideology works. This issue throws more light on the problem of coherence within an ideology. Martin Seliger, in his magisterial study of ideology, draws a distinction between the *fundamental* and *operative* levels of ideology. Although arguing that 'politics is inseparable from ideology', Seliger maintains that the distinctive mark of ideology, as compared with philosophy, *is* the action-orientation of ideology. This latter point has been disputed above. For Seliger, the fundamental principles, beliefs and prescriptions of ideology are faced continually by the demand for action or operation in the world, which inevitably compromises the principles. Thus, as Seliger remarks, 'Compromises cause ideology to bifurcate into the purer, and hence more dogmatic, fundamental dimensions of argumentation and the more diluted, and hence more pragmatic, operative dimension. In the latter, morally based prescriptions are often attenuated ... by technical prescriptions'.[32] The result of this for Seliger is a constant tension between the fundamental and operative/technical spheres of ideology. Fundamental principles are often changed or revised, not only through conflict with other fundamental principles, but also via technical and operative demands. On the other hand, the operative and technical questions are also examined, judged and modified before the stringent court of moral and ideological purity.

Some ideologies, like liberalism, have been more concerned with, and more adept and successful at, operationalizing their concerns. Others, like anarchism, have remained for various reasons more caught up in the area of fundamental principles. Comparatively, anarchism has had far less chance to face technical operational questions than has liberalism or socialism. This can give rise to the mistaken judgement that liberalism is basically a more truthful, pragmatic and non-ideological doctrine, whereas anarchism lives in a world of principled ideological dreams, which cannot be put into practice. However, it is not a question of ultimate truth here, but of the level at which an ideology has tended to function, coupled with the interpretative judgement that liberalism enables one to cope better in the world. Yet even if an ideology has functioned more operationally, this still does not diminish the tension that exists with the fundamental theoretical level within that ideology. The history of liberal policy-making is continually punctuated with the question – is this really liberalism?

The above fundamental/operational distinction is also useful in discussing ideological change. Change, for Seliger, can either mean 'the re-adaptation of operative principles to the original specifications or fundamental specifications of fundamental principles, or the adaptation of specifications to what is actually being done or to possible alternatives'.[33] In other words, change can occur in both the operative and the fundamental dimensions, but most often in the latter, partly because it is most subject to strain from the contingencies of the world. Contingencies can both reinforce and undermine fundamental principles. The only point to add to this is that the perception of contingencies still relates to ideological views. There are no absolute unmediated contingencies to which ideologies must correspond. As the recent affiliates of conceptual history (*Begriffsgeschichte*) have argued, one must understand political change conceptually. We live in a world of words; they determine who and what we are. We are tied by words and all we do 'is deeply delimited by the conceptual, argumentative and rhetorical resource of our language. The limits of my moral and political language, we might say, mark the limits of my moral and political world.'[34] All perceptions of the necessity of contingencies are conceptually mediated. As another of the group writes, 'To understand conceptual change is in large part to understand political change, and vice versa. And such understanding must of necessity be historical'.[36]

A further point to note is the interweaving and overlapping of ideological continuums at both fundamental and operational levels. Often, the same basic unit, idea, argument, technique or thinker will be used by apparently quite alien ideologies for different reasons and outcomes. This overlap and interweaving increases the problem of clear identification and often gives rise to titles like liberal socialist, liberal conservative, Marxist feminist, communist anarchist and anarcho-capitalist. Ideologies are complex structures of discourse which carry immense amounts of inherited, interwoven intellectual baggage, often increasing by the year. Every ideology is therefore a conjunction of intellectual hybrids.

Such overlapping of themes must lead to scepticism concerning ideologists who claim to be the inheritors of *a* true doctrine. The mantle of Elijah has apparently descended upon them. This 'true doctrine' approach is what makes them at once easier to understand, firm, coherent and impressive in argument, and potentially worrying in terms of their powers of conversion. They do not seem to be overly burdened by guilt, scepticism or doubt. Such a mentality appears in all the ideological positions. The mantle of conservatism, socialism and liberalism has fallen on a multitude of Elishas, so many up to the present day that it must by now be a finely shredded robe. Not all ideological positions are so burdened, but given time the syndrome will develop. Some of the most perplexing of such Elishas are those who claim to be writing *about* the concept of ideology itself in an academic manner. They offer the reader something which claims to be an impartial judgement on ideology, but is in fact subtly part of another ideological perspective. There is a danger of this tendency in all writing on ideology, though some writers seem less aware of it or less prepared to admit it than others. It is a matter of fine, almost aesthetic judgement to get the discussion of ideology right, and even then doubts will always return.

One consequence of the above is the frequent desire to maintain the purity of an ideology. There are many who assume that there is clearly something *out there* called conservatism, feminism or socialism. This objective 'thing' is self-standing, impermeable, like a brick wall, and must remain unsullied and pure. For theorists, this takes the form of a defence of a doctrine which is wholly unique and leads to clear imperatives for policy. Sometimes this purity is retained by great intellectual subtlety. It is also closely connected to the previous issue: namely, the pure doctrine is seen to run ahistorically through certain important figures in an unbroken descent from some Mount Sinai (sometimes *the* Mount Sinai). A related problem might be called the 'need for ancestors'. Most ideologies claim ancient lineage, indicating in some cases that they correspond to perennial ahistorical human needs, implicit in human nature. This gives their theories more *gravitas*. Thus it is contended that we are all naturally anarchists or conservatives; that palaeolithic peoples were ecologists; or that the 'woman question' has existed since the dawn of time. In my own reading, ideologies are all comparatively recent forms of thought, stemming from the immediate post-French revolutionary era. In addition, there are no pristine doctrines. All ideologies are internally complex, intermixed and overlapping. There is no *one* pure socialist or liberal view of the world. Claims to purity, as claims to greater truth, are usually bogus or misleading.

Another problem is the 'truth and illusion' argument which has already been touched upon. This basically assumes that an ideology *is* the truth about the world; that all other forms of thought are illusions and must be resisted. In its simplest format it asserts: 'We are neutral, you are biased'. The illusion tag appears in various formats. All ideologies have their own icons and demonology of illusions. Sometimes this argument is very difficult to perceive and is obscured by the appearance of balance. It is hard for us to take so seriously the truth/illusion distinction in ideologies which are long in the tooth. When the prophets of conservatism or socialism address us on truth, we usually view their distinctions with an interested but glassy eye. It is not so easy when an ideology is at the stage of vigorous infancy, flexing its arguments and analyses. Then the purveyors of truth and illusion come to us with so much force, zeal and credibility that their arguments are more difficult to resist. For the interested observer, it is usually the more outrageous or comic components of such ideologies which wake us up with a jolt.

We examine ideology as fellow sufferers, not as neutral observers. There are no absolute Archimedean onlookers on the ideological scene. It is a central contention of this book that there is no given world to which ideologies do, or do not, approximate. There is also no way of excluding our own presuppositions. Embodying our own assumptions, we encounter ideologies as conceptions of reality and the world. We cannot step completely outside these conceptions and compare or validate them with some definite external thing, although we can compare worlds. Ideologies do not stand side by side with something objective or real, rather they subtly constitute this reality. However, even though we are sufferers we are not complete sufferers. We can both belong and also, to a degree, distance ourselves in the very fact of theorizing self-consciously.[36] Studying ideologies is a process of encountering a number of such worlds, some of which are quite febrile and limiting, others of which are expansive. The study of ideology itself is an attempt to combine self-consciously our scheme of understanding with that of another, which can be an enriching experience. In this context it becomes more problematic to speak of the truth or falsity of ideologies. Rather, some ideologies enrich us, some diminish us. Some appear to enable us to cope and function in the world, others less so.

THE TEXT

There are multiple dangers when walking into the field of ideology, not least that there are many who claim proprietorial rights to the ground and become enraged and agitated that others should ramble there. It is also a field filled with snares and hidden hollows. Yet I make no apologies for rambling. The rights of way are disputed and remain unsettled. This particular text is written to serve two functions. Primarily, it is designed for courses on ideologies. In such a controversial area, one cannot help but interpret, and there are a series of arguments running through this work which mark out certain idiosyncratic views.

Each chapter is written in a structured manner. In this sense it is hoped that it can be read in discrete sections if necessary. There is an initial introduction and examination of the particular terminology (i.e. fascism, liberalism, etc.), followed by a brief review of the accounts of the origin and history of the ideology at issue. The next section deals with the nature of the ideology. Under this rubric one main issue is discussed which is crucial for grasping the sections that follow. The ideology at issue is broken down loosely into various 'schools of thought' which are unpacked and clarified. The etymological character of the particular ideology, the history and origins, and the analysis of the nature of the schools, vary in complexity between ideologies, thus the length of this section will vary from chapter to chapter. There then follow a series of sections which encapsulate the more general and formal themes characterizing the ideology. These skeletal structures are fleshed out by the varying contributions of 'schools of thought' and individual thinkers. Some of the more complex issues of differing intellectual interpretation and overlap are dealt with in these sections. Each chapter concludes with some brief critical remarks.

An ideologies course, for teacher and taught alike, can be both a deeply rewarding and a highly frustrating experience. On the one hand, the student tries to articulate the coherence of a body of thought, assuming that it has some kind of identity. On the other hand, dealing with this body of thought requires examining both differing schools of thought 'within' the ideology *and* contributions by individual thinkers. This latter task places problems before the student. Examining Burke, for example, entails speaking of his contribution to something called conservatism (possibly), a conservatism which in another thinker looks markedly different. The problem is multiplied if one takes on board the many scholarly interpretations of Burke. In addition, does one approach the ideology via the thinkers or the thinkers via the ideology? Both paths carry dangers. The danger of the former method is of becoming lost in a morass of interpretation and contextualist questions. The danger of the latter is of circumscribing the richness of the intellectual content. Finally, what are the ideological views of the interpreter? Do they impinge on the ideological study? An ideologies course often moves along with these internal tensions, which can both exacerbate as well as enliven and enrich debate.

2
LIBERALISM
—

Liberalism is the most complex and intricate of ideologies. It has permeated so deeply into the cultural life of the West that it is difficult to disentangle the partisan from the more objective commentary. Much academic study (in fact the notion of the liberal academic mind) is founded on the assumptions of individualism, tolerance, progress. A great deal of contemporary political theory, specifically in the writings of major figures like John Rawls, Robert Nozick, Michael Walzer and Friedrich Hayek, deals with liberal themes.

The oldest apolitical use of the word liberal denotes a type of education. From the Middle Ages it implied two things: first, a broad or wide-ranging education; second, the education of a gentleman and freeman (*liber*). We have not lost the first sense of the term, although it seems to come into periodic disfavour in educational and political circles. The notion of a 'liberal education' is now often strongly linked with the disciplines of the humanities. The liberal education is said to cultivate a certain disposition or habit of mind. Yet the term can be complimentary or pejorative. The complimentary sense implies broadmindedness, tolerance or generosity (the latter is more easily caught in the word *liberality*) seen as a virtue. From the late sixteenth century there was another sense of the term which was opprobrious, namely, where liberal implied licence. This is close to the word *libertine*, which from the sixteenth century implied both sexual licence, lack of regard for moral laws, or addiction to antinomian opinions in religion. In *Othello*, when Desdemona refers to Iago as 'a most profane and liberal counsellor', she was not, we can assume, complimenting him. This opprobrious, more abusive sense of liberal is still in use today.

A third sense identifies the *concept* liberal with certain kinds of moral values. In other words, there are a series of values (tolerance, progress, liberty, individualism), which pre-date the *word* liberal by centuries, but are none the less seen to be characteristic of the 'liberal mind' from the nineteenth century. It is this sense of the term liberal which is used to describe thinkers like John Locke or Montesquieu who pre-date the existence of the ideology and the word liberalism in European thought. Additionally the term liberal, because of its connotations of breadth of mind, tolerance, openness and generosity of spirit, was often equated with a philosophical demeanour. The broadest and most liberal minds were philosophical in character. In this sense, philosophy was the queen of the liberal arts.

The final sense of the term liberal settles on its political usage. It must be realized that it is a comparatively new political word in the European vocabulary. The first explicit use of the term to denote a political allegiance or faction was in Spain between 1810 and 1820. *Liberales* was used to describe a group who opposed the more traditional royalist factions (sometimes referred to as *serviles* – namely, the nobles, clergy and deputies of the estates).[1] The *liberales*, under the influence of events in France, were in favour of the establishment of a secular constitution and freedom of the press. The term was partly abusive, coined by the royalist faction to imply dangerous reformism and licence. In fact, events soon overtook the Spanish *liberales* with the return of royalist absolutism. This pejorative sense of the term became common currency in Europe after 1820. The Tory Prime Minister of Britain, Castlereagh, scathingly referred to some of the then Whig Party as 'English *liberales*' or 'English *libéraux*', implying radicalism and republicanism – the sentiments of revolutionaries. Presumably because of the older complimentary uses of the term liberal, this opprobrium was not lasting. By the late 1850s it was more generally used in England to denote a member of Gladstone's party.

It is worth noting here that not all European societies followed Britain on this particular political course and the term liberal did not commonly denote membership of a particular party. Figures like Guizot, Thiers, Constant and Mazzini believed in a broad, over-arching political attitude, which typified generalized optimistic beliefs about human nature, constitutional government, free institutions, limited democracy and social progress, and which could contribute towards the improvement of the human species, but which did not have to be associated with a party. This political attitude, an affirmation of certain values outside party allegiance, is still highly significant. Many claimed, quite reasonably, that they could not become members of a Liberal Party because they *were* liberal. The history of the British Liberal Party is strewn with cases of those who left the party, and sometimes joined other parties, because they felt liberalism was not being effectively represented and might be better found in the Conservative or Socialist factions. It can be confusing, but it is important to bear in mind, that a non-Liberal is not necessarily illiberal and a Liberal is not necessarily liberal.

A discussion of political liberalism, in the words of one commentator, 'provides an ideological map of many of the major developments which have occurred in Britain and elsewhere since the seventeenth century'.[2] There is an inevitable overlap with other ideologies – no pure doctrine of liberalism exists. There are no central core texts or thinkers to liberalism. There are also no unequivocal liberal themes. But there are formal core ideas which work differently in distinct contexts and for different thinkers. The past two centuries are cluttered with examples of liberal experimentation. Such diversity is not necessarily incoherent. It implies that there is a continual process of reflection within liberalism. It is this continuing reflection which makes it one of the most pervasive and stimulating ideologies in the contemporary world.

THE ORIGINS OF LIBERAL THOUGHT

There are a number of debates concerning the origins of liberalism. Some scholars identify liberalism in the context of the history of nation-states. German, Italian, Spanish, French and British liberalisms developed in unique political and socio-cultural environments. The push for national unification in Italy and Germany in the nineteenth century, the effects of the 1789 revolution in France and the comparative isolation of Britain, tempered the character of liberalism in these countries. There is thus no overall coherence in liberalism, only different national traditions. While there is some truth to this, it can be over-emphasized.

Another approach focuses on the character of particular liberal ideological traditions. The most usual path here is to argue for a distinction between Continental and British liberalisms.[3] British liberalism is usually seen to be of greater antiquity and more empirical in character. Continental liberalism is related more to the French Enlightenment and the overactive use of 'abstract reason' in human affairs. The coherence here lies in the two different ideological traditions. Each is located within distinct cultural histories. This distinction can become narrowed down to British liberalism being the 'true' liberalism and others being revisionary or misleading doctrines. These particular views are not very helpful in accounting for the origins of the liberal movement, which are very much more complex and inchoate.

A third approach to the origin of liberalism locates it in the development of a particular type of economy. In the words of one writer: 'So long as capitalism survives, so will liberalism in its various alternative forms.'[4] The rise of industrial capitalism can be seen as coterminous with liberalism (although this argument neglects the fact that it is equally coterminous with most ideologies). Liberalism is thus seen as the ideology of capitalism. This is a view which expresses primarily, though not exclusively, the

Marxist and more general socialist reading of liberalism, and it can be found in a number of commentators on liberalism.[5] In this view, private property tends to figure prominently in the liberal pantheon of values. Liberalism therefore needs to be unmasked and exposed to show its acquisitive sins. Writers like Arblaster believe that liberalism generally has had far too good a press over the last two centuries.[6] Such an argument represents, though, an unduly restrictive and limited perspective on liberalism.

My own preference in accounting for the origins of liberalism is to see it as a focus, in the nineteenth century, of the constitutionalist tradition in European thought. In the last century constitutionalism became virtually identified with liberalism. The two doctrines of liberalism and constitutionalism have subsequently become virtually coterminous. It is prudent to note, however, that such an identification is historically a relatively recent phenomenon.

It is unnecessary to trace the highly complex European constitutionalist tradition, the roots of which lie in the late medieval revival of Roman law, conciliarist ideas, the elaborate theories of resistance in Reformation and Counter-reformation writers and the immensely tangled debates of the French Wars of Religion and the English Civil War.[7] Out of these movements and events ideas on individual rights, individual freedoms, consent, the separation of the private and public realms, contract, limited and balanced government, popular sovereignty, increasingly became common political currency throughout Europe. Paradoxically, such ideas often derived from profoundly illiberal but vociferous sects, like Calvinists or Jesuits, who were fighting for their own liberty of conscience within opposed religious majorities. However, without two further developments, constitutionalist thought would have remained somewhat one-dimensional: first, the Enlightenment and its offspring in France, England and Scotland; and second, the revolutions in America, culminating in the Declaration of Independence in 1776, and in France in 1789.

The Enlightenment signalled the full and experimental use of reason in human affairs. Theology, economics, politics, law and philosophy were all profoundly affected. No longer was authority in religion or politics unquestioned. In philosophy, the methods of the Enlightenment were prefigured in thinkers like Descartes (1596–1650) and Hobbes (1588–1679). For Descartes, nothing was accepted unless it was judged defensible by individual reason. The effects of the Enlightenment are often seen to vary across different societies. Some contemporary theorists, like Hayek, in fact wish to make a fairly rigorous distinction between the effects of the Enlightenment on the Continent and in Scotland. In Scotland the major offspring was the Scottish school of political economy, whose most notable representatives were Adam Smith and Adam Ferguson. The use of reason by the latter was seen to be balanced, sceptical, empirical and limited in scope. In German and French thought the claims for reason were far more ambitious.

The revolutions in America, and more particularly in France, brought many ideas on popular sovereignty, natural rights, consent and contractualism into sharp political focus. The idealism of those, like Tom Paine, who had sketched out utopian schemes for contractual societies based on individual equality, rights and freedom, seemed to be coming to fruition. The various constitutional documents and bills of human rights began to spread throughout Europe. The impetus of this movement has not ended to this day. One must recall here that it was a mere twenty years after the French Revolution that we find the word 'liberal' being coined for a definite faction, the Spanish *liberales*, who had been much influenced by events in France. It was also the campaigns of the revolutionary armies of the French Republic in the 1790s and 1800s which helped to spread these ideas on the Continent.

The legacy of the Revolution was extremely ambiguous, however. The more balanced constitutionalist view found itself at loggerheads with the even more radical ideas of the *sans culottes*, those who advocated direct participatory democracy and, on occasions, communistic theories of property. Benjamin Constant, a key representative of the more balanced liberal constitutionalist persuasion, blamed the more extreme *étatiste* aspects of the Revolution on J. J. Rousseau and his theory of the General Will.[8] Constant's judgement has been supported in this century by post-Second World War liberal writers like J. L. Talmon.[9] In France, after the Revolution, liberal opinion thus divided between the radical *étatiste* and the more conventional constitutional liberals.[10] In Britain it also divided between the Whigs and the radicals.

Once we move into the 1820s and 1830s we begin to encounter the fully self-conscious liberal ideology. Constitutionalism is focused at this point within liberalism. In British and European thought, the heyday of liberalism coincides with the growth of industrialization and the expansion of markets in goods, capital and labour. Some contemporary liberal thinkers still look back nostalgically to a golden age of liberalism in the mid-nineteenth century, roughly dating in Britain from the Catholic Emancipation Act of 1829 to Cobden's Free Trade Treaty with France of 1860.

The 1870s are sometimes seen as marking the beginning of a decline or radical change in liberalism. Liberalism, in this reading, went too far down the road of collectivism, though not all agree with such an assessment, as we shall see in later sections. In Europe, liberal ideas waned in France from the 1850s and in Germany from the 1870s with the rise of Bismarck.[11] Its longest period of effective political and economic activity was in Britain. In the shape of the Liberal Party it dates from the 1840s until 1922, when the last Prime Minister who could be described as liberal, David Lloyd George, fell from office. A form of Liberal Party has carried on in Britain up to the present day. Adherents of liberalism have been found increasingly outside the ranks of the party; in fact, liberalism now seems to have stronger support in other political factions than in the Liberal Party itself.

This very cursory survey of the origins of liberalism in constitutionalist thought suggests that some of the impetus behind ideas on rights, liberties, limitations on authority and tolerance, derives from profoundly illiberal sources. No one would immediately describe either Jesuits or Calvinists as advocates of tolerance or individual liberty. Yet it was often the intolerant minorities, ruthlessly maintaining their independence in hostile environments, and searching for arguments to justify their independence, that were paradoxically driven to express ideas which, in the words of one scholar, 'put forth a theory of political liberty, which was the direct parent of the doctrines triumphant in 1688, and through Locke the ancestor of those in 1789'.[12] Even the exponents of popular sovereignty were not democrats. Locke, although preparing the ground for discussion of majority rule, was clearly not in the least interested in extending this to suffrage, periodic elections, or even parliamentary supremacy. There is thus something profoundly fortuitous about the growth of constitutionalism and liberalism.

THE NATURE OF LIBERALISM

In this section, certain schools of liberal thought will be examined. There is some debate, though, as to the key representative thinkers of liberalism. For example, the late-nineteenth-century thinker Herbert Spencer is variously cited as both the great summation of nineteenth-century liberalism and a complete 'maverick' who stood outside the mainstream beliefs.[13] A similar contradictory fate has befallen figures like John Locke, Adam Smith, Jeremy Bentham, Alexis de Tocqueville, Immanuel Kant, John Stuart Mill and, more recently, Friedrich Hayek and John Rawls. It is thus a hazardous task trying to isolate the key liberal thinkers and this will not be attempted.

Some theorists have seen a definite single clear doctrine of liberalism. However, the more common line of interpretation has been to delineate schools of liberalism. The contention of this study is that there are different schools of liberal thought and it will proceed along these lines as a means of clarifying an immensely complex tradition of discourse. The two principal schools that will be reviewed are classical liberalism and social, or new, liberalism.[14]

The background to classical liberalism is complex. One important strand, particularly in Britain, lies in Whiggism. Over the nineteenth century Whiggism became increasingly associated with conservatism. Because classical liberalism itself was not a simple entity it could also be actively promoted within conservative factions. Whiggism came to prominence in Britain after 1688. The major preoccupations of Whigs then became the defence of parliamentary supremacy, upholding the rule of law and the defence of their landed property. Many were deeply attached to the mythology of the ancient constitution and the fundamental rights embodied in it. Some supported notions of freedom of the press and speech as such fundamental rights.

The ancient constitution was an idea promulgated by Whig figures like Viscount Molesworth, who contended that there was an ancient British constitution going back to the Anglo-Saxons and possibly to the Goths and even the Trojans[15] The ancient constitution did not, it should be added, embody Locke's natural rights. It rather incorporated immemorial customary rights justified by long and ancient usage. Many Whigs believed that vigilance was needed to protect such rights against any return to the arbitrariness and absolutist tendencies of the Stuarts. Monarchical power had to be retained, but as a limited component within a balanced constitution which required that power be constrained by a judicious balance of elements. Whiggism represented a curious mixture of defence of privilege combined with resistance to arbitrary rule. Whigs believed in limited suffrage and, unlike many Tories, learnt some lessons from the French Revolution. Yet even in 1832 they still saw the vote as a limited privilege and not as a right.

By the time of the French Revolution, Whiggism had begun to mutate. Older Whig factions still identified with the ancient constitution ideas. Lockian Whigs never really gained much of a foothold between the 1680s and 1776.[16] Others began to identify with commercial wealth, enlightenment and progress. These newer Whigs included the more optimistic Whiggery of Adam Smith, as well as the much more sceptical Whiggery of David Hume: figures like Edmund Burke who, despite applauding the 1688 Settlement, identified neither with the ancient constitution Whigs nor with Locke's, Hume's or Smith's positions. The French Revolution was a catalyst. The older Whig ideas still persisted but new forms of discourse developed: the commercial ideas of Adam Smith; Jeremy Bentham's systematic use of utilitarianism; and Price and Priestly's radical distillation of Lockian language.

Tom Paine was the first and most effective voice of radicalism who tried to link the events of 1688 and 1789. His *Rights of Man* (1791) was immensely popular in Britain. Other important writers to explore this theme were Joseph Priestly, Richard Price, James Mackintosh, William Godwin, Mary Wollstonecraft and Percy Shelley. The core of such radicalism lay in an interpretation of Locke's *Two Treatises* (1689) and Rousseau's *Social Contract* (1762), although some of Paine's language seems to have strong echoes of the 1640s Levellers. The basic thesis was the familiar one, that sovereignty did not lie in either monarchy or some privileged aristocratic faction, but in the people. Governments should only govern on the basis of the consent of the whole people, a consent which, as Locke made plain in the final chapter of his *Second Treatise*, could be withdrawn. The natural rights of the people should be enshrined or codified in constitutional documents, as in America and France. It was this radicalism that paved the way for the great age of constitution-making and bills of rights.

Much of the British radicalism, from the 1790s up to the 1820s, concentrated on the theme of parliamentary and electoral reform. This increasingly centred on groups like the London Corresponding Society (founded in 1792). The language of such groups was based, like Paine's, on natural rights and popular sovereignty theory. In 1794, the London Corresponding Society and its related groups planned a national constitutional convention, virtually on the French revolutionary model. This led to the arrest of the leaders, Horne Tooke, John Thelwell and Thomas Hardy, for high treason. The conflict between France and Britain at the time aroused the suspicions of the government, and despite the acquittal of the leaders of the Corresponding Society, they were subject to harassment and continual fear of rearrest. Such government activity blunted the practical impact of the movement. In spite of this, the radicals established a vocabulary for speaking of the democratic and natural rights of the sovereign people which became assimilated, during the next century, into the growing labour and socialist movements, and also remained as a strand within liberal thought.[17]

Whiggery and radicalism both fed into nineteenth-century classical liberalism. Classical liberalism is a peculiar blend of ideas and strategies about how best to acquire or defend liberty. Some elements of Whiggery became far more closely identified with conservatism. Many of the older Whigs also felt increasingly uncomfortable with the new commercial industrial spirit expressed by many liberals. Liberal Party figures in Britain, like Bright and Cobden in the 1840s, expressed utter contempt for landed aristocratic privilege, whether it appeared in Tory or Whig form. They traced many of the ills of Britain to this class and its ownership of large tracts of land which held back the development of a class of yeoman freeholders. This latter argument in fact goes back to the seventeenth century.

Unlike Whiggery, there is a formal unity to classical liberalism. It was clearly committed to the doctrine of individualism. Individualism can be defined as a political and moral doctrine which extols the value of the individual human being. Secondly, such liberalism was pledged to uphold liberty and the equal right of all individuals to equal freedom. Conventionally this freedom was understood negatively, namely, as freedom from arbitrary coercion. One of the areas where freedom was most in demand was in the economy. A free economy was most conducive to the satisfaction of human beings and the fulfilment of their interests. A free economy, where all have relatively equal rights to produce and consume, implies that the government must retain only minimal functions, like maintaining the rule of law, internal order, the defence of private property and security.

Zealous government is thus to be mistrusted. The most vigorous support for these arguments can be found in Britain between 1830 and 1914. It came most notably, from the classical political economy school, the utilitarians, the Manchester school of economics, plus many individual theorists like J. S. Mill, Herbert Spencer and Henry Sidgwick. In Europe such ideas, though far less concerned with political economy, were associated with the views of thinkers like Benjamin Constant, Guizot, Charles de Rémusat, Mazzini, Alexis de Tocqueville, and Wilhelm von Humboldt.

It has been argued that this form of liberalism died in 1914. George Dangerfield, in his book *The Strange Death of Liberal England*, spoke of Britain in 1910 as 'about to shrug from its shoulders ... a venerable burden, a kind of sack. It was about to get rid of its Liberalism'.[18] Yet the reports of liberalism's demise have been greatly exaggerated. In the post-1945 era, specifically from the late 1970s, liberalism has been anything but dead. Some have had the temerity to call this a 'New Enlightenment'.[19] Like the nineteenth-century variant, this modern form of classical liberalism embodies a number of diverse views. Notable among these are the views of the Austrian school of economics, whose most famous offspring is Hayek; the Chicago school, whose most avid popularizer is Milton Friedman; the Virginia public-choice school associated with the work of James Buchanan; and a number of individual writers and philosophers like Ayn Rand and Robert Nozick. In Britain it has had support both from academics and politicians, and from research and propagandist bodies like the Institute of Economic Affairs.

From the late 1880s liberalism was seen to change direction.[20] There is an immense amount of scholarly debate on this issue, particularly in Britain.[21] Some wish to deny that the new liberalism really was liberal. Formally, the new liberalism was committed to a 'social individualism': the good of the individual was seen as tied to the good of the whole community. The atomism of the formal classical view came to be regarded as morally and sociologically naive. The social consequences of industrialization had to be dealt with at a much broader level and should not be left to individual charity. Poverty, unemployment and illness were not just the concern of the single individual, but were communal or social issues, and dealing with them transcended individual capacities. Further, liberty was not just leaving people alone, but was actually identified with the fuller life of genuine citizenship. Citizens should possess the economic, cultural, political and social means to partake of worthwhile lives. Such ideas were taken up in the present century by most European reformist socialist parties. This new liberalism is identified with figures like T. H. Green, L. T. Hobhouse and J. A. Hobson from the 1880s up to 1914. In fact it also tends, in different ways, to characterize the general social democratic trends of Britain and other West European states from the 1930s to the early 1970s. It is important, though, to realize that there are variations within this new social democratic liberalism which are only now beginning to be explored by scholars.[22]

There remains a complex and unresolved debate on the relation between the classical and new liberalism. One view is that classical liberalism was the pristine doctrine which was betrayed by the quasi-socialist new liberalism. There are other interpretations on the theme of decline and betrayal. J. H. Hallowell saw the demise of integral liberalism through its loss of moral content. Religious respect for the individual soul had collapsed into moral relativism.[23] The most popular line among historians up to the 1970s was that liberalism had two faces — the individualist and the collectivist. The new collectivist liberals adapted liberalism to the needs of a new age and thus seismic shifts took place in the ideology. In the last two decades this idea has been subject to critical scrutiny.[24] It has been argued that there was really no division at all between the classical and new liberalism. They were all part of a broad-church doctrine.[25]

Classical liberalism was not simply reconciled to the new liberalism. Such terminology obscures a profound and subtle movement at work within liberal thought. Formal ideas were given substance in different contexts. They were worked and reworked. There were no seismic shifts but a fluid development of interpretations around certain ideas. Many of these formal ideas were explored by other political movements. The major point to keep in mind is that much of this change in the character of liberalism was internal to the ideology. It was not externally imposed. Many of the ideas that were associated with classical liberalism were flexible enough to be used by the new liberals. One conclusion from this is that liberals in government progressively found themselves enacting measures which they felt increasingly uneasy about at a level of fundamental principle. As we will see in the following sections, there were often reasons both to oppose and to support the legislation.

Although a distinction has been drawn between classical and new liberalism, this should not be taken as hard and fast for two important reasons. First, the schools of liberalism are not wholly distinct. The arguments of classical liberalism seem to evolve at certain points into the new liberalism. There are thus no sudden transitions. The second, related point is that liberal thinkers do not fit together neatly into the same school. The intellectual and moral preoccupations of classical liberals quite often differ markedly. We ignore such differences at our cost. In fact, at times such thinkers seem to fit into different ideologies. David Hume, Alexis de Tocqueville, Edmund Burke and Friedrich Hayek can be classified both as liberals and as conservatives. L. T. Hobhouse, J. A. Hobson, John Dewey and John Rawls have been classified both as social liberals and as socialists. There should be nothing disturbing in this.

INDIVIDUALISM

It is difficult to generalize on the liberal view of human nature, partly because the accounts are so diverse and complex. There is, however, one concept which figures consistently in liberal discussion, which can act as an important leitmotif. This is the concept of individualism. Liberals have been, and are, *formally* committed to individualism. It is the metaphysical and ontological core of liberal thought and the basis of moral, political, economic, and cultural existence. The individual is both more real than, and prior to, society. This priority has been differently interpreted: it could be natural or moral.[26] Values are also tied to the individual. The individual is the touchstone of morality and truth. Individualism therefore tends, as such, towards a form of egalitarianism. Each person is seen to be of equal value.

Yet these ideas of equality and individualism do not tell us a great deal about the more substantive views of liberals. The briefest acquaintance with liberal literature will throw up distinctions between types of individualism. The American liberal philosopher John Dewey was not alone, in his book *Individualism – Old and New*, in distinguishing between the 'abstract individual' of early-nineteenth-century liberalism, and a more communal understanding of the individual found in the social liberalism.[27] This distinction is used differently by Hayek in his essay 'Individualism: True and False', where he distinguishes a rationalistic individualism (in writers like Wilhelm von Humboldt and J. S. Mill) from a true individualism (which is more in line with the traditions and conventions of a market society).[28] Purely rational individualism, for Hayek, is unworkable. Such distinctions are fairly commonplace in many works on liberalism.[29]

In the classical liberal format, the 'individual' is usually understood as a single, self-enclosed being 'shut up in his own subjectivity'.[30] The limits of the body are the limits of the individual. The individual owns his or her own body, in terms of a natural right. This notion is often linked with the 'possessive individualist' theory, in the sense that a person is the 'proprietor' of their own body and its capacities and owes nothing to society. The goods which that person produces are seen as extensions of the proprietorial rights to the body.

The desires and interests of the individual are seen to be sovereign. Reason is instrumental to the achievement of one's desires. Each person is driven from within by desires and passions and is, by definition, the best judge of his or her own interests. In this sense, institutions should avoid judging for individuals. There could not be any collective or institutional responsibility, since only individuals can be responsible for themselves. The only good is individual good.

There are, however, a number of possible variations on the above theme. The purest and most consistent form of individualism is 'unconstrained individualism'. There is no morality or doctrine which can constrain the individual. Nobody can dictate to it, since it, logically, *is* the source of all value. This implies total individuality and autonomy. There is absolutely no possibility here of formulating any theory of public goods. The ultimate fruition of such a doctrine can be found in individualistic anarchy, of which the best European example is Max Stirner whose theories will be examined in chapter 5.

Such an argument cannot uphold property rights or even a market economy. Yet it must be stressed that it *is* the logical direction of individualist argument. Most liberals stop short well before these conclusions but there are some who draw close to them, teetering on the brink of anarchism. Some recent libertarian thought, although linking itself with liberalism, is better discussed under the umbrella of anarchy. This is partially recognized in the popular denotation 'anarcho-capitalism' for the writings of figures like Murray Rothbard.[31] In Britain at the turn of this century some of the more extreme disciples of Herbert Spencer, like Auberon Herbert and Wordsworth Donisthorpe, also came very close to anarchism through their individualism.

Auberon Herbert, in the words of a contemporary, 'out-Herberts Mr Herbert Spencer'.[32] Herbert even criticized the deeply individualist Liberty and Property Defence League, which he claimed was 'a little more warmly attached to the fair sister Property than . . . to the fair sister Liberty'.[33] He became obsessed with the liberty of the individual, advocating a voluntary state and voluntary taxation, redolent of some recent anarcho-capitalists. He also found Spencer's later views distinctly conservative, yearning for the idealism of Spencer's early work, *Social Statics*. In America Ayn Rand argued for more total liberty for the individual from an entirely different philosophical standpoint. A rational life for Rand was the pursuit of pure egoism by each individual. The philosophical premises of this doctrine lie in Rand's odd use of Aristotelian and Thomist thought. As one recent writer has noted, 'Man's purpose [for Rand] lies in his own self-realization and it would be a perversion of that purpose for him to sacrifice himself for others, least of all for some fictitious entity called "society"'.[34] Rand enshrined this idea in a doctrine entitled 'the virtue of selfishness'.[35] The individual's own life and survival are the sole criteria of value. Egoism is thus the only basis to ethics. A rational life is purely self-interested. Altruism is moral cannibalism. Capitalism is the only type of arrangement which maximizes the possibility of such a life. Thus Rand contends that liberals 'must fight for capitalism, not as a "practical" issue, not as an economic issue, but, with the most righteous pride, as a *moral* issue'.[36]

Despite appearances, neither Auberon Herbert nor Ayn Rand were prepared to accept the full logic of this individualistic argument. Herbert was enough of a Lockian and Spencerian to believe in the constraint of natural rights, and thus argued for the necessity of mutual respect and consent, something of which a pure individualist like Stirner was duly contemptuous. Rand, deeply critical of anarchism, also believed in an objective, rational order and saw the necessity of some form of state.

In Herbert Spencer and the Liberty and Property Defence League we find a type of 'constrained individualism', although it is worth recalling that its members were regarded by many liberal contemporaries as extremists. Spencer's main political concern was that, in the past, liberalism habitually stood for individual freedom versus state coercion. His famous book, *The Man Versus the State* (1884), was meant to re-call liberals to their true origins and away from Gladstone's empirical socialism and the sins of the legislators. For Spencer, individuals owned themselves by way of natural rights. Each had an equal right to equal freedom. Natural rights originated in a biological process of mutual limitation and contractualism which was necessary for social aggregation. The important point to note about Spencer is that his argument for individuality is rooted in an ambitious naturalistic evolutionary metaphysics. It was designed to free the individual from coercion. Only an industrial society which maximized such individuality could be genuinely liberal.

In Germany, the much earlier liberalism of von Humboldt is worth comparing briefly with that of Spencer. Like Spencer, Humboldt detested the idea of the state's interference with individuality. Spencer would have had little trouble agreeing with Humboldt's comment that 'the State is to abstain from all solicitude for the positive welfare of the citizens, and not to proceed a step further than is necesary for their mutual security and protection against foreign enemies'.[37] However, Humboldt's definition of individualism is markedly different from Spencer's. Humboldt wanted freedom for the maximum aesthetic development of the individual (*Bildung*), an idea explored extensively in German literature in the *Bildungsroman* tradition. Each person develops his or her own sensibilities. This is essentially an organic process. For Humboldt, 'the richer a man's feelings become in ideas, and his ideas in feelings, the more transcendent his nobility'.[38] The individual grows, develops, and becomes more cultured through diverse experiences. Freedom is the possibility for this *Bildung*. The ultimate aim 'is the highest and most harmonious development ... to a complete and consistent whole', an idea which J. S. Mill was to employ in *On Liberty*.[39] State coercion stifles such aesthetic development.

The idea of society being based on mutual individual limitation and contract, which can be found in Spencer, struck a not dissimilar note with another classical liberal, Henry Sidgwick, in his *Elements of Politics* (1897) For Sidgwick, contract is of fundamental importance to the individualistic system. The contract is essential to unite the individual atoms of society. However, the comparison with Spencer ends here, for Sidgwick was at pains to distance his moderate utilitarian individualism from Spencer's 'extreme individualism'. Whereas Spencer had been obdurate in his opposition to the Poor Law and public provision of education, Sidgwick saw a *via media* between Spencer's extremism and the empirical socialism of Gladstone's 1880s administration. The minimum of personal security, enforcement of contracts and rights to private property are not total guarantees of individual well-being. There is a form of individualistic interference which aims 'to secure [the individual] from pain and loss'.[40] The care of children, the prescription of weights and measures, precautionary legislation on sanitary matters, housing and medical training, are matters best supervised by the state. They are also clearly compatible with individualism. Sidgwick maintained that individuals do not in fact always know their own best interest, and that they should not be allowed to suffer from their ignorance or profit by the debilitation of others.

Despite being critical of the 1880s Liberal administration, which was, in his view, paternalist in the worst sense of the term, Sidgwick was far closer to this type of social liberalism than Spencer. Spencer held that suffering, pain and squalor are equivalent to the biological warning system of the body. Adversity is the efficient school for the transgressor. The artificial support of a backward individual lowers the whole evolutionary genus. As Spencer put it: 'Fostering the good-for-nothings at the expense of the good-for-somethings is an extreme cruelty'.[41] Most of the measures mentioned by Sidgwick are explicitly repudiated by Spencer as totally incompatible with true individualism.

Spencer's opposition to Sidgwick's utilitarian individualism was an extension of his general opposition to Benthamism as a philosophy of expediency. Despite A. V. Dicey's judgement on Benthamism as 'nothing else than systematized individualism' totally congruent with *laissez-faire*, Spencer maintained that such a philosophy was wide open to authoritarian abuse.[42] The 'greatest happiness' principle, as deployed by Bentham and later by J. S. Mill, could never be the basis for sound liberal legislation. Spencer is not alone in this judgement. Despite the reputation of figures like Bentham and J. S. Mill as founding figures of liberalism, some liberals, like Spencer and more recently Robert Nozick, have doubted their credentials.[43] Nozick has argued that one of the fundamental errors of utilitarianism is that in trying to aggregate utility it destroys the separateness and value of individuals.

Hayek has comparable objections. He doubts the rationalist premise built into utilitarianism, namely that anyone *could* calculate the general happiness of society. He argues that reason is a limited practical tool which guides individuals to the satisfaction of their interests. No one can stand above their interests.[44] Utilitarians commit the philosophical mistake of not identifying the limits to reason and, whereas J. S. Mill wanted to free the individual from conventions, Hayek believes that social and moral traditions constitute individuality.[45]

Hayek's argument on the social constitution of the individual, although used very differently to the new liberals, forms a convenient bridge to the conception of individuality employed *by* the new liberals. One of the principal motifs of the new liberal grasp of individuality was that it could be reconciled with community. In the case of the idealist liberals, the argument was quite directly metaphysical. Individuality was seen as the product of an ethical state. The individual who determined his or her actions within rational social parameters was essentially the rational citizen of an ethical state.

T. H. Green argued, on idealist grounds, that society was a means for individual self-realization and character development. Politics exists to draw forth the potentialities of the individual. The possibility for such development depends upon the existence of social institutions. Each individual is a spiritual possibility which can be realized through society. Green stated: 'The good which a man seeks for himself is not a succession of pleasures, but objects which, when realized, are permanent contributions to a social good which thus satisfies the permanent self'.[46] The permanent self is at one with the common good. Civic institutions are the outward form or expression of moral ideals. The only justification for institutions is the contribution they make towards the moral development of individuals. The communal good cannot therefore be divorced from the individual. Individuals only have rights and duties as members of the community.

A similar doctrine can be found in L. T. Hobhouse. As Hobhouse argued in his seminal work, *Liberalism*, liberalism was founded on the self-directing individual, yet 'in realizing his capacities of feeling, of living, of mental and physical energy ... in Green's phrase, he finds his own good in the common good'.[47] Social life provides the setting and conditions where humans can develop. A society is free 'where all minds have that fullness of scope, which can only be obtained if certain fundamental conditions of their mutual intercourse are maintained by organized effort'.[48]

Such an idea did not represent a reversal of any commitment to individualism. It argued that individuality develops in a community and that part of individuality is a recognition of common goals. Liberals, in this argument, have been interested primarily in civic individualism. As Michael Freeden comments: 'New Liberals ... interpreted the assumption of communal responsibility for defined areas of human activity as itself conducive to the development and perfection of individuals'.[49] Individuality, especially for the idealist liberals, and J. S. Mill to some degree, was a process of development towards a fuller life. Our personal development involves interdependence.[50] We cannot divorce our own good from the good of others.

Many of the more traditional popular nineteenth-century views on individualism, associated with figures like Samuel Smiles or Harriet Martineau, which concentrated on character, self-help, and self-reliance, were subtly transformed in new liberal arguments. Self-reliance and self-help became moulded into self-realization. It became easier in this context for social reformers to speak of material obstacles to self-realization (and thus obstacles to self-help and character formation). Increasingly, measures of the 1890s and 1900s, like National Insurance and old-age pensions, were justified as providing a firmer basis to self-help. Some even described National Insurance as the nationalization of thrift.

One point to note here is that individualism and human nature remain ambiguous in liberalism. There is certainly no clear, unequivocal distinction between 'individualism' and 'collectivism'. These terms conceal more than they reveal. Further, there are different forms and perceptions of individualism justified from differing philosophical and occasionally incommensurable stand points. Finally, the various views on individualism hover between complete antipathy to, and clear acceptance of the necessity for, state intervention.

THE VALUE OF LIBERTY

Liberty is a crucial value for liberals. We should, however, take note of Michael Freeden's comment: 'To observe that a belief in liberty is a core element in liberal thought is a truism. To hold that liberals were ideologically united through a belief in liberty is an error. Like other concepts, liberty covers a wide range of positions'.[51] The conventional distinction made within the concept is between negative and positive liberty.[52] In addition, it is often argued that positive liberty is not really part of liberalism. Hayek, for example, sees the decline of British liberalism from the 1870s as 'closely connected with a reinterpretation of freedom'.[53] The present account rejects such an assessment.

If the classical liberal literature is scanned it is not hard to find a commitment to the negative idea. Writers like Benjamin Constant, Alexis de Tocqueville, Humboldt, Spencer, Sidgwick and, more recently, Isaiah Berlin, Hayek, Milton Friedman and Robert Nozick, adhere to such a definition. The individual is free when left uncoerced or unrestrained. Much state intervention, conventionally, is seen to undermine individual initiative and offend against basic liberty.

The important question here is the meaning of restraint. It is obviously profoundly significant for establishing whether or not liberty has been violated. There are fairly precise conditions for the identification of restraint. First, restraints are usually regarded as physical in character — prisons and pointed guns. Second, they are external to the individual: a restraint is something that X imposes on Y. Finally, restraint involves deliberate intentional action. One cannot, in this reading, unintentionally restrain someone. Hayek in fact prefers the word 'coercion' to the more slippery term 'restraint', unless it is evident that there is a 'restraining agent'.[54] It is not clear here why coercion or restraint *have* to be intentional, other than that it is stipulated that this must be the case.

Hayek is also insistent that we should not confuse liberty with some inner sense of feeling free. Furthermore, inability, lack of capacity or power are not restraints. An ability or power might provide possibilities for the use of liberty, but they are not synonymous with liberty. Liberty should not therefore be confused with the conditions under which it is exercised. This argument implies that disease, illness, old age, physical disability, poverty, unemployment or lack of opportunities are nothing to do with liberty since they are not intentional restraints.

Such a notion of liberty is often connected with property. From John Locke onwards, the issue of property has been intimately linked with liberty. John Gray, following Hayek, comments that 'private property is the embodiment of individual liberty'.[55] Property becomes an extension of bodily rights. Many of the arguments used by liberals on freedom can often be traced to claims about 'freedom from' coercion or restraint by the state in bodily and property rights. The state usually figures high in such coercion stakes. In the case of the constitutional tradition, this is understandable, since most constitutional writing developed in the context of highly arbitrary absolutist rule. This fear of arbitrary state action was as true for classical liberals, like Constant in France in the early 1800s, as for classical liberals in the twentieth century who have opposed state socialism.

The justifications for negative liberty are, though, broader than simply the defence of property. Most of its proponents would also tend to claim that it is necessary for both genius and creativity. Negative liberty does not propound any single monolithic moral structure for individuals. In fact, it is supposed to rest on recognition, tolerance and respect for diversity. Individualism thus implies a diversity of goods. It is usually contended that positive liberty does the precise opposite of this.

Liberal arguments on restraint are not so straightforward in practice. The main initial constitutionalist concern of Whigs, struggling with an absolutist legacy in government, was to uphold civil freedoms of speech, worship and the like. The point was to try to extend constitutional guarantees. In some Whigs and radicals the onus of restraint switched to political freedoms from the 1790s. Interest moved towards the extension of the franchise. However, as early as the 1750s the Whig Josiah Tucker was also calling for a 'Glorious Revolution' in the economic sphere.[56] The demand for economic freedom centred in the 1840s on the ark of free trade and the repeal of the Corn Laws. In a sense, such economic freedom was seen by liberals like Bright and Cobden as an extension of political freedom. Economic freedom was freedom from another of the political privileges of the aristocratic land-owning class who were artificially holding up the price of basic foodstuffs through their monopolistic control. The demand for such freedom reached a peak in the Anti-Corn Law League.

By the 1870s many liberals had become more and more concerned by the restraint on individuals involved in an industrial culture. The concern focused increasingly on social freedoms. Social freedom often involved (like political and civil freedom) an extension of state regulation. As one of Spencer's contemporaries argued, people needed the state guarantee of enough education to be able to understand Spencer's argument about the need for the exclusion of state involvement from education.[57]

What can be observed in the above is the shifting ground of restraint. From Adam Smith onwards, there have been stipulations on the necessity for different forms of legal restraint. Classical liberals, though suspicious of the range of state action, certainly did not envisage doing without it. The same point holds true for many more recent liberals. Even the minimalist liberal Robert Nozick envisages a 'state equivalent' – the Dominant Protection Agency – emerging naturally and spontaneously to provide protective services.[58]

Thus there seem to be implicit distinctions, within liberal thought, between justifiable and unjustifiable restraint. There are three points to note here. First, there is little consistency between those practices which liberals see as restraints; second, there is little indication of the reach of the argument on justifiable restraint; and third, how does one define justifiable restraint without actually indicating what is worthwhile in certain types of action?

It is clear that the concept of negative liberty as such does not provide any guidance on state activity. C. B. Macpherson, for example, uses a redefined negative liberty argument to support a socialist-orientated transformation of social and economic relations in Western industrialized societies.[59] This can hardly inspire confidence in the classical liberal mind. In addition, no classical liberals accept the principle that restraint *qua* restraint is an evil. State action *qua* state action is not necessarily a restraint. Much state action can be perfectly innocuous. In fact, restraint is a movable feast in liberal thought. The extension of its application, as argued earlier, continued unabated through to the new liberal theories at the turn of the century. The character of some restraints has required more state activity than others. Certain restraints are justifiable partly because they help to remove unjustifiable restraints. This is specifically the case where unemployment, poverty, illness or old age have been viewed in the latter category. Here we see a fluid movement into the new liberalism.

The second point concerns the degree to which the argument on restraint can be extended. Some contemporary liberals, like Hayek or Berlin, would tend to argue that the notion of restraint cannot encompass such items as poverty or unemployment. There are only 'positive external restraints' which involve intentional restraining agents. Thus no one intends that poverty or unemployment should exist. This is the only sense in which Hayek will accept the equivalent use of 'restraint' and 'coercion'. Yet, are there overriding reasons why the concept of restraint or coercion should be limited in this way? Severe migraines, debilitating illness, ignorance, lack of skills, poverty and unemployment are restraints upon individuals which could be said to coerce them into patterns of activity. To claim exclusivity solely for 'positive external restraint' is both conceptually unwarranted and historically and semantically odd. It also appears that many classical liberals did not adhere to such a limited idea.

Liberals have extended the restraint argument well into the twentieth century, although they have also added to it. This is where we touch upon the more positive view of liberty. How does one ascertain what a justifiable restraint is, without indicating what is worthwhile in certain actions? Unless one takes an extreme view, arguing that all restraint *qua* restraint is evil, which is recognized by the majority of liberals as plainly absurd, one is committed to a formal distinction between unjustifiable and justifiable restraint. In so doing one is qualitatively discriminating between actions and, therefore, moving beyond the immediate remit of negative liberty. Liberty thus comes to be identified with certain types of worthwhile action. This is the domain of a more positive understanding of liberty.

T. H. Green argued in the 1880s that freedom cannot be understood as the absence of restraint or compulsion. He contended that 'we do not mean merely freedom to do as we like. We do not mean freedom that can be enjoyed by one man ... at the cost of a loss of freedom to others.' Freedom, he continues, is 'a positive power of doing or enjoying, and that, too, something that we do or enjoy in common with others'.[60] The important points to note here are that progress in society is measured by the advance of such freedom, which Green believed was perfectly in accord with the development of liberalism, and that society is the precondition to the exercise of such freedom which cannot be premised on others' unfreedom. Freedom coincides with the common good. In this way the freedom of the individual is reconciled with that of society. It is the maximum power of all members of society to make the best of themselves. Thus Green contended that it was justifiable, on grounds of freedom, to interfere in the sale and consumption of alcohol, housing, public health provisions, employment, land ownership and education. Such action, although coercive, none the less removed unjustifiable coercion and so provided conditions for the genuine exercise of freedom. Law could thus contribute to the lives of the overworked, underfed, ill-housed and undereducated.

These themes on positive freedom are echoed in many new liberal writings. As Herbert Samuel remarked: 'There could be no true liberty if a man was confined and oppressed by poverty, by excessive hours of labour, by insecurity of livelihood ... To be truly free he must be liberated from these things also. In many cases, it was only the power of law that could effect this. More law might often mean more liberty.'[61] Similar points are put by new liberal figures like Hobhouse, Winston Churchill and H. H.

Asquith.[62] It is this understanding of social freedom which lies behind the Liberal administrations of 1906—14 and their welfare legislation. It is also this line of thought which has carried on into some aspects of the social democratic tradition of the twentieth century.

JUSTICE AND EQUALITY

Justice for classical liberalism involves the maintenance of a general body of formal rules and procedures. It provides the over-arching structure, the rule of law within which individuals are protected in the pursuit of their interests. Law does not exist to interfere in particular human activities and choices. It is concerned with the conditions in which individuals express their preferences. Justice is not concerned with the outcomes of preferences. Poverty, economic inequality or unemployment are not in themselves issues of justice. This particular notion of justice has been called 'commutative justice' and it has been contended that it is the essence of what liberals mean by justice.[63]

Commutative justice is contrasted with distributive justice, which is often seen to be a misunderstanding of justice. Much distributive justice is the attempt to ameliorate social suffering and distress. However, theorists like Hayek argue that there are no recognizable principles for welfare distribution in society. Even if such central principles were found, they could not be put into practice in a society 'whose productivity rests on individuals being free to use their knowledge and abilities for their own purposes'.[64] Distribution implies a plan, and planners who will attempt to impose their principles upon others. Such processes inevitably create injustices by their very arbitrariness. This was the major theme of Hayek's *The Road to Serfdom* (1944). It was also predicted by Herbert Spencer in his notion of a decline from industrial society into a militant society.

Some writers have also seen the impetus behind distributive justice simply as envy.[65] Those who do not succeed as entrepreneurs find other ways to undermine the successful, namely, by extracting their property through taxation. For Spencer, one of the major problems that distributive justice tries to address is suffering and pain caused by inequality of resources; this very suffering is equivalent to the biological warning system of the body. The unfit, idle and feckless should be weeded out. To save such individuals by redistributing resources to them is a misplaced paternalism. It is also a reversal of the whole evolutionary process.[66]

The above arguments tie in closely with those used in the sphere of equality. Classical liberalism promoted a largely formal understanding of equality. Inequality arose as a natural fact, or an outcome, of impersonal processes. Equality before the law in terms of civil rights was essential. Economic equality meant equal access to the market. Everyone should have the same freedom to follow their interests, provided they do not infringe an equal right of others to do so. False egalitarianism, from this position, tries to achieve better distribution of wealth via state action. This is Spencer's feared 'militant society'. Spencer argued in 1903 that his aim was 'not the equality of man, but the equality of their claims to make the best of themselves'.[67] The pursuit of substantive economic and social equality inevitably undermines the market process and destroys freedom. Freedom is thus always at loggerheads with equality. For many classical liberals the pursuit of substantive equality always leads to coercion and bullying by the state.[68]

Despite the fulminations of some classical liberals against the notions of distributive justice and substantive equality, it is clear that these latter ideas have an honoured place in the liberal tradition, going back to radicals like Tom Paine. As G. F. Gaus has observed: 'All modern liberals — Rawls and Mill included — argue that we ought to accord others equal opportunities for development'.[69] If it is acknowledged that each person has an equal right to equal freedom, and freedom is understood as the power to do something worth doing, then the liberal argument moves on. To guarantee equal freedom is likely to entail some substantive redistributive actions by the state.

New liberals were quite clear that gross disparities of wealth were unjust and needed to be remedied by a limited form of redistribution. They did not want to undermine the market system, but they felt that its effects could be moderated. As T. H. Green argued: 'Left to itself, or to the operation of casual benevolence, a degraded population perpetuates and increases itself'.[70] The new liberalism recognized the need for some form of redistribution for the sake of genuine freedom, equality and justice. This particular idea has been pursued with great sophistication in recent years in the social liberal ideas of John Rawls.[71] In the early part of this century, new liberal ideas on a minimum wage, health and unemployment insurance, school meals, old-age pensions and so on were the result of such lines of thought. This was not a move towards socialism but rather an extension of arguments about equal rights to equal freedoms.

RIGHTS AND DEMOCRACY

The place of natural rights in liberal thought is often traced back to thinkers like John Locke. Behind the original natural rights ideas was the panoply of natural law ideas and an optimistic deism which saw the world as ruled by laws of God implanted in our reasoning. Such rights were seen to be asocial, universal, inalienable claims premised on human nature. The possession and respect for such rights was the precondition to human flourishing.

In the hands of John Locke and, more specifically, the American colonists and French revolutionaries, natural rights became a radical and disturbing doctrine. It represented a standing protest to established government. It was a tendency which quickly moved from demands for life, property, free speech, political self-determination and religious freedom into claims for minorities, racial groups, women, and the poor. Many radicals, like Paine, wanted these rights to be codified in constitutional documents. It should be noted, though, that not all these rights were commensurate. The right to freedom and the right to property were at odds in North America, where slaves were initially seen as part of the natural right to property.

The pursuit of substantive equality derived from natural rights eventually developed into the socialist movements of the later nineteenth century. The other aspect of natural rights arguments mutated, and occasionally calcified, into a dogmatic defence of existing property rights. In other words, natural rights became simply a defence of the existing economic and social order. D. G. Ritchie commented on this process as providing 'another illustration of the way in which the conservative of one generation may take up the ideas of a past generation of Radicals'.[72]

The notion of natural rights, specifically the concentration on natural rights to property, was subtly transformed by the end of the nineteenth century by certain liberals. T. H. Green argued that the idea of the asocial 'state of nature' is false. Humans are social creatures by nature. There are no 'natural' rights antecedent to society. Rights always imply normative recognition within society. Thus, natural rights are seen by Green as shorthand for those rights which contribute to both the individual good of the person and the common good of society. For Green, they are the negative conditions for the realization of individual capacities and powers.

Such arguments are particularly pertinent to the question of property rights. As most classical liberals affirmed, property is the preconditon to the development of the person. To interfere with property is a gross infringement of rights and liberties. However, this argument has another side. If property is an important precondition to human development, then surely a liberal society is duty bound to guarantee everyone access to some property. A Spencerian or a Hayekian, on the other hand, would tend to say negatively that only equality of access or opportunity must be guaranteed. No one must stop the individual participating in the market, but the outcome, whether failure or success, is solely the concern of the individual. The reverse of this argument contends that more substantive equality of property must be guaranteed. In other words, belief in the importance of property for individual development implies the wider redistribution of wealth and the diffusion of property to all citizens. Individuality is premised upon property.

The more negative proponents might claim that the above argument will entail intervention in others' property rights, which are supposed to be sacrosanct. Some new liberals had ways round this. First, natural rights are not asocial claims but claims congruent with the common good. They imply normative social recognition. If some people have massive property holdings giving them power over others, who consequently cannot realize their potential, such property is then not a genuine right, since rights are dependent on the common good and on social recognition. Liberty cannot be gained by the loss of liberty to others. Second, if property is a pre-condition to liberty, then all members of society ought to recognize a duty, via the common good, to provide the means for liberty to their fellow citizens. Finally, property was sometimes distinguished between property for use, or that which was genuinely earned, and property for power, quite often derived from unearned income. It was the former which was seen to be the fundamental right, not the latter. This argument located an area of wealth which could be used for redistribution. The unearned increment of property values was in fact the main target for new liberal proposals on progressive taxation.

Admittedly, not all classical liberals have been at home with natural rights doctrine. In the nineteenth century the Benthamites were the clearest earliest example of a rejection of natural rights doctrine. For Benthamites, rights were institutional arrangements for the protection of interests, pre-mised ultimately on the science of utility. There were no pre-institutional or pre-social natural rights; such rights Bentham described as 'nonsense upon stilts'. In this century liberals like Hayek adopt a more Kantian legalistic and procedural stance on rights. As John Gray comments, in Hayek 'we specify the content of the Liberal rights by reflecting on the demands of justice ... rather than by pondering the scope of Lockian rights in an imaginary state of nature'.[73] This kind of argument is usually premised on a distinction between the 'right' and the 'good'. The function of rights is to provide a fair procedural framework within which individuals can pursue their *own* good. Such a notion of rights does not propound any particular conception of the good.[74] However, the more Kantian 'right'-based approach has come in for criticism in recent discussion by com-munitarian critics like Michael Sandel.[75] There is almost a return here to the themes of the idealist liberals, such as T. H. Green, who insisted that we must take the social dimension seriously and consider the common purposes and ends of social existence in discussing any conception of rights.[76]

One other significant issue here is the relation of liberalism to democracy. It might be assumed that liberalism has some kind of intrinsic tie to democracy. Such a notion is excessively misleading. First, classical liberalism is conventionally distinguished from liberal democracy. A form of democracy — representative democracy — became identified as one of the consti-tutional devices of liberalism from the nineteenth century. After the excesses in participatory democracy of the 1789 revolution, liberals, particularly in France, had little trust in complete democracy. In Britain, Whiggery also had very little interest in democracy. Whigs were still deeply elitist about political rule, despite their occasional forays into consent and popular sovereignty. Such dislike of the extension of the franchise was in fact characteristic of some liberal writers into the twentieth century.

There was, though, an aspect of the liberal tradition which demanded an extension of the franchise as the basic right of property-owning citizens. Benthamites saw the franchise extension as a useful device for attaining maximum happiness by restraining and balancing the various interests of society so that neither sinister aristocratic interests nor the unruly mob could dominate. Such a conception of democracy was not educative or character-building but protective of basic property interests.

J. S. Mill was probably the most optimistic theorist on democracy, believing that it could have a beneficial effect on the moral development of citizens. This more developmental view of democracy can be found in some of the new liberals like Green, Hobhouse and Dewey. However, in the twentieth century the scepticism about the role and need for democracy within classical liberalism still continues. The problem with democracy, for some liberals, is that it does not always produce liberal policies. Jefferson had noted this problem in the eighteenth century, arguing in favour of the need for 'auxiliary precautions' against democracy. Hayek also sees democracy and liberty as having different goals which may or may not coincide. Limited protective democracy may protect liberty. But there are dangers. Hayek remarks: 'Perhaps the fact that we have seen millions voting themselves into complete dependence on a tyrant has made our generation understand that to choose one's government is not necessarily to secure freedom.'[77]

THE ECONOMY

All liberals are aware of the value of the free market economy. There are, however, very different views on its nature. It is doubtful that its origins were perceived either in terms of its efficiency or its value in promoting freedom. As Albert Hirschman has argued, from the Renaissance onwards there has been a view of humans as creatures dominated by their passions. The question arises as to how one deals with these passions. Various ideas had been canvassed – namely, the suppression of the passions; the use of countervailing passions, where the love of pleasure is restrained by the love of gain; and finally, the harnessing of the passions in some innocent or socially innocuous activity. Hirschman shows how the term 'passion' became subtly transformed into the term 'interests'. These interests finally became economic interests, moving slowly from the council chambers of state to the economy. Interest 'bestowed on money-making – a *positive* and *curative* connotation'.[78] Money-making was increasingly viewed through the lenses of interest and innocence. Traders were regarded as peaceful and inoffensive. Many believed that the spirit of conquest would be replaced by the spirit of commerce. All, including Adam Smith, were at this stage generally optimistic as to the effects of unhindered commerce on human civilization.

Although Adam Smith was keen on the development of commercial values, he was also concerned about its effects on martial virtues and civil order. The value of the free economy was its capacity for harnessing wayward passions. In addition, many liberals, from Tom Paine onwards, have seen participation in the market and property ownership as giving rise to responsible civic virtues. The promotion of liberty and efficiency are not therefore necessarily the prime effects of the market. In fact, there are many reasons why free market economies might be valued. They teach self-reliance and self-discipline. They produce peace and order. Some theorists value the market order in itself, others the valuable consequences it produces. The most extreme example of the former is the praxeology of Ludwig von Mises, which argues that markets are good a priori, regardless of their consequences. Not many liberals follow this particular line.

One of the slightly uncomfortable factors behind the idea of the natural harmony of the free economy is that there is often an unspecified metaphysics underpinning the discussion. In writers like Smith, the invisible hand is encapsulated within an optimistic deism. God was really controlling the apparently random events of the market. Apart from Hayek's attempt at specifying this metaphysics, in his notion of a spontaneous or catallactic order, this factor remains inert and unargued in most modern liberals.[79]

Certain liberals contend that there was a golden age of the liberal economy. Even certain critics tend to agree.[80] Sometimes it is called an age of *laissez-faire*. Some maintain that no coherent philosophy of state intervention was developed until the second half of the nineteenth century. The prevailing principle was non-intervention or *laissez-faire*.[81] It is important to remember that *laissez-faire* was never an exclusively liberal idea. After its inception, it was quickly appropriated by the conservatives and has been used periodically by them since the mid-nineteenth century. For liberals during the last century, it was seen as a useful device to employ, initially, against privilege and monopoly. Its most active use was by the Manchester school of economists whose supporters perceived the aristocratic landed monopoly which controlled basic foodstuffs as one of the greatest of evils. This was more of an anti-feudal rhetoric. Bright, like his admirer T. H. Green, traced many of the ills of Britain to the Norman land-owning families.

Although there are figures like Herbert Spencer who appear to be closely identified with the doctrine of *laissez-faire*, it is most clearly seen in Britain in organizations like the Liberty and Property Defence League, which was in fact peopled by many conservatives like its president, Lord Wemyss.

Even extreme individualist critics of the League, like Auberon Herbert, started his political life in the Conservative Party. While *laissez-faire* figured in many popular liberal discussions from 1830 onwards, by the 1880s it was largely dropping out of the mainstream of liberal thought and has never really re-entered since. In fact, many scholars have doubted whether it actually existed during the middle years of the nineteenth century.[82]

Certain proponents of classical liberalism, in their desire to compartmentalize their own version of liberalism, argue that other liberals, like the Benthamites, progressively gave up their commitment to the free economy and became obsessed with state intervention. In fact, this is misleading. If one examines the arguments of liberals over the nineteenth and twentieth centuries, one finds a continual and slowly developing commitment to the role of the state.[83] The new liberalism is an extension of this general thesis, a recognition that every citizen has the equal right to enjoy basic economic, political and cultural resources. This process entails some intervention and control of economic life. As J. A. Hobson argued: 'Liberals ... never committed themselves to the theory or policy of this narrow *laissez-faire* individualism.'[84] Enlargement of the sphere of the state, for new liberals, usually entails an increase in individual liberty.

It should be noted that none of the new liberals wanted to abandon the market economy. Many pre-1914 new liberals wanted to moralize capitalism. In the case of liberal economists like Keynes in the 1930s the emphasis was different, shifting to more technical economic argument concerning the state supervision of the market system in order to increase its effectiveness in reducing unemployment and poverty and thus to release the full productive capacities of capitalism. This had become a major theme of new liberalism in the 1920s, culminating in 1928 with *Britain's Industrial Future*. Known as the Yellow Book, from its cover, this was an extensive programme of state-led action involving public works, diffusion of ownership, extension of progressive taxation and encouragement of saving. In sum, it was suggesting a form of planned or managed capitalism. Keynes himself did not seem unduly aware of the problem of poverty, except as an underused economic resource. Comprehensive social policies on poverty were developed by W. H. Beveridge in his 1942 *Report on Social Insurance and Allied Services*, which laid the foundations for the social security system in Britain. It is clear that most of the major policy changes in economic and social spheres in Britain this century, until the 1970s, were developed by new or social liberals. This social policy development is not necessarily at odds with classical liberalism. There was a gradual extension and mutation of ideas over the nineteenth and twentieth centuries, which gave rise to increasing state involvement in economic and social policy.

POLITICS AND THE STATE

The liberal notion of the state arose from the much older intellectual tradition of constitutionalism. Liberalism has focused on constitutional themes since its inception. Of course, many early constitutional writers had no perception of many of the themes that we might now associate with liberalism, yet liberalism fed upon, and eventually virtually identified itself with, the constitutional tradition. The principal concern of this constitutional tradition, as in liberalism, was to limit the scope of the state, to make it accountable and responsible for its actions and to ensure that it was committed to certain values.

It has been contended that liberalism is committed to a minimal state, one limited to the tasks of internal order and external defence and distinguishing between the private and public realms. Although some classical liberals are periodically thrown into paroxysms of anxiety over how to limit the state, they are hamstrung by the fact that liberal constitutionalism is a theory of the state and concerned with the public good. If there are limitations, they are constructed within a state. The *sine qua non* of the limitations is the state itself. The boundary that is supposed to exist between public and private is a continually shifting one. The liberal state is formally committed to respect the realm of the private, and yet, as we have seen in previous sections, there is no hard-and-fast rule to distinguish the private from the public. Manifestly, in times of war, liberal states do, as a matter of course, change the boundaries.

As in the section on the economy, we find a slow and growing commitment by liberals over the nineteenth and twentieth centuries to the positive role of the state. The arguments of liberals have varied, once again, between those who hover close to anarchy, disliking the state or seeing it as an unfortunate necessity, and those who see a positive and active role for it in promoting genuine individuality and civic virtue.

In the minimalist case of figures like Auberon Herbert, a totally voluntary state is advocated. More recent liberals, like Robert Nozick, are concerned to argue for a more definite, compulsory minimal state, limited by the side-constraints of natural rights. Yet Nozick has been criticized by some Hayekian liberals for being too minimalist in scope.[85] Herbert Spencer saw the state as an unfortunate but necessary 'committee of management'. Spencer had an extensive list of 'do nots' for the state. He viewed the statute-book of Britain as an unmitigated disaster: legislation piled on more legislation to cure the defects of previous legislation. Such state growth interfered with social evolution towards the industrial society by cultivating dependence in the population and undermining individual self-reliance. The state, for Spencer, should therefore have no concern with aiding the poor, factory legislation, public health, drainage, sewage, and vaccination. Spencer, unlike Humboldt, Adam Smith and Malthus, also disapproved of any form of state involvement in education on the same grounds. He objected to state-organized postal networks and lighthouses, and, oddly, he took exception to the British Nursing Association and National Society for the Prevention of Cruelty to Children as overly 'collective' groups undermining individualism. On the other hand, Spencer did suggest the state control of libel laws and the regulation of pollution, noise and smoke. He toyed with a scheme for land nationalization by the state, land ownership being regarded as an aggression against individual rights. Later in life he also conceded the need for state involvement in the upkeep of roads, pavements and sewerage. All this greatly disappointed some of his disciples.

A similar ambivalence towards the state can be seen in the utilitarian liberals. Bentham, Mill and Sidgwick, despite overt commitment to a limited state, allowed it to perform progressively more tasks, going well beyond Spencer's proposals. The science of utility allowed utilitarians to assess the value of legislative activity. There were no intrinsic grounds to oppose state activity *per se*. None of the Continental liberals, such as Constant, rivalled Spencer's minimalism. Constant and Tocqueville were looking more for limitations through balance and separation of powers within the state structure. Their major fear was the growth of popular dictatorship and the consequent decline of individual freedom. More recent classical liberals, like Hayek, are not in favour of any ultra-minimalist or even minimalist state in the Nozickean sense, although they are clearly at odds with the utilitarian tradition from Bentham onwards.

The more positive view of the state is therefore neither the result of a sudden transition nor a fundamental revision of liberal thought. It is the result of a slow movement within liberal ideas. It would be true to say that this movement was somewhat accelerated by prominent thinkers like Green. The idealist notion of the state envisages it as having a positive ethical role in society. The state is not just an abstract institution, but an outgrowth of the wills and aspirations of the citizens comprising it. It is an organic entity designed for the realization of the common purposes of humanity, which are coincidental with true individuality and freedom. Institutions in the state represent objectified ethical purposes. The meaning and significance of the state is dependent on the improvement of its members, thus it is still in an important sense individualist and committed to individual liberty. Such liberty, though, requires the state to provide the necessary conditions for all citizens to develop.

These ideas, plus more radical uses of utilitarian and evolutionary thought, lay firmly behind the advent of the new liberalism in Britain. For thinkers such as Hobson and Hobhouse, and in America, Dewey and Rawls, the state was increasingly viewed as an integral part of the economic and social life of the community. It was not just concerned with freeing individuals from obstacles to their economic activity, but was actively involved in the promotion of a better life for its citizens. Liberals, up to the present day, have never been completely content with the state. The two major world wars of the twentieth century and the penetration of the state into many spheres, has genuinely unsettled them. This unease was true of new liberals in Britain during and after the First World War, who felt deeply unhappy about issues like military conscription. However, discontent with the state has never stopped liberals from using it to promote freedom, utilizing distributive justice, establishing a legal framework for economic relations, promoting a mixed economy and providing certain public goods. The state in this sense can be an enabling institution for the good life for all citizens.

CONCLUSION

The main criticisms that may be encountered by the student of liberal thought will now be reviewed. Some of these are more generally directed at the whole liberal mentality, others are aimed at specific forms of liberal ideology. For the sake of convenience such criticisms will be divided into three main topics: the critique of the individualist mentality; the critique of the reality and illusion of liberal ideology; finally, some ideas on the direction and culmination of liberal thought in the twentieth century.

The critique of the individualist mentality encompasses a large body of arguments which can only be briefly mentioned here. First, it is contended that liberals find it immensely difficult to formulate any clear and realistic concept of social life. They have been accused of a sociological naivety by both socialist and conservative critics. If liberalism conceives of the fundamental units of experience as being isolated atoms, how can any collective notions be formed?

If one tried to formulate any genuine theory of individual consent, would it not be impossibly impractical, since it would assume that every act by a government would have to have the consent of every individual? In practice, liberals never argue this and thus are regarded as inconsistent with the general direction of their arguments. It is clear that many liberals have been quite prepared to accept that individuals should be coerced, which again seems utterly inconsistent with an individualist premise. In the same vein, some critics would contend that liberals try surreptitiously to smuggle in a moral or social consensus by the back door. Hayek, after long disquisitions on the importance of individual responsibility and the inconsistency of collective responsibility, refuses to face up to the logic of his own argument and tries to hold society together by subliminal moral conventions which all individuals are supposed to accept without thinking. This can look like sleight of hand. In one sense, the best liberal, who judges the world according to purely individual self-interest, would be the free-rider, regardless of the cost to others. Free-riding would be the most rational path, as long as others were publicly responsible.

If it is difficult to aggregate individual interests, it is virtually impossible to formulate any satisfactory theory of public goods or to reconcile the individual with public authority. Individualism implies, so critics argue, that all goods are purely private. How can one aggregate these? Individual preferences simply cannot be aggregated to provide public provisions, which in the end usually have to be imposed. Overall, it appears that liberals, though valuing individuals, are not really prepared to take on board the full logic of individualism. Individualism in its most radical sense implies solipsism and relativism in all matters of morality and truth. There appears to be no way to distinguish between the individual's true and false interests. In fact, the very idea of real interests appears faulty from a purely individualist perspective. This is one reason why so many complex moral issues are generated by liberal thought. Can we condemn abortion, euthanasia or surrogate motherhood? Have we any right to censor pornography? It is the importance and value of individuals and their liberty which lies behind such questions of policy.

The fundamental weakness in this line of criticism is that it only applies to a limited number of liberals. There is a social individualism which can be found in many liberal writers, from the nineteenth century onwards, which does not have to respond to this because it already acknowledges certain societal values in the social constitution of the individual. In consequence, the criticism tends to miss the mark in terms of the liberal tradition as a whole.

The second body of criticism focuses on the reality and illusion of liberal ideology. This criticism can be encapsulated in a number of contradictions. Liberals, it is argued, celebrate the freedom of those who cannot use it, proclaim equal citizenship for all and make it innocuous for a majority. Liberalism is far more interested, in this sense, in civil rights than in hungry people. Many liberals would contend that it is preferable to be starving in a liberal society than well-fed and unfree in an authoritarian or totalitarian society. How well-fed liberals can know this has often struck critics as puzzling. Liberals speak in glowing terms of the importance of property, but effectively, through their economic institutions and markets, deny it to millions. In fact liberals, especially over the nineteenth century, were noted for the harshness of their treatment of the poor and hungry. One only has to recall the words and actions of the Liberal administrations during the great Irish famines, or the attitudes of figures like Malthus to the labouring poor, for confirmation of this thesis. Liberalism proclaims the common human values of civilization and then praises selfish individualism – a position most neatly summed up in Ayn Rand's doctrine of the virtue of selfishness. Liberalism is interested in legal equality for all, but not in equality of property or power. It sees no conflict between property ownership and equality of opportunity. Liberals have, in the eyes of certain critics, had far too favourable a press on their positive side. One has to consider the reality behind the illusion, or at least the bad as well as the good aspects.

What use is freedom or equal legal citizenship to an individual who is starving and ill? Liberalism does not see that unequal ownership of property can lead to unequal powers, which can then distort the interrelation of human beings. Poverty is seen somehow to be the fault of the individual. The poor must be made to be responsible. Property is said to be fundamental, but the capitalist system recognizes that many will not partake in it. To interfere with someone's property is then seen to be a gross infringement of rights. So the sick individual, dying in a gutter, is free and no injustices have been perpetrated, whereas a multi-millionaire subject to progressive taxation is the victim of injustice. Thus Robert Nozick describes taxation of the wealthy as a form of forced labour or slavery. Many have found such conclusions unpalatable.

A number of these criticisms strike at classical liberals. Yet as we have seen in this chapter, different notions of freedom, citizenship, rights and property have been promulgated within liberalism. One only has to recall those social liberals who argued that freedom is not just about being left alone but about leading a worthwhile life, to see the potential variety of perspectives.

The final set of criticisms focuses on the destiny of liberalism in the twentieth century. In a sense it is a criticism with a more positive note attached. The contention is that the particular freedoms and rights that have been sought by liberals have only been experienced by limited groups in society. The doctrine of equality and freedom has been veiled from certain other groups who should have benefited equally. As Ruggiero commented: 'Beneath the veil of a universal liberalism, the bourgeoisie disguised a privilege similar to that once flaunted by the aristocracy; and thus the proletariat's efforts to overthrow the new privilege, though anti-liberal in appearance, were in reality to bring into existence a wider liberalism'.[86] Until the twentieth century, the broad working masses and women were excluded from the benefits of liberal civilization, in terms of equal political, cultural, economic and social rights. The character of liberalism is changing due to its extension to these groups. This took place initially with working-class groups and, in the twentieth century, extended to women. Thus, as Ruggiero argued, the growing cooperation of liberal and labour groups from the 1890s 'is not an accident or an expression of political opportunism, but is deeply rooted in the necessities of the new democracy'.[87] It is arguable whether this process is still continuing within liberal thought.

There is a further twist to this argument. From the 1930s, a number of Marxist critics of liberalism argued that liberalism was unable to cope with this natural extension of its logic, because to do so would have had tremendous repercussions on capitalism, profit maximization and property ownership. Liberalism had not realized that 'the political democracy it brought into being was established on the unstated assumption that it would leave untouched the private ownership of the means of production'.[88] It was so obsessed with political forms that it failed adequately to take into account the economic foundations they expressed. The only way out for liberals was to seek some means to stop the whole process. They found this, so it is argued, in fascism. Fascism protected capital accumulation and oppressed the rising proletariat. Thus fascism 'emerges as the institutional technique of capitalism in its phase of contradiction'.[89] This argument, of course, envisages liberalism as a declining creed tied indissolubly to a particular mode of production. The end of capitalism means the end of liberalism. One major weakness of this argument is that it does not explain why, in the 1920s, fascism occurred in a country with a very weak liberal tradition (Germany), and, compared with Britain, one with a very undeveloped capitalist industrial base (Italy).

Liberalism has in fact stayed on the scene in European thought, although two world wars have altered the liberal mind. Much of the optimistic perfectibilism of the nineteenth- and early-twentieth-century liberals was dashed on the fields of the Somme, Ypres, and by the later knowledge of Dachau and Buchenwald. It became difficult to feel very hopeful about the human species. This led, in some liberals, to a loss of hope and a sense of disgust with nationalism. In the 1930s, for those not caught up with the appeal of fascism or socialism, the siren call of scepticism, individual self-cultivation and self-examination was heeded by many. Although one must not forget the vigorous thinking conducted in the 1920s and 1930s in the progressive wing of the British Liberal Party, specifically in the summer school.[90]

In the post-Second World War period, liberalism has reappeared in a number of political forms. In the 1950s it was typified in the Cold War, 'end of ideology' group, discussed in chapter 1, which had a considerable impact in both America and Europe. Liberalism stood, paradoxically, against the ideological mind. The ideological mind always seemed to be either partially or totally totalitarian. Liberalism, at this time, appealed to consensual politics, which it mistook for non-ideological politics. Politics was only seen to take place, for some, in the liberal domain. Out of this anti-totalitarian demeanour another strand of liberal thought developed, which repudiated the 'end of ideology' consensual mentality. This was probably best expressed in the writings of Hayek. It was an attempt to return Western societies to the pristine clarity of a somewhat mythical and utopian vision of classical individualistic liberalism. This is the mentality which has come into such high profile in Western industrial societies in the last two decades. However, it is important to put this into perspective.

There is nothing pure or pristine in such classical or Whiggish liberalism. The Hayekian scheme is as narrow and stultifying a vision of genuine liberalism as the 'end of ideology' mentality. A third manifestation of liberalism, which is more contentious, is the continuance of diverse streams of more social liberal thought. The *prima facie* electoral demise of liberalism, in Britain and other countries, has not meant the demise of liberal thinking. It is arguable that most of the reformist and revisionist socialist parties in Europe (and certainly the British Labour Party) have taken on the mantle of social liberalism. In fact, this social liberalism is manifest in most parties. The present debates in British politics look increasingly like a dialogue between the more classical liberals and social liberals, rather than a debate between conservatives and socialists.

One final manifestation of liberalism, which has had some impact on politics, is the vigorous efflorescence of liberal political philosophy, specifically in the USA, which also represents the diverse and contradictory impulses of the liberal ideology. Writers like John Rawls, Robert Nozick, Ronald Dworkin, Michael Walzer and others are thinking through many of the major issues of politics from the diverse angles of liberal thought. Nozick appeals to the more libertarian individualist liberals, whereas Rawls is rapidly becoming the patron saint of the social liberal persuasion. It is not only liberals like Keynes and Beveridge who have influenced Labour Party thought and policy in Britain. It appears now that Rawls' ideas are being recruited in the restructuring of present Labour thinking, which does admittedly set the liberal balance straighter in terms of the influence of writers like Hayek on conservative ideas in the 1980s. The only problem with the current manifestation of liberal philosophy is that it does not seem to be very self-conscious about its ideological roots and context. In the case of Rawls, Nozick and Hayek it is also very selective and limited in its conception of the liberal tradition, picking up what confirms its present vision and rejecting what does not. Such selectivity impoverishes our understanding of the liberal tradition. One other danger implicit in this tradition is its ahistorical character. When these present thinkers address issues of justice, rights and freedom, it is almost as if we are to assume that liberal thought *is* philosophy or philosophical method. Thus we are supposed to see their studies simply as analytical, philosophical arguments. The major problem here is again a lack of awareness that this is only *one* form of philosophical thought which has historical roots.

Liberal values and ideas developed slowly from the seventeenth century. The ideology itself crystallized in the early 1800s as a way of thinking and seeing ourselves and our relation to others. It has penetrated much of our thought, but we should be careful about viewing it as the truth about the world and humankind.

3
CONSERVATISM

—

Like liberalism, conservatism is often seen to have both an ordinary and a more technical usage. The ordinary usage generally focuses on the idea of conserving or 'keeping something intact'. This idea has been dated to the fourteenth century. Contemporary writers on conservatism, such as Russell Kirk and Robert Nisbet, place a heavy emphasis on this medieval origin. Kirk, for example, traces back the conservative perspective to 'conservators' (the guardians of medieval cities), the unwitting Chaucer and English justices of the peace — 'Custodes paces'.[1]

The more overt political use is usually dated, like liberalism, after the French Revolution. Most scholars admit that the actual political origin dates, more precisely, from the early 1800s in America, as an epithet implying a low or moderate estimate of a state of affairs. Some early American National Republicans styled themselves conservative in this sense. In France, the term was first coined in Chateaubriand's journal, *Le Conservateur*, in the 1820s. This periodical was designed to propagate ideas on clerical and political restoration. In Britain, the term first occurred in the *Quarterly Review* journal in 1830. By 1835 it became the more official designation for the Tory Party. Blake remarks that its gradual adoption from 1832 onwards 'was a deliberate attempt to purge the party of its old associations and symbolize, if not a break with the past, at least a change of course'.[2] The term spread throughout Europe from the 1840s. The political upheavals of 1829–30 and 1848 focused the attention of conservative thought on the dangers of revolution, although industrialization and democratization also played a significant role.

There is a perennial debate on the relation between the more ordinary and the technical political uses. Many proponents of political conservatism see certain advantages in rooting their political sentiments in the ordinary use. There is some truth to the proposition that we are all a little conservative immediately after a good dinner. Some political conservatives have wanted to exploit this 'disposition' and have argued that we are all, in fact, conservative 'by nature'. Conservatism, it is concluded, is not only a political doctrine but is also embedded in the stuff of life itself. Such an idea makes humanity, *en masse*, conservative. The difficulty of such a notion is in explaining allegiances to other ideologies and articulating the beliefs to which all conservatives would supposedly adhere. It also bypasses the point that conservatism is historically a specific ideology, arising at the same time as liberalism and socialism, and sharing some of their sentiments. Some commentators have therefore concluded that the ordinary use of conservatism provides very little insight into the technical political sense.[3] In the urge to provide a coherent ideology, the simple notion of 'conserving' is seen to be both crude and unhelpful.[4]

Before moving on to the debates about the origins and nature of conservative ideology, a definitional problem should be considered. We should not assume that there is a definite body of ideas to which all conservatives adhere. In fact, there are many conservatives who would deny the attribution of ideology to their beliefs. This has been called conservatism's 'political anti-philosophy'.[5] In some cases this denial of theory is less convincing, in others it is rather better thought out.

There are five broad interpretations of the character of conservatism, which have very different implications. These can be schematized as follows: the aristocratic ideology; the pragmatic ideological position; the situational or positional view; conservatism as a disposition of habit or mind; and finally, the ideological interpretation.

In the first view, conservatism is perceived as the negative doctrine of reaction expressed by a semi-feudal agrarian aristocratic class, specifically after the challenge of the French Revolution. Conservatism thus functioned in a highly specific historical and economic context. It represented the negative defensive posture of a declining aristocratic class in European societies. In this sense, the time span of conservatism can be roughly dated from 1790 to 1914. In Britain, 1832 (rather than 1914) was a crucial watershed, with the advent of growing democratization. The development of enfranchisement, industrialization and the success of the Anti-Corn Law League in the 1840s were mortal blows to the Tory Party. This view is recognized by commentators who draw a distinction between the older Toryism and the post-1832 ideas. Once the political and economic significance of this aristocratic class had faded, then the ideology also withered and was subtly but decisively superseded by classical liberal practice. Hence conservatism can be seen as a temporary historical phenomenon, representing the views of a class which was in serious political and economic decline.

The second argument is the least satisfactory. Conservatism is seen primarily as a form of political pragmatism – a doctrine with no principled content. It simply absorbs the prevailing political, cultural and economic ethos. Other political credos always make the running. Thus, it is contended, with a grain of truth, that in the last two hundred years conservatism has taken its policies from other political ideologies and defended them all at one time or another. If something works and is accepted, then it is legitimate material for conservative policy. Conservatism, as a number of scholars have noted, can be found espousing both statist and extreme libertarian sentiments. This argument does, though, over-play the negativism of conservative thought.

The above pragmatic view can sometimes be confused with the two further interpretations. The first of these — the situational or positional perspective — is in fact more in tune with ordinary discourse.[6] It is revealed in commentators and journalists who, quite unwittingly, speak of conservative factions within, say, a socialist party. Conservatism, in this reading, is not tied to any particular class, historical events, pragmatism or even to a specific disposition. Like the pragmatic view, the situational perspective does not possess any definite substance. It has no ideal or utopia to strive for. Conversely, it reflects the self-conscious defensive posture of any *institutionalized* political doctrine. Political schemes which are not institutionalized, transcend any present political realities and offer to change the world in line with the transcendent ideas, are the natural enemies of conservatism. Conservatives are those rooted in an institutionalized way of life, offering an immanent defence of a particular order. The defence usually only arises in a 'situation' of challenge to institutions confronted with transcendent ideas. Conservatives thus stand for the existing order, whatever its political complexion, against the chaos of change and reform. In this situational reading it becomes possible to speak of a 'Conservative Left'. There is therefore no content to conservative ideology. Any institutional order (communism or liberalism) can be conservative.

The fourth interpretation focuses on the idea of a disposition. There are two arguments here. The first is premised on the earlier claim that conservatism is part of the stuff of life itself. Lord Hugh Cecil called this 'natural conservatism', which he defined as 'a tendency of the human mind. It is a disposition averse to change and it springs partly from a distrust of the unknown and a corresponding reliance on experience rather than on theoretic reasoning.'[7] The important point to note is that conservatism is not being viewed as an ideology; rather it is the natural disposition of human beings, preferring the tried habits or tools to the new and unfamiliar. This idea carries over very easily into politics. Imperfect established practices or institutions are preferred to the novel.

The second argument embodied in the dispositional claim is a more sophisticated philosophical defence of natural conservatism. It focuses on subtle distinctions between types of reasoning (namely, theoretical and practical reason) and also inquires into the origin of human motivation.

There is an ingenious if misleading argument at work here. The philosophical defence of the disposition thesis maintains, on the one hand, that conservatism is a non-ideational and natural phenomenon, and on the other hand, tries to persuade us of the truth of this idea in an argument full of subtle ideational elements. This is what was referred to earlier as the 'political anti-philosophy', although 'philosophical anti-philosophy' might be a more appropriate term. The more sophisticated argument on the conservative disposition straddles the fourth ideological interpretation.

In the final category, conservatism is an unequivocal ideology which cannot be compromised by any pragmatic or situational considerations. It is not defined by its historical situation and is not necessarily identified with any class. It is also far more than a natural disposition. It is a body of ideas with a prescriptive content. Edmund Burke is often taken to be the founder of this ideology, which is seen to be profoundly relevant today. Conservatives, in this view, have consistently tried to oppose certain ideas, which have often been generated and used in revolutionary situations: namely, the perfectibility of the human species through social and political conditions; the progress and development of human nature towards some ultimate good society; equality and liberty as individual human goals and the economic and political implications which follow from such ideas; the belief in the triumph of human reason in the world; the neglect or disparagement of authority, privilege, hierarchy and tradition. Initially, in France and Germany, conservative criticism was directed at the Enlightenment and *Philosophes* tradition and its extreme offshoot – revolutionary Jacobinism. In Britain, the early radical liberal tradition (Paine and Price) also came in for sustained assault and, later, the utilitarians and liberal economists. Finally, in the nineteenth and twentieth centuries, the various manifestations of socialism have caused the greatest consternation in conservative ranks.

The non-ideological perception of conservatism will arise again in this discussion and its pervasiveness and influence cannot be neglected. It is also worth noting that this argument will be re-encountered in the discussion of other ideologies. Conservatism is not alone in trying to make itself appear non-ideological. Having noted the definitional problems with conservatism, it is the latter ideological account which will occupy the rest of this chapter.

THE ORIGINS OF CONSERVATIVE THOUGHT

Most writers on conservatism observe that the real watershed of conservative thought was the French Revolution. It was the events in France which spawned the famous reflections of Burke and, of course, it is not until the early 1800s that we find the first use of the word conservative in the political sense. However, some scholars see important themes before 1789 which, though not self-consciously conservative, none the less contribute towards the conservative perspective. This might be said to be an 'unconscious conservatism'. There is something worryingly anachronistic and spurious in such claims.

The earliest inception of conservatism is seen in Greek and Roman thought. The writers most often cited here are Plato and the Roman Stoics, though the dramatist Aristophanes makes an appearance in Russell Kirk.[8] A selection of Conservative writings published in 1976 begins with excerpts from Plato's *Republic*.[9] Another writer comments that 'It is essential that a work on Conservatism begins with Plato's *Republic*'.[10] The next most favoured beginning is the Middle Ages, but it is difficult to feel confident about Morton Auerbach's description of the twelfth-century book, *Policraticus* by John of Salisbury, as a work of 'pure conservatism'.[11] Nisbet, even more extravagantly, places the whole nineteenth- and twentieth-century Conservative movement firmly under the banner of a recovery of medievalism. For Nisbet, it is a mistake to see Burke as a Whig. Burke was really trying to revivify the local communities and guilds structures of a feudal society. Much has also been made of Burke's medieval natural law sentiments, but this is a different and more subtle argument.[12] Neo-Medievalism is also seen in groups like the mid-nineteenth-century Disraelian Young England Group. Paul Smith describes the group as a 'revivified and spiritualized feudalism', although it is worth noting that he later depicts them as a form of *opéra bouffe.* [13] Many recent scholars have found the medievalist reading of both Burke and conservatism far-fetched.[14] There is a strong element of nostalgia, anachronism and wishful thinking in these views.

Such anachronism continues into later periods. Whereas Keith Feiling and Hugh Cecil focus on the Reformation period as the source of conservative ideology, writers such as Anthony Quinton, Huntington and Robert Eccleshall begin with Richard Hooker and the Elizabethan Settlement.[15] For Eccleshall, Hooker is the grandfather of conservatism. He remarks that 'There is a line of development running through Hooker and Filmer to the formation of the Tory party in the latter part of the seventeenth century'.[16] He parallels Hooker's attack on the Puritans with Burke's later attack on the Jacobins.[17] However, Frank O'Gorman has commented that the Elizabethan Settlement lacks 'the historical perspective on social and political institutions proper to modern conservatism'.[18]

Other scholars see the roots of conservative ideology in the doctrines of divine right and patriarchalism. For Gordon Schochet, Filmer's *Patriarcha* was the backbone of Tory thinking.[19] The doctrines of divine right — that government is ordained by God, non-resistance and passive obedience are religious duties, society is natural to humans and resembles a family with an inbuilt natural hierarchy — are still, it is contended, implicit in nineteenth-century conservative thought. Opinions may have changed within conservatism about the source but not about the nature and sacred quality of national sovereignty. Sovereignty had simply moved from monarchy to Parliament.[20]

O'Gorman favours the 1660s Restoration, when the term 'Tory' came into political use. As he states: 'It is more rewarding to note the emergence of a specifically "Tory" attitude to politics in the second half of the seventeenth century than it is to wrangle over spurious pedigrees'.[21] Others appear to prefer the 1688 Settlement as the decisive moment. The Marquis of Halifax is often seen as the key conservative figure at this point. There are hazards, though, in all these ideas. The doctrines of the Whigs and Tories after 1688 were closely allied. Neither group were parties in the modern sense. They had no formal rules, discipline, or strict criteria of membership. They might better be described as shifting alliances of interests. Trying to identify a consistent conservative position in these periods is erroneous.[22] Also, it is worth recalling that Burke was a Whig, not a Tory. He was an enthusiastic supporter of both the 1688 revolution and the American colonists in the 1770s. Unlike Tom Paine, he wanted to keep these revolutions distinct from that of 1789.[23]

One other eighteenth-century philosopher who is often mentioned by conservative writers as a founding figure is David Hume, although he is as frequently claimed for the liberal pantheon. Opinions are divided about Hume. Some writers hail him as the great inspiration to conservative thought.[24] Another conservative writer, Ian Gilmour, has remarked of Hume: 'How could a man whose scepticism demolished God, the soul, miracles, causation, natural law, matter, and induction, be a good conservative?'.[25] Hume's deeply secular and destructive scepticism is not always to the taste of conservatives. Dr Johnson was not alone when, in conversation with Boswell, he described Hume as a 'Tory by chance'.[26]

Most scholars agree that the self-conscious ideology of conservatism was worked out in response to the French Revolution. The period 1789–1914 is often taken as the heyday of conservative thought and practice.[27] The 1789 revolution gave rise to Burke's famous *Reflections* and also to the word 'conservatism' itself. European writers associated with conservatism, such as Coleridge, Maistre, Bonald, Lammenais, Chateaubriand, Novalis and Müller, all clarified their ideas in relation to the revolutionary events, often taking Burke as their exemplar. Burke's position in conservative thought has remained pre-eminent to the present day for both admirers and critics. For Burke, the French Revolution was dynamically new. It was not of the same character as the revolutions of 1688 and 1776. Its central ideas proposed that humans were both equal and perfectible. Such improvement could be advanced by the cultivation of human reason and the reform of social and political institutions. For Burke, such ideas had profound implications for politics. It was these implications which he and subsequent conservatives resisted. Such resistance formed the real catalyst to the ideology of conservatism.

The subsequent history of conservative ideology over the nineteenth century was characterized by a number of negative themes. Conservatives, specifically in Britain, tried to acclimatize themselves to the growth of democracy, but it was not a smooth passage.[28] Conservatives have often been unwilling to accord popular sovereignty or manhood suffrage much credence. They have usually kept the 'people' distinct from the 'rabble'. The people with property had some right to be represented, but not the ignorant rabble or mob. Stability and an interest in the common good of the community related to property ownership. Writers such as Matthew Arnold, Thomas Carlyle, Sir Henry Maine and W. H. Lecky, and particularly politicians like Lord Salisbury, were still bewailing the enfranchisement of the ignorant masses at the close of the nineteenth century. Even the property owners were subdivided by Burke, who argued for 'virtual representation', namely, 'the notion that even without the franchise, individuals could be "virtually" represented through others in their community'.[29] Burke reckoned on a property-owning vote of roughly four hundred thousand citizens. British conservatives, however, adapted more pragmatically to democracy than their European counterparts.

Conservatives in the nineteenth century also had a very ambivalent reaction to industrialization and the rise of liberal political economy. There has been a strong anti-industrial, anti-individualistic strain in conservatism from Möser and Coleridge, through Cobbett and Disraeli, to Charles Maurras, T. S. Eliot and Christopher Dawson in this century. Industrialization and individualism meant the decline of community, tradition, order and religion. There is therefore a recognizably anti-capitalist streak in conservative thought.[30] None the less, the political success of the Conservative Party in Britain into the twentieth century has been based on its ability to adapt and find a *modus vivendi* (at times an immensely enthusiastic one) with the industrial and democratic ethos.[31]

THE NATURE OF CONSERVATISM

There are three broad approaches to the study of conservatism: the historical nation-state, chronological and conceptual approaches. These are not mutually exclusive. They often overlap quite considerably in some studies. None of these approaches, except one dimension of the conceptual view, identifies any distinctive or necessary ideological conservative position.

The historical nation-state idea argues that conservatism can only really be classified in terms of the particular historical and cultural circumstances of the nation-state in which it occurs. In other words, it is German, British and French conservatism which are of most interest, not some over-arching theory. O'Sullivan toys with this stance, but combines it with a formal conceptual emphasis on imperfection. Thus French conservatism was attached initially to a more religious and moralistic vision of the world, appealing to eternal religious verities and order. German conservatism, by contrast, tended towards a more metaphysical and historical vision which emphasized a strong philosophical theory of history. Karl Mannheim concurs with this view, commenting that in German conservatism we have 'a philosophical deepening of the points Burke had posed, which are then combined with genuinely German elements ... Germany achieved for the ideology of conservatism what France did for progressive Enlightenment – she worked it out most fully to its logical conclusions'.[32] Finally, in Britain we see a sceptical and empiricist vision, which is intellectually messy, compromising and less coherent, but none the less in the end more politically successful.[33]

There is some value to this approach. In the USA many apparent conservatives have in fact been defending classical liberalism. For Louis Hartz, the Right in America is exemplified in the tradition of big propertied liberalism.[34] Those in the USA in the 1930s who defended traditional classical liberal doctrine against the New Deal were branded conservative, whereas Roosevelt and Woodrow Wilson were considered liberal.[35] In Germany also the particular problems of political unification in the nineteenth century, a vociferous nationalist movement emphasizing *völkisch* ideas, the dominant position of the authoritarian Prussian Junkers, and the heavily metaphysical approach of their leading thinkers, inevitably coloured the approach to conservative ideology. By the late 1920s most nationalist and conservative thought had been influenced by the impact of national socialism.[36] Indigenous historical, cultural and political issues affect the character of conservatism in most states.

The second approach classifies conservatisms in chronological terms. The classification follows the fracture-lines and fortunes of Conservative Parties. In the British context, Peelite conservatism was superseded by Disraeli, Salisbury, and so on until the 'middle way' of Macmillan and 'Thatcherism' in the 1980s. Each phase of conservatism is stamped by the dominant personalities and exigencies of the period. Such a chronology, despite being more easily grasped, can obscure the ideological coherence.

The final interpretation of conservatism focuses on conceptual classification. There are two general positions taken on the conceptual view. The first argues that there is one pure doctrine of conservatism. There are no conservatisms, even if there are different philosophical roots. It is therefore useless to try to classify types of conservatism.[37] The second, more popular view sees differing schools of conservatism. There may be some formal unity on values and ideas, but the manner in which these ideas are interpreted can lead to radically different conclusions. The problem with this latter view is that there are a bewildering variety of classifications in the literature. Sometimes conservatives are drawn distinct from Tories, traditionalists and reactionaries. Within conservatism itself we can find twofold classifications – collectivist and libertarian conservatives or sub-

stantive and procedural conservatives.[38] There are threefold classifications
– reactionary, status quo and reformist conservatives or liberal empiricist,
liberal rationalist and anti-liberal intuitive conservatives.[39] There are also
even more extensive classifications in the literature.[40]

There is obviously little consensus here. To make sense of the diversity
of conservative thought it is necessary to consider a fivefold classification:
traditionalist, romantic, paternalistic, liberal and New Right conservatives.
The latter is the most recent and most problematic area. Yet none of these
provides a totally airtight category. There is continual overlap and much
of the time it is a matter of emphasis.

Traditionalist conservatism places greatest emphasis on the notions of
custom, convention and tradition. This is the conservatism that we are
most familiar with in the usual image of Burke. Theoretical reason is
disparaged over and against prejudice and practical reason. The state is a
communal enterprise with spiritual and organic qualities. The constitution
of the community is not a human artefact but the cumulative, unpredictable
result of years of practice. Change is something which, if it does happen,
is not the result of intentional reasoned thought. It flows naturally out of
the traditions of the community. Leadership, authority and hierarchy are
again natural products. We obey as easily as we breathe. Our liberties and
rights are rooted in our communal norms.

Romantic conservatism is characteristic specifically of many of the
German theorists such as Justus Möser, Adam Müller, the Schlegels, Friedrich Novalis, as well as English conservatives like S. T. Coleridge, William
Wordsworth, Sir Walter Scott, William Cobbett and T. S. Eliot. In many
of these theorists we find a strong nostalgia for an idealized pastoral, rural,
often quasi-feudal past, often combined with a well-worked-out utopian
vision of what that restored society could look like. The general tenor of
thought amongst the romantic conservatives was anti-industrial. They
disliked the alienation and dehumanization of mechanistic industrial
culture and were deeply critical of the view of humanity and the values
expressed through the commercial mentality. Liberal political economy
was seen to be fundamentally wrong about human nature. Romantic
conservatives favoured a form of life which was simpler, religious, and
saturated with communal sentiments. There would be a natural hierarchy,
as in traditionalist conservatism, which would incorporate chivalrous,
heroic values, as in many of the characters of Scott's novels or Carlyle's
imaginary heroes. This form of conservatism tends to be far less concerned
to disparage the role of reason. The rationalism of the Jacobin revolutionaries was not attacked from the basis of either instinct or practical
reason, but from the dizzy heights of speculative reason (or Reason with a
capital R – *Vernunft*). This can be identified clearly in Coleridge's approach.

Paternalist conservatism is implicit in some aspects of the traditionalist
and romantic perspectives. It interprets the duties of rule to imply fairly

wide-ranging state activity to foster a good life for all citizens – a form of responsible aristocratic *noblesse oblige*. This principle has led many conservatives down the more *dirigiste* road.[41] Government is envisaged as a benevolent paternal figure setting goals and ensuring fair play and equal opportunity. Paternalist conservatism has been seen regularly over the last two centuries, from the work of Shaftesbury in the 1830s, through Disraeli and Chamberlain, up to the middle-way and more corporatist conservatism of Macmillan and Heath. It is also present in aspects of European Christian Democracy in Germany and Italy in the post-1945 era.

Combined with the elitist responsibility was a strong humanitarian element. In Britain this can initially be seen in the thinking of men like Oastler, Sadler, and Shaftesbury, and their work on the Factory Acts. They engaged in a sustained critique of individualism, Benthamism and classical political economy. They disliked the New Poor Law (1834) and believed fervently in the role of the state in guaranteeing decent housing, working conditions, wages and treatment of the poor. Later in the century in Britain this concern to uphold decent conditions for all took on the title, 'one-nation' conservatism. It is debatable as to how effective it was, certainly in the nineteenth century.

One other motivation entered this paternalist strand from the 1830s. This was an electoral realism: a realism concerning the changing character of the electorate. It was signalled by Sir Robert Peel in his Tamworth Manifesto (1834).[42] The Manifesto was not a detailed body of ideas, in fact it seems to have been put together hastily for an election. Yet most scholars agree that it reflected a change of mood, attempting to reconcile the older Tory Party with the new electorate of the 1832 Representation of the People Act. Strong government, law and order, the traditional constitution, and existing property interests had to be linked with a new middle-class electorate. If the Conservative Party was to survive electorally, it had to adapt. This message came home to sections of the party, particularly after the repeal of the Corn Laws in 1846.

Disraeli consolidated the Peelite movement. The Young England group, with which he was associated, was a more rhetorical version of this paternalism and realism concerning the new electorate. Their aim, which was espoused in Disraeli's novel *Sybil or the Two Nations* (1845), was the founding of a national Conservative Party, repudiating wealth-making for its own sake, liberal individualism and class divisions. Disraelian conservatism looked for both political representation and improved industrial and social conditions. This was to be linked with a renewed reverence for the Crown and the ancient constitution. In sum, its aim was 'one nation'. Disraeli's admiration for the older constitution was expressed in his early work *Vindication of the English Constitution* (1835), which paid homage to both Burke and Coleridge. The improvement of social and economic conditions was fairly superficial. However, the achievement of Disraeli's vision, apart from internal party reorganization, lay in the extension of the franchise movement in the 1867 Representation of the People Act.

The paternalist tradition has played a significant role in the Conservative Party for over a century. The emphasis on the responsibility of property, the extension of political rights, a preparedness to use the state for the welfare of the nation, were self-consciously upheld by figures like Lord Randolph Churchill, Joseph Chamberlain, and by his son Neville in the 1920s. This approach also characterised the middle-way conservatism of Macmillan in the 1950s and some aspects of Edward Heath's premiership. One of its more recent advocates in the British Conservative Party is Sir Ian Gilmour. In *Britain Can Work* (1983) Gilmour argued against the rise in unemployment in the 1980s on the grounds of its undermining the one-nation doctrine. Gilmour linked this idea with the conservative tradition. The critique of the New Poor Law, the lenient attitude of Disraeli to the Chartists, the concern for factory legislation, are all seen to be part of a healthy conservative tradition. In consequence, Gilmour expressed deep disquiet concerning the classical liberal view taken by many of his fellow party members in the 1980s. Although a free economy is desirable, to some degree, it should not become the dominant value for a conservative. For Gilmour, politics should always be prior to economics.[43]

The maxim of liberal conservatism is the reverse of Gilmour's. Economics is prior to politics. There is an identifiable continuity of liberal-minded conservatism dating back to the nineteenth century. Some would include here thinkers such as Constant and De Tocqueville. Yet it would still be a matter of debate as to whether this is a correct categorization. The liberal conservative tends to accept most of the formal tenets of classical liberalism: the emphasis on individualism, negative liberty, personal rights and a minimal rule-of-law state. But this conception of the state, sometimes combined with an imperial destiny, is usually more extreme than would normally be accepted by classical liberals. The post-1945 revival of liberal conservatism, in many European societies, has focused its attack on public-sector ownership and welfare state policies.

This form of liberal conservatism has been traced to Burke's *Thoughts and Details on Scarcity*. Others see the late 1880s as a safer starting-point. In Britain in the 1880s, it is identifiable among the conservative membership of the Spencerian Liberty and Property Defence League. Organizations with membership connections to the Conservative Party, like the Personal Rights Association, the Political Evolution Society (later State Resistance Union), the British Constitution Association, Anti-Socialist Union and Industrial Freedom League, also manifested the general temper of liberal conservatism. The campaigns of such groups were usually devoted to attacks on state growth. Deregulation and privatization were the desired ends.[44]

This particular tradition has been carried on by a number of societies in the post-war period and has had a growing impact throughout Europe and America, specifically in the last few decades. Probably the most famous of these intellectual groups is the Mont Pelerin Society. In Britain the torch has been carried by the Institute of Economic Affairs, Aims of Industry and, more recently, by the Adam Smith Institute, the Freedom Association and the Centre for Policy Studies. Over the late 1970s and early 1980s, many of the leading figures in the British Conservative Party were completely absorbed by liberal conservatism, almost to the exclusion of other themes in the conservative tradition. Sir Keith Joseph, and a host of lesser figures, had all the enthusiasm of Damascus road converts (not a common characteristic of conservatives) to a new faith, involving the dogmatic and slavish reiteration of the virtues of the liberal free market. Their statements appeared virtually indistinguishable at times from classical liberalism.

The final category of conservatism, the New Right, is the most problematic. It is not something which is easy to describe, partly because it incorporates such a diverse membership. It is clearly very different to the older traditionalist, romantic and paternalist traditions. Liberal conservatism, paradoxically, could be said to be one of the strands of the New Right. Its immediate origins lie first in the persistence and durability of the liberal conservative tradition; second, in the anti-totalitarian critiques of the 1950s, specifically in writers like Hayek and Oakeshott, who engaged in a running battle with all forms of socialism and social liberalism. Further, the electoral defeats of the paternalist conservatives, over the 1960s and early 1970s, convinced many that a change of direction was needed. Finally, people believed that the policies and strategies of nationalization, corporatism, Keynesian demand management and the welfare state had failed. This disillusion coincided with deep-rooted fears of inflation in Western economies in the 1970s.

Who to include under the rubric of the New Right remains puzzling. It is usually seen as an amalgam of traditional liberal conservatism, Austrian liberal economic theory (Ludwig von Mises and Hayek), extreme libertarianism (anarcho-capitalism) and crude populism.[45] David Green, in his apologia, widens the liberal dimension to include the Friedmanite Chicago school and the ideas of the Virginia public-choice school.[46] None of these elements are necessarily intellectually commensurable. Some texts, like Green's, though widening the study of the neo-liberal aspect, are not prepared to countenance the inclusion of the neo-conservative or neo-authoritarian elements. Roger Scruton and other members of the Salisbury Group are ruled out from discussion. Although one can see why this should be — since it fragments even further the ideological coherence of the New Right — none the less it does little justice to the movement.[47]

The *prima facie* ideological coherence stands some chance if it is limited to the neo-liberal element. The neo-liberal policy emphasis has been enthusiastically orientated to the free market. State intervention is perceived to have failed totally. The consensual post-war politics of planning, state welfare, high taxation, public spending, bureaucratic growth, wages unrelated to productivity, and corporatism, are seen to be redundant. There is no alternative to the free market, which should be the final arbiter for virtually all social issues (including health and education).

The policy objectives have been the emancipation of the individual from state regulation, cuts in taxation, reduction of state welfare, controlling budgetary deficits and the money supply, and privatizing state monopolies. The difference from the liberal conservative tradition is that there has been an even greater reliance, in the neo-liberal New Right, on market criteria. Anarcho-capitalist or extreme libertarian elements in the New Right have called for the deregulation of hard drugs, pornography and in some cases criminal activity like blackmail. It has been contended that these would no longer be problems if they were available on the free market. If an individual values their reputation and can settle a contract with someone not to reveal information about them, then even blackmail is conceivable on market criteria as a legitimate mode of exchange. No liberal conservatives would accept these ideas. In fact, a liberal conservative like Enoch Powell in Britain is not prepared to countenance either health or education being subject to market principles. There is thus a far-reaching dispute on the extent of the market.

Not many market theorists feel comfortable with the agenda of the neo-conservative New Right, namely, nationalistic fervour, patriotism, national culture, purity of race, natural inequality, the importance of disciplined family life and patriarchal authority, and compulsory Christian religious education. The neo-conservatism of Scruton or Maurice Cowling has more in common with some traditionalist conservatism.[48] They repudiate both paternalist and liberal conservatism with equal fervour. Freedom and equality are of little or no interest. Citizens have in fact had too much freedom and equality in the post-war era. For Cowling, both Marxism and liberalism should be equally subject to conservative ridicule and incredulity. One of the self-conscious aims of the Salisbury Group was in fact to correct the trend toward liberalism within the Conservative administration. True conservatives, for Cowling, should be concerned with issues like upholding private property, having freedom over one's earnings, and the restoration of national identity.[49]

HUMAN NATURE

Conservatism has a relatively constant judgement on human nature, except for the schools of liberal conservatism and the New Right which have absorbed much of the classical liberal perspective. For traditionalist, romantic and paternalist conservatisms humanity has a limited capacity for altruism, usually extending to family, neighbours and friends. We are naturally but not exclusively selfish. Our acquisitive instincts make us potentially corruptible, yet our laziness and liking for the tried and tested tends to limit the reach of such corruption. We cannot, in this sense, be rational utility maximizers. Such a notion of rationality is inappropriate to the complexities of the human condition. Humans may at times value their freedom and the maximization of their interests, but not to the exclusion of their love of leisure, natural laziness and enjoyment of life. Humans are not rational machines, they are a complex mesh of emotions, thoughts and often contradictory motivations. There is nothing to be ashamed of here. To seek for complete consistency is a rationalist myth. It is a superficial view of humans to see their primary motivation as reason. This observation also gives rise to a sceptical attitude towards the aspirations for human rationality. The latter point is linked with one of the primary objections voiced by conservative critics of liberal conservatism, namely, that it simplifies and misunderstands human nature.

For many conservatives, neither the idea of mass society nor of atomized individuals is meaningful. The critique of individuality has given rise to acerbic interchanges between liberal conservatives and the other conservative schools. Both notions (individuality and mass society) are often seen as two sides of the same bad coin; the mass being constituted by alienated and isolated individuals. For many conservatives, human beings grow up within a complex process of historical and social acculturation. Individual freedom is the result of years of social development within a particular national tradition. Language, customs and thought are acquired pre-reflectively in the family, peer groups, schools and social interaction. Abstract individuals and cosmopolitan humanity are figments of the imagination. As Joseph de Maistre argued: 'The Constitution of 1795, like its predecessors, was made for *man*. But there is no such thing as *man* in the world. In my lifetime I have seen Frenchmen, Italians, Russians, etc.; thanks to Montesquieu, I even know that *one can be Persian*. But as for *man*, I declare I have never in my life met him; if he exists, he is unknown to me'.[50] Roger Scruton makes the same point when he comments: 'Individuality . . . is an artifact, an achievement which depends upon the social life of man'.[51]

Despite the acclaimed historical sensitivity of much conservative writing, its vision of human nature is both universal and ahistorical. This universality is something conservative thinkers share with liberalism. Historical awareness can lead to the relativization of human nature. In the conservative case, despite being children of our time and community, our basic nature and motivations remain unchanged. Nature still moulds us in certain universal ways. On the one hand, this historical awareness has led conservatives to repudiate the doctrines of natural rights, contract theory and the state of nature. These doctrines are seen to alienate humans from the particular national traditions and institutions which make sense of their lives. Human beings cannot be imagined outside society. On the other hand, conservatives still envisage humans remaining constant over time and circumstances. Although this argues a compatibility between historical change and our unchanging nature, it is not convincing. Conservative writers want the benefits but none of the relativistic costs of historical consciousness.

Because we are socially and historically determinate creatures, we necessarily reflect the natural patterns of inequality in abilities and status in society. Authority is always necessary in society and authority entails inequality. Someone in authority gives the orders and others obey them. Conservatives have faith in the natural leadership powers of certain groups or individuals.[52] Inequality is rooted in both natural and political circumstances. Some people are naturally superior, both intellectually and morally. Such inequality is nothing to be ashamed of. It cannot be eradicated by social or political means. Some are born to lead and some to be led. However, it should be noted at this point that some twentieth-century conservatives, both those who have assimilated liberal ideas and those following a more paternalist line, have been far more influenced by arguments for equality of opportunity and equal citizenship.

Finally, conservatism is concerned with the ineradicable and universal *imperfection of human nature*. This notion implies that humans will always remain flawed creatures and cannot be perfected in any way. This is an idea which no doubt gave rise to Viereck's comment that conservatism may be described as the 'political secularization of the doctrine of original sin'.[53] There are two main sources to this vision of imperfection in human nature: the theological and the practical. The theological is the oldest view. In Christian theology the idea relates primarily to the doctrine of original sin. We live in a fallen sinful world. Nothing can be done except a holding operation by individuals and societies against corruption. This is the human condition. In the city of man (to use the appropriate Augustinian term) all that political authority can do is to make the best of a bad job. As Maistre commented, 'In the works of man, everything is as wretched as their author'.[54] Maistre was far more concerned about the wretched and sinful character of humanity than Edmund Burke.[55]

In spite of the fact that there are conservatives this century who hold to the idea of religious imperfection, many others are unable to accept such a view.[56] Some have in fact directly repudiated the religious theme. There is a strong tradition of secular conservatism which has undoubted intellectual pre-eminence this century. Secular conservatives hold to what broadly may be called the practical doctrine of imperfection. This calls upon the resources of moral theory, epistemology, and psychology. The basic contention is that humans are imperfect in terms of their capacities to understand the world. We all have a very small stock of information at our command. We are also historically and socially limited in our horizons. The reach of human reason and knowledge is very small and not to be relied upon. Custom and tradition are therefore far safer guides for conduct. This limited knowledge and inability to determine the good of others with any precision is not something that will change. It is again a universal fact about humans. As the total stock of human knowledge increases, even within our own culture, we are doomed to increasing ignorance of the whole. Practical imperfection is inevitable. Thus, apart from the liberal conservative persuasion, the more general assumption of conservatism is that human nature is flawed and imperfect and will remain so whatever the politics.[57] A politics involving human perfectibilism therefore remains anathema.

REASON AND ACTION

Before proceeding to any discussion of the economic and political ideas of conservatism it is important to grasp one of the central and most elusive arguments of conservative ideology. This argument concerns the explanation of the nature of human action and the role of reason. This has been touched upon briefly in the previous sections and must now be expanded.

Because the inception of conservatism was linked with the refutation of ultra-rationalist arguments from the French Revolution, there has always been an impression of an anti-rationalist element in conservative ideology. The conservative view is sceptical concerning the relevance of rationalism to politics; in the words of Russell Kirk, 'Any informed conservative is reluctant to condense profound and intricate intellectual systems to a few pretentious phrases; he prefers to leave that technique to the enthusiasm of the radicals'.[58] The dislike of systematic political philosophy, the belief in a more pragmatic, sceptical and expedient approach to politics, has led conservatives from Burke to Oakeshott to repudiate the exclusive role of reason in politics. Yet it would be a mistake to call the more traditionalist, romantic and paternalist conservatives irrationalist. As Scruton has observed: 'Because there is no universal conservative policy, the illusion has arisen that there *is* no conservative thought'.[59]

Essentially, many conservatives have noted a distinction between two types of reason. This distinction between 'practical' and 'theoretical' reason, which goes back to Aristotle, can be found deployed by certain of the early traditionalist conservatives at the time of the French Revolution. For some, the distinction is not so clear and appears between 'reason' and 'instinct', or 'reason' and 'intuition'. In Maistre, philosophy generally 'corroded the cement that united men'. Modern philosophy, he contended, 'is at the same time too materialistic and too presumptuous to perceive the real mainsprings of the political world'. It is not reason which differentiates us from animal creation, but our ability to intuit a spiritual world. True legislators 'act on instinct and impulse more than on reasoning'.[60] In Justus Möser this argument appears as a confrontation between *thought*, which is rigid and immobile, as against *life*, which is active and growing but also rooted in time-honoured custom.[61]

Burke deployed a distinction between *abstraction* and *principle*.[62] Principles, which Burke used with great reluctance, were rooted in custom and tradition, as distinct from the dry abstractions of metaphysical reason. Burke's sentiments on the metaphysics of Enlightenment reason are clearly stated in the *Reflections*:

> Four hundred years have gone over us; but I believe we are not materially changed ... Thanks to our sullen resistance to innovation, thanks to the cold sluggishness of our national character, we still bear the stamp of our forefathers. We have not (as I conceive) lost the generosity and dignity of thinking of the fourteenth century; nor as yet have we subtilized ourselves into savages. We are not the converts of Rousseau; we are not the disciples of Voltaire; Helvetius has made no progress amongst us ... We know that *we* have made no discoveries, and we think that no discoveries are to be made, in morality; nor many in the great principles of government.[63]

Burke's point was not to undermine all reason in politics, but to suggest that politics should not be determined by abstract theoretical notions like natural rights. The fact of the existence over time of an institution or custom was evidence of an intrinsic practical rationality, something which might not always be obvious to the observer. Change might be needed but it should not be premised on a priori abstract ideas, but rather on a close attention to the concrete problems and spirit of the institutions concerned. To wipe out institutions and to start again on rational premises was the primary error of the French revolutionaries. Such an idea was nicely encapsulated in Justus Möser's remark: 'Whenever I encounter an old custom or habit which does not square with our modern notions I tell myself there is no reason to believe that our ancestors were fools. I then explore the problem until I find a reasonable explanation ... having found it I can return and ridicule those who have ignorantly attacked old customs.'[64] Michael Oakeshott's terminology for this is the primacy of practical over technical knowledge. Practical knowledge works within a tradition, attending sensitively to its 'flow of sympathy'. Rational technical knowledge distorts and simplifies.[65]

Not all conservatives fit neatly into the above framework. Romantic conservatives, like Coleridge, placed a heavy emphasis on the Germanic notion of 'philosophical reason' as against the 'understanding'. Philosophical reason grasped the sense of the *whole*, as against the fragmentary nature of the understanding.[66] Reason became almost a symbol of the organic wholeness of society. Benthamism and liberal political economy became examples (in Coleridge's mind) of the more fragmentary false *understanding* of society. Yet liberal conservatives, who in fact rely on the more instrumentalist notion of reason present in liberal political economy, inhabit an Enlightenment rationalist world which is repudiated by most traditionalist and romantic conservatives.

The argument on two types of reason leads many conservatives to the notion of two types of truth. These are the truths of reason and logic which exist in the realm of ideas. Such truths may have little or no relevance to the empirical world we inhabit on a day-by-day basis. Practical truth is found in customs and traditions. True legislators act by such practical impulses.[67] As Möser argued: 'Practice which adapts itself closely to every individual circumstance and knows how to make use of it is bound to be more competent than theory which in its high flights is bound to overlook many circumstances'.[68] When the truths of theoretical reason are applied to the world, distortion ensues. This was the root of Maistre's fulmination against the building of the city of Washington, which he predicted would fail simply because it was the result of rational calculation and decision.[69] It is also the basis to Michael Oakeshott's discussions of the fallacy of learning to cook or ride a bicycle by reading a book. Such practices cannot be learnt from technical rules.[70]

The distinction between types of reason also throws some light on the conservative reputation for scepticism. There are, to continue the above theme, two forms of scepticism. Pure scepticism is a radical critical doubt of every human belief, which uses the tools of reason to turn reason on its head. Conservatives do not hold this view. This line of scepticism is present potentially in David Hume with his experimental method of reasoning. Hume does not, though, take his scepticism very far in politics or political economy. He is more inclined to view the latter in terms of history, human nature and custom.[71] Hume's real target is abstract Enlightenment reason in epistemology and morality. Many conservatives have sensed the general direction of Hume's arguments, especially in his writings on religion, and drawn back in horror.

The second form of scepticism, which is characteristic of traditionalist and paternalist conservatives, is a limited, tempering one, pessimistic about the reach of theoretical reason. It expresses a philosophic doubt as to whether rational ideals can be achieved or, in fact, whether they mean anything.[72] The exceptions to the above arguments are, first, many of the romantic conservatives. As mentioned earlier, these tend to deploy confidently the notion of philosophic reason. There is little room here for scepticism. Secondly, the liberal conservatives also have assured beliefs concerning human nature, instrumental reason and the nature of economic activity, which eschew any wavering doubts. In liberal conservatives and the market-orientated aspects of the New Right there is a breezy sense of abstract rational truth.

In traditionalist conservatism the basis of human action is not theoretical reason, but custom, prejudice and habit. Such practices embody practical reason. For Maistre, the cradle should be surrounded by prejudice in order to give secure content to the mind of the child. Such prejudices and habits are derived from the historical and social circumstances of the individual. Prejudice is not simply blind or irrational behaviour; conversely, it is 'pre-judgement', a distillation of experience over generations. It is a way of knowing *what* to do, which is innately superior to abstract reason. Prejudice allows the agent to know what to do, without reflections, in morality and politics. To act on prejudice is to act as one's forebears acted. It is, in essence, tradition. Scruton thus remarks that 'When a man acts from tradition he sees what he *now* does as belonging to a pattern that transcends the focus of his present interest, binding it to what has previously been done, and done successfully'.[73] Burke aptly called this 'wisdom without reflection'. As Hampsher-Monk notes, Burke's view of prejudice 'is a defence of the unexamined assumptions which, as a result of associations formed in our society's past, make up its political and moral beliefs ... he [Burke] defends prejudice itself without regard to the content because it renders human behaviour within society more predictable and manageable'.[74] Prejudices, because of their durability, form the substance of traditions and human action. Jacobinism and other such political creeds represent the attempt to eradicate prejudice in the name of enlightenment. No wonder Burke could assert, with gusto, 'Thank God we are not enlightened'.

Paradoxically, one of the results of the concentration on prejudice, habit and custom, and thus tradition, is that history acquires a higher profile. Burke was led by his arguments on tradition towards a rich sense of history. Unwittingly, he was preparing the ground for the enormous burgeoning of nineteenth-century historical thought, specifically in Germany. This has led to some comparisons between Hegel and Burke. It is in this area that we find romantic and traditionalist conservatives in agreement. Both read history teleologically as the embodiment of a deeper and more spiritual purpose. The point at which most conservatives part company with such historical thought is where history becomes non-teleological, namely, where human thought and activity become simply the expression of a particular historical moment with no meaning or purpose above or beyond that moment. Conservatives, understandably, cannot abide such historical relativism.

POLITICS AND THE STATE

For most conservative schools, political life is viewed organically. Such conservatism also tends to be communitarian and suspicious of individualism. Finally, society is viewed hierarchically, namely, leadership and political judgement are skills limited to a few. Political judgement is for the connoisseur. The marked exception to this perspective is the liberal conservative persuasion, specifically the more extreme, market-orientated theorists of the New Right.

The organic view of society conveys the idea that society is not an artifice or mechanism but is a mutually dependent interrelation of parts. Most conservatives, with rare exceptions, use organicism analogically. Each individual has a place in the organic whole. Change or reform has to be consonant with the pace of the whole organism. Theorists such as Lammenais, Maistre and Müller gave this organic idea a religious and mystical reading. Probably the most extreme example of this tendency was Friedrich Novalis in *Christianity or Europe*, who interpreted the state as a vast organic *makroanthropos*.[75] More secular-minded conservatives have simply used the organic analogy to symbolize the importance of community or nationhood.

Political life is seen to be part of a much larger drama, whether religious or secular. There is an order implicit in the world. Political or moral order cannot be invented or imposed; rather it is internal to political and moral institutions. It is taken *from* the world at large. Thus Cobban remarks that Burke 'spent his life on his knees before the great mystery of social life'.[76] Conservative writers have read the nature of this order in different ways. The more religiously-minded, like Maistre, saw God as the author of order. As he remarked, institutions are 'only strong and durable to the degree that they are, so to speak, *deified*'.[77] For Maistre (and Burke to a much lesser degree) the French Revolution was an evil act against a divine order. Such a religious reading of order is still to be found in some conservative interpretations this century.[78] Other writers identify the secular historical development of society and tradition as the meaningful order. In some case this involves a clear repudiation of the religious theme. In post-1945 Britain, Michael Oakeshott is the best example of such secular conservatism.[79]

The communitarian and anti-individualist tendencies of conservatism derive, to some extent, from the organic analogy. The individual is part of an organic whole and cannot be understood except through the whole organism. The notion of community remains somewhat inchoate, however. For Nisbet, it is 'a fusion of tradition and commitment, of membership and volition'. It was used as an oppositional theme against Enlightenment individualism. Nisbet contends that the family, kindred, parish, village, church or folk are 'all obviously the historically formed molecules of the greater reality of society. These, and not abstract, atomistic individuals of natural law fancy are the true subjects of a true science of man.'[80] The idea of community suggests that a deeper identity and sense of belonging was the source of human contentment and sanity. Such a theme is present in Coleridge, Disraeli and later in T. S. Eliot's and Christopher Dawson's barely disguised contempt for the individualism of liberal society, as against the virtues of the more pastoral and semi-feudal community.

One of the implications of the organic community is a veneration for established customs. Piety to the established order is a necessary concomitant to realizing the importance of tradition. Tradition incorporates more wisdom than the individual, since it embodies a concrete manner of life over generations. Traditions can be trusted, unlike abstract theories. Change, in itself, within a tradition is not repudiated, but rather the 'selfish spirit of innovation' which changes on rational grounds for the sake of change.

Finally, such piety to the established order means that we respect the existing natural hierarchy and inequality of society. All the conservative schools, except liberal conservatism, adhere to this idea. Social order will always entail authority and a natural leadership group or elite. As Allison comments: 'Hierarchy, authority and coercion are necessary if there are to be "arts, letters and society"'.[81] Burke referred to this leadership as a natural aristocracy. Whereas Burke, Maistre, Möser and Novalis thought in terms of a more fixed hereditary and landed aristocracy, Coleridge and Eliot included a broader elite – incorporating an intelligentsia – namely, Coleridge's 'national clerisy' and Eliot's 'Community of Christians'.[82] Others, like W. H. Mallock, in *Aristocracy and Evolution*, put forward the idea of an entrepreneurial meritocratic aristocracy, premised on its evolutionary fitness to rule.[83] Another conservative writer argued that the important point was not the content of the elite aristocracy, but the moral qualities of the leaders of 'dutiful public service, insistence on quality and standards, the decorum and inner ethical check of *noblesse oblige*'.[84]

Government is needed because of the imperfection of human nature. For conservatives, government is a positive but not unmixed blessing. There is also some variation on the nature of government. Writers like Maistre and Möser obviously felt more at ease with quasi-feudal and monarchical regimes. Even in nineteenth-century Britain Thomas Carlyle, hovering on the edges of conservative thought, showed deep impatience with the British parliamentary structure and longed for both hero-worship and a strong dictatorial leader like Oliver Cromwell. However, Burke and the majority of the British conservative tradition have felt happier with the balanced constitution and parliamentary government.

Government should provide a strong framework of procedural rules and customs which maintain peace, justice, liberty and property. For the majority of conservatives, government is a necessity of life which can have positive or negative aspects. Apart from liberal and market-orientated aspects, conservatives have not been frightened to use the powers of the state. Romantic and paternalist conservatives have been fairly open in their intention to use the state to help provide a better life for citizens. The 'middle-way' conservatism of Macmillan and others utilized corporatist ideas, Keynesian demand management, and actively promoted state involvement in social security, education and health-care. The British Conservative Party was the first to begin the nationalization process in the inter-war years, as well as initiating the state broadcasting system. Furthermore, the concept of the welfare state in most European societies owes as much to conservatism as to other ideologies.

Although there are no very specific conservative ideals of government, there are general features worth noting. First, conservatives have tended to repudiate purely autocratic rule. They are not proponents of weak government, but favour something which is both strong enough to cope with internal or external order and yet is still constitutionally limited or balanced. They do not usually believe in liberal constitutionalism. A constitution understood as a body of created written rules and rights has no real meaning. Rules and rights are the result of years of social and political development.[85] Written laws are declarations of the pre-existing customs which make society cohere. As Maistre commented: 'Although written laws are merely declarations of anterior rights, it is far from true that everything can be written down; in fact there are always some things in every constitution that cannot be written and that must be allowed to remain dark ... on pain of upsetting the state.'[86] Constitutions, for Maistre, are not created by human deliberation but germinate unconsciously with God's help. Burke does not go as far as Maistre, but the same basic idea of the unconscious immemorial constitution is still present in his thinking. Even a recent conservative writer, like Nisbet, feels compelled to redeem the American constitution from the clutches of liberal constitutionalism, arguing, in effect, that apart from the Bill of Rights, much else in the constitution, like the separation of powers, is intrinsically informed by unwritten immemorial customs.[87]

Such a customary constitutional settlement involves a command structure, fixed inequalities of powers, and a natural leadership or aristocracy. These were premised on a limitation on powers, a defence of certain rights to liberty and property, and some separation between state and civil society. This latter point did not involve a doctrinaire, fixed separation, as in the formal account of classical liberal thought. In fact, a fixed separation in an organic community was regarded as suspect. If the citizen was part of an interrelated whole, how could any firm separation occur? None the less, conservatives have acknowledged the moral and political importance of the private realm, particularly the liberal conservatives.

The traditionalist, romantic and paternalist conservatives place considerable value on rights. Such rights are not those of liberal individualism. They are not private, natural or pre-social. Rights are legal concessions from the community. In other words, rights are problem-solving devices within political communities. As a conservative propagandist has argued: 'Just as you cannot have a private language, because words derive their meaning from use, and therefore it is inevitable that language inheres in community ..., so you cannot have private rights which no one else acknowledges. When we talk about rights, we are talking about communal life.'[88]

Although the right to property is fundamental, it is not an absolute right which is located in the individual. Conversely, it is a right which is acknowledged and conceded as such (for secular or religious reasons) by the political community. It may be accorded fundamental importance in terms of social stability, but it is still not a totally private entity. It also, for many conservatives, implies duties and responsibilities.[89]

Property is also linked with freedom − 'No man is fully free unless possessing some rights of property'.[90] Freedom is not regarded as an abstract liberal freedom − the right to engage in unconstrained or uncoerced action.[91] Freedom is usually viewed by traditionalist and paternalist conservatives as a legal right *within* the parameters of tradition and the rule of law. It is premised on established institutional life. This is an important theme in the conservative tradition.[92] Freedom is concerned with the protection of the individual (usually in the context of the family) and their property. Freedom is not, however, an absolute value. It is relative to the ends of the community. Incessant liberation undermines the social order. Freedom is not attained by allowing everyone greater liberty to participate in the political process. This was the great error of the Jacobins and later socialists. Freedom is experienced by the citizen of a state with sound authority and the rule of law.

It is worth mentioning at this point that conservatives in general, even those of the more liberal persuasion, have not been overly sympathetic to the value of democracy. For a host of writers including Burke, Maistre, Charles Maurras, Maurice Barrés, Sir Henry Maine, William Lecky, W. H. Mallock, T. S. Eliot and Christopher Dawson, perfect democracy implied perfect despotism and the destruction of sane political life and liberty. Fear of the mass mediocrity of democracy was also present in the liberal writings of Constant, Tocqueville, J. S. Mill and Hayek, as well as in a wide spectrum of European writers like Jacob Burckhardt, Friedrich Nietzsche, and probably most notably Ortega y Gasset, in his famous book, *The Revolt of the Masses*.[93] It was thus not a fear shared simply by conservatives.

Democracy, in its more unlimited participatory form, was seen to be implicit in most revolutionary movements. It was also linked with the worrying doctrine of popular sovereignty. For most schools of conservatism, humans cannot govern themselves; they need the wise guidance of prejudice and a natural governing elite. Freedom is not acquired through democracy. Maurras in France and Dawson in Britain were led by the same logic to criticize even limited representative parliamentary democracy.[94] In the 1920s and 1930s, this was also a tempting path for the conservative elements of Germany and Italy, but it had different consequences to those in France and Britain. Society needs authority and hierarchy, which are incompatible with popular rule. For conservatives, pure democracy implies rampant self-interest, a destruction of community into an alienated, atomized mass, and the end of authority and civilization.

Many conservatives have accepted a limited, controlled and representative democracy. There are qualifications within this idea, however. Burke, for example, put forward the idea of 'virtual representation', namely, that even without any franchise, individuals could still be represented by others. Burke had in mind a minuscule franchise. This notion has been influential in the British conservative tradition. Martin Pugh catches the spirit of the point well when he remarks that late-nineteenth-century conservatives (and liberals):

> did not claim that their system was democratic, a term that smacked of conti-
> nental abstraction and implied an excess of equality characteristic of American
> society; rather, it produced effective government, it guaranteed 'liberty', and
> it was representative. What it represented directly was those considered fit
> by reason of their independence, their material stake in society, their education
> and political knowledge to exercise the parliamentary franchise.[95]

Non-electors could be spoken for: labourers by landowners, wives and children by husbands, the illiterate and propertyless by the literate and property owner. One can still sense an intense irritation with democracy, at the turn of this century, in the Conservative Prime Minister Lord Salisbury.[96] More recently, Roger Scruton refers to democracy as a 'contagion' in British society. In remarking on the relation of the state to trade unions, he continues, in a sinister tone: 'The true nature of the relation between state and trade union will be understood only when the democratic principle has been put aside'.[97] In consequence it seems logical for Scruton, in the 1980s, to have helped to found the Conservative propagandist journal, *The Salisbury Review*.

Genuine freedom therefore requires communal constraint. Even recent conservatives argue that post-war Britain has had (to use the title of an essay by Peregrine Worsthorne) too much freedom. Worsthorne, warning against the rise of liberal conservatism in the 1980s, argues that: 'The urgent need today is for the State to regain control over "the people", to re-exert its authority, and it is useless to imagine that this will be helped by some libertarian mish-mash drawn from the writings of Adam Smith, John Stuart Mill, and the warmed-up milk of nineteenth-century liberalism'.[98] Freedom is not about individual autonomy but, conversely, about upholding certain traditional rights in an established state.

This idea of liberty is clearly at odds with all but the most minimal or formal view of equality — as in equality before the law. Demands for substantive social, economic or political equality are associated, in the conservative mind, with the levelling demands of Jacobinism or socialism.

People should know their place in society. For most traditionalist, romantic and paternalist conservatives, humans are naturally unequal. Some are cleverer and will receive greater benefits, some are luckier in terms of family, others are more adept at ruling. Society is necessarily and inevitably an unequal hierarchy.

THE ECONOMY

There are two basic positions taken on the economy within conservative ideology. The first, reflected in the traditionalist, romantic and paternalist schools, tends to adopt a more sceptical stance to the notion of a free-market economy. The other position is the pro-market view of liberal conservatism and aspects of the New Right.

The debate on the economic views of conservatism goes back to one of the founding fathers, Edmund Burke. Some commentators see him as a clear exponent of a free-market view, specifically in his essay *Thoughts and Details on Scarcity* (1795). It is argued that there is very little distinction between the thought of Burke and Adam Smith. Robert Eccleshall remarks that in Burke 'for the first time, bourgeois economics was fused with the older conception of society as a command structure'.[99] Others appear less impressed with this view. Ian Gilmour sees Burke's political economy writings as an aberration, incorporating some 'barbarous metaphysics'.[100] On the other hand, Iain Hampsher-Monk observes astutely that in Burke 'the real political argument for regulated free trade as against taxation was that free trade limited the Crown's access to the spoils of empire and consequently its resources for political management at home. Burke did not need Adam Smith's economic arguments for free trade.'[101] In this sense, there were political rather than directly economic factors at work in Burke's arguments.

Despite the significance of liberal conservatives over the last decade, and the emphasis on the free market, most of their ideas reflect the formal themes of classical liberalism. There is therefore little point in rehearsing arguments for markets which have already been discussed in chapter 2. However, it should be noted that liberal conservatives tend to be slightly less optimistic about human capacities than classical liberals. For them, the market needs a stronger, more secure framework of law and order than would normally be contemplated by classical liberals. In this sense, liberal conservatives are more willing to use the state to defend or promote market interests, although internal debates do arise over imperatives towards markets and social controls, particularly in relation to some of the New Right proposals.[102]

Despite the dominance of liberal conservatism and the New Right in Europe and America in the last decade, it would be a truism to say that historically many conservatives have been committed to a statist view and sceptical of unregulated markets. This does not mean that such traditionalist and paternalist conservatives have been in favour of anything like a command economy. They have usually adopted a more pragmatic and flexible approach containing markets within certain socially defined parameters. In fact, the European Christian Democratic idea of the 'social market economy' appears far more consonant with the conservative tradition.

The development of industrialization and the market economy entails the pursuit of private interest and accumulation of capital. There are subtle responses to this issue within conservatism. Some romantic conservatives obviously had very mixed feelings about industrialization and the market economy, others were tolerant as long as such processes did not impinge on prior values like community. Writers as diverse as Coleridge, Southey, Lammenais, Maurras and Eliot expressed profound anxiety as to whether liberal market economies were conducive to genuine community. Eliot, in his *Idea of a Christian Society* (1939), bewailed the fact that:

> the dominant vice of our time ... will be proved to be Avarice. Surely there is something wrong in our attitude to money. The acquisitive, rather than the creative and spiritual instincts, are encouraged ... I am by no means sure that it is right for me to improve my income by investing in the shares of a company, making I know not what, operating perhaps thousands of miles away ... I am still less sure of the morality of my being a moneylender.[103]

In encouraging private gain and cupidity over all else, market ideas atomized society, encouraged philistinism in tastes, and undermined education and culture.[104]

Furthermore, in creating poverty (Coleridge used to refer to liberal political economy as the 'poverty-making wealth machine'), the market economy only aggravated existing tensions in society.[105] Such tensions seemed, in fact, to be incipient in the market process. For Nisbet, Southey's *Letters from England* (1807) reads like a late-nineteenth-century socialist indictment of the factory system.[106] The same could be said of some of Cobbett's outbursts. Cobbett, like Coleridge and Southey, detested liberal political economy, directing some marvellous sallies at Malthus in his *Rural Rides*.[107]

One commentator on Coleridge compares favourably his views on taxation with twentieth-century under-consumptionist economic theories. Coleridge had called for a replacement of the 'spirit of commerce' with the 'spirit of the state'. For Coleridge, the business cycles of the market economy 'bring not only hardship to the poor, but moral decay to the rest of society'.[108] In addition, the whole conception of life and humanity present within classical liberal economics was regarded as false. It was a technical, arid and mechanistic view. Humans were not, for Coleridge, simply acquisitive machines. The health of a nation could not be measured by its economic prosperity. Such a narrow notion of life destroyed everything of value. The spirit of commerce was thus viewed as incarnate philistinism. Coleridge was echoing sentiments also found in German romantic conservatism. In this century, Maurras and Action Française showed an equally intense dislike of liberal capitalism and its implicit materialism and found more in common with Sorelian syndicalism.[109] Maurras's disquiet was shared by Dawson and Eliot.

However, conservatives and classical liberal economists were mutually agreed on the importance of private property. Yet there were differences in their views. Acquiring property through liberal market processes could interfere with the traditional pattern of stable property rights. There was an implicit struggle here between what may broadly be called landed aristocratic property and financial property. For liberals, anyone, regardless of social status, could theoretically become a financial property owner and lose that property as quickly through the market. Such a notion appeared horrific to the more traditional conservative interests. How would people know their place in the hierarchy of society if such wealth could be gained by anyone, without proper status? This unstable pattern undermined landed property rights and corroded the traditional social structures and authority patterns of society.[110] Society became a mass of competing, restless, anomic and self-interested individuals.

In British conservatism, from Coleridge and Disraeli onwards, 'one nation' concerns have often been seen as prior to the interests of the liberal market economy. Recent writers and practitioners of conservatism still reflect this sentiment in their own idiosyncratic ways.[111] One of the clearer expositions of this outlook has been by Ian Gilmour. He contends that 'Economics is not a self-contained science ... Economics and its objectives are the means to wider ends'.[112] For Gilmour, liberal economists, like Marxists, do not appear to live in the real world. The Austrian liberal economist, Ludwig von Mises, is taken to be a precise dogmatic mirror-image of Marx. Both theorists subsist in 'mystical' realms. Gilmour contends that their views of human nature and society are equally false. Conservatives should never have succumbed to liberal theories, partly because they have 'habitually treated theory as subordinate to practice and ... traditionally had a far greater liking for facts than for doctrine'.[113] Historically, conservatives have often favoured the careful use of the state to curb the market. As Herbert Spencer noted in *The Man Versus the State*, conservatives have a disposition towards a more controlled militant society. For Gilmour, a moderate Keynesianism and a mixed economy has much to be said for it. Keynesianism was not the cause of the decline of the post-war British economy, which Gilmour attributes to factors like primitive trade union practices, poor management and too much 'stop-go' government policy. He looks therefore to the return of economic sanity in the Conservative Party.[114]

Overall, it is clear that conservatism has had a very ambivalent attitude to economic policy, reflecting quite diverse positions. However, the dominant view has been that of a more flexible and pragmatic recognition that markets are useful within certain social and political parameters.

CONCLUSION

One of the most elusive arguments within conservatism, mentioned earlier, is that it is not an ideology in the ordinary sense of the term. The paradox here is that it is a theory which rejects theory. The anti-intellectualism is, in other words, apparent rather than actual. The most convincing account which lies behind some of the theoretical dismissals of theory is that a different kind of theory is at work. Practical reason is distinct from theoretical reason. Theoretical reason, based upon preconceived a priori ideas, is seen to be inappropriate to politics. In this sense conservatives cannot, by definition, have clearly worked-out *theoretical* answers to political questions. Some see this as a weakness; others argue that it is an implicit strength.[115]

One problem is that the anti-intellectualism is not a consistent feature of all conservatism. Romantic and liberal conservatives are a case in point. Further, there is something quite misleading and self-contradictory in such denials of abstract theorizing. It is odd to construct a clearly reasoned attack *against* the use of reason in politics, especially when such an attack has strong implications for political life. The usual way out of this dilemma is to appeal to practical reason. Yet, is practical reason so clearly different from theoretical reason? Some conservatives argue that practical reason is based on tradition and practice, but this is often a very selective and partial reading of practice and tradition. Tradition is not a single unequivocal thing waiting to be read or discovered. There are multiple traditions of all types. There can, after all, be traditions of rationalism and radical political traditions. Moreover, some traditions might not be worth retaining, certainly not *just* because they are traditions. Traditions or prejudices like cannibalism, anti-Semitism or slavery are profoundly objectionable and unquestionably worth abandoning. Why, therefore, should 'tradition' or 'prejudice' *per se* be regarded as valuable? Traditions have to be critically assessed by certain rational standards.

There is surely nothing intrinsically mistaken about theoretical change within traditions. Such a process is commonplace. Theoretical ideas are also often tried out in practice. From physics to morality, technical knowledge is applied to the world. Individuals read cookery books, cycling or computer manuals before they cook, cycle or compute, and they perform far better than if they had not read these books. Abstract theories and rational technical knowledge permeate practices in all spheres of human activity, including politics.

Like other ideologies, there are clearly theoretical differences between forms of conservatism. As we have seen, even more so than in liberalism, ideas that are canonized by some conservatives are utterly rejected by others. Some conservatives, specifically the romantics and the traditionalists, are haunted by a form of regret and nostalgia. Novalis's medieval Europe, Eliot's pastoral society, De Maistre's *ancien régime*, are caught up with certain *idées fixes*, which seem incapable of looking forward. Other conservatives, who accept change, are trapped by a self-contradictory logic: having resisted certain ideas, once these become integrated they begin to praise the immemorial wisdom of ages which has incorporated such ideas. Tradition becomes whatever happens to be the case. Liberal conservatives, on the other hand, appear to accept certain changes with open arms. In fact, it would be no exaggeration to say that much of the really radical and disturbing social and economic change of the last decade in many industrialized societies, has been fomented by liberal conservatism, particularly in Britain and America. Many find this a strange contradiction. It will be curious to see if the older aspects of traditionalist or paternalist conservatism reassert themselves again before the next century. Given the unerring ability of conservatives to survive politically, no doubt some change will take place.

4
SOCIALISM
—

The word 'socialism' finds its root in the Latin *sociare*, which means to combine or to share. The related, more technical term, in Roman and then medieval law, was *societas*. This latter word could mean companionship and fellowship as well as the more legalistic idea of a consensual contract between freemen. We find two distinct senses of the term 'social' here which have implications for the much later use of the word socialism. 'Social' could refer either to a more formal legalistic contractual relation between free citizens or a more emotive relationship of fellowship and companionship.

For some commentators, the more legalistic and contractual use of the term 'social' implied something distinct from the state and therefore, some would argue, from politics in general. Individuals make contracts and confer obligations upon themselves, thus reinforcing the common distinction between a 'society' of free contracting individuals and a rule-of-law 'state'.[1] The contractual use is also connected to the contrast, which dates from the 1800s, between a political and social revolution. For example, some writers argued that the failure of the French Revolution, and its collapse into Napoleonic dictatorship, was due to the fact that it had only been a political revolution at the level of the state apparatus. It was not a social revolution (in the socialist sense) of the people and of their attitudes and mode of existence. This was basically Marx's interpretation of the revolution as an act of bourgeois politics.[2] This critique, with enormous amounts of supplementation, has carried on into twentieth-century socialist and anarchist assessments of revolution.

The notion of 'civil society', which is also rooted in the contractual idea, entered into European political economy and particularly into ideologies like classical liberalism. Yet it was not without some impact on early socialism and anarchism. The anarchist Pierre-Joseph Proudhon's notion of society was firmly rooted in the contractual idea. Usually, though, civil society became part of the opposition to the alternative meaning of the word social, namely, the sense which implied fellowship and community. Society, in the fellowship sense, was contrasted to the negativity of individualism (as embodied in one meaning of civil society). We would recognize this distinction better now under the rubric of the opposition between socialism and individualism, or collectivism versus individualism, which became popular in European thought from the 1880s.

Another implication of the communal and fellowship understanding of the word social was its connection with the idea of the *populus* (the sovereign people). If 'society' were identified with the whole community, it could legitimately be seen as equivalent to the entire people. Thus the 'social will' could imply the popular or general will. Social ownership was ownership by the people. Socialized property was owned by the whole. Social welfare or socialized medicine would be available for all the people. Social participation in government was popular participation. Social, in this sense, formed strong connections with the ideas of democracy and popular sovereignty. These ideas have a long conceptual pedigree in European thought but they acquired their characteristic present form during the era of the French Revolution. Furthermore, because moral significance was often accorded to the popular democratic will, the term social also took on a moral lustre.

In a similar manner, the other sense of 'social' (*qua* civil society and contractualism) was often subtly linked with moral and political individualism and formed one of the elements of the later theory of representative liberal democracy. By the 1840s, the connection of 'social' and 'democracy' was firmly in place, as in the parallel link between 'liberal' and 'democracy'. Terms like social democracy, democratic socialist and socialist democrat were relatively well-known throughout Europe, although enormous ambiguities still remained.[3]

Socialism, indicating a political stance and set of beliefs, has been fairly precisely dated by a number of scholars. Like conservatism and liberalism it is a child of the post-French Revolution era. There is some argument as to where exactly it first appeared. France and Britain are the main contenders.[4] However, no one disagrees that the 1820s and 1830s are the critical periods. The word *socialisme* appeared in February 1832 in the Saint-Simonian journal *La Globe* edited by Pierre Lerroux. Before this it had figured briefly in 1827 in the Owenite journal *The Cooperative Magazine*. The Owenites in Britain and the Saint-Simonians and Fourierists in France were the first to use the word self-consciously. Marx was later to tag these as the 'utopian socialists' in *The Communist Manifesto*, a label which had unfortunate and misleading connotations.

The concept of socialism has had a chequered and tortuous relation to a number of other concepts, particularly collectivism, communism and social democracy. This relation will be examined briefly to clear up any potential misunderstandings. Collectivism is a late-nineteenth-century concept originating in France. It denotes, with reasonable consistency up to the present day, the use of the state and governmental apparatus to control, command and regulate sectors of the economy and civil society. It is an instrumental device of public policy. It usually entails, in varying degrees, central state planning. Since the late nineteenth century the notion of collectivism has often been linked with socialism. There are a number of problems with such an identification, however. First, despite the fact that many socialists have used collectivism in practice, a significant number have either ignored it or repudiated it. Second, many other ideologies like conservatism and liberalism, as we have already seen, have been prepared to use collectivist methods. Finally, it is worth emphasizing that collectivism refers to an instrumental device, *not* a thesis or set of beliefs about human nature and equality, as one would expect to find in socialism. Collectivism, in itself, is thus much narrower, more formal and procedural than socialism.

We will now briefly turn to certain other concepts which are closely linked with socialism. In Durkheim's *Socialism and Saint-Simon*, communism is seen as a much older and more primitive form of organization than socialism. Communism is concerned to regulate human consumption in an egalitarian manner. It had been practised in early monastic communities and some more primitive tribal units. Socialism, on the other hand, is viewed by Durkheim as a very modern device of industrialized societies, which regulates productive relations. Here we see a clear separation of the terms, though not all would accept such a distinction.

The term communism, denoting a self-conscious political adherence, pre-dates socialism by only a few years. In France, Gracchus Babeuf and the Society of Equals, which appeared on the political scene between 1794 and 1797, were often called the Babouvists and occasionally 'communionists'. Babeuf was in fact guillotined in 1797 under the orders of the Directory. The Society of Equals was essentially a conspiratorial sect devoted to revolutionary overthrow, the establishment of a dictatorship and a community based upon perfect substantive equality. The communist element, oddly, did not appear in Babeuf's trial; it became more significant in the politics of his followers, Buonarroti and Blanqui. It has also been subsequently traced through to the Russian Populists and the young Lenin in the 1890s. Another French writer to explore this radical equality and communal ownership, but from a very imaginative utopian angle, was Étienne Cabet in the late 1830s. His elaborate imaginary world of Icaria is often described as utopian communism.[5]

Marx in his earliest writings saw communism as a primitive form of socialism, but by 1848, in *The Communist Manifesto*, a firm contrast appeared between 'revolutionary communism' and 'utopian socialism'; although, under the influence of the anthropologist Lewis Morgan, both

Engels and Marx still accepted the notion of primitive communism.[6] Marx gradually formed an antipathy to the word socialism, which lasted right up to his last works in the late 1870s. Socialism appeared to denote a softer, classless, utopian, in sum, *bourgeois* doctrine. Despite this, Engels referred to *The Communist Manifesto* in a later preface of 1888 as 'socialist literature'.[7] Marx's antipathy reappears among some of the Bolsheviks in 1917, who saw communism as a more mature historical phase beyond socialism. In Britain, William Morris and H. M. Hyndman (the founder of the first British Marxist group) also preferred not to use the denotation socialist, associating it with reformist Fabian socialism. Despite these circumlocutions, it is hard to fix a definite barrier between the terms. Revolutionary fervour is certainly not the test or standard. If one compares the profoundly constitutional views of many Eurocommunists of the 1960s and 1970s with the multiple revolutionary splinter groups of the same period calling themselves 'socialist', then the term 'revolutionary' appears to attach itself more closely to socialism than to communism.

'Social democracy' is subject to a similar ambivalence. H. M. Hyndman referred to himself as a social democrat, indicating thereby his adherence to Marxism. He was following here the German example. The driving force of Marxism from the Second International, which dominated European Marxism up to 1914, was the German Sozialdemokratische Partei Deutschlands (SPD), deriving originally from the 1869 Social Democratic Workers' Party.[8] Despite some ambivalence, social democracy became virtually equivalent to organized Marxism. Marxism, as social democracy, set its theoretical face firmly against the revisionist socialism of Eduard Bernstein.[9] After the break-up of the Second International, with the outbreak of the First World War, the Soviet Union began to take over as the central interpreter of Marxism. The Bolsheviks changed their name from the Social Democratic Labour Party to the Communist Party of the Soviet Union. Because of their dominance of the Third International it became essential that the term communist replaced social democracy for all groups who wished to be part of the International. Before the First World War, ambivalences were already creeping in, with the title social democracy being taken over by some revisionists, ethical socialists and new or social liberals. After 1920, and up to the present, the term social democracy has had its strongest links with the related reformist socialism and the social liberal tradition. In this sense, the founding of the Social Democratic Party in Britain in the early 1980s was not that novel or significant.

In sum, we should be careful about attributing definite parameters to socialism, either to say that all socialists are collectivists, or that communism is wholly distinct from socialism, or that social democracy is a non-socialist tradition. All of these judgements are both historically and ideologically misleading. There is a complex overlap of discourses between these various elements.

THE ORIGINS OF SOCIALIST THOUGHT

Although the roots of socialist thought are contested, they are less tangled than conservatism and liberalism. There are two broad accounts of the origins of socialist thought. The first covers a lot of ground, usually tracing socialist themes back to movements of ideas in the early modern period. The second account focuses on the post-French Revolution period.

In terms of the first account the two figures most often discussed are Sir Thomas More, because of his book *Utopia*, and the anabaptist Thomas Münster. The doyen of German Marxism, Karl Kautsky (often referred to as the 'Pope of Marxism'), wrote *Thomas More and his Utopia* to demonstrate this particular origin. The claim has been repeated again recently.[10] The other main hunting ground of this same period is the English Civil War. Groups like the Levellers and Diggers are often given a high profile in such an interpretation.[11] For example, Christopher Hill remarks on the Diggers' leader:

> Winstanley was working out a collectivist theory which looks forward to nineteenth and twentieth century socialism and communism ... Winstanley had grasped a crucial point in modern political thinking: that state power is related to the property system and to the body of ideas which supports that system. He is modern too in wanting a revolution which would replace competition by concern for the community, in insisting that political freedom is impossible without economic equality.[12]

There do seem to be worrying problems with this type of analysis, partly because at the time no body of beliefs existed equivalent to nineteenth- and twentieth-century socialism. It could be argued that the concept preceded the word. Yet the theological and cultural context within which the arguments of the Diggers appeared seems to be ignored in such accounts. There is a danger of reading our present concerns into the past, which, as argued in chapter 1, can be an anachronistic and misleading enterprise.

The second account focuses upon the immediate post-French Revolution period. The interplay with the Industrial Revolution is also explored by some scholars.[13] Lichtheim comments on the 1790s: 'A history of socialism must begin with the French Revolution, for the simple reason that France was the cradle of "utopian socialism" and "utopian communism" alike ... both currents stemmed from the great upheaval of 1789−99'.[14] The revolution was the crucible from which socialism derived, both the word socialism itself and the social movements which adhered self-consciously to the ideology. All these phenomena find their roots in the revolution and post-revolution period. The vigorous attempts to extend democracy, rights, justice and equality, through radical social and political action, although hardly beneficent in all their effects, sent immense shock waves through European thought which are still reverberating today.

In many ways the Industrial Revolution also acted as a further catalyst, not least because it facilitated the growth of capitalism and the maturation of the urban working class, who became the focus and vital membership of many socialist movements. This particular point becomes more problematic if we take into consideration some of the notions developed by Maoism or by Frantz Fanon, which relied heavily on the revolutionary potential of the agricultural peasantry.[15] Industrial capitalism also created the tensions and conflicts which became the crucial target for socialist criticism. Capitalism was initially seen by most socialists as the *bête noire*, the source of all injustice and inequality. In criticizing capitalism and trying to find alternative policies, socialists drew upon the language of the radical French Revolution tradition which incorporated demands for the extension of democratic suffrage, trade union rights, parliamentary reform and social justice for working people. As the French revolutionaries had demonstrated, such ideas could be pursued successfully through the use of mass movements.

The above account does not, however, negate the point that many of the ideas utilized by socialists were derived from previous intellectual traditions, in some cases pre-dating the revolution. Socialism, in fact, took on ideas from diverse sources: civic republicanism, Enlightenment rationalism, romanticism, forms of materialism, Christianity (both Catholic and Protestant), natural law and natural rights theory, utilitarianism and liberal political economy. All these and more form the backdrop for socialist theorizing. Various elements of the socialist movement coalesced around certain of these intellectual traditions, thus formulating their proponents' arguments in markedly different ways.

As already stated, the first self-conscious socialist movements developed in the 1820s and 1830s. The Owenites, Saint-Simonians and Fourierists provided a series of coherent analyses and interpretations of society. They also, especially in the case of the Owenites, overlapped with a number of other working-class movements like the Chartists. The radical tradition, as expressed in groups like the Chartists, trade unions and the like, often indirectly coincided with, rather than directly pursued, socialist aims. By the 1880s socialist discourse was coming to be widely accepted as the most adequate account of working-class aspirations.

After a brief hiatus, from the late 1840s until the late 1860s, another surge of socialist development took place in Europe. Socialism through this period, up to the 1880s, was gradually maturing and becoming self-conscious of its ideological content. The crucial place of Marx in the socialist pantheon is in part due to the fact that he provided such an intellectually powerful synthesis of ideas and convincing explanations at such a pivotal moment. With the exception of Britain, Marxist language set the tone of much subsequent European socialist discussion. The Marxist German SPD party became the dominant force in European socialism up to 1914, imposing its ideological pattern on the French socialists under Guesde. This dominance and consensus gave rise to the description 'the golden age of Marxism' during the period of the Second International.

However, the phenomenon of most of the major Marxist-orientated parties in France, Germany and Austria voting for war credits in 1914, rapidly undermined all sense of international unity or solidarity. The Third International, which emerged out of the furnace of the 1914–18 war, was this time premised on the Bolsheviks in the USSR. Lenin was now the leading figure and Marxist-Leninism became the key official doctrine. Yet from the 1930s further polarization of the movement took place. Marxist revisionism, which had been festering since the early 1900s, carried on unabated throughout Europe. The German SPD moved gradually towards a more revisionist democratic socialist stance, especially in the post-1945 era. British socialism continued to take its own unique and idiosyncratic reformist course. Further deep fissures developed within Marxism, which widened into chasms through the post-1945 era. Trotskyism, Stalinism, Leninism, revisionist Marxism, humanistic Marxism, Maoism, African Marxism, existential Marxism, Eurocommunism, structuralist Marxism, feminist Marxism and many other currents proliferated. A vast scholastic catalogue of often mutually hostile Marxisms developed, each claiming orthodox truth. The river had run into the multiple silted channels of the estuary. The surviving socialism which is rethinking itself in the 1990s is by and large reformist, democratic and revisionist in nature. If there is a future for socialism it lies in this format.

THE NATURE OF SOCIALISM

The first point which should already be obvious is that there is no such single thing as socialism. There are rather socialisms, which often overlap with other ideologies. No pristine doctrine exists. One has to be very careful at this juncture since the dominant position of Marxism in the history of the movement has often led to a reading of socialism through Marxist eyes. Marxism is not the true socialism, Marxism is a species within the genus of socialism. Whether Marxist-inclined or not, it is easy, too easy, to adopt unthinkingly the terminology and categories of Marxism. A typical case is the distinction between utopian and scientific socialism or the assertion of the importance of class to socialism. There are, in fact, no such neat demarcations in the discussion of socialism. There are multiple definitions of the concept and numerous ways of actually conceptualizing it. Should socialisms be identified by beliefs, values or political strategies? Socialism is a rich body of formal arguments and values which are interpreted in different ways by the varying schools.

There are a number of possible ways of distinguishing forms of socialism. Marx and Engels (the latter particularly) started the process of categorizing types of socialism. One of the early distinctions was between revolutionary scientific socialism as against utopian socialism. This distinction, apart from its essentialist reading of socialism, ignores many of the scientific pretensions of the utopians and the commonality of beliefs within Marxism itself. Another mode of classification of socialisms is by strategies. The neatest division here would appear between revolutionary and reformist traditions, although this would not necessarily catch all the subtle and occasionally stark differences *within* each category. The differing views on revolution of Luxemburg and Lenin or Stalin and Trotsky would need to be accounted for within such a distinction. Furthermore, if another typology were adopted, distinguishing authoritarian and libertarian socialisms, then reformist socialists like the Webbs could be seen as 'reformist authoritarians', whereas Rosa Luxemburg or, in a different setting, Wilhelm Reich and Herbert Marcuse, might be considered 'revolutionary libertarians'. W. H. Greenleaf adopts a slightly different categorization, namely, collectivist organizational socialism as against libertarian socialism.[16] Again, a number of cross-cutting issues arise. Some collectivists have been concerned with libertarian issues. Collectivists could also be authoritarian, revolutionary or reformist. Similar problems arise with libertarianism. In this sense, these more simple distinctions do not catch quite enough of the nuances.

One of the major problems here is that socialism inherits a number of intellectual traditions and values. It has accepted wholeheartedly *and* repudiated the role of Enlightenment rationalism. It has fulsomely praised the growth of industrialism *and* resisted it in a longing for pastoral communes. It has embraced modernity *and* opposed it. It has utilized the state *and* attacked it. Some theorists, in despair of finding a consistent pattern, have sought to delineate certain core themes. R. N. Berki is a good example of this tendency. He sees four values: egalitarianism, moralism, rationalism and libertarianism. These exist in harmony and disharmony in different socialist thinkers. When combined in various formats they inevitably yield very different views.[17]

My own approach will be to try to distinguish certain schools of socialism according to a dominant pattern in their argument or approach. The particular schools outlined are not hard-and-fast categories. The thinkers within them often have very different perceptions on certain issues. The typology is an attempt to make sense of a diverse, complex, and nuanced tradition without undue simplification. A number of arguments and beliefs within these schools overlap not only with other socialisms but also with other ideologies. The schools of socialism are: utopian socialism, revolutionary socialism (Marxism), reformist state socialism, ethical socialism, pluralist group-based socialism, and market socialism.

Utopian socialism is not just a primitive phase leading to Marxism. Each of the early utopian socialists – Saint-Simon (1760–1825), Charles Fourier (1772–1837), Robert Owen (1771–1858) – are interesting and significant people in their own right. The distinguishing feature of utopian socialism, which figures in socialist thought into the twentieth century, is its attempt to sketch out, sometimes in minute detail, the ordering of a possible form of social life which corresponds to the true nature of humanity, including even the reproduction pattern, family arrangements, diet or dress of community members.[18] Such a well-structured society, in harmony with the natural springs of human nature, would provide the conditions for fully satisfied, happy and virtuous human beings. The utopians did not specify static social structures. Their societies were dynamic and creative entities allowing for (especially in the case of Fourier) the full flowering of humans.[19] Such utopias – Fourier's *Phalanstery*, Owen's New Harmony, Saint-Simon's Administered Industrial society – were placed in the context of a historical development and required radical changes in the economies and property relations of existing societies.[20]

Revolutionary socialism is best expressed through the medium of Marxism. Marxism provided the most powerful and masterful integrating theory of socialism, premised upon a critical combination of Enlightenment materialism, Hegelian idealism, liberal political economy and utopian socialism. The main distinguishing feature of Marxism is a powerful historical interpretation of societies. The material and economic conditions of life form the basis for all social and political structures, as well as for human consciousness. Relations of production are the real foundations upon which the legal and political superstructures arise. The state reflects the intrinsic class struggle which takes place at the economic base of society. As material conditions, productive relations and modes of exchange alter, so do class and political relations. Ultimately, societies will develop into the capitalist mode of production where a particular configuration of classes occurs – confrontation between proletarians and bourgeois capitalists. The end to this conflict will be the revolutionary overthrow of capitalism.

The major philosophical division that has subsequently occurred within Marxism is between more humanistic and scientific claims. The former is often identified with the writings of Antonio Gramsci, Karl Korsch and Georg Lukács, and tries to incorporate a much stronger element of human autonomy into the social and economic theory. The other side of the debate is the more stultifying legacy of scientific socialism, which derives from the later writings of Engels and Karl Kautsky, and leads through in a more veiled form to the structuralist Marxism of the 1960s and the writings of Louis Althusser. This theory discerns certain objective determining structural laws of development. The autonomy or individuality of the human subject counts for very little in this brand of Marxism.

Reformist state socialism is being employed as a broad category here.

The use of the notion of collectivism, as synonymous with socialism, reveals comething of the conceptual ancestry of this idea. Reformist state socialism incorporates the revisionism of Eduard Bernstein, the Fabians (at least a number of the important Fabians), the post-1945 German SPD and British Croslandite socialism from the 1950s. It is also very close to the tradition of social liberalism. The characteristic features of this form of socialism are, first, that by and large it has always either repudiated or tried to revise Marxism. Second, it has always, from the 1880s, advocated democratic gradualism and constitutional reform as the path to socialism. Socialism has never wanted to dispense with parliaments, adversarial parties, or representative democracy. Third, it has nearly always accepted a role for the free market, usually within the framework of a mixed economy. Fourth, its critique of capitalism is more often than not conducted in instrumental terms. Capitalism is seen to be primarily inefficient and wasteful rather than immoral. This is not to say that there are no ethical concerns within this category; these have taken a slightly different path and are dealt with under a separate category. Finally, and most significantly, it has advocated the use of the state to achieve its aims of greater efficiency, equality, social justice and rights. Reformist state socialism, which has been most prominent in political practice in the post-1945 era, has also been closely associated with the development of welfare states throughout Europe.

Ethical socialism is closely allied to reformist state socialism. In fact, in many aspects it overlaps directly with it, although its perception of the state is often distinct. Furthermore, reformist state socialism has often utilized ethical motifs, but it usually only accords them a secondary significance. The distinguishing characteristic of ethical socialism is its emphasis on the ethical dimension. Socialism is concerned with correct or true values. Capitalism is not adjudged economically inefficient, but ethically deficient. Political, social or economic reforms in themselves are not enough. The establishment of material entitlements to welfare, social security, free health-care or unemployment benefit do not constitute genuine socialism. Rather, moral change in the citizens themselves precedes adequate political change. State action can facilitate this moral change through education but it is not crucially necessary. Education cannot make humans moral. The Christian Socialists in Britain, France and Germany over the nineteenth and twentieth centuries have, by and large, held to this position. This is an attitude which also seems to inform the twentieth-century exponents of 'liberation theology', although their views are usually a unique amalgam of humanistic Marxism and Christian ethics. Many of the early ILP leaders, such as Keir Hardie, Robert Blatchford, and J. Bruce Glasier, also had ethical views of socialism. These figures derived their ethical socialism from writers like Ruskin, Carlyle, Dickens and Thoreau. Such a view is also characteristic of many in the social liberal tradition, like L. T. Hobhouse.

In twentieth-century Britain, R. H. Tawney is probably the best-known representative. He undoubtedly perceived the state as an institution having ethical functions.[21]

Pluralist socialism is to be found in various formats. In using the word 'pluralism' I am not suggesting any necessary connotation of moral or political pluralism. In other words, there is no allusion here to the tolerance or co-existence of moral, political or economic alternatives. Beliefs in 'moral pluralism' can also be found in forms of ethical and reformist state socialism. Conversely, many proponents of pluralist socialism present 'totalizing' perspectives, acknowledging no alternatives to their own. In my own use of 'pluralist', the basic distinguishing feature is that the state is not regarded as a device for introducing or furthering socialism. Socialism can *only* come about from a plurality of groups of self-organized workers: producer associations which would gradually take over all the functions of administration and welfare (previously performed by the state) for themselves. The category of pluralist socialism therefore covers those socialists who have had no truck with the state and prefer to rely on the plurality of workers' associations. There is a strong overlap here with some schools of anarchy.

Such a pluralist view is, paradoxically, present in the conciliar communism of Gramsci. It is half-heartedly present in Lenin's call for 'all power to the Soviets'. Marx partially and unwittingly supports it in his comments on the 1871 commune in France in *The Civil Wars in France*, and his advocacy of decentralized communes.[22] It found a firm endorsement, moving into the border regions of anarchism, in the syndicalist and anarcho-syndicalist movement. Theorists like Gustav Landauer or Pierre-Joseph Proudhon also subscribed to such a view; however, their general theories appear difficult to categorize, hanging precariously between pluralist socialism and anarchy.[23] Finally, and most representatively, the view found a clear expression in the guild socialist movement in Britain, which developed in the Edwardian era. There are also some loose parallels to be drawn with the cooperative and shop stewards' movement in the post-1945 era. The state, in the pluralist view, was seen to replace the coercion of the market with the coercion of bureaucracy or centralized administration. There are, though, undoubtedly broad differences between these pluralists. Conciliar communism and syndicalism were totalizing perspectives, believing in violent revolution and dismissive of constitutional and reformist procedures, whereas the guild socialists were, in the main, the precise opposite. Despite these marked differences, they shared an antipathy to the state as a vehicle for socialism and favoured instead group activity.

Market socialism is a fairly recent phenomenon of the 1980s, although some trace its ancestry further back, finding sources of the doctrine in Marx.[24] It is premised, largely, on the perceived failure of reformist state socialism in the twentieth century. The most important distinguishing features of market socialism is the notion that the market economy can be decoupled from capitalism. Many socialists in other schools would find such an idea immediately unacceptable. For market socialists, capitalism may be impossible without markets, but markets can function without capitalism; in fact they can be used to further socialist aims, bringing a concern for equality, welfare and ethics together with economic efficiency. Market socialists tend to be suspicious of the state, favouring more decentralized economic decision-making premised on market activity. Liberty is also seen to be a neglected value by market socialists. But liberty needs an effective ability to choose. Market socialism is thus concerned to maximize the possibility for choice. Because markets are accepted as an allocative device, this does not mean that some limited indicative planning cannot be used with care. Some market socialists are also, with certain qualifications, supportive of workers' cooperatives.[25]

HUMAN NATURE

It is always difficult to generalize in any area of ideology. However, socialists usually have an optimistic developmental view of human beings; they tend to embrace, to some degree, a perfectibility thesis. Human beings can grow and improve in moral stature.[26] Socialists also tend to see the roots of human nature in social life. We are not simply asocial impervious individuals. We are part of one another through a common social life. The conditions under which humans develop explain a great deal about their character and nature. In other words, both the material and moral condition of human beings must be understood in the context of a society. Furthermore, for many socialists, humans are seen to be capable of reason and self-development. Like liberalism, and unlike much conservatism, socialism tends towards a more cosmopolitan doctrine. The belief is that *all* humans are capable of self-development, regardless of country, class, sex or race.

Despite these more common formal beliefs about human nature, there are subtly distinct and often contradictory ontologies at work in socialism. Such ontologies do not fall neatly into any of the types of socialism; instead they tend to cross-cut the various schools. In the writings of certain of the early utopian socialists such as Robert Owen and Saint-Simon, in the arguments of many early Fabians, and also in 'scientific Marxism', there is an Enlightenment rationalist stance on humanity. This is an ontology which rejects tradition and believes that human nature can be manipulated, controlled or built afresh through the use of reason and the right circumstances. Socialism becomes, in this context, a rational modernizing doctrine. If one can modernize and improve the conditions for human development, then the character of humans can be formed anew. Marx's historical materialism is one example of this tendency. It tells us how humans will act under certain conditions or material circumstances. If the material circumstances can be changed, then human nature will also be modified.

On the other hand, in the more romantic and humanistic ontology of socialist thought there is a powerful belief in the autonomy of individuals. Humans cannot simply be built anew from material circumstances. They have to be persuaded and educated to identify moral truths. Humans are also creatures of tradition. They do not reject the past or always seek to radically modernize social life. In addition, they do not necessarily associate progress with rapid industrial development; in fact, in some cases it is the precise opposite. There are socialisms which look on a slower pastoral existence as the ideal form of life.[27] Human beings are creative creatures who can fulfil themselves through thoughtful labour. The ideas of Arthur Penty and William Morris concerning creative labour, of ethical socialists on the moral development of humans, and of Antonio Gramsci on humanistic Marxism, reveal different aspects of this general ontology.

One debate which reveals much of the ambiguity of human nature under socialism focuses on the perennial issue of morality and science in socialism. The debate does not break down into a simple argument between a rigidly rationalist science inimical to free will and morality. There is an ethical passion present in the thinking of nearly all socialists, however deeply obscured in scientific jargon.

The grounds for scientifically orientated socialism lie, first, in the Enlightenment project to explain reality via the principles of reason and thus to repudiate all superstition and, often, tradition; the second premise is the late-nineteenth-century admiration for the empirical sciences. Natural science during the last century was increasingly associated with 'truth'. Socialism, in order to appear more truthful, often utilized the language of natural science. The original grounding of scientific socialism can be found in the utopians. They were impressed with the project of finding the precise inner structure of human nature. If the structure could be identified and tabulated, then societies could be designed to fulfil all the aspirations of human nature. Food, sexual activity, clothing, architecture, and even the most minute human desires could be catered for. Fourier's idea of the basic passions of each individual, precisely balanced and matched within the utopian *Phalanstery*, is typical of this process.[28] Equally, it is not accidental that Owenites were the first to popularize the idea of social science in Britain.[29]

The real dynamism for scientific socialism came with Marx and Engels. Engels particularly embraced a crude positivism in popular works such as *Socialism Utopian and Scientific, Anti-Dühring* and *Dialectics of Nature*.[30] *Anti-Dühring* was particularly influential in developing the scientific perspective. It is questionable exactly how far down this road Marx was prepared to go. Marx's application of materialism was more tentative and finely balanced than that of Engels. As far as is known, Marx never anticipated the application of dialectics to nature. Engels set the tone of this particular strand of Marxist socialism, allying it with scientific development in general. As he stated at the graveside of Marx: 'Just as Darwin discovered the law of development of organic nature, so Marx discovered the law of development of human history'.[31] This line of thought was closely followed not only by German Marxists, like Kautsky and Bebel, but also by the Russian Marxist Plekhanov, in works like *Materialism Militant*, by Lenin in *Materialism and Empirio-Criticism*, and subsequently by Bukharin and Stalin.[32] Many viewed Marx through Engels' eyes. In this reading, humans were material creatures determined by certain objective 'dialectical laws' operating both in nature and society. The individual was identified with a class which had a determinate role in the economic process. The material base of society determined the superstructure of human thought. It was this doctrine which became embodied in the official SPD party programme, agreed in the city of Erfurt in 1891 – subsequently known as the Erfurt programme.[33] The same doctrine was rejected by the revisionist Eduard Bernstein. In more recent times the claims of scientific socialism have been regarded with considerably greater scepticism.

The Marxists were not the only socialists to utilize the notion of science. Many of the early Fabians in Britain 'were inspired by a belief in the possibility, and indeed the necessity, of rational and scientific reform and administration'.[34] For the Fabian Webbs, good socialism was premised on sound social science. Social science was a process of strict systematic empirical investigation.[35] The Webbs showed very little overt patience with talk of ethics or socialist values. Their language was permeated with social Darwinism (in the case of Beatrice Webb, most probably derived from Herbert Spencer), eugenics, Comtian positivism, neo-classical political economy and radical utilitarianism.[36]

One of the initial Fabian Tracts – *Facts for Socialists* – established a general trend of thinking for many socialists in Britain. It was confidently asserted that 'no reasonable person who knows the facts can fail to become a socialist'.[37] The case for the scientific inevitability of socialism was to be made on an empirical level. Progress through socialism was to be revealed by empirical social science. Doubters were to be overwhelmed with the sheer mass of factual detail concerning the efficiency and cost-effectiveness of socialism and the inefficiency of capitalism. Socialism, in this case, was the politics of rational controls and good filing systems. Such efficiency not only included an elite of trained social science experts controlling affairs by precise plans, but also, ultimately, controlled breeding and work camps for the work-shy. How much actual science existed in this perspective is open to doubt. None of the major Fabians were scientifically trained or even fully scientifically literate. The term science (although having strong roots in economic science) was more of a term of approbation. As one scholar has remarked, 'constant repetition [of the word science] was intended to inspire confidence'.[38]

The judgement of capitalism in these cases was premised on its inevitable collapse, a demise based either on its inherent class tensions or alternatively, for the Fabians, on its total inefficiency and waste. Where a clear difference exists between Marxism and the Fabians it is over the issue of distribution. The Fabians, in general, did not accept any notion of historical determinism, namely, that all depends on the historical stage of an economy and its production. They believed in governmental action and the distribution of resources, not necessarily on moral grounds but rather on grounds of national and economic efficiency. Marxists, on the other hand, placed little theoretical value on distribution via the state. Influenced by Engels' perspective, up to 1914 the state in vulgar Marxist theory always reflected class interests and could never achieve social justice.

Yet, with regard to the above point, nothing could be farther from the judgement of other socialist schools. The case to be made against capitalism for many socialists *was* its immorality. This moralistic stance can be found, paradoxically, also in some of the early utopians like Owen and Saint-Simon, combined with their enlightened rationalism. Neither Saint-Simon nor Owen were Christians, but Saint-Simon's final work, *The New Christianity*, which was taken up vigorously by the Saint-Simonian school as a quasi-religious doctrine, and Owen's later oracular spiritualism, had all the resonance of the prophecy of a future spiritual golden age.[39] Fourier also saw his role in cosmic and prophetic terms. The utopians frequently commented on capitalism and liberal political economy in tones of high moral disapproval[40] This theme can be found expressed strongly in the work of mid-nineteenth-century Christian socialists like Charles Kingsley, who overtly linked Christianity and socialism. It can equally be found in the twentieth-century exponents of liberation theology.

This view is also reflected in another aspect of Marxism: Marx's early philosophical writings. The so-called *Economic and Philosophical Manuscripts* in particular, discovered in the 1920s, reveal another side to Marx, namely, one which is concerned with the autonomous human self and free will.[41] Alienation, in these early writings, is a moral and philosophical dilemma, not just inherent in capitalism. History is not concerned with rigid objective laws, but with loose tendencies and the redemption of humans from spiritual alienation. Consciousness and moral beliefs are seen to have a definite role in human affairs. This general current of thought, carried on into the twentieth century, is associated with the work of writers such as Gramsci, Marcuse, Lukács, Korsch and the Frankfurt school.[42] In more recent years it has been revived by a number of social theorists like Agnes Heller and Ferenc Fehér. These writers, as intellectual disciples of Lukács, try to accommodate the themes of autonomy and morality within the Marxist perspective.

The issues of morality and autonomy also figure in the revisionist debates. Eduard Bernstein, one of the key figures in the German SPD until his expulsion, argued that the case for socialism should be made on moral grounds, citing Kant as his mentor.[43] This theme is also by no means absent from the Fabian ranks. Writers like Sydney Olivier and Sidney Ball, contrary to the Webbs, premised their whole case on the morality of socialism.[44] Their position had strong affinities with many in the social liberal faction, like L. T. Hobhouse.

The ethical and religious tendency also figures prominently in British socialism. Some commentators trace it back as an important facet of British political culture for several centuries.[45] From the late nineteenth century both William Morris and Belfort Bax looked to socialism as a remoralized order in society. Similarly, most of the early ILP figures, including Keir Hardie, spoke of their socialism continually in religious language. As one commentator has put it, in the 1880s 'the conversion to socialism seems often to have involved all the intense emotion of religious experience'.[46] R. H. Tawney, who in Tony Wright's words 'shaped and expressed the thinking of a whole generation of British socialists', provides the clearest example of this ethical and religious theme.[47] His attack on capitalism and the acquisitive society was premised upon its immorality and anti-Christian nature. Capitalism was both sinful and encouraged immoral tendencies in citizens.[48] In fact, Tawney came close to saying that to be a genuine Christian was to be a socialist. A functional socialist society would be a correct ordering and instantiation of Christian values, which would automatically deny a role for capitalism. Material progress required, first of all, moral progress and social evolution of the human personality.

In this stance humans are seen to shape their own order, whether moral or immoral. They make history autonomously. The major criticism directed by such moralists at the more scientific socialism was not only its hollow scientific pretensions but also its denial of the prime motivation for socialist criticism—morality. The scientifically minded socialists allowed little room for moral choice and moral critique. Determinism cuts away the foundation of socialism itself. A socialist cannot, from the scientific perspective, pursue values like rights, social justice or equality, since socialism, by definition, is not about values at all. From a scientific socialist stand-point, the subsequent discussion of this chapter might be considered rela-tively worthless. Values and morality, as many Marxists have seen them, are bourgeois illusions.

A critique of this rigid determinism, in a veiled form can even be found within Marxism, in Gramsci's condemnation of 'economism' and, most significantly, within the loose intellectual association of the Frankfurt school. The problem with the ethical position, apart from the danger of

'high-minded moral whistling', is the very diversity of moral beliefs which have characterized the socialist critiques. Christian, Kantian, utilitarian, Hegelian idealism, natural law and natural rights theory and many others have constituted the bases of socialist morality. Such a diversity of often mutually hostile beliefs weakens the claim of socialism to any objective moral stance.

Other related perspectives which link up with questions of human nature and morality in socialism are the values associated with cooperation, fellowship, fraternity and community.[49] There is a strong core of belief, from the utopians up to twentieth-century socialism, that humans are cooperative creatures. Society is ontologically prior to the individual. Furthermore, cooperation and community are superior values to individualism and egoism. Individualism denoted isolation and competition. Socialists have often argued that we are part of one another. This idea can be found even within Marxism in a more muted form. One sense of the term 'social' definitely implies commonality, mutuality and sharing. It can be identified in the earliest trade unions, friendly societies and cooperative societies. Despite this commitment to mutuality, it is clear that socialism was more directly communitarian in its earlier phases, where community denoted a more stateless decentralized situation. Later in the nineteenth century, many reformist and Marxist socialists tended, conversely, to rely on the state apparatus to achieve common aims via social welfare policy. However, the communal tendency, as found in groups like the guild socialists, was certainly not absent in the twentieth century. It is still a strong value in the writings of New Left figures like Raymond Williams.[50]

There are both strong and weak senses of community and cooperation in socialism. The stronger sense of community is usually premised on a belief in a more objective, identifiable moral or religious consensus. The belief in common reason, common religious or moral beliefs or, in more restrained terms, what George Orwell might have called a common belief in the decency of humans, pervades much socialist writing.[51] The kind of society envisaged is more directly homogeneous and consensual. Such a notion, although superficially attractive, is difficult to uphold in an industrial scenario with rapid social, political and economic mobility. Many twentieth-century socialists have, in the face of industrialism, contemplated much weaker and more formal understandings of community, premised on the mutual respect of citizens.[52] This tendency can be seen most clearly in reformist state socialism and the recent expositions of market socialism. One factor which has contributed to this weaker sense of community is the perception that strong communitarianism can be either simply foolishly nostalgic or reactionary. It must be recalled that over the nineteenth and twentieth centuries a number of conservative and fascist writers have appealed with immense enthusiasm to the value of traditional communities.[53]

EQUALITY AND LIBERTY

Many commentators on socialism have taken equality as the key socialist value. All socialists, it is argued, must be first and foremost egalitarian. Conversely, liberty is not so often cited. The division between equality and liberty is frequently stressed by critics of socialism at this point. It is argued that to uphold equality (as is pointed out *ad nauseam* by Hayek and his disciples) is to deny the possibility of liberty. To uphold liberty is therefore to deny the possibility of equality. Thus it is contended that socialists cannot uphold liberty.

Equality is undoubtedly a crucial socialist value, but a number of questions remain to be answered. Have all socialists believed in equality? Further, have all socialists adhered to the same concept of equality? Finally, is equality automatically in contradiction with liberty? In other words, can there be a socialist conception of liberty which does not conflict with equality?

It is a common misapprehension to believe that all socialists have adhered to the value of equality. Primarily a lot depends on what sense of equality is being discussed. Furthermore, it is not a value which figures prominently with all the utopian socialists. Fourier regarded egalitarian ideas as a poison. He accepted that there would be, in the socialist utopia, hierarchical orders, and wide inequalities in abilities, wealth and position. The rich were assured by Fourier that they could retain and gain in wealth in a *Phalanstery*. Saint-Simon had similar beliefs to Fourier, although not quite so stark. Saint-Simon held that various orders of society should be maintained. Given that both thinkers relied on the prospect of bankers and entrepreneurs financing their projects, they could hardly have wished to attack such privileges too vigorously.

Marx also, from a different perspective, was critical of egalitarian beliefs, seeing such normative claims and arguments as liberal bourgeois theorizing. As Allen Wood comments, Marx was 'no friend to the idea that "equality" is something good in itself'.[54] The end result of communism might be egalitarian, but it would be pointless utopianism to speculate about such things. We could not *know* what society would look like until the consequences which flowed from given economic conditions gave shape to particular forms of life. In this latter argument we see an aspect of Marx's scientific legacy. Regardless of this, Marx did occasionally lapse into some speculation on equality and justice, although this tells us very little systematically about any egalitarian beliefs that he may or may not have had.

One common theme on equality within socialism, including Marx, is the wholesale rejection of the notion of literal factual equality, which is one of the most over-exploited and hackneyed myths concerning socialism.[55] The nearest we come to such literal equality is in some of the more extreme communist views of Gracchus Babeuf or Cabet. The greater part of the socialist tradition has regarded such notions as absurd. Literal factual equality is nothing but a straw man set up by rival ideologies. The only mild exception to this is the claim advanced by some socialists, particularly in welfare state theories, that 'need' can be an empirical egalitarian principle for distribution in society. The concept of need is difficult to articulate and has a number of intrinsic problems.[56] Despite these problems, 'need' still falls far short of any sense of literal factual equality, as exemplified in some critiques of socialism. The response to need also does not imply universally equal treatment, as is often insinuated in the idea of literal equality.

A related question concerns whether socialists hold the same concept of equality. The answer to this must be somewhat negative. We must disentangle a number of points here to illustrate the complexity of this question. First, equality as a value is distinct from any literal or factual assertions about human equality. Second, the various justifications for the value of equality should be analysed. Third, 'equality as a goal' must be kept distinct from 'equality as a condition'. Finally, the means to achieve equality should not be confused with the goals of equality.

Firstly, contrary to the claims of some critics, socialists, with some rare exeptions, adhere to the belief that equality is something that 'ought' to be pursued. It is not an empirical or factual notion (apart from some of the claims made for need). Socialists do not assert that humans are, or can be, literally equal in physical or mental abilities. Conversely, they argue that regardless of natural differences in race, sex, abilities or class, there are valuable morally relevant qualities which should direct us to treat individuals equally. However, to move on to the second point, the moral justifications for such equality have varied considerably. The most mundane has been the Fabian belief that greater equality would lead to greater efficiency. Equality in this sense is an instrumental value, although not all Fabians were so impressed with equality, even in this minimal sense.[57] Most justifications of equality either involve, somewhat negatively, a questioning of the acceptance of inequality, or a more positive advancement of reasons for equal treatment.

On the positive side, i.e., justifying substantive equality, the Christian socialists, Tawney and the like, have focused on the Judaeo-Christian idea of the equality of souls before God.[58] Many ethical and state socialists have utilized variations of idealist, natural rights, Kantian and utilitarian arguments, particularly the latter two. The equality in the last two arguments is premised, first, on each individual being considered equal in terms of possessing a rational will, which is of equal worth and deserving of equal respect; and second, on each individual being capable of satisfying their interests and of achieving happiness and thus meriting equal consideration in both respects.[59]

The third theme is that equality as a goal or outcome should be kept distinct from equality as a condition. Socialism has been predominantly associated with achieving the goal of equality in society. The outcomes of human endeavours should not give rise to inequality. Socialism has also advocated the idea that equality can be a condition or opportunity for the development of human beings, what is now sometimes referred to as a 'starting-gate' equality. Without a basic minimum of educational, health and welfare conditions as a point of departure, individuals cannot develop their potentialities and powers. Social and economic outcomes, from this original starting-point, could reflect moderate levels of inequality. Such a notion of equality is more compatible with liberty than 'equality as a goal'.[60]

Finally, the *means* to achieve equality should not be confused with either the justifications, goals or conditions of equality. Because nationalization (in Britain) or a command economy (in what was the USSR) have been associated with socialism, it is occasionally assumed that all egalitarian socialists are seeking to justify these particular means, and that all socialists therefore believe in command economies or nationalization. This is plainly wrong. The means for achieving equality have been reflected across a wide spectrum of proposals. Certainly, command economies and nationalization have been adopted as means. Socialists (including Marxists in France, Italy and Britain) have also advocated equality within both mixed and market economies. There are many shades of grey within these arguments. In the attempt to achieve economic equality, at one extreme, equality of income has been suggested by such diverse figures as the Fabian, George Bernard Shaw, and the Bolshevik Lenin. However, the redistribution of wealth through progressive taxation, welfare benefits and established national minimums are probably the most popular option adopted by revisionist, state and ethical socialism this century. There are, in sum, a bewildering range of methods utilized in this area.

Socialists have not limited themselves to economic equality. They have also shared with some liberals the demands for political equality of suffrage for all citizens. The call for full legal equality of civil rights has been another characteristic theme. Social equality, in terms of equal rights to a modicum of civilized existence, implying equality in health and education, has been another important facet of the idea. In recent years there has been a strong tendency to extend all these dimensions of equality towards gender questions, the argument being that women have been subtly excluded from such developments in the past. This question will be taken up within the later chapter on feminism. Admittedly all these entitlement rights and justice-based proposals have been more characteristic of the reformist traditions within socialism. Classical Marxism tended to repudiate rights-based theories, although in recent decades many Communist Parties, for example, that in Britain and the Italian PCI (now PDS), have moved substantially towards the constitutional socialist position and, in some cases, close to market socialism. In this sense, the picture is now becoming increasingly complex.

It should be recalled, though, that pluralist socialists have not accepted the statist methods but have favoured distributing power and authority to decentralized groups or organizations of producers. Guild socialists and syndicalists, particularly, favoured a very minimal or non-state situation.[61] Equality, in this case, would be attained within groups of workers. Thus, overall, equality within socialism has many means available to it and should not be irrevocably tied to any particular one.

Finally, the rigid separation between equality and liberty should be regarded with considerable scepticism. The separation is premised upon an equally rigid definition of negative liberty as 'non-restraint', 'restraint' being understood also in very limited stipulative terms, as examined in chapter 2. If it is argued that liberty is concerned with maximizing choices and the development of the individual (which many socialists have believed), then creating the equal conditions for making informed choices (implying adequate education, health and income) and thus developing human potential, denotes the compatibility of the values of liberty and equality. A socialist conception of liberty is thus a perfectly feasible idea and does not necessarily conflict with equality as a conditional notion.

STATE AND DEMOCRACY

It is sometimes presumed that all socialists are statists. It is also assumed that all state socialists hold to the same concept of the state and that all are equally self-conscious about the state. These assumptions are quite simply inaccurate. It is undeniable that from the 1880s onwards a dominant strain of reformist socialism, and also Marxism in institutional practice rather than theory, has been overtly statist. It should not, however, be assumed that such statism characterizes the whole movement, or that such statist practice implies some form of coherent theory. Both points are questionable. There are a number of profoundly difficult questions on the issue of the state in relation to socialism which need to be unpacked. A relatively convenient heuristic distinction can be made initially between, on the one hand, the more state-organizational socialism, and on the other hand, the pluralist and libertarian socialisms.

The notion of state-organizational socialism is often regarded as synonymous with collectivism. This synonymity has already been questioned. Collectivism is not only a method which transcends socialism, but also implies a number of different potential strategies, and has been repudiated by many socialists. Furthermore, despite the fact that Marxism is often regarded as a deeply statist doctrine and is conventionally taken as the archetype of the centralized socialist state, one looks in vain within the corpus of Marx and Engels' writings for any positive theory of the state. What one finds is an overwhelmingly negative analysis of the state.[62]

A basic summary of Marx's position would be that the material conditions of life are primary. These form the base for social and political structures as well as for human consciousness. Humans must produce in order to survive before they can think in any systematic way. Classes form or condense around economic interests within a mode of production, at any particular epoch in history. Individuals are defined by their class position. They relate to each other as members of classes. Because classes receive differential rewards of power and property and such differences are a consequence of exploitative relations, the state structure is premised upon certain property, class and, thus, exploitative interests. The state is not a product of human thought or intention. Conversely, it is determined by class and the struggle between classes. The state is usually, therefore, regarded as an oppressive agent for a particular class.

There are a number of difficulties with this more conventional view. First, Marx never offers a precise account as to what the state embraces. Does it include all administration – educational institutions, police, local government – as well as the executive, judiciary and legislature? No clear guidance on this is offered in any of the writings of Marx and Engels. In addition, no systematic account is given of the alternatives to the state, only vague hints on federalized communes which bear a closer relationship to anarchy. Furthermore, no clear description is given of the nature of class, its precise relation to property ownership and the state.

Occasionally Marx and Engels see the state as simply emerging from the material base. *The Communist Manifesto*, and other popular writings, often identify the state as simply an expression or instrument of class rule–the executive committee of the bourgeoisie, which had to be smashed by revolution. This was a doctrine which not only dominated the official views of the German SPD, but later became enshrined in the Russian-dominated Comintern. At other points, in writings like *The Eighteenth Brumaire of Louis Bonaparte*, the state appears as a more complex structure, possessing some autonomy and also independent of any particular class. Marx even suggested that countries like Britain might not require a revolution for the transformation to socialism. Later writers in the Marxist tradition, particularly those influenced by the work of Gramsci, see the state as having considerable autonomy and have consequently criticized the crude deterministic 'economism' and positivism which are particularly characteristic of Engels' views.

Marxism is not alone in this ambivalence on the state. Reformist state socialists, like the Fabians, have also been notoriously vague on the question. As one writer has put it, 'Early Fabian writings contain scant examination or description of what the state might actually be'.[63] Much the same could be said of most Fabian writings into the 1990s. There are some doubts raised about the state in Fabian circles, even, oddly, by the Webbs, but overall the tendency of the Fabians has been to see the state as a neutral instrumental device or apparatus, won over by representative democracy and utilized for the purpose of greater social and economic efficiency. Salvation would come about through a trained expert bureaucracy. In spite of the fact that the name Fabianism earlier this century was associated with local or municipal government and even industrial democracy, the Webbs and their acolytes none the less favoured centralized elite control and a benevolent paternal state apparatus.

The above view of many of the Fabians, particularly the Webbs, also links up with their idea of democracy. Some still see democracy as crucial to the whole socialist position.[64] Yet, if one looks more closely at the socialist tradition, not all Fabians share this view. At least, they share different visions of democracy. For the Webbs or G. B. Shaw, extending suffrage or even women's rights had limited appeal. They had little faith in the average citizen. Government was generally *for* the people, not *by* the people. In the case of the early utopian writers there was also little interest *per se* in democracy , certainly that associated with representation. Robert Owen was extremely doubtful of parliamentary democracy as being anything but a loose veil over corruption and injustice. Neither did Marx show much interest in the topic. The nearest he came to this was in his unsystematic speculations about direct democracy in the Paris Commune. This vision of direct participatory democracy lurks in the wings of both anarchy and some later Marxist socialists. However, for Marx and Engels democracy looked more like another capitalist and bourgeois illusion obscuring real class interests. Such a view would not represent the ideas of more recent Communist Parties in Europe where there has been a great deal of rethinking and name-changing. Whether it is still legitimate to describe, for example, the Italian PCI (now PDS) as Marxist, is an open question.[65]

Reformist state socialists this century, as in the British Labour and French socialist parties and the German SPD, market socialists and some ethical socialists, have accepted the notion of representative parliamentary democracy. Reformist state socialism has acquired some relative electoral success although if one looks now (with the century drawing to a close) at the periods of the Labour Party or German SPD in political office, the results are not terribly impressive. There has also been some tentative interest in industrial democracy and cooperatives, usually muted by scepticism about their true efficacy or efficiency. Direct participatory democracy has had little interest for the mainstream of reformist state socialism.

The above tendency has not reflected the totality of the socialist response on either the state or democracy. Within the Marxist tradition, as indicated, there has been a strong anti-statist tendency which derives from Marx

and Engels' own views. In the case of Lenin's *The State and Revolution*
there was a vision of a non-state, commune-based society, run by local
soviets of workers. This 'odd' line of thought in Lenin (associated as he
later was with totalitarian views of the state) was taken very seriously
in Gramsci's council communism premised on his experiences in Turin.
Such a conciliar communism was closely tied to Gramsci's theoretical
position which emphasized the proletariats' self-organization. Organic
working-class intellectuals could formulate and express this new proletarian
consciousness.[66]

Within guild socialism in Britain there was also a strong anti-state and
pluralist line of thought at work, although it should be noted that there
was no one clear position on this. Without trying to complicate matters
unduly, there were a number of tendencies within the movement, particularly the medieval as against the national guildists.[67]. The guild socialists
not only suggested that authority, welfare and the like should be devolved
to producer groups; they also subscribed, even in the national guild scheme,
to very minimal functions for the state. In the case of G. D. H. Cole and
S. G. Hobson, geographical representative democracy was to be supplemented by both direct participatory democracy, within producer groups,
and functional democracy premised upon producer associations, forming
more or less an industrial parliament. Tawney's dislike of the policy of
nationalization and his discussions of a functional society owe much to
the guild perspective.[68] The guild perspective has had a perennial appeal
for generations of socialists up to the present. It has even reappeared on
the peripheries of the very recent discussions of market socialism. Its
support still raises the temperature and diversity of contemporary political
debate within socialism.[69]

The prevailing problem of the state in socialism is that in Britain — a
political culture which has not been historically receptive to state theory —
the socialist tradition has not formulated a clear or consistent theory of
the state. In many other European countries, like Germany and France,
which do have self-conscious state traditions, the socialist discussion has
historically been more dominated by Marxian vocabulary and has incorporated three tendencies: a deeply negative critique of the state; an
ambivalence about what happens to the state under communism; and, in
Eastern Europe, an institutional record which has been depressingly
authoritarian and distant from all socialist aspirations. The question of
democracy has cross-cut all these issues. There is therefore no consistent
socialist picture on either democracy or the state within socialism.

In the same manner, there is very little consistency on socialist proposals
for social and political change. The extremities of socialist strategy lie in
revolution and constitutional reform. In between these extremes lie a bewildering range of proposals. Originally utopians sought the help of wealthy
bankers to set up experimental socialist communities, which would generate

further communities by example. They assumed, too, common resources of reason. This notion of creating an example for others to admire and follow was also suggested by guild socialists in the twentieth century.

By the later nineteenth century a number of dominant strategies had developed. Reformist state socialists advocated setting up constitutional socialist parties committed to the existing representational democratic arrangements. Socialism would gradually evolve through the electoral process. This method was often called socialist gradualism. In the case of the Fabians it was sometimes coupled with the strategy of placing trained experts in key political and administrative positions, thereby gradually permeating government and administration with socialism.

On the more revolutionary side, some guild socialists toyed with the syndicalist notion of direct action, namely, the latter's crucial concept of the 'general strike' of all workers which would bring about a capitalist collapse. Those influenced by Lenin favoured a more direct insurrectionary tactic through a vanguard party of trained and disciplined revolutionaries. This was attacked by other Marxists as employing the means of Jacobin revolutionaries and not working with the proletariat. Within the mainstream of Marxism, strategy was an immensely sore issue. Marx and Engels had formulated no single consistent view, thus support could be found in their writings for most methods: a long-term proletarian struggle; short-term insurrection; waiting for industrial capitalism to come to fruition with all its attendant contradictions, when revolution would happen inevitably; a proletarian revolutionary party committed to educating the proletariat; a self-organized conciliar structure within the proletariat, committed to intellectual and political struggle against bourgeois hegemony; revolution in one country; world revolution, and so on. All these strategies, and more, have found support within the Marxist tradition.

This uncertainty over strategy is reflected in the ambiguities as to who should carry it through. Who are the actors of socialism? The most popular contender is that elusive entity 'the working class'. Many socialists have doubts now about the existence of the working class.[70] There are even ambiguities in Marx's accounts as to who, or what, constitutes their ranks. However, while the working class have constituted an electoral majority this century in all European states, they have been equally active in support of deeply conservative, liberal, national socialist and fascist groups. There is nothing intrinsically socialist here.

It is also clear that many socialists have not believed in the working class as the chief actor of socialism. The utopians had virtually no conceptions of class; socialism was to be brought about by prophetic figures like themselves, with the support of wealthy patrons. Lenin, in a different context, in his famous *What Is to Be Done?*, suggested that socialist consciousness had to be injected into the working class from outside by the true socialist actors, an elite of vanguardist revolutionaries. Others, like Rosa Luxemburg, advocated a much wider proletarian party taking the lead with an intrinsically revolutionary proletariat. Gramsci added organic intellectuals to a self-organized proletariat. Mao Tse-tung identified the agricultural peasantry as the revolutionary actors. The more syndicalist-inspired cooperative socialists and guild socialists have seen producer groups, like cooperatives and trade unions, as the true actors of socialism. Yet for the Fabians, like Shaw and the Webbs, both trade unionists and the working class in general were viewed as ignorant and stupid.[71] The true socialist actors were an expert bureaucracy trained in the social sciences. In the broad reformist tradition, socialists have veered away from classes and elites and seen socialism as pursued by all men and women of good sense and goodwill. Thus, again one looks in vain for a consistent account of the true actors of socialism.

MARKETS AND THE ECONOMY

If there is one view which purports to be socialist, it is that socialism is always critical of free markets and capitalism and proposes a planned economy as the alternative. This is an essential part of the popular myth about socialism. It is, however, an odd view. There are varieties of both public ownership and state action in the economy, as there are also varieties of market activity.

On a very simple level, public ownership could imply total collective control and ownership of an industry by the state. This is usually the archetype of ownership. It could also mean ownership of the commanding industries, banks and insurance companies of an economy. This alone would allow a vast private sector. Alternatively, it could imply the ownership of what are sometimes regarded as natural monopolies, as in communications and water supplies. Furthermore, ownership could be decentralized to a company; in the latter case, the state could keep a weather eye on industry, with the option of some indirect influence on major policy or strategic investment decisions, or possibly allowing grants or financial incentives to certain enterprises. This is perfectly consistent with privatization initiatives. The nature of state involvement in the economy, in whatever format, could also vary considerably. Apart from outright ownership, managers could be state-appointed, with responsibility to a minister. They could be expected to set financial targets. The state could take a majority shareholding, a significant shareholding, or simply lay down broad policy parameters. It could also provide a financial environment, training, or preferential finance to benefit certain industries. It is, in fact, difficult to see any economy where some of these conditions do not exist. The most dynamic economies in the present situation, like Japan and Germany, have very sensitive and diverse forms of state activity within their economies. Indeed, it is worth noting that even some European Communist Parties, as in Italy, have advocated very diverse policies sensitive to the logic of markets, and consequently repudiating the older centralist and nationalization methods.

Such diversity in the understanding of state action in the economy needs to be extended to the understanding of markets and capitalism. Capitalism has varied considerably according to the societies in which it has appeared. Also, although markets are necessary to the existence of capitalism – which itself has an obscure and odd history often linked closely to the development of the state – it is questionable as to whether markets *per se* necessarily require capitalism. Even in the heyday of the lumbering command economy of what was the USSR, markets existed and in some cases flourished both in the black economy and in the state sector. The notion of a market cannot therefore be restricted to capitalism.[72]

It is true that socialism has been overtly critical of capitalism. Yet the substance of that criticism has been discordant. Generally capitalism has been linked, since the mid-nineteenth century, with poverty, unemployment and social distress. This has been a perennial reproach. Further, capitalism is seen both to generate and to exacerbate inequalities, creating deep social tension. It fosters harmful, anti-social and competitive attitudes. Private consumption and want satisfaction are encouraged, whereas public goods and the satisfaction of genuine human needs are neglected. Consequently capitalism undermines fellowship, solidarity and cooperation. The patterns of distribution in capitalist societies are uncontrolled and arbitrary. Profit is always prioritized over the creative production of goods. Capitalism therefore destroys the enjoyment and aesthetic pleasure of production. It ignores the costs to people, unless they can be measured as tangible profits or losses. People themselves are viewed as commodities which can be bought or sold.

Many socialists have tended to see the above amalgam of criticisms through moral lenses. Capitalism, for Tawney and the ethical socialists, was basically immoral. It adhered to the wrong value order. While such capitalist values remained, society could never be redeemed, reformed or improved. Yet the classical Marxist tradition, even within the humanist perspective, tended to take a more historical view of capitalism. As a mode of production, capitalism would be historically superseded, whether by the inevitabilities of materialist dialectics, direct revolutionary overthrow, or by the subtle strategies of intellectual and political manoeuvre. Ethics was not significant in this reading. More recently some European Communist Parties, as mentioned, have considerably modified this approach. The upshot of Fabian criticism, on the other hand, was that capitalism was both inefficient and wasteful. There was no interest in this latter argument in either historical inevitability or morality. Capitalism should be superseded by a socialist-controlled state apparatus to bring about efficiency in the economy. Inequality was not so much ethically suspect as wasteful of human resources.

It should also be noted that within this same argument the sources of socialist economic theory have been as varied as their criticisms of capitalism. Marxian economic theory, Ricardian and classical economic theory, the neo-classical writings of Wicksteed and Edgworth, Keynesianism, have all been utilized by the diverse schools of socialism in their analyses of capitalism. In fact, in terms of reformist state socialism in Britain, from 1945 up to the 1970s, the social liberal Maynard Keynes has undoubtedly been the most influential economist.

Equally, if we look for socialist alternatives to capitalism we find many different and often contradictory projects. The initial ideas developed by some utopians were anti-political in nature. In the case of writers as diverse as William Morris and Charles Fourier we are presented with a non-industrial future, non-statist, communal and pastoral. In this form of society, work would become an aesthetic and sensual pleasure. No roles or tasks would be fixed. Production would be for basic well-made goods to satisfy human needs. Marxism, as it developed, despite its often vague decentralist communist suggestions for a future society, became associated in practice with highly industrialized 'total' societies, organized and commanded by a state apparatus. The future abundance would be determined by state direction of industries. As the anarchist Bakunin had predicted during the early years of classical Marxism, a new state despotism would result from such Marxian doctrine. In recent years Marxism has tried to adapt itself to aspects of market behaviour, especially since the collapse of the USSR.

Reformist state socialists this century have accepted industrial development with open arms, but usually with a mix of private and public ownership, a developed nationalization programme with a vigorous free-market sector. Pluralist socialists have varied in their response. Some, like A. J. Penty, called for a return to an anti-industrial, pastoral, and medieval guild-based society. Others, like Cole, argued for the abandonment of capitalism (but not industrialism) and the wage system, and the adoption of an economy premised upon industrial guilds.[73] These would control prices, wages and the welfare of their members. Such a policy would be decentralist and emphatically not statist. This view is still criticized by state-orientated socialists.[74]

Finally, in recent years, there has been a vigorous attempt to make socialists rethink the notion of a market and to decouple it from capitalism. In Britain, to some extent, this idea was prefigured in Hugh Gaitskell and Evan Durban. It also embodies many of the ideas of the social market economy promulgated in German politics. In Britain some in the Fabian Society and Socialist Philosophers Group have advocated market socialism in the last decade as a response to the advances of the New Right ideology. Communist Parties, like that in Italy, have also developed a more sensitive policy to markets during this period. The basic idea is that market socialism is neither committed to full-blooded capitalism nor to state centralization. It is, though, interested in a society 'where power is more widely distributed ... where the interests of owners of capital, of workers, and of consumers, are all taken into account with none taking automatic priority'.[75] The market, decoupled from capitalism, can be retained as a useful allocator of goods and services. All citizens ought to be enabled to enter the market on as fair terms as possible. The equal *worth* of liberty, for all citizens, is as important as the principle of equal liberty. To take advantage of the market, to use our liberty and shape our lives, we need to be enabled to do so. Adequate health care and education can form the basis and means for adequate choice. In this context a socialist market economy can flourish, allowing for the maximum compatibility of equality and liberty. Planning would still exist, but it would very be different in character, indicative rather than directly interventionary.

In sum, the usual charge made against socialism of being attached to state-run command economies, wholesale nationalization, and opposed to markets (caricatured particularly in the East European post-1945 experience) is simply false. Socialism, like most ideologies, embodies deep, subtle and often contradictory views.

CONCLUSION

The future of one form of socialism now seems to be at an end. One of most dominant elements of the socialist tradition in the twentieth century (institutionalized Marxist-Leninism) has received some fatal body-blows in the last decade with the collapse of Eastern Europe, and the transition of what remains of the USSR into market economies, or at least the aspiration to develop along these lines. Although this may be fatal for the stultified association of Marxist socialism with command economies, it is by no means fatal to the broad socialist tradition (which still incorporates Marxism in a different format), which has not necessarily looked to overthrow markets. Reformist state socialism has come in for less severe criticism in the last decade, though its attachment to certain types of nationalization policy has been perceived to fail. However, given that such nationalization policies have also been supported by certain schools of both conservatism and liberalism, this is hardly a fault to be laid at the door of reformist socialism. The more ethical, reformist state and market socialist perspectives are well able to adapt to contemporary views on the value of the market.

The notions of market socialism and the social market economy are being explored by a number of socialist theorists. In fact, because of the considerable overlap between these traditions and social democratic and new liberal traditions, they provide one of the most constructive alternatives to both conservative and liberal capitalism, which have dominated ideological discussion in the last decade in Europe and the USA. Socialism, despite the manifest dangers in some of its formats, its tendency towards communal nostalgia and its occasional attachment to a mechanistic statism and elitism, is still a fruitful and adaptable ideological tradition which reflects in the twentieth century an immensely important mode of human self-understanding and moral aspiration.

5
ANARCHISM

—

The discussion of socialism leads fairly naturally on to anarchism, with which it shares a number of ideological affinities. In point of fact, some of the ideas and schools of anarchy have been categorized as forms of socialism, although equally it should not be forgotten that some have been classified as liberal. Indeed, anarchy clearly overlaps with both ideologies.

The word anarchy is a compound of two Greek words, *an* and *arkhê*, which means, literally, the absence of government or rulers. More commonly the term 'state' (in place of government or rulers) is used through the nineteeth and twentieth centuries. An ambiguity creeps in here which can be destructive of a clearer understanding of the ideology. The idea of being 'without a state and government' can slip into the notion of being 'without authority or rules' which can in turn become, by verbal slippage, an equivalent to disorder, chaos or confusion. We can recognize these two senses in ordinary speech, namely where anarchy can refer to a way of life without the state, or, more commonly, it can denote complete mayhem. The latter is sometimes personified and parodied in the cartoon caricature of the anarchist about to throw a smoking bomb.[1]

Anarchists rightly object to such confusions in speech. Yet, they have not always discouraged the idea that anarchy might involve destruction and mayhem. There has been a certain humour and pleasure in the confusing implications of the idea of anarchy, a confusion emphasized by proponents and critics alike. The Russian anarchist Bakunin's famous, if ambiguous, comment that 'the destructive urge is a creative urge' catches something of the flavour of this playful duplicity. Certainly late nineteenth- and early-twentieth century literature which portrayed anarchists, such as Joseph Conrad's *The Secret Agent* or Emile Zola's *Germinal*, plays upon this ambiguity.

Yet anarchy itself, as an ideological movement, is, as most commentators agree, difficult to pin down with precision. Like other ideologies it incorporates a wide spectrum of opinions.[2] It should therefore not be over-simplified. This is not only due to the multiplicity of anarchy's exponents, but also to the problematic questions at the very centre of the ideology. For example, does the notion of 'doing without the state' automatically imply 'doing without government'? Do anarchists reject all authority or do they distinguish between types of authority? Is there a distinction to be drawn between authoritarian domination and moral authority? If the state, and possibly government, are absent, does any form of collective identity, like society, remain? Is society simply an aggregation of contracting individuals or an organic unity?

As in the ideologies previously discussed, the word anarchy is of comparatively recent origin. It entered into political currency fairly late in the nineteenth century. The first use of the term to denote a political position is to be found in Pierre-Joseph Proudhon's work *What is Property? An Inquiry into the Principle of Right and Government* (1840). This work not only coined the notoriously equivocal remark 'all property is theft', but also contained a clear assertion of, and commitment to, anarchy. As Proudhon stated: 'As man seeks justice in equality, so society seeks order in anarchy. Anarchy – the form of government to which we are every day approximating.' Proudhon defined anarchy as the 'absence of a master, of a sovereign'.[3] This and other similar statements in the book gave rise to the appellation 'father of anarchy', in respect of Proudhon, though the man has remained a profoundly confusing figure.

Before Proudhon, anarchy was used more as an abusive term, implying disorder. It retained connotations of abuse even up to the First International. Thus Bakunin initially did not utilize the term as a means of self-description. From the late 1860s he preferred the term 'collectivist', partly indeed to dissociate himself from the followers of Proudhon.[4] In addition, collectivists were not necessarily anti-statist, a point which has continued to make some anarchists uncomfortable with Bakunin. Marx, on the other hand, did employ the word 'anarchist' as an insult, indicating not only utopian impracticality, but also those individuals who, in his view, wanted to destroy the International. His target was most often Bakunin who, in consequence, initially tried to distance himself from the term. The nomenclature 'anarchy' subsequently followed a tortured and circuitous history in the congresses and heated debates of the International through the 1870s. It was not until the 1880s that it began to be used more widely in Europe and America to denote a comprehensive movement and a distinct ideological position.[5]

THE ORIGINS OF ANARCHIST THOUGHT

Debates about the origins of anarchism can be broken down into three main types. The first of these need not detain us long. There are those who claim that anarchism is essentially an all-pervasive universal and ahistorical libertarian disposition. It is argued that from the Ancient Greek writers onward we can find anarchist sentiments expressed. In the same vein it is also asserted that anarchist themes are to be found within ancient Chinese texts like the *Tao te Ching*. The contemporary American anarchist writer, John Clark, describes this Taoist work as 'one of the great anarchist classics'.[6] General libertarian-inclined movements and thinkers, from the time of Socrates, are all in imminent danger of being incorporated into this 'catch-all' perspective. Sophists, ranters, anabaptists and counter-culture movements from the 1960s become part of the same libertarian disposition. There is an intellectual weak-mindedness here that ignores historical and sociological factors. A similarly shallow view can be found, at some point, in the explanation of most ideologies. There is a strong demand for an 'ancient lineage' in all ideologies which often overwhelms intellectual caution.

The second perspective enjoys a more substantial credibility. It is rooted in the anthropological investigation that began in earnest in the nineteenth century with writers such as Lewis Morgan. Here, the basic claim is that anarchism either has strong parallels with, or (more forcefully) that anarchism can be found in embryo in, primitive acephalus forms of society throughout the world. The greatest early example of the stronger thesis is to be found in Peter Kropotkin's work *Mutual Aid* (1902). A modern form of the claim, with different intellectual roots, is represented by Michael Taylor's *Community, Anarchy and Liberty* (1982). As Taylor argues: 'During almost all the time since *Homo Sapiens* emerged, he has lived in stateless "primitive" communities'.[7] Many of these societies can be described as primitive anarchies. He distinguishes between certain types of primitive societies, finding that 'acephalus' societies approach 'much more closely to the pure anarchy'.[8] Defending his thesis, Taylor remarks:

> I do not see how anyone interested in anarchy or in community can or ought to avoid examining these communities, for they constitute the chief, almost the only historical examples of anarchy and quasi-anarchy and they are important examples of community on almost any account of the concept.[9]

This view of the origins of anarchy presents a number of problems. There is still a facet of the 'ancient lineage' perspective here, although less pronounced, which lays it open to the charge of sociological and historical anachronism. A false conceptual universalism pervades this view, even though it is premised on the more respectable concepts of nineteenth-century anthropological positivism. There is also a certain ingenuousness concerning the types of organization. Because something is stateless, or headless, does not ncessarily mean that it has to be placed under a very particular nineteenth-century rubric of anarchy. Why not conceive of it as another form of social organization? Why the desire to incorporate such phenomena into the categories of contemporary ideologies? Furthermore, the religious and social views of such primitive societies appear very different to the world of nineteenth- and twentieth-century anarchy. Again there is an element of almost romantic parochialism in the attempt to assimilate such different worlds. Rousseau's noble savage appears to lurk behind the neat public-good arguments. The forms of belief and the forms of control in such primitive societies might in fact now be considered considerably worse than state control.[10] Many of these primitive societies, despite not having over-arching authority, were immersed in sorcery, magic, cruelty, threat, mutual hostility, and certainly do not look like exemplars of mutual respect or liberty. As one investigation of such primitive groups argued:

> The absence of the State as a method of social organization does not *necessarily* involve the absence of those other undesirable features of western society that we would like to see abolished: competition, class division, status seeking, authoritarianism, restrictions on individual freedom, and so on. The acceptance of this myth is partly a result of the nineteenth-century tendency to seek universal monocausal explanations.[11]

The third view of the origins of anarchism locates it as a comparatively late offspring of the Enlightenment and the French Revolutionary era.[12] Apart from William Godwin (1756–1836) – who certainly expressed much of the sense of the concept of anarchy, feeding into one of the diverse currents of the French Revolution – anarchy itself was a product of the later nineteenth century. Its forceful appearance in the 1880s was not fortuitous. Anarchy can be seen as a confluence, or an interstice, between liberalism and socialism. As the German anarchist Rudolf Rocker aptly put it, anarchism is 'the confluence of the two great currents which during and since the French Revolution have found such characteristic expression in the intellectual life of Europe: Socialism and Liberalism'.[13] This does not mean that there is nothing distinctive about anarchy, yet it does signify considerable overlaps between it and other ideologies.

The period of the anarchist movement can be dated from approximately the 1880s until the 1930s. The Spanish Civil War saw the last vigorous attempts to set up anarchistic communes, unless that is, one includes the counter-culture movement of the 1960s.[14] Anarchists were essentially involved on the edge of two major revolutions: in Russia and in Spain. In both cases they were fairly quickly eliminated. In the example of the Ukrainian anarchists led by Nestor Makhno after the Russian Revolution, their success was prolonged through war conditions. Whether Makhno's movement was genuinely anarchist, given the extreme conditions of the war, is debatable.[15]

Some writers have contended, as suggested, that a return to anarchist themes can be seen in the counter-culture movements of the 1960s. Issues like growing industrialization, nuclear power, pollution, the threat of global ecological crisis, the escalation of state power and warfare, have radicalized a new generation with anarchistic sentiments. Anarchist writers from the 1960s such as Paul Goodman, Alex Comfort, Colin Ward and more particularly Murray Bookchin, all addressed these themes from within an anarchist perspective.[16] A new generation of journals like *Black Rose, Harbinger, Telos* and *The Raven* have continued to promote the anarchist critique. In addition, the Freedom Press and Black Rose Press still publish large amounts of anarchist literature.[17]

The question as to why anarchism developed from the 1860s and 1870s is immensely complex, the answer often being specific to particular societies. For example, the reasons for the development of Russian anarchism might be very different to the reasons for the development of the American, Spanish or French variants. To some extent there is also an intellectual dimension to the origin of different forms of anarchy, a point that will be discussed in the next section. Thus the origin of individualist anarchism has closer intellectual affinities to classical liberalism, whereas communist and collectivist anarchism were forged in the heated intellectual debates with Blanquism and Marxism in the International. From the 1880s onwards, anarchisms appeared in all European societies, as well as in India, South America, Japan and the USA.

It is not really possible to uncover a transparent rationale underlying the development of anarchism. A rough guide would include the following points. In the nineteenth century we see certain crucial historical developments. Most important was the growth and increasing centralization of nation-states, something which a number of ideologies, including liberalism, have found profoundly worrying. In addition, there was the marked expansion of industrial capitalism and the tremendous social, economic and political upheavals and distress attendant upon it. One consequence of this, particularly in more rural societies, was a clash between industrial and agricultural ways of life. It was not by accident that anarchism had, until the 1930s, its most vigorous support in the more rural, peasant-based societies of India, Russia, Spain and Italy.

The above social development coincided with a powerful European revolutionary tradition. Certain dates in this tradition became part of the iconography of socialism and anarchism, each with its accompanying hagiograhy and provoking violent disagreement as to its true meaning. The revolutions of 1789, 1830, 1848, 1871, 1917, and 1930 were seen as a developmental sequence imbued with a sacred teleology of liberation. This iconography was given its imprimatur and propagandized in the great debates of the First, Second and Third Internationals from the 1860s onward. The anarchists saw themselves as part of this process of liberation. In many cases their opposition to the state and to wide-scale industrialism took its cue from an opposition to Marxism which it saw as betraying the task of liberation and selling out to a form of state capitalism.

THE NATURE OF ANARCHISM

Anarchism, like socialism, is subject to a great deal of critical contestation. Most commentators, and many anarchists themselves, recognize a diversity of view. This is to be expected in one sense, given the strong belief in liberty of opinion implicit within much anarchist argument. Also, like most ideologies, there are a number of ways in which the movement can be categorized. We can either classify anarchisms according to the particular ideas and goals promulgated, or by the particular tactics employed, i.e., pacifist or violent.[18]

There is, in addition, considerable disagreement as to the number of schools of anarchy. My own preference is to distinguish between individualist, collectivist, communist, mutualist and anarcho-syndicalist versions. The typology adopted here includes some sub-variants. For example, one of the more popular versions of individualist anarchist thinking in the USA in the last decade had been associated with the name of Murray Rothbard and has acquired the nomenclature 'anarcho-capitalism'. There are other possible variants on this scheme. Some of the more extreme 'propaganda of the deed' anarchists in the 1880s and 1890s verged upon nihilism. More recently, the American anarchist Murray Bookchin has cited himself as an 'eco-anarchist'. Some recent writings have also spoken of 'feminist anarchism'. I have chosen to follow the more established typology. Thus, nihilist anarchism, eco-anarchism and feminist anarchism will not be considered as separate categories. While there is a much stronger case to be made for Bookchin, the present account will treat him as an exponent of communist anarchism.[19]

Individualist anarchy can be clearly observed in American writers such as Josiah Warren, Benjamin Tucker, Albert Jay Nock and Murray Rothbard. Rothbard does not fit so easily within this category on account of his particular obsession with capitalism. Although individualists differ markedly on many issues, the common thread that holds them in an uneasy alliance is their rigorous commitment to the sovereign individual, and, in many cases, their affirmation of the central importance of individual liberty. In the American tradition there is also an assertion of the value of private property. However, their firmest commitment is to complete individualism. Beyond this, disparities arise. Apart from the central importance of the individual, the ideas of Max Stirner do not fit very easily with other individualist anarchists. The same point holds for William Godwin and Leo Tolstoy who, despite their focus on the individual, do not cohere with the American conception of individualism.

Collectivist anarchism was primarily associated with the ideas of Michael Bakunin. Apart from his idiosyncratic pan-Slavist ideas and anti-German sentiments, Bakunin was celebrated for his belief in revolutionary spontaneity, his theoretical solemnization of the destructive urge, his virulent anti-Marxism and his conception of revolutionary anarchist dictatorship.

In organizational terms Bakunin believed in the collectivization of the means of production, where distribution would be determined by the criteria of work. Kropotkin thus argued that collectivist anarchists had a very different conception of justice to the communist anarchists, who thought in terms of need.[20]

Communist anarchism is one of the strongest components of anarchist thought to the present day. Kropotkin is the best-known early exponent of this variant. Others included Errico Malatesta, Alexander Berkman, Emma Goldmann, Colin Ward and Murray Bookchin. Communist anarchism is committed to the common ownership principle, in terms of property, production and housing. In the case of Kropotkin, distribution is premised on need. Such a commitment overlaps with some aspects of reformist socialism and social liberalism. Communist anarchists also assert the necessity of social solidarity and cooperative dispositions. Such notions are seen to be implicit in human nature. This tendency is repeated by Bookchin in his writings and linked with themes of ecological balance and harmony.[21] The first communist anarchist work to present this case was Kropotkin's *Mutual Aid*. Freedom remains a slightly ambivalent issue in communist anarchy. It is usually related to the moral growth and self-development of the individual within a community, which might be better understood as a positive concept of liberty, yet there are exceptions to this within some communist anarchist writings. Finally, like collectivist anarchism, communist anarchy disapproves of market activity and the private production of goods.

Mutualist anarchy was associated with the 'father of anarchy', Pierre-Joseph Proudhon. Proudhon's views changed during his life time. He later even balked at the title 'anarchist'. His early views on anarchy can be summarized by the term 'mutualism'. He surmised that political organization premised on the state would be replaced by economic organization. Governments and states would disappear and individuals would relate to one another through mutual economic contracts. Mutualism, sometimes also called 'guaranteeism', was a form of contractarian anarchy. The only organization which would not be contractual was the family, which remained unradicalized, hierarchical and patriarchal. Women were, by and large, excluded from the benefits of anarchy. Men would possess private property (so long as they were not exploiting or abusing others), and work for themselves. They could start businesses by borrowing credit, without interest, from a 'mutual credit bank'. Their products could also be exchanged for credit notes guaranteed by the bank. Distribution would be unpatterned and dependent upon work and productivity. Despite this, there was still a background of substantive egalitarianism and liberty. Contracts could not be made under economic duress or under conditions of unequal liberty. A just society would be one in which equality and freedom of contract were upheld. Proudhon called his contractarian notion of justice 'commutative justice'.

The final strain of anarchism is anarcho-syndicalism, which grew out of the broader and slightly older movement of syndicalism.[22] The term 'syndicalism' has two meanings. It can denote simply trade unionism in a neutral sense. On the other hand, it signifies revolutionary or militant trade unionism, devoted to the overthrow of capitalism and the state. The usual mechanism of overthrow was the general strike. Syndicalism envisaged the eventual reconstruction of society according to a non-state, federalized format, premised on existing syndicalist producer groups. This movement had been growing during the 1880s and 1890s in France. In the early 1900s it spread to the USA with the famous International Workers of the World (Wobblies), acquiring highly effective, if idiosyncratic, exponents in Eugene Debs and Daniel de Leon. It also developed in Italy, Spain, Australia, Latin America and Britain among other countries. In Britain its effect was felt most intensely in the South Wales coalfields before 1914, though its precise role and effect in fomenting industrial unrest is still hotly disputed.[23]

Because of its militant anti-political and anti-state stance, syndicalism attracted the support and interest of some anarchists, though not all. They were drawn by its deeply anti-political organizational roots within the working class. Communes did not have to be constructed, revolutionary culture and popular decentralist structures were already in place. After a 1907 anarchist congress in Amsterdam many anarchists tried to unify with syndicalism, hence the title 'anarcho-syndicalism'. Some like the German anarchist Rudolf Rocker, regarded anarcho-syndicalism as the future path for anarchy to take. Others, in mainstream syndicalism, like Victor Griffuehles, and in mainstream anarchism, like Malatesta and Kropotkin, repudiated any relationship between anarchism and syndicalism.

Basically anarcho-syndicalism rejected all state-orientated politics − parties, parliaments, democracy and the like. It also displayed a strong anti-intellectual tendency, rejecting bourgeois education and forms of thought. It advocated class war and the destruction of capitalism by armed violence and general strikes. Producer groups would form the nuclei of the new society. These would be democratically self-organized and self-directing federated associations of workers who would create their own social, political and economic culture and do so even before the revolution. This autonomy had been vigorously advocated by the syndicalist Pelloutier, the leading light of early French syndicalism, as one important component of his concept of the *Bourse du Travail*. The *Bourse* was envisaged as a meeting-house within a locality for workers of all syndicates. It had many functions: as a labour exchange, meeting-place, holding a strike chest, and as an educational centre with a library. As well as serving practical and strategic functions, the *Bourse* would also enable a new workers' culture to be built.

Before moving on to discuss features of anarchist thought, one problem within this scenario of 'schools of anarchy' needs to be reviewed. Can all the above schools be described as anarchist? Within the literature there have been a number of attempts to limit the field. Apart from the communist anarchists, nearly all the schools of anarchy are subject to this attempt at restriction. For example, from the time of its inception many considered that anarcho-syndicalism was outside the main anarchist movement. Yet, even if anarcho-syndicalism is considered to be part of anarchy, writers who are popularly associated with this school, such as Georges Sorel, E. Berth and H. Lagardelle, are often dismissed as having contributed little to it. Thus Rudolf Rocker commented that none of these figures had 'any mentionable influence' on either anarchy or anarcho-syndicalism.[24] A modern commentator like David Miller also remarks that syndicalism was 'always an alliance between ideologically disparate elements', and that it was 'not explicitly anarchist in character'.[25] Yet Rocker, amongst others, did not share this latter judgement. He saw anarcho-syndicalism as the vital centre of anarchy.

Another particular favourite for exclusion is Max Stirner. As John Carroll noted in his introduction to Stirner's *The Ego and His Own*: 'intellectual studies of anarchism have tended to exhibit a deep hostility to the philosopher of the self'.[26] Carroll suggests that Stirner might better be considered a nihilist than an anarchist, and he is not alone in this assessment. He continues: 'Stirner's uncompromising advocacy of self-realization sets him apart from other anarchist philosophers, especially Proudhon and Kropotkin'.[27] Not all agree with this judgement, however. John Clark, in his study *Max Stirner's Egoism*, fiercely contends that Stirner's 'influence on individualist anarchism has continued to the present, and I strongly suspect that it is in fact growing'.[28]

Again Gaus and Chapman, in an introduction to a volume of essays on anarchy, have suggested that not only should 'anarcho-syndicalism' be ruled out but also individualist 'anarcho-capitalism'. This point is repeated in a later essay in this volume by David Wieck who comments that the latter movement is 'entirely outside the mainstream of anarchist theoretical writings'.[29] Those within the communist anarchist movement have been particularly keen to expunge individualist anarchists like Rothbard. It is obviously uncomfortable to find themselves as bedfellows with such antipathetic ideas. Rothbard himself does not appear to be worried by this, and still sees his own affinities as lying with an individualist libertarian anarchism.

If one looks more closely at the anarchist movement this process can be repeated *ad infinitum*. Most communist and collectivist anarchists expressed distaste for Proudhon's contractarian anarchism, which was seen to evince a 'shopkeeper's mentality'.[30] They also felt uncomfortable with his labour theory of value, his notion of a market-based commutative justice, his patriarchal view of the family, his striving to become a parliamentary candidate, his support of the South and slavery in the

American Civil War and, not least, his later belief in the role of a federal state. In the same vein, recent anarchist commentators, including Vernon Richards and Daniel Guérin, have seen Bakunin's collectivism as conforming more to a Marxist position than to anarchism.[31] This process of mutual repudiation and delimitation is potentially endless and does not appear to be a very profitable path to follow.

Finally, it is worth remarking that various schools of anarchism have existed in a tense, overlapping and immensely complex relationship with both Marxism and liberalism. This point will not be dealt with separately, but will be touched upon in the course of the discussion.[32]. Having outlined the schools of anarchy, some of the elements of anarchist thought will now be examined throught the lenses of the various schools.

HUMAN NATURE

There are three essential points to note in respect of the issue of human nature. First, anarchists most emphatically do not all hold to the same concept of human nature. There are marked differences evident between thinkers and schools of anarchy. Second, their notions of human nature do not always evince optimism or perfectibilism. They are often accused of holding naively optimistic beliefs, but as Rothbard notes: 'I confess that I do not understand the basis for this charge ... I assume with most observers that mankind is a mixture of good and evil, of cooperative and criminal tendencies'.[33] Earlier this century the communist anarchist Malatesta made exactly the same point with regard to the fallibility of human nature.[34] Third, anarchists do not necessarily all hold an absolute or fixed concept of human nature. In the case of writers like Kropotkin and Elisée Reclus, human beings were still seen to be biologically evolving. Both Kropotkin and Reclus were geographers and natural scientists by training and inclination. Their explanations of human behaviour were ultimately premised on the natural sciences. Other anarchists, both earlier and later, have believed that humans gradually change through the cultivation and development of reason. With the growth of literacy and the availability of books, human society must ultimately progress. Godwin articulated this from an Enlightenment perspective, whereas writers from Bakunin to Bookchin have linked this theme with a more Hegelian standpoint on the growth of reason.

The idea of human nature, however, remains central to anarchist thought. What differentiates perspectives within the anarchist movement are their starting-points. These may, crudely, be seen as individual and social. One perspective locates human beings as independent autonomous agents framing their own plans of the life outside society; the other portrays

humans developing within a community and achieving freedom and individuality through it. These represent broad tendencies within anarchist
thought.

One of the most famous examples of the social tendency can be found
in the work of Kropotkin. He rejected the dominance of the competitive
notion of evolution. From his study of animal behaviour and primitive
communities in Siberia, and stimulated by the work of the zoologist Karl
Kessler, he came to the conclusion that animals, including human beings,
only flourish in cooperative communities. As a result of his observations
of many animal species he was led to remark: 'In all these scenes of animal
life which passed before my eyes, I saw Mutual Aid and Mutual Support
carried on to an extent which made me suspect in it a feature of the
greatest importance for the maintenance of life, the preservation of each
species, and its further evolution'.[35] Social solidarity and mutual aid come
naturally to human beings. It is part of the law of nature. Kropotkin
was profoundly optimistic about the cooperative, creative and altruistic
qualities of human nature. Nature was the teacher of morality − a claim
that Kropotkin explored in a book on ethics. Kropotkin did not deny the
element of struggle, but suggested that it had been overemphasized by
Darwin's acolytes. Fallow deer, pelicans, bees, badgers, are all taken as
corroboration of the mutual aid hypothesis. Linking this with political
theory, Kropotkin noted with due seriousness: 'The ants and termites
have renounced the "Hobbesian war" and they are better for it'.[36]

The basic thesis was that the biologically fittest were the most cooperative. Nature is not red in tooth and claw. Even for primitive human
communities this is obvious.[37] Kropotkin notes that primitive peoples
find it as impossible to grasp our individualism as we do their cooperation. For primitives, 'self-sacrifice in the interests of the clan are of daily
occurrence'.[38] In subsequent chapters of *Mutual Aid* Kropotkin traces,
this human solidarity through village communes, medieval cities and
guilds. Competitive life in the state, for Kropotkin, is an historical aberration. Cooperation and mutual aid in fact still go on regardless of the
existence of the state.

Kropotkin clearly had a touching and optimistic faith in the mass of
human beings, an attitude that even led some fellow communist anarchists
to accuse him of naivety.[39] His faith in nature still finds an echo in the
writings of the contemporary communist anarchist Murray Bookchin,
who comments that: 'Ecology recognizes no hierarchy on the level of the
ecosystem. There are no "kings of the beasts" and no "lowly ants" ...
Virtually all that lives ... plays its coequal role in maintaining the
balance and integrity of the whole'.[40] Nature is thus intrinsically anarchic
to Bookchin. This belief in 'natural' anarchy has some parallel with the
remark of Alexander Berkman that all children 'show an instinctive
tendency to individuality and independence, to non-conformity manifested

in open and secret defiance' and thus may be considered to be naturally anarchistic.[41]

Not all socially orientated anarchists shared this faith in nature. Bakunin, for one, disliked the idea of set rational patterns of progress towards anarchy. History, like nature, was to a large extent irrational and unsystematic, and characterized by sudden unexpected explosions of instinctual and spontaneous activity.[42] In the same vein, Bakunin spoke of the 'revolt of life against science'. Preordained laws or rules were to be rejected in favour of anti-intellectualism and instinct. The instincts of the uneducated peasant were more reliable than the intellectual systems of the educated. Revolution was instinctively present in such people. As he commented, 'The most renowned geniuses have done nothing, or very little, specifically for the people ... Popular life, popular development, popular progress belong exclusively to the people themselves.'[43]

Leaving aside the question as to whether George Sorel was, or was not, a spokesman for anarcho-syndicalism, this reliance on instinct was also characteristic of Sorel's general position in *Reflections on Violence*. In the case of Sorel it was not the peasants who experienced this instinctual response; conversely, it was the industrial proletariat. The instinct was to be channelled through myths like the general strike. The instinctual psychology which dominated Sorel's thinking had deeper theoretical roots than it had for Bakunin, namely, in the work of Gustav Le Bon, Eduard von Hartmann, Friedrich Nietzsche and Henri Bergson.[44] Furthermore, the epic state of mind of such proletarians was clearly at odds with anything that Bakunin would have comprehended.[45]

On the individualist reading of human nature further disparities arise. William Godwin was noted for his individualistic stance. He believed the nature of human beings to be determined by their environment. In other words, human beings were ductile. They were also possessed of the capacity to reason. The particular moral theory he embraced was utilitarianism. True happiness lies in the development of our individuality. The individual alone can be a judge of his or her utility. This led Godwin to suggest that all forms of cooperative activity should be regarded with suspicion. As he put it: 'Everything that is usually understood by the term cooperation is in some degree evil'.[46] Anything which prevents someone from thinking for themselves – communal labour, communal meals, marriage, even theatrical or musical performances – could be seen to be an invasion of individuality. Humans ought to be able to stand without one another. As Godwin stated: 'He is the most perfect man to whom society is not a necessity of life but a luxury'.[47]

The above position bears some similarities to the twentieth-century individualist Murray Rothbard, except that Rothbard repudiates utilitarianism in favour of a natural rights theory. For Rothbard, human beings have a definite specifiable nature. We are self-interested acquisitive beings, who are capable of rationality. We feel, think, and act as individuals and should be allowed the liberty to learn and to develop our faculties. We fundamentally 'own' ourselves. We can cooperate with others, but this is an individual choice that we make. Rothbard calls this the 'self-ownership principle'. Individuals recognize the self-ownership principle, acknowledge the right of property embodied in it, and thus relate to each other through the free market.

Another individualist, Max Stirner, certainly accepted the self-ownership principle, but his notion of *Eigenheit* implied a great deal more.[48] Stirner argued so rigorously for individualism that even the recognition of others' rights to private property, the contractual basis of interaction, and the important role of the market, were regarded as mere fabrications placed over the individual. The 'ownness' of the solitary ego even comes before liberty. Stirner's human being is totally self-enclosed, constructing its own world and values. This is anarchistic individualism taken to its ultimate degree. Even pure altruism is seen to be profoundly egoistic. This doctrine has been called 'psychological egoism'. Its roots lie in a very different intellectual debate within the peripheries of Hegelianism, more precisely in Stirner's critique of some his fellow young Hegelians. Each individual ego is the only arbiter of reality. In this scenario nothing is important except the ontological supremacy of each ego.

It can be seen from the above examples drawn from anarchy that there is no one clear reading of human nature. In fact, anarchy appears to be more subject than other ideologies to enormous diversity on this issue. This makes the discussion of anarchist politics that much more complicated.

CRITIQUE OF THE STATE

If there is one theme which recurs in discussions on anarchism it is the critique, and rejection, of the 'state', and also sometimes 'government' and 'authority'. There are a number of problems with such a rejection. First, there is a lack of clarification in anarchist writings as to what these terms mean. Consequently it is difficult, on occasion, to ascertain *what* is being rejected. Second, anarchists often differ markedly as to whether concepts like government, authority and the state should be considered to be synonymous or separate. In other words, can authority be maintained under anarchy without a state or government? Third, the normative grounds on which anarchists attack the state and justify alternatives to it are premised on amazingly diverse moral sources. Lockian natural rights theory, radical utilitarianism, psychological egoism, neo-Kantianism, Hegelianism, evolutionary theory and Christian principles, are just the better-known among the normative resources.[49] This diversity of moral justification alone makes the arguments difficult to discuss coherently.

I will briefly examine the the meaning of these terms and then turn to the question of why the state is rejected.

Oddly, there is remarkably little written by anarchists on what is meant by the state. Usually they have in mind the institutional structures of legislative, executive, judicial and bureaucratic administration, also occasionally the police, armed forces, and for some, religion and education. Some concentrate on the structure of coercion, others on a psychological disposition.[50] None of these assessments are particularly sensitive to the nuances of the state tradition. In addition, some of Proudhon's writings appear to treat government, state, sovereignty, law and authority as virtually synonymous. Proudhon speaks of the abolition of the state as the abolition of both government and authority.[51] On the other hand, the American anarchist Albert Jay Nock in *Our Enemy the State* distinguished sharply between government and state. Government was concerned with intervention to secure natural rights to life, liberty and property.[52] A state is always an oppressive structure, in fact it is a criminal organization. Rothbard follows the same line of argument, interpreting taxation as a more sophisticated form of robbery.[53]

What, therefore, is wrong with the state and government? Again anarchist responses vary. Generally the state is seen to be an artificial and alien institution which, in its worst aspect, is a brigand or criminal organization writ large. As Alexander Herzen put it vividly, the state is 'Genghis Khan with the telegraph', although today a computer might be more apt. Such a view stretches across the schools of anarchy. A state denotes the centralization of coercion and violence. Historically, states are usually built on the back of military dominance. Their resources are always legalized plunder. The existence of the state thus implies the total denial of liberty. As Bakunin commented: 'States can find no other grounds for joint action than the concerted enslavement of the masses who constitute the overall basis and purpose of their existence'.[54] Furthermore, because states involve hierarchy and domination, they also necessarily entail the denial of human equality. Most anarchists contend that the state structure is defended by a caste of academics, priests and intellectuals. This judgement goes some way towards accounting for the anti-intellectualism redolent of some anarchists.

Individualist anarchists focus primarily on the state's denial of individual rights and freedoms, particularly the freedoms of the market and property. This is especially true for many of the American individualists. Individualist anarchists, in concert, tend to mistrust any talk of collective, corporate or communal entities, the state being the most heinous of such collectivities. For Godwin, Stirner and Rothbard, as we have seen, cooperation or collective action are intrinsically mistrusted. For Stirner, given the ontological primacy of the ego, society is inevitably viewed as another mental 'spook'.[55] Godwin rejected cooperation on the grounds of his individualistic utilitarianism. Rothbard, from a natural rights base, similarly denies the very existence of society, commenting that, 'There is no existing entity called "society"; there are only interacting individuals'.[56] Humans are intrinsically egoistic. Society can only be a convenient label for interacting individuals.

The collectivist, mutualist and communist anarchists also have their own idiosyncratic views on this issue. Proudhon and Bakunin tend to see the state as a brutal but passing phase in the development of society. For Bakunin, the Germans were the only really committed statists in Europe. He made direct links in this context, not without some passing amusement, between Marx and Bismarck. He also looked with interest and sympathy on American federalism and considered that the British did not really have a state tradition at all.[57]

Kropotkin's work (and, in this century, Bookchin's) is more wide-ranging and optimistic than that of Bakunin. For Kropotkin the state does not undermine and destroy individuals *per se*, but rather the natural, harmonious, organic communities in which individuals develop. Bookchin calls such natural communities 'affinity groups'. Kropotkin sees a pattern in the development of societies, remarking that 'whenever mankind made a new start in civilization, in Greece, Rome, or middle Europe, it passed through the same stages – the tribe, the village, community, the free city, the state – each one naturally evolving out of the preceding stage'.[58] The state exists to destroy all natural forms of federated union. For Kropotkin this destruction was the policy of popes, Continental monarchs, parliaments, and even the revolutionary convention of France. Kropotkin believed, though, that beneath this stifling state control, mutual aid still lived in an 'infinity of associations'.[59] The task of anarchy was to encourage the full re-emergence of these natural associations.

It is important to realize that for the majority of anarchists *nothing* redeems the state. Proudhon and Bakunin are exceptions to this point.[60] The liberal constitutional tradition, the Jacobin state, liberal parliamentary democracy, and more especially the socialist state, are seen as illusions by virtually all the schools of anarchy. Thus Bakunin used to refer to the Marxist state as the 'great lie of the century – red bureaucracy'.[61] And Kropotkin declared with equal disdain: 'The modern radical is a centralizer, a State partisan, a Jacobin to the core, and the Socialist walks in his footsteps'.[62]

LIBERTY AND EQUALITY

For many anarchists the reason why the state is to be abhorred is that it is the root of all compulsion. As Berkman argued: 'A life without compulsion means liberty'. The anarchist commitment to the value of liberty necessarily entailed a rejection of the state.[63] Liberty was not, on this reading, an abstract philosophical 'end' to aim for, but, as Rocker maintained, it was 'the vital concrete possibility for every human being'.[64]

It might be assumed from this that all anarchists were committed to the value of liberty. Two problems arise here, one more complex than the other.[65] To take the simpler one first: it is not clear that all anarchists have valued liberty or autonomy above all else. Stirner, for one, explicitly elevates 'ownness', or *Eigenheit*, above liberty. Liberty is, in other words, always subordinate to the value of the ego. Similarly, for Stirner, much of the supposed value and content of liberty was nothing more than a series of unauthentic illusions and mental 'spooks' of the bourgeois mind. As Stirner put it in his stark prose: '"Freedom" awakens your *rage* against everything that is not you; "egoism" calls you to *joy* over yourselves, to self-enjoyment; "freedom" is and remains a *longing*, a romantic plaint, a Christian hope ... "ownness" is a reality'.[66] Even when Stirner discusses freedom, it is far from clear whether he accepts either the negative or positive notions. The American anarchist writer John Clark, following Stirner's insight, comments that 'Anarchism is the one major political theory which has attempted to synthesize the values of negative and positive freedom into a single, more comprehensive view of human liberty'.[67]

Yet this desire for synthesis is certainly not shared by the majority of anarchists. This leads to the second problem, namely that, similar to the case of liberalism, there are major differences of interpretation regarding the meaning of liberty. As with liberalism, these distinct senses of liberty carry differing social and economic implications. The most orthodox view of anarchists is that they share a conception of negative liberty, virtually the same as that of many of the classical liberals.[68] Liberty is read in this context as a paucity of intentional physical coercion or compulsion. This view is particularly characteristic of American anarchism. Rothbard quite clearly defines coercion as 'aggressive physical violence against person and property'.[69] Thus, like Berkman (a communist anarchist), he contends that the abolition of the state will mean the abolition of the main source of coercion, and hence the enhancement of liberty. Rothbard's argument links up with his self-ownership principle and non-aggression axiom: that if individuals have absolute rights of ownership over their bodies, then no one should coerce them. Thus everyone has 'the absolute right to be "free" from aggression'.[70]

On the other hand, some communist anarchists appear to be arguing more in the vein of positive liberty. This particular notion of positive liberty has not facilitated a more benign attitude to the role or function of the state, however, as it did with the social liberalism of T. H. Green. Anarchists who have entertained a more positive understanding of liberty are as vociferous as the individualists in their rejection of the state. There are several elements present in this positive conception of liberty. First, liberty was not just about lack of compulsion, although it is clear that compulsion was still accepted as an important factor in examining liberty. In this sense liberty was freedom from compulsion in order to pursue a positive goal. Positive liberty involved self-government, legislating to oneself, choosing one's own goals autonomously. One particular neo-Kantian variant of this argument, R. P. Wolff's *In Defense of Anarchism*, has attained particular publicity in some academic circles. In spite of showing very little grasp of the diversity of anarchist thought, Wolff offers a powerful philosophical argument aimed at showing that the recognition of authority is inconsistent with our overriding obligation to act as autonomous self-directing agents. Any duty to obey authority *de jure* implies an abdication of autonomy. Wolff's argument has generated a minority taste of philosophical literature in the last twenty years. But, despite its intrinsic interest, it is peripheral to the mainstream of anarchist thought and practice.[71]

Second, liberty is concerned with choosing goals which, minimally, do not abuse, exploit or demean others. In other words, the goals must have a moral dimension. This moral dimension is part of the constitutive meaning of liberty.[72] Third, liberty is concerned with the self-development of human beings, or as Rocker put it, bringing 'to full development all the powers, capacities, and talents with which nature has endowed him'.[73] Finally, the constitutive moral goals must be embedded in a community. In fact, the goals and purpose themselves are derived from a community or from the natural communal instincts of our natures. This is a fundamental premise of communist anarchism.[74]

In respect of equality, anarchist beliefs vary according to their conceptions of human nature and the character of value. The starkest view of equality — that of Stirnerite egoism — sees everything over and above the ego as illusory. Egos may thus be taken as formally or procedurally equal. All claims to hierarchy or superiority should be treated as bogus by the egoist. In the case of other individualist anarchists the nature of equality becomes more explicit. With Godwin's position, every human is equally possessed of the capacity to reason and judge his or her own interests and happiness. No hierarchy was acceptable, each individual should be approached as equally capable of reason. In the American anarchist tradition, equality stems from the isolated ego demanding the natural right to property in his or her own body and not to suffer aggression, and also to have equal access to the market. In the case of Leo Tolstoy, equality was based on the Judaeo-Christian principle of equality of souls. For Tolstoy, the kingdom of God was within each of us and implied mutual religious respect for each person.[75]

The more formal reading of equality in individualism can be contrasted with the more substantive vision of equality to be found in the commuist anarchists. For communist and collectivist anarchists, political, legal or economic equality were not viewed as adequate. Equality was something more far-reaching. In the case of Kropotkin, equality was premised on need. Each person had certain fundamental physical, mental, and cultural needs which ought to be met equally within society. These needs constituted the well-being of the human individual. In the case of the communist anarchists, specifically, equality in a substantive social sense tied in closely with the achievement of genuine positive liberty. In the case of individualists, the more formal procedural reading of equality linked up with negative liberty — in the form of an equal right to equal liberty. The attempt to establish individual substantive needs, and satisfy them through a community, would have struck most individualists as a denial of liberty.

JUSTICE, PROPERTY AND THE ECONOMY

Another of the values widely appealed to by anarchists was justice. Justice was usually considered independently from law. The concept of law was linked with the practices of government, state and authority.[76] Thus, if there were any relation between the two it would be that justice acted as an evaluative yardstick to set against legislative practices. Hence the notion of the morally just society is central to anarchist thought, but the question remains — what is justice? There are two distinct senses in which the notion of justice is deployed in anarchist thought. As with the concept of equality, one is linked with a more procedural understanding and the other to a more substantive and distributive model.

The above points are also revealing about the nature of anarchist views on the economy. Generally it can be said that all anarchist schools oppose the notion of state capitalism and the state-based command economy. Apart from this more negative judgement, it becomes difficult to identify a common ground. There is certainly some vague attachment to a decentralized economy. With the American individualists — the anarcho-capitalists in particular — the totally unregulated market becomes the model. Production becomes a very different question to distribution. In communist anarchy, production and distribution are both completely linked and communalized. Proudhon's contractarian market model and social individualism hangs midway between these ideas. Proudhon's theory is more or less equivalent to an anarchist form of market socialism.

The first anarchist to deploy the concept of justice robustly in his discussion of society was Proudhon. However, it should be mentioned that, despite any *prima facie* radical reputation, his understanding is economistic and comparable to some forms of classical liberalism. Proudhon, paralleling something of Sir Henry Maine's 'status to contract' argument and Spencer's 'militant to industrial society' idea, argued that societies as they developed and grew towards anarchy moved from government to contract. This was not a contract *with* any government. Proudhon was deeply critical of 'contract of government' theorists like Locke and Rousseau. For Proudhon, contract *replaced* government. Contract, he maintained, is opposed to authority and denotes mutuality.[77] People would take the responsibility for their own lives and interact via contract and exchange. The contract is a totally self-assumed obligation. For Proudhon, therefore, it is an ideal vehicle for anarchy. The only exception to this contractarian vision was the family which Proudhon still conceived of, inexplicably, in hierarchical and patriarchal terms. In general Proudhon was adamant that there must be substantive equality of contract and it is this substantive equality that differentiates him from later individualist anarchists.

Contract served two functions: first, it entailed the guarantee of equivalent economic exchange; second, contract guarantees liberty, since relations are purely voluntary and free from coercion. Contract was to characterize the new form of society, something that Proudhon also called a 'guaranteeist society'. Proudhon came to speak of this society in almost mystical and religious terms.[78] What is unsurprising, and yet puzzling, is the notion of justice deployed by Proudhon. Justice is concerned with equal contracts. Proudhon calls this 'commutative justice'. In the present era we are more used to hearing Hayek and his acolytes deploying this idea, which only reinforces Proudhon's more market-orientated appearance. Proudhon notes: '*Commutative justice*, the *reign of contract*, the *industrial* or *economic system*, such are the different synonyms for the idea'. Of significance here is the fact that in arguing for this procedural and commutative idea, Proudhon poured scorn on the distributive senses of justice, which we might now tend to associate with reformist socialism and social liberalism. Distributive justice, he argued, relates to authority, law and government. It implied that someone was planning and patterning. Like Herbert Spencer, Proudhon saw distributive justice as feudal in character. It is important, however, to grasp that despite his dislike of communism and distributive justice, he had no love for the idea of an unregulated market.[79]

Later individualist writers, especially in the American tradition, recall some of Proudhon's ideas. Certainly there is a clear opposition to distributive justice. In the case of writers like Rothbard, the natural right to one's body, property and liberty are of supreme importance. This entails a far more formal understanding of procedural justice. Rothbard is not concerned with the substantive equality of parties to contracts, only that individuals should not be prohibited from contracting. Property rights in one's body, and capital, should not be interfered with and one should not be subject to harm or aggression. Justice is concerned with sustaining a voluntary 'libertarian law code', focused on formal individual rights.[80] Rothbard ignores all large accumulations of property and social handicaps which might affect the ability to contract. Neither Proudhon, Stirner nor Godwin would have accepted this latter argument, especially the sacred quality that Rothbard confers upon property rights. Each would have rejected the argument for very different reasons. Proudhon, in particular, rejected the absolute right to property as encouraging its utter abuse. This is what lay behind his elusive statement, 'All property is theft'.

The American individualists thus endorse a very much more rigid application of a free market. The difference between individualist anarchists and minimalist classical liberals is slight on this point, namely, that many classical liberals believe that human beings are egoistic and self-interested and cannot be trusted in a completely unregulated forum. In addition, given that each ego recognizes this, it is rational that individuals would agree on a minimal state apparatus to perform certain public functions. Certainly this is the direction of contemporary liberal writers such as Robert Nozick and James Buchanan. On the other hand, individualist anarcho-capitalists either suggest that humans will adapt to a purely unregulated condition or that individuals would hire out services (previously performed by governments) on the free market, including policing and judicial work.

For communist and collectivist anarchists, justice was seen almost exclusively in distributive terms. For Kropotkin, this was tied to an evolutionary development. As he stated: 'Feelings of justice develop, more or less, with all gregarious animals ... Sociability thus puts a limit to physical struggle, and leaves room for the development of better moral feelings'.[81] There were differences in the respective criteria for distribution. Bakunin's belief in distribution was premised upon the performance of work or labour in a commune. Kropotkin regarded such a process as faulty since it contained the seeds of unequal treatment.[82] Desert, or work, were replaced in Kropotkin by 'need' as the key distributive principle. In fact, distribution is a misleading word since no one would be *doing* the distribution; rather there would be a change in the character of production and in the way people consumed.

Kropotkin's analysis was premised on the argument that no production was individual. It is the human race which creates wealth. This wealth is seized illegitimately by a few. Private property is therefore at odds with the nature of production and wealth creation. For human beings to develop fully, wealth must be reappropriated for humanity. The principle, as Kropotkin put it, should be: 'All is for all! ... What we proclaim is THE RIGHT TO WELL-BEING: WELL-BEING FOR ALL!'[83] Everyone has the right to live. To live is to have needs, and such needs are met when wealth is reappropriated and redistributed according to needs. Needs are both physical in respect of food, clothing and housing, and cultural in respect of education. In this context, the communist anarchist view of the economy becomes markedly distinct from that of the individualist anarchist. Production and distribution are envisaged as integrated communal enterprises, in which goods are produced to meet the needs of all.

Kropotkin defines the science of political economy as 'The study of the needs of mankind, and the means of satisfying them with the least possible waste of human energy', or as he renames it: 'the Physiology of Society'.[84]

THE PROBLEM OF POLITICAL ORGANIZATION

One of the major problems for anarchy in formulating any account of political organization is the accusation that anarchy is a distinctly unrealistic, naive and utopian doctrine that is unlikely to work. Anarchy has been replete with models of the ideal society. Some anarchist writers have undoubtedly been wild and impractical in their proposals, whilst others have been more balanced, pragmatic and piecemeal in their approach. Those who have worked through the medium of education on anarchist themes have obviously had a longer-term view.[85]

There are some common beliefs within anarchism concerning the organizational base of society. Most anarchists hold that any future society would be non-hierarchial, non-coercive and libertarian. Furthermore, the nation-state is quite definitely seen as passing from the historical scene, with its bureaucracies, judiciary, police and army. If some elemental government were to remain it would be minimized and premised upon consent. It would be, as one writer has put it, 'government without politics'.[86] There might be, in some cases, loose non-compulsory federations, but 'decentralization' would be the watchword. Beyond this minimal agreement a number of different views arise.

With the American individualists, and in particular the anarcho-capitalists, much previous government or state activity could be carried out by individuals in a free market. As the American anarchist Benjamin Tucker put it, 'genuine anarchism is consistent Manchesterism'.[87] Anarchy exists where there is 'no possibility for coercive aggression against the person or property of any individual'.[88] To be opposed to the state, for Rothbard, is not necessarily to be opposed to the services it performs. Rothbard envisages a situation of complete voluntaristic individualism. Even the word 'society' is seen as a collective fiction. As long as individuals voluntarily agree to arbitration they would be able to hire out even judicial courts and police. Rothbard contends that people could be invited to attend a court and be judged under a libertarian code of law. Of course, in the final analysis, there is nothing that could compel individual compliance except a feeling that a libertarian consensus *ought* to develop if all individuals acknowledged natural rights (which, of course, they do not). Moreover, it is difficult to see what could be done in the individualist perspective about a mass murderer, the physically handicapped or the insane. Also, as many have noted, the evidence that exists on private security and policing firms does not inspire great confidence. There is nothing to stop criminals themselves setting up as police or security firms. In the end, punishment becomes a matter of retaliation. If no agreement can be reached, then violence is the only resort. In this situation the market would not encourage order but lethal disorder. Rothbard comforts his audience here with the bland observation that there would nevertheless be no state-led equivalent to Hiroshima or Dresden in such localized conflict.

Max Stirner at least was not so sanguine about consensual libertarian agreement. He appears more directly honest and hard-headed about individualism than Rothbard. Stirner believed that punishment would be replaced by retaliation between egos. Since all the mental 'spooks' of the bourgeois mind – including natural rights, property and markets – would be ruled out, the most that could be hoped for would be a vague 'union of egoists', where each would be seeking to satisfy his or her own interest.[89] Society simply would not exist. It would be replaced by nothing but the solipsistic ego. As Stirner commented, 'Every people, every State, is unjust towards the egoist'.[90] On this reading of social life, as Stirner was prepared to admit, crime was as valid an enterprise as punishment or retaliation.

In the case of the communist anarchists a much stronger moral claim is made for communal values and organization. This in turn makes it more problematic to account for individual liberty or autonomy. In responding to the individualist case, communist anarchists contended that individualism was anachronistic and flawed, too reliant on the vagaries of markets to achieve liberty or substantive equality, and ultimately set for collapse into state capitalism. The communists and collectivists envisaged humans living in small-scale decentralized, federated, non-hierarchical communes linking up with age-old village community traditions.[91] Bookchin calls them 'affinity groups'.[92] Communes would be voluntary. Yet most anarchists of this persuasion believed that people would flourish, develop, and desire to live in this context. Kropotkin gave this claim a strong biological gloss with his theory of mutual aid. Interestingly, Kropotkin was also inspired in some of his writings by the voluntary efforts of the Red Cross and British Lifeboat Association, as well as his better-known admiration for medieval guilds and cities.[93] Such communes would be spontaneous, solidaristic and altruistic. They would be small-scale in terms of membership, functionally specific, and would produce for local needs.[94] Technology would be scaled down to meet these. Bookchin therefore, in his work, calls for a 'peoples' technology'.[95] Physical and mental labour would be integrated and production performed on a human scale in self-governing workshops. Most communist anarchists have been particularly keen to overcome the separation between hand and brain, mental and physical labour. Many looked to the reform of the family and marriage. Kropotkin was adamant that communist anarchy would lead to the true emancipation of women from both patriarchal and domestic drudgery. One of his suggestions was that labour-saving machinery in the home would help to achieve this.[96]

In the case of Proudhon we encounter a different vision, one which incorporates elements from individualism, communism and liberalism. Thus Proudhon has been described as a 'liberal in proletarian clothes'.[97] His opinions altered during his lifetime, but he is usually identified with a form of contractual federation peopled by social individualists. Society would be constituted primarily through contracts between individuals and groups which would replace the need for government and politics. Federated groups would also make agreements for national defence and the arbitration of disputes. Proudhon's view later shifted back to the support of a federal state, something that he had espoused in his early years. Most notably, his conception of a mutual credit bank would play a crucial role in any future federal society. This would issue labour notes and interest-free credit to enable individuals to set up in business. What Proudhon really objected to was not private property and private business as such but 'the earning of income from the labour of others through such means as rent, interest and wage labour'.[98]

Revolutionary syndicalism and anarcho-syndicalism were both anti-political and anti-statist movements that concentrated 'on the revolutionary potential of working-class economic organization, notably the trade union or industrial union'.[99] Syndicalism, in general, had no faith in representative democracy. It rejected all forms of state organization, whether capitalist or socialist. In Britain the ILP, official unionism and social democratic liberalism were treated with equal disdain.[100] The market economy was as objectionable as the centralized command economy and nationalized industries. The British syndicalists were deeply antagonistic to the new liberal welfare reforms in the period 1906–14. As one writer has commented, the syndicalists saw the first elements of the welfare state as simply 'designed to promote industrial efficiency and social discipline'.[101]

The principal economic actors for syndicalism and anarcho-syndicalism were the working-class producer groups, not the consumers. Both the state and capitalism had to be destroyed by the revolutionary 'direct action' of such producers. Violence was fully legitimated in such action. Georges Sorel, in his *Reflections on Violence*, made much of this particular theme. Unions were not only conceived of as the means to revolutionary direct action, but also as the nuclei for a future decentralized federal society. Workers in a locality would be members of a union. Unions would then link together in a central cartel or *Bourse*. This would propagandize, educate, and prepare workers to take control of their lives. Labour cartels would unite or federate in a region and eventually form a national federation. Such great industrial alliances would not only form the basis for revolt but also for a future society. Although they tended to despise abstract theory and bourgeois intellectualism, syndicalists none the less placed considerable emphasis on working-class self-education. This is something that can be seen in Pelloutier's *Bourse du Travail* in France, in the Plebs

League, the Industrial Syndicalist Education League and the Central Labour College in Britain.[102]

There is a problem in anarchist theory of reconciling authoritative organization with the liberty or autonomy of the individual. If political authority entails the right to rule, and those subject to it do not have the choice of whether or not to obey (otherwise it would not *be* an authority), then liberty appears to be negated. This is a particular dilemma for communist and collectivist anarchists confronted with the issue of the need and desire for some form of community and authority. The individualist does not face this problem so directly, but simply sidesteps it by denying its relevance.

One way of tackling this difficulty is to utilize the notion of democracy. Democracy mediates and carries the individual's autonomous decision into the public sphere. Authority therefore derives from the will of the people. There are, however, problems with this argument too. First, as one commentator has recently noted: 'The relationship between anarchism and democratic theory has always been ambiguous'.[103] Despite a more overt sympathy for the participatory model of democracy, all anarchist schools have been profoundly critical of democracy *in toto* for a number of reasons. Primarily majoritarianism appears dangerous even to communist anarchists. Majorities can make grossly immoral decisions. Potentially, they can crush individual liberty. Furthermore, democratic parties are both manipulative and intolerant, voters being at the mercy of unscrupulous party machinations. It is the liberty of the individual, or of the minority, that is at particular risk in democracy. For the American individualists, democracy can even undermine and destroy private property. As Proudhon remarked, in a different context, there is little to choose between the tyranny of an absolute monarch and the tyranny of popular sovereignty. Both can rule the individual in a despotic manner.[104]

Representative democracy came in for particular criticism. Electoral change and universal suffrage make no difference, according to Proudhon. They simply place a veil over state coercion. Universal suffrage, as Proudhon noted, meant universal despotism. Representation is always viewed as false by anarchists. Bakunin therefore criticized the 'pseudo-sovereignty of a sham popular will, supposedly expressed by pseudo-representatives of the people in sham popular assemblies'.[105] Ultimately, for many anarchists, representative democracy linked up with party politics and statism. Direct participatory democracy fared somewhat better than the representative model, especially as it was seen in the Paris Commune. Nevertheless, even this was viewed with suspicion.[106] The premise once again was that individual liberty was of primary importance and that it could easily be swamped by majorities, even in fully participating assemblies. For this reason democracy does not necessarily allow anarchists the means to bypass the problem of authority and liberty.

One final problem in anarchist theory concerns the method of achieving the new form of political organization. Virtually all anarchists wanted to bring this about through revolution, whether peaceful or not. The nature of the revolution was usually perceived in terms of social change. Political or economic revolution was not enough. There had to be a change in social attitudes and dispositions. Proudhon and Rothbard argued that anarchism could be achieved by reformist means, working through existing state structures. For Bakunin, this was anathema; the destruction of state structures was the essential preliminary for all change. Godwin, on the other hand, believed in the power of reasoned persuasion. This idea has by no means disappeared. In fact, persuading others through education and the printed word appears to be the most favoured route for anarchists today. The idea of setting an example or sponsoring alternative communities has also had perennial appeal. This is somewhat reminiscent of the clearly pacifist anarchist methods of Tolstoy and his admirer Gandhi.

On the other hand, as is well known from the various caricatures of nineteenth-century anarchists, the path of violence has also had immense appeal. The forms of direct violent action proposed have varied. At one extreme was the so-called 'Propaganda of the Deed' movement which engaged, usually on an individual basis, in random acts of bomb-throwing or assassination. Parallel to this was the advocacy of criminality and brigandage as anarchy. The most extreme exponent of the latter tendency was the short-lived companion of Bakunin, Sergei Nechaev. Nechaev (with or without Bakunin's help) constructed the notorious *Revolutionary Catechism* pamphlet, which advocated total criminal terrorism as the way forward. Others favoured more organized armed insurrection but this presented problems owing to the fact that anarchists are, almost by definition, not good organizers. Anarchists have also looked to various forms of strike activity. Although they have used the sympathy strike, the form favoured by most syndicalists and anarcho-syndicalists was the general strike. This entailed a total stoppage of work and, ultimately, the collapse of the political and economic system. Within the workplace anarchists and anarcho-syndicalists also advocated boycotts and sabotage as ways of undermining regimes.

In anarchist literature violence was often distinguished, in a vague manner, from force. Force was exercised illegitimately by states and police. Violence was legitimated in terms of its objectives. This left Kropotkin feeling distinctly uncomfortable with such a position. In one sense violence, certainly in the manner in which anarcho-syndicalists and Bakunin spoke of it, was conceived of as cathartic or therapeutic; it was a way of cleansing the Augean stables of bourgeois society. However, such a cleansing could be dangerous in terms of unleashing unnecessary destruction and loss of innocent life.

CONCLUSION

More than other ideologies, anarchy suffers from a profound divergence of views and tactics. Yet it still has a perennial appeal. The reasons for this are apparent. Not only does it contain a continual plea for the liberty of the individual against all forms of regimentation and coercion, something which has struck a deep note in European thought since the Reformation and the Enlightenment, but it also represents a continual questioning and challenge to group life, particularly the associated life of the state. This very logic has trapped anarchism in a number of insoluble dilemmas. On the one hand, anarchism is committed to the importance of individualism. Yet the strict logic of individualism carries it to the boundaries of absurdity. Stirner's psychological egoism is the most hard-headed reading of this logic. If the individual is the supreme value and the sole arbiter of value, then anything over and above the individual is of necessity suspect. Other anarchists, like Rothbard, Godwin or Tolstoy, never carry the underlying logic of individualism to its conclusion. They always seek some consensual terminus, whether it be reason, natural rights, markets or the Sermon on the Mount. These provide bulwarks against facing the full implications of radical individualism head on.

On the other hand, those communal anarchists who find such radical atomized individualism intolerable face a different problem. Potentially, communal values and objectives stand as a barrier to individual freedoms. Once a community is organized it seems that immediate limitations are placed by it upon individuals. In such circumstances liberty is almost inevitably curtailed. There are, of course, ways round this. Kropotkin suggested that human nature evolved naturally to embrace this communal condition; in other words, free will does not enter into the argument. Individual behaviour would be biologically determinate. Others suggested that true freedom was experienced within a community and its values. Kropotkin's biology now appears very shaky and the positive freedom argument places communal anarchists in close proximity to ardent statists who see the state embodying such freedom. The particular difficulty of the freedom of the individual within a community, for anarchists, can be seen in their attempts to deal with crime, punishment, laziness and social deviance. The answers to these issues verge on the naive. Some anarchists argued that crime and social deviance were overrated. They were the offspring of statism, capitalism and social hierarchies. Individuals could be persuaded and educated, or, if all else fails, socially ignored or excluded from a community. As much as some of these suggested solutions may appear reasonable, it is difficult to believe that they would really meet the problems of criminality and deviance. It is also hard to reconcile such anarchist practices with the value of liberty. They do not appear to be very different conditions to living under a formal rule of law; in fact, they might be far worse.

When anarchists do speak of their hoped-for communities, unless there is an anachronistic and anthropologically weak-minded appeal to past primitive village communities, the whole position appears as charming, but unrealistic and deeply nostalgic. Apart from some of the more rigid and strange absurdities of individualist anarchists, the communist, collectivist and mutualist anarchists express a millennial vision of what we would really like to be in our better moments, but which we know is relatively hopeless.

6
FASCISM

—

The word fascism is a product of this century.* One noted scholar of fascism has remarked that even in 1920 'the word "fascism" was known to very few people in Europe, and even Mussolini placed it between quotation marks as being a neologism.'[1] Its late emergence on the political scene is viewed by some political sociologists as profoundly significant for the somewhat heterogeneous character of the movement.[2]

The word fascism derives etymologically from the Latin *fasces*, bundles of rods bound together symbolizing strength in unity, which were traditionally carried before consuls in the Roman Republic, indicating their authority. It is not certain that the word was chosen for its association with ancient Rome, although this was later emphasized by the fascists in the 1920s.[3] It had initially sentimental, more socialist connotations in revolutionary Sicilian groups who referred to themselves as *fasci* in 1892. The term retained this socialist connotation up to 1914 when *fascio* groups called for intervention in the First World War and declared themselves against neutralism. The national defence groups organized after the Italian defeat at Caporetto in 1917 also called themselves *fasci*. The word thus had strong socialist origins and later came to imply extra-parliamentary and non-party nationalist activity. The young socialist Mussolini became involved in, and then led, the Milan *fascio* in 1915. After the war, in 1919 Mussolini reconstituted the Milan *fascio* under the title Fasci di Combattimento. Even Mussolini did not initially publicize the term fascism. It was only after the somewhat mythical March on

* In this chapter, unless indicated otherwise, I will use the word 'fascism' as a generic which includes 'national socialism', although this should not be taken to mean that I regard them as identical, or that Italian fascism was *the* model. In the course of the chapter, the differences between Italian fascism and German national socialism are examined.

Rome that fascism moved self-consciously, and with startling rapidity, into European political debates. This was especially the case after the consolidation of the fascist regime in Italy from 1922–3.

There are a number of problems in examining fascism. Of all the ideologies that we have dealt with, fascism, virtually alone, has given ideology a bad press. Despite its innocuous image to all but the communists in Europe in 1920, it now conjures up, justifiably, visions of horrifying pogrom and unprecedented European destruction. From the 1950s this negativity has contributed to its hackneyed use as a term of political abuse.

Another problem concerns the relationship between 'fascism' and 'national socialism'. Although there are marked differences between the movements, there are also enough affinities to treat them as part of the same generic compound. An additional key problem, which recurs throughout the assessment of fascism and national socialism, is the fact that the ideology is tied to particular nationalisms. This national particularity has the effect of limiting its universal applicability. The problem was very acute for those who conceived of a Fascist International in 1935. It is still a serious problem in the post-1945 era for those who see fascism as a legitimate descriptive term to use in contemporary political science or historical work. If fascism is so tied to the ends of particular nations, it is difficult to see how it can have universal appeal or application, except in so far as it asserts, formally, universally conflicting nationalisms.

There is an additional problem concerning the relations between fascism as an ideology, the political movements which espoused it, and the actual activity of fascists whilst in power. This problem appears in other ideologies, yet in fascism it is particularly perplexing. The ideology is at times self-consciously anti-ideological, disparaging the whole effort to engage in rational discourse. The movements which espoused it, and the governments who claimed to be fascist, do not therefore appear to be easily explicable in rational terms. As one commentator remarked on fascism: 'Some observers were reminded of the magic mirror in which everyone, whether militaristic, reactionary or extreme pacifist on the left, could see his heart's desire'.[4] Fascism often occupies a middle ground somewhere between rational political ideology on the one hand and opportunistic adventurism on the other. Stated purposes do not always tell us much, although they can sometimes be very revealing. There is some truth, though, to the point that fascism was initially more of a technique or method of acquiring power, and that the ideological doctrine was *ex post facto* elaboration. Yet even if it was *ex post facto* this still should not lead us to underrate or totally ignore it.

A number of difficulties must be faced in trying to characterize the ideology. Fascism is profoundly eclectic and occasionally bizarre. Many of its statements appear as simple-minded, vague rhetoric and propaganda. Yet should we always expect consistency and high levels of analysis from ideology? In other words, is there always such a clear, hard-and-fast distinction to be drawn between ideology and propaganda?[5] Ideology can appear in many guises, from the simple to the most complex. We should not disregard something *because* it is bizarre, simplistic, eclectic or propagandist in intent.

Another difficulty concerns the relation of fascism to other ideologies. This is a complex area which can only be touched upon. On the one hand there were clearly puzzling relations between socialism, syndicalism and fascism. The appellation 'national socialism' was not accidental. Early fascists in Italy also called themselves 'national syndicalists'. It should not be forgotten that many fascists, like Mussolini in Italy or Mosley in Britain, had early socialist affiliations. There were also strong affinities with forms of conservatism. Overall as Oswald Mosley's biographer has commented, 'To the historian fascism is Janus-faced. One face looks forward, in the spirit of the Enlightenment, to the rational control and direction of human life; the other face looks backwards to a much simpler, more primitive, life when men struggled to live'.[6] Ideologically, fascism was neither clearly socialist nor conservative in character. This ambiguity, especially in its early years, contributed to its initial reception by some intellectuals.

THE ORIGINS OF FASCIST AND NATIONAL SOCIALIST THOUGHT

There are two main issues dealt with in this section. The first is concerned with the origin and history of fascism and national socialism. The second considers the diversity of scholarly approaches to the ideology and the movement. The two issues are not unrelated, partly because many of the attempts to explain the nature of fascism incorporate diverse perspectives on its origin and history. To try to keep this discussion within manageable proportions, the origin and history will only be reviewed in outline. The key focus will be on the second main issue: the diversity of scholarly approaches.

There are roughly four points of origin to which fascism is traced. The first sees fascism as an instinctual state of mind found in all forms of social organization from the beginning of civilization. This was articulated, from a more positive standpoint within fascism itself, by those German commentators who linked national socialism with the 'folk consciousness' and history of the Nordic race, or the Italian fascists who related their vision to the history of the Roman Empire. In addition, some psychological explanations this century have merged fascism with a certain type of universal personality structure, a structure which is implicit potentially in all humans. The second point of origin, which appears particularly in

Italian fascism, sees it emerging from European cultural movements like the Renaissance or the Enlightenment. The Italian fascist, Alfredo Rocco, saw, for example, Machiavelli as the founding father of fascism. Rocco maintained that 'Fascism learns from him not only its doctrines but its actions as well'.[7] Rocco also discusses Vico and Mazzini in a similarly anachronistic vein.

The third, more viable point of origin, regards fascism and national socialism as tardy aspects of the complex negative reaction to the French Revolution in European thought. The critical and fatalistic response by many European thinkers and regimes to the growth of liberalism, egalitarianism, democracy, rationalism, industrialization and later socialism, over the course of the nineteenth century, forms a backdrop to fascism. As one commentator has noted: 'The growth of fascism ... cannot be understood, or fully explained, unless it is seen in the intellectual, moral, and cultural context which prevailed in Europe at the end of the nineteenth century'.[8] In this context, the intellectual movements of German romanticism, *völkisch* thought, social Darwinism, elite theory, syndicalism, corporatism, vitalism, and the like, are often discussed as components of such a response. Works like Mussolini's 'Doctrine of Fascism' or Hitler's *Mein Kampf* can, in this sense, be seen as the simplistic, shallow topdressing to a much older intellectual tradition. A large amount of scholarly interpretation congregates in this area.[9]

The final point of origin is the 1920s. As F. L. Carsten remarked: 'There was no "Fascism" anywhere in Europe before the end of the First World War'.[10] Ernst Nolte, in his *Three Faces of Fascism*, more or less accepted this view. One of its best-known expositors is Hugh Trevor-Roper who commented that:

> The public appearance of fascism as a dominant force in Europe is the phenomenon of a few years only. It can be precisely dated. It began in 1922–3 with the emergence of the Italian fascist party ... It came of age in the 1930s ... It ended in 1945 with the defeat of the two dictators.[11]

Trevor-Roper does not deny that there were precursors to fascism. Yet, in terms of the public history of fascism, they were not significant. Fascism was 'inseparable from the special experience of one generation'.[12] In this reading, fascism was a recent and short-lived ideology which had little or no relevance outside of the inter-war years. The experiences and legacies of the First World War, the effects of the Versailles Treaty, the great world depression, and the collapse of the Weimar Republic, were a unique concatenation of events.

Moving now to the second main issue of this section, concerned with the diversity of scholarly explanations of fascism: many of these explanations show little or no interest in political ideas. In fact, it would be appropriate to note here that by far the most popular accounts of fascism have been non-ideological. It is these non-ideological views which will now be examined. In some cases the concern for non-ideological explanation is quite self-consciously pursued, ideology being regarded as offering very little help in grasping the nature of fascism. The ideology is viewed as either too fragmented, eclectic, bizarre or confused to be of any use whatsoever. Some explanations assume this to be the case without further discussion. Although it is necessary to cover these differing non-ideological accounts, in order to give a comprehensive coverage of fascism, the bulk of the discussion in this chapter is none the less given over to the ideology itself. Although I am persuaded that there are economic, political and even pathological dimensions to fascism, I still believe that it is necessary to analyse its ideas and values. They should not be simply dismissed as absurd, partly because they often overlap and have close affinities with other ideologies. The non-ideological explanations can be dealt with under five main categories: Marxist, psychological, religious and moral, historical and sociological and, finally, political.

By far the most popular explanation of the fascist era of the 1930s was Marxist. There was no single, consistent account within Marxism, however. Fascism was basically explicable through the underlying economic laws or logic of capitalism. In general terms it was part of the crisis of monopoly capitalism.[13] As Herbert Marcuse argued, 'The roots of fascism are traceable to the antagonisms between growing industrial monopolization and the democratic system'.[14] The argument, in sum, was that in order to allow monopoly capitalism to survive, the democratic and working-class opposition had to be neutralized. Accordingly, existing democratic institutions could no longer serve as a vessel for capitalism; in fact, increasing democratization was threatening capitalism. Interestingly, this latter view is still shared by classical liberals like Hayek. Thus, for production to continue and profits to be maintained, totalitarian terror had to be instituted. Fascism was a tool of monopoly capitalism at a particular stage of its development. It was used to repress the working class in the interests of big business, banks and financial concerns. Fascism was therefore causally related to the development of capitalist economies.

Some argued that fascism was the particular agent of finance capitalism alone and not necessarily of industrial or agrarian capital. This early view on fascism was encapsulated in the 1933 Comintern definition of fascism as 'the openly terroristic dictatorship of the most reactionary, most chauvinistic and most imperialist elements of finance capital'.[15] Others saw fascists as the anti-communist and anti-trade union shock troops for industrial manufacturing capital. Some Marxists also adapted Marx's argument from the *Eighteenth Brumaire* and saw fascism as a form of Bonapartism or Caesarism, whereby an extra-parliamentary group exploited the difference of interests between finance and industrial capital and ran the state autonomously. Fascists, in this sense, were not the pawns of any class.

Antonio Gramsci, despite his association with the Caesarist view, was the first Marxist writer to note that the ideology of fascism was a material force. It appeared to meet many of the ideals and aspirations of the masses. Thus the ideological hegemony of fascism could not simply be ignored. For Gramsci it had to be combated as a body of ideas as well as a political and economic practice. It was too simple to dismiss fascism as absurd. It was not by accident that Gramsci's *Prison Notebooks* should have scrutinized in such detail the mechanism for the production and maintenance of hegemony. Gramsci's friend and a founding member of the PCI, Palmiro Togliatti, also noted the power of fascism to successfully coalesce and mobilize the masses. In fact, it was acknowledged that fascism was far better at such mobilization in times of crisis than either liberalism or socialism. Togliatti was probably one of the first to realize the significance of Gramsci's notion of hegemony. However, the mainstream of Marxism in the 1930s could not accommodate the idea of an extreme right-wing political movement enjoying a significant influence on public consciousness.

There are numerous problems with the Marxist position. Apart from the disagreements on interpretation within Marxism, there is the unanswered question as to why there was such a body of anti-capitalist argument within fascism. In addition, many of the practices pursued under fascism, as in the racial extermination programmes under national socialism, cannot be easily accounted for using capitalist criteria. Furthermore, how could fascism appear in non-capitalist (or at least very low-level capitalist) societies like Italy or Hungary, and dominate in some highly industrialized societies like Germany but not in others like Britain? If there was a transparent deterministic relation between capitalism and fascism, how did it fit into the above scenario? Also it is not clear that manufacturing, industrial and financial interests consistently supported fascism politically or financially.[16] Moreover, as certain Marxist writers have noted, there appears to be no explicit one-to-one relation between fascism and particular social classes.[17] There is often a blind spot for certain Marxists on the instrumental relation of classes and political power.

A second non-ideological explanation of fascism concentrates on the psychology of fascists. The basic thesis of the psychological explanation, with many subtle variations, is that fascism needs to be explained in terms of certain forms of personality types and/or disorders. The ideology or historical determinants of fascism are of secondary significance to the basic personality traits. Like the Marxist argument there are many possible variations. Some approach fascism purely from within the structures of Freudian, Jungian or other schools of psychoanalysis. The particular use of this approach in historical work has given rise to the epithet 'psychohistory'. Others focus on the psychological character of certain classes, or generational factors, particularly the lower middle class and socially deprived adolescents after the First World War. Finally, some of the Frankfurt school of Marxists, like Erich Fromm, Theodor Adorno and Wilhelm Reich, tried to bridge the economic and psychological explanation, linking Marx with Freud.

Psychohistory tends to look at the childhood of fascists to reveal the deep structure of their later beliefs. Certain forms of isolation, displacement, sublimation and projection, often relating back to childhood, are seen to be characteristics of fascist personalities. The repression of early sexuality in authoritarian families (genital repression), denial of creativity, the Oedipus complex, and fear of castration in males, can lead to a sense of frustration, guilt and powerlessness. This in turn can give rise to aggression and sado-masochism, which can express itself politically in the bizarre male fantasies of fascism. The psychologist Erik Erikson remarked of Hitler's childhood that 'Now and again, history does seem to permit a man the joint fulfilment of national fantasies and of his own provincial and personal daydreams'.[18] Richard Koenigsberg, in *Hitler's Ideology: A Study in Psychoanalytic Sociology*, also notes that Hitler's ideology offered 'a means whereby his fantasies might be expressed and discharged at the level of social reality'.[19]

Wilhelm Reich, in *The Mass Psychology of Fascism* (1975), also saw fascism growing out of the suppression of infantile and adolescent sexuality. In this sense, all humans were potentially fascists. Fascism was the political expression of the average human character when exposed to certain conditions. It had nothing to do with race, nations or parties. Whereas Marx had called for a social and economic revolution for liberation, Reich called for a sexual revolution. At this point his thoughts drifted into the virtues of sexual freedom to avoid the fascist mentality. Another German compatriot of Reich was Adorno, who postulated the idea of the authoritarian personality.[20] The lower middle class, suffering alienation, self-hatred and loss of security after the First World War, developed sadistic and masochistic traits of character, which constituted the authoritarian personality. Noël O'Sullivan sums up this authoritarian personality as follows:

> a wretched creature, overwhelmed inwardly by sexual deprivation and afflicted outwardly by the ruthless economic order of capitalism, constantly liable to panic under the burden of a freedom for which he really has no use ... In a desperate endeavour to escape from his misery, he welcomes political extremism.[21]

The weaknesses of the psychological approach stem from the dearth of evidence on the childhoods of major fascists like Hitler. Too much reliance is placed on sketchy personal testimonies. There are also doubts concerning the 'scientific' status of the psychoanalytic approach. Furthermore, it is difficult to see how such studies can be used for explaining mass electoral support or mass membership of fascist groups. Finally, if the psychological perspective is true then we might as well all train to be psychologists, since it would explain the whole of history and politics, which is not a particularly convincing hypothesis.

The third non-ideological explanation was again characteristic of the late 1930s, although it can even now be found in some discussions. The basic idea was that fascism was an aspect or symptom of a moral and religious crisis or malaise in Western civilization.[22] This perspective was more ready to consider the ideological content of fascism, although there was still a tendency to see the practice of fascism as the result of a deeper religious or moral cause. In the late 1930s and early 1940s, philosophers like Benedetto Croce and R. G. Collingwood saw fascism as a negative challenge and a denial of human liberty. For Croce, fascism was a corruption of the Italian tradition of liberty. He argued that 'authoritarian governments endure only among decadent peoples'.[23] In Britain, Collingwood also viewed fascism as a new form of barbarism and a sign of a loss of faith in liberty and liberalism. Liberty for Collingwood had been 'distilled from the body of Christian practice'. The barbarism and paganism of fascism and national socialism challenged the whole Christian tradition.[24]

Other writers have expressed similar views. One of the first critical German commentators saw national socialism specifically as a form of profound cultural and moral nihilism.[25] Fascism has also been seen as an aspect of the 'death of God' movement in European thought, dating from the work of Friedrich Nietzsche, and the overall loss of religious belief and transcendent values. Catholic writers such as Jacques Maritain, following this line, saw it as a form of pagan 'demonic pantheism'.[26] More recent scholars, like Robert Pois, have argued a similar point. Pois comments that 'Nazism was most definitely a rebellion against the Judaeo-Christian tradition' and that it 'was singular in its efforts to consciously supplant Judaeo-Christian forms'.[27] Other writers, such as G. L. Mosse, Fritz Stern and P. J. Pulzer, have seen fascism, and more particularly national socialism, as a deeply rooted cultural malaise.[28]

Some commentators dismiss this view, finding little hard evidence for it, just a series of generalized assertions about moral decline or cultural despair.[29] Such a judgement seems unnecessarily severe. There is now a great deal more scholarship backing some of these explanations than in fact can be found in many of the Marxist or psychological accounts.

The fourth, now rather dated, explanation concentrated on the historical and sociological context of fascism. The basic claim was that fascism was the result of rapid development and modernization, or sometimes the particular manner of industrialization, in certain societies. The aim of such studies was to gain more empirically respectable economic and statistical indices for the occurrence of fascism. A. F. Organski, and later Barrington Moore, were initially associated with this line of thought.[30] All traditional societies, over the nineteenth and twentieth centuries, were subject to transformation, comprising rapid industrialization, urbanization, secularization and rationalization. Various paths were taken to modernization, and fascism was one possible route. However, compared to Germany, industrialization and modernization came late to Italy. This raises an immediate problem. If Germany was highly industrialized by the 1920s, but Italy was not, then in terms of the socio-economic modernizing criteria, as one writer puts it, 'Italian fascism and Nazism do not belong in the same category'.[31] If fascism is linked closely with rapid modernization and industrialization, then it does not appear to explain what happened in Italy and Germany. Thus it remains a deeply unsatisfactory account.[32]

A final broad band of explanations is 'political' in character. The term 'political' is used rather loosely here.[33] To some extent this explanation is set against the background of a crisis of parliamentary democracy. It was one of the key fascist arguments that parliamentary democracy had failed. The most traditional political explanation of fascism sees it as old-fashioned tyranny and personal aggrandizement by figures like Hitler. The task is therefore to unpack the biographical features, actions and thoughts of tyrants. Alan Bullock's unsurpassed work, *Hitler: A Study in Tyranny*, and Dennis Mack Smith's *Mussolini*, broadly follow this line. It is also to some extent present in the writings of Hugh Trevor-Roper and Ernst Nolte. Discussing contrasting attitudes among the national socialists, Bullock remarks that 'To Strasser National Socialism was a real political movement, not, as it was to Hitler, the instrument of his ambition. He took its programme seriously, as Hitler never had.'[34] Some would argue that over-concentration on tyrannical personalities gives the wrong impression of fascist movements. Not only does it appear to absolve many others from responsibility, making the fascist parties totally monolithic and focused on their leaders; it also ignores the deep inner confusion, bitter infighting and power struggles which took place in all fascist groups.[35]

Another popular line of political explanation was to incorporate fascism, with communism and Stalinism, under the general rubric of 'totalitarianism', or alternatively under the rubric of mass politics. These views, particularly the former, were developed in the Cold War period of the 1950s. Initially, totalitarianism was explored in a more philosophical manner in works like Hannah Arendt's *The Origins of Totalitarianism* and Karl Popper's *The Open Society*. However, it soon became part of the conventional language of academic political science, as expressed in the writings of J. L. Talmon, C. J. Friedrich and Z. K. Brzezinski amongst many others.[36] Fascism, as totalitarianism, was characterized by a monolithic single party, no separation between state and society, complete control of the state structure and the economy, total mobilization of the masses, and domination of mass communication. The masses in this context become rootless, isolated and atomized.[37]

The weakness of the totalitarian approach is that it plays down the deep chaos, general incompetence and internal feuding which in fact characterized fascism. In other words, it overrates the totalitarian capacities of, particularly, Germany and Italy. It is doubtful whether any of the features associated with totalitarianism were actually instantiated completely in either country. The approach also underplays the role of authoritarian conservatism within fascism. Further, it ignores the differences between communism and fascism, by lumping them under the same category. In addition, within national socialism, it is far from clear that either Hitler or many of the key protagonists actually wanted totalitarian statism.[38]

Finally, despite the fact that many scholars associate fascism with the lower middle class, others argue that fascism was a latecomer to the political scene, cross-cutting existing structural, political and social allegiances.[39] It was thus a 'conjunctural phenomenon' combining heterogeneous social class and generational support. As Juan B. Linz suggests, this accounts 'for the often quite different social composition of the initial nucleus'.[40] For Linz, the vagaries of war and foreign aid helped fascism fortuitously to play a political role, but as a pragmatic and ideological mix. Fascist parties, in fact, prefigure the post-1945 development of ideologically mixed political parties in Western Europe. Linz adds that, 'The more fluid social structure, the exhaustion of ideological passion, the needs of national reconstruction in post-fascist Europe made programmatically eclectic heterogeneous parties possible and successful'.[41] Linz insists, however, that any full study of fascism has to take into account the unique sociological, political and historical context of each society. Thus he notes that the only kind of viable empirical generalization is that 'Fascism was that novel response to the crisis ... of the pre-war social structure and party system'.[42] Linz's view is in fact characteristic of much political sociology in recent decades.

THE NATURE OF FASCISM

In examining the nature of fascism there is an immediate problem of which writers to include and which to exclude. Some scholars include French writers like Maurice Barrès and Charles Maurras, with particular reference to French organizations like Action Française.[43] Others see these as pre-fascist, reactionary, or authoritarian Right groups as distinct from fascism.[44] Spain before 1933 and the Falange, despite having a rightist anti-parliamentary Movimento Nacional, still did not have an overt fascist grouping.[45] In Germany, whereas the more traditional Right had little of a worked-out programme, the national socialist group quite clearly did.[46]

Related to this whole debate is the question as to how broadly fascism can be extended. Were Jean Degrelles Rexists in Belgium, the Rumanian Legion of the Archangel Michael, Portugal under Salazar, Argentina under Peron or the later Junta, Hungary under General Gombüs, Japan during the Second World War, or France under de Gaulle − to name but a few of the suggestions − all fascist?[47] Despite the concentration on Italy and Germany in this chapter, it should not be assumed that all the above movements were automatically non-fascist or pre-fascist. This is a vast and unresolved scholarly debate which can only be mentioned in passing. Germany and Italy have been dealt with on grounds of space and as being the most obvious cases.

Most commentators on fascism agree that it incorporated many groups and tendencies. On the most general level, there are ideological differences between German national socialism and other European fascisms in Italy, France, Spain and Britain. For some, these differences are so great that they balk at including national socialism in the same genus as Italian or Spanish fascism.[48] The most profound difference is the centrality of the issue of race. There is also an absence of a strong *Volk* tradition in other variants, whereas it is central to the German case. This Germanic *Volk* factor alone alienated French fascists like Brasillach and Drieu de Rochelle, Spanish fascists like Primo de Rivera, and even Italians like Mussolini. Mussolini used to refer to Germany in the 1930s as a 'racialist lunatic asylum'.[49] Certainly in many of the ideological tracts from Italy, Spain, France and Britain over the 1920s and 1930s, there is no mention either of the race question or of the virtual cosmic significance of anti-Semitism which obsessed so many national socialists. Italian and other such fascist groups only gradually assumed a more anti-Semitic stance in the late 1930s. In spite of this, they never reached the intense and vitriolic levels that prevailed in Germany. The intensity of controlled violence and terror is another distinguishing mark of Germany as distinct, certainly, from Italy.[50] In addition, little attention is given outside Germany to the *Lebensraum* issue. This question was of particular concern to Hitler and lay behind his obsessive foreign policy (quite clearly articulated in the closing chapters of *Mein Kampf*) for the eastward expansion of Germany into Russia and the decimation of the Slavic peoples. In Italy, expansion was usually conceived of in terms of traditional European aggressive imperialism. In Germany it was again tied obsessively to the issue of race.

Finally, whereas fascism in Italy was premised, with some qualification, on a more traditional Western rationalism, German national socialism was self-consciously committed to an irrationalist position, where every human artefact, the arts, sciences, societies and history, were judged from one salient perspective − race. Alternatively, in Italy there was often a definite impetus, in some though not all sectors of the fascist movement, towards rational modernization, where the state would play a dominant creative role. In Germany, the race question overshadowed all such endeavour, at least in the ideological output. The German state in fact was irrevocably subservient to the *Volk* and to racial issues.

Within the various national groupings of fascism, including the German, there were again quite marked subdivisions. There are a number of ways of conceptualizing these subdivisions. Nolte speaks of early, normal and radical fascism (as well as his category of pre-fascism). Alexander de Grand, in his study of Italian fascism, speaks of conservative, national, technocratic, *Squadrismo* ruralist and national syndicalist fascism.[51] A somewhat simpler basic ideological subdivision occurred between more socialist- and more capitalist-inclined wings. Some were prepared, within a disciplined societal order, to give capitalism a full head, others wanted to seriously curtail it. In Italy, Mussolini was initially, in the early 1920s, and at the end of his life in the Republic of Salò, associated with the socialist stance. During the late 1920s he tried to sit astride both tendencies.[52] The national syndicalist and corporatist catholic input into fascism ensured the continuance of the socialist line of thought. One Italian writer, Angelo Olivetti, placed Left fascism firmly in the tradition of Proudhonian socialism![53]

A similar division of opinion occurred among the national socialists in Germany. Party activists like Gottfried Feder and Gregor Strasser were much more inclined towards socialist methods. Feder, for example, called for wide-scale nationalization; a centralized state-controlled banking system; state management of public utilities, transport, credit; and control of prices and wages with state confiscation of excessive profits. The famous Twenty-Five Points of the NSDAP programme of 1920–3, the Agricultural Programme 1930 and the Full Employment Programme of 1932 incorporated a great deal of anti-capitalist material.[55] Alfred Rosenberg, Hitler and Goebbels did not appear to be as enthused by this line. This does not mean that they wished to pursue a more overtly capitalist policy. In the case of Rosenberg, the racial line was far more significant.

In the context of the common fascist denigration of intellectualism, it is often difficult to pick out important fascist themes, programmes and ideologists. Italian fascism had some clever apologists, like Giovanni Gentile, who constructed (so it subsequently appears) much of the 'Doctrine of Fascism' article for Mussolini, as well as writing a sophisticated political treatise, *The Genesis and Structure of Society*. Critics are none the less divided on how representative Gentile is of fascism.[55] The national socialists did not have anyone so distinguished as Gentile. Hitler's *Mein Kampf*, which Mussolini described as 'a boring tome that I have never been able to read', does not really serve as a foundational text although there are undoubtedly influential ideas present within it.[56] Rosenberg contributed his own rather disjointed rambling on the Nordic race. There were also writings on national socialist themes by Strasser, Feder, and Goebbels. More sceptical academic figures on the sidelines, like Carl Schmitt or Martin Heidegger, added some element of respectability to the literature.[57]

Given the above points it is difficult to find common ground for a discussion of fascism(s). One starting-point is the negative ideological 'anti's' of fascism. As Linz suggests, 'The various "anti's" of fascism served to define its identity'.[58] The majority of fascists were anti-liberal, anti-marxist, anti-parliamentary, anti-individualist and anti-bourgeois. They felt that the bourgeois age was spiritually empty, hypocritical and materialistic, estranged from the actual world, and lacking any sense of community. These were undoubtedly common themes, but they do not tell us a great deal. The discussion will now turn to a consideration of fascist views on human nature, ideas on nationalism, race, the state, leadership and the economy.

HUMAN NATURE

The intellectual background to the fascist understanding of human nature is an odd mixture. The ideas promulgated were a peculiar concoction of social Darwinism, nineteenth-century racial theory, intuitivist and vitalist philosophies, syndicalism, elite theory, romanticism, crowd psychology and the psychology of the unconscious. Out of this unholy brew a number of recurring, more formal, themes on the character of human beings can be discerned.

First, human nature was characterized by the primacy of will and activism. Humans were first and foremost creatures of volition and action. Thought was something which appeared almost *ex post facto*. Abstract thought distorted or diverted us from action. In exercising our will and acting in the world we express our true natures. It was argued that we should act on the basis of instinct and intuition rather than on the basis of reasoned argument. The philosophical roots to this line of thinking lie in a number of sources, but more particularly in Henri Bergson's and Friedrich Nietzsche's distinct vitalism, William James's pragmatism and German *Lebensphilosophie*.

It is important to grasp the context of such activism and vitalism and the manner in which it was manipulated and distorted by fascists. A large percentage of recruits to early fascist groups had fought in the First World War (this included Hitler, Mussolini and Mosley). In the case of Italy, France and Germany, many of the Squadristi, Camelot du Roi, Freikorps, Brownshirts and SS were initially ex-servicemen. The post-1918 generation was brutalized and militarized, both acclimatized and accustomed to death and extreme levels of violence. In peacetime many still thrived on an atmosphere of intimidation, which they fomented. In this sense, the violence and activism of fascists appeared as self-justifying, especially since the same tactic was also adopted by their communist opponents. Pre-war liberal tolerance was seen as a cause both of the war and of post-war social distress. It was also utterly inappropriate to the new world. Beating up communists, Jews, trade unionists, or political opponents was the fascist stock-in-trade. Hitler's murder of Ernst Röhm and the Brownshirts, *Kristallnacht*, Mussolini's murder of his political opponent Matteotti, the beating-up of the communist deputy Misiano in parliament, and the regular street battles, normalized violence. Fascist instinctivism and activism were contrasted with ineffectual flabby parliamentary liberal rationalism. The mythology and symbolism of fascist movements were expressed in terms of active battles, marches and *Putsche*.

Such politically orchestrated violence was given the intellectual gloss of social poetry. Violence had almost an aesthetic appeal.[59] Writers like Georges Sorel, in *Reflections on Violence*, were influential here in linking philosophical vitalism with political violence. In fact, given its instinctual and emotive base, vitalism could be allied, by almost imperceptible shifts of logic, to all artistic creative experience, via the all-inclusiveness of concepts like intuition and instinct. In the same way that it is difficult to unpack the emotional experience of artistic creation into abstract theory, so equally with heroic, crusading political violence. Violence becomes alchemically transmuted into an aesthetic mystery.

In one sense this link between art and violence was consciously pursued in some of the writings of Italian futurists as a kind of *fin de siècle* aestheticism. Many talented artists were drawn to fascism, particularly in the initial stages before the murder of Matteotti. Mussolini's mistress, Margherita Sarfatti, was especially enthusiatic about patronizing the arts, although she personally favoured the link between fascism and a form of neo-classicism, rather than futurism. Futurism itself came out of the same cultural matrix as fascism, emphasizing direct action, life, instinct and creativity over reason and system. The author of *The Futurist Manifesto*, Filippo Marinetti, saw futurism as the art of fascism, but it is not so certain that Mussolini shared this view. Marinetti declared, in the opening sections of the *Manifesto*, some of the main elements of his credo:

1 We want to sing the love of danger, the habit of energy and rashness.
2 The essential elements of our poetry will be courage, audacity and revolt.
3 Literature has up to now magnified pensive immobility ... We want to exalt movements of aggression, feverish sleeplessness, the double march, the perilous leap, the slap and the blow with the fist.
4 We declare the splendour of the world has been enriched by a new beauty, the beauty of speed. A racing automobile with its bonnet adorned with great tubes like serpents with explosive breath ... a roaring motor car which seems to run on machine-gun fire.[60]

Younger fascists were thus encouraged to think of violence in romantic, crusading, almost chivalrous terms. When Sorel linked violence with Bergson's *élan vital* (a spontaneous evolving creative 'life force' which lifted the whole human species to higher levels of development), and others linked it with the achievement of the historic mission of racial purity, violence took on cosmic significance. Such violence was not the same as the force exercised by liberal states. Violence was instinctual, linking the individual with unconscious spiritual depths. It encouraged the epic state of mind of the hero, or *Übermensch*. It was a cathartic, character-changing experience. As the Italian fascist Giovanni Papini noted: 'While the democratic mob raise outcry against war ... we look on it as the greatest possible tonic to restore flagging energy, as a swift and heroic means to attain power'.[61] We might recognize here a mundane but, in this case, glossy platitude, namely, that human nature can be transformed in situations of dire hardship and danger. This is often stated by those who have never experienced dire hardship.

Within such a scenario, fascist writers frequently referred to the ideology as not so much a programme but a state of mind or a way of being. Primo de Rivera, the leading light of the Spanish Falange, commented: 'Our movement will not be understood if it is thought to be merely a way of thinking; it is not a way of thinking, it is a way of being.' Papini also noted: 'We are not putting forward programmes but a passionate attitude of mind to make an end to words and turn programmes into action.'[62] It was in a similar vein that Nazis often proclaimed that one should think 'with the blood'.

It is not surprising in this context that fascism should be seen as an anti-intellectual doctrine. The philosophical premise incorporates an implicit assumption that it is the unconscious depths – will, creative emotion, instinct, intuition, *élan*, blood and so on – which really characterize human nature. This is contrasted to the superficial 'intellectual' surface. This attitude constituted part of the very attraction of fascism for many artists, writers and intellectuals, particularly the two former groups. Gentile's response (as a Hegelian and thus an anti-intuitivist) to the question of whether human beings were motivated by rationality or irrational/volitional drives, was to argue that we should not conclude that fascism was 'a blind praxis or purely instinctive method'. Fascism, for Gentile, was the heart of reality, 'living thought', in other words, concrete as opposed to abstract thought.[63] Fascism is only anti-intellectual if, as Gentile notes, one divorces 'knowledge from life, ... brain from heart, ... theory from practice'.[64] Fascism is thus seen to be immanent in reality itself.

Another aspect of this vitalism was that the masses were often viewed as instinctual and herd-like. Their instincts could be manipulated by the superior few. Crude forms of social Darwinism, combined with the doctrine of the *Herrenvolk*, suggested that the less fit or corrupt specimens of humanity could be removed in the same way that we would engage in the selective breeding of any domestic animal. Humans could thus be regarded *en masse* with benevolent contempt. Mussolini indeed appears to have had an abysmal view of human beings. He generally assumed that everyone was utterly selfish and untrustworthy. This parallels Bullock's summary of Hitler, where 'Distrust was matched by contempt. Men [for Hitler] were moved by fear, greed, lust for power, envy, often by mean and petty motives. Politics . . . is the art of knowing how to use these weaknesses for one's own ends'.[65] Mussolini's major criticism of Machiavelli's credentials for being a founding fascist was that he did not have enough contempt for the masses. Overall Mussolini regarded the masses as easy to deceive and dominate. Essentially they were like children who had to be scolded and rewarded in turn. As Mack Smith comments, Mussolini 'was glad to find that the herd − this was the word he liked to use − would gratefully accept inequality and discipline'.[66]

Most fascists considered that humans were social or communal creatures by nature. No fascists denied this thesis, although they had different understandings of it. One common critical target, which appears in the work of nearly every fascist writer at some point, is classical liberal individualism. Thus Alfredo Rocco argued that, contrary to liberal individualism, 'A human being outside the pole of society is an inconceivable thing − a non-man. Humankind in its entirety lives in social groups'. For Rocco, fascism 'replaces therefore the old atomistic and mechanical state theory which was at the basis of the liberal and democratic doctrines'.[67] There was, as indicated, a marked difference of understanding of this social nature, particularly between the Italian and German writers. In the writings of Gentile, Rocco and Mussolini, the 'social' dimension was understood more conventionally through the concept of the nation-state. Gentile, in his article 'The Philosophic Basis of Fascism', argued that 'Since the State is a principle, the individual becomes a consequence'.[68] In his last systematic treatise he expressed it thus: 'At the root of the "I" there is the "we". The community to which an individual belongs is the basis of his spiritual existence'.[69] The gist of Gentile's point was that for European peoples − from the satisfaction of the most basic needs to the realization of freedom and morality − the development of the individual is integral to the existence of the state. In fact, the state and the individual are of the same substance. As Gentile noted: 'The State is the universal aspect of the individual . . . it is not a presupposition of his existence . . . but the concrete actuality of his will'.[70]

The national socialist interpretation of the term 'social' was distinct from that of the Italian fascists. National socialists tended to focus their attention on the racial and *völkisch* dimension rather than on the state. An individual was constituted through the community. This community was constituted in terms of a racial or folk soul (*Volkseele*). A romanticized conception of nature lay behind this claim. Nature was not understood as a lifeless, orderly mechanism which could be coldly observed; conversely, it was understood as a 'life force' which animated and gave purpose and meaning to both humans and their *Volk*.[71] The instinctive, emotive life of human beings linked them not only with their *Volk* but also with the inner 'life force' of nature. Human beings could be glorified, therefore, according to their oneness with nature, not through their dominance of it. Unlike the Italian fascists, national socialists celebrated, in a bogus, mystical sense, nature, pastoral landscape and rural peasant life. The soul of a people was supposedly present in their landscape. It should not be forgotten that the national socialists were the first in Europe to set up nature reserves and pursue deciduous woodland reforestation schemes, for nationalistic ecological reasons.[72]

A further point here was that unconditional inequality was biologically determined and irremovable. All Nazis accepted an inequality of races and folk souls. The Aryan, at one with the landscape and people, was superior in all respects to Jews, Slavs or Negroes. Hitler described Aryans as the 'genius race'. The unconditional inequality of peoples did not alter inequalities within the Aryans themselves. There were some, for example, the genius or hero-figure, who were born superior. Great things could only be accomplished by peoples through the efforts of great individuals. As Hitler put it: 'The progress and culture of humanity are not a product of the majority, but rest exclusively on the genius and energy of the personality'.[73]

A related point about genius or leader figures was made in Italian fascism. In this latter case it was not premised on hazy accounts of racial or biological genius, but on an interpretation of the sociological writings on elitism of Vilfredo Pareto, Gaetano Mosca and Robert Michels. Elite writers not only contributed to the theories of leadership, but also helped to generate suspicions concerning parliamentary democracy, suspicions which were rife among fascists. It should be noted that only Michels became an open supporter of fascism. Admittedly, this more intellectual side of Italian fascism was not always evident. The element of self-deluding pomposity and neurosis was also a strong feature of Mussolini's (and Hitler's) visions of their own role.[74]

All fascists suggested that because of the corruption of human nature brought about in liberal democratic societies some change had to be contemplated. In the case of national socialism this campaign had to produce, as Ernst Krieck put it, a '*Volk*-bound German man'.[75] For Mussolini, the fascist Italian was to be created on a par with the Renaissance Italian. The attempt to bring about the fascist man had its absurdly amusing side, as in the campaign against pasta as an anti-fascist food, spaghetti not being the right 'food for fighters'.[76] Mussolini anticipated that the new Italian man would be more heroic, optimistic, less critical and individualistic, more serious, hard-working, courageous, less talkative, abjuring comfort and spending less money on pleasurable food or wine, sleeping less and being physically fit.[77]

The major difference between the German and Italian visions of a reform of human nature was that for Mussolini the new man was already present, but had to be disencumbered. For some Nazis, like Rosenberg, the blond Aryan also existed (Tacitus had, after all, noted him lurking in Teutonic forests) but had to be protected against racial admixture. For Himmler and the *Waffen*-SS, the new man had to be eugenically and selectively bred for the future and other 'race units' had to be eliminated.

NATION, RACE AND VOLK

Fascist thinking on human nature is further elucidated if we consider the issues of nationalism, race and *Volk* in a little more depth. In fascist terms, human beings, as should be obvious by now, are first and foremost creatures of a nation, race or *Volk*. There is therefore no human *per se*, only a German, Frenchman, Italian and so on. This idea runs directly counter to Enlightenment and later liberal and socialist internationalism and cosmopolitanism.

Fascist nationalism was distinct from nineteenth-century liberal nationalism. When Gottfried Herder examined the linguistic character of nations he did not suggest the notion of either superiority, conquest or mutual national hatred. In many ways the more insular, xenophobic and aggressive use of nationalism was already integral to more authoritarian conservative groups at the close of the nineteenth century; fascists simply adopted it.

The common features of fascist nationalism were, first, the older conservative contrast to liberal or socialist internationalism. As Papini noted, socialism is 'an international, that is to say anti-national party', and 'in order to love something deeply you need to hate something else', thus the true nationalist cannot possibly be internationalist.[78] Second, fascist nationalism was orientated to a communitarian ideal. True identity was found in the community of the nation and the nation was prior to the individual. As the Italian fascist Charter of Labour stated: 'The Italian nation is an organic whole having life, purposes and means of action superior in power and duration to those of individuals ... of which it is composed'.[79] Third, nationalism was used as a counterbalance to class struggle. The nation transcended such division. As Primo de Rivera put it: 'The class struggle disregards the unity of the fatherland because it destroys the integrity of the concept of *national production*'.[80] In addition, nationalism was opposed to the liberal bourgeois conception of life. Nationalism prepared the nation for heroism, self-sacrifice, conflict and, ultimately, war. The bourgeoisie undermined such ambitions and wasted time on materialistic longings and parliamentary politics. Before the First World War, Enrico Corradini summarized this contempt as follows:

Every sign of decrepitude, sentimentalism, doctrinairism, outmoded respect
for transient human life, outmoded pity for the weak and humble, utility
and mediocrity seen as wisdom, neglect of the higher potentialities of mankind, the ridiculing of heroism, every foul sign of loathsome decrepitude of
degenerate people can be found in the contemplative life of our ruling and
governing class, the Italian bourgeoisie.[81]

Finally, nationalism was used as a device to bestow legitimacy on certain
senses of democracy and socialism. These were often referred to in fascist
writings as the 'nobler democracy' and 'nobler socialism'.[82] Socialism and
democracy, when devoted to the primacy of the nation, were seen as
superior to, on the one hand, bourgeois representative democracy, and
on the other, to internationalist socialism. The worst of all worlds was
the mutual contamination of socialism and democracy. In this case the
best aspects of socialism and democracy – their collective devotion to
nation – were lost in the mists of internationalism and the false equality
between peoples.

The major difference between the German and Italian variants of
nationalism again rests on the race issue. With Italian fascism, nationalism was a more traditional form of xenophobic imperialism and patriotism.
In national socialism, the German nation expressed the *Volk* spirit and
was underpinned by a biological doctrine of racial purity. To be German
was to be of a particular racial stock. More significantly, in Italian fascism,
as Mussolini put it, 'It is not the nation that generates the State ... Rather
the nation is created by the State'.[83] Yet conversely, in Nazism, as Hitler
put it, 'The *state* in itself does not create a specific cultural level; it can
only preserve the race which conditions this level'. He continued, 'We,
as Aryans, can conceive of the state only as the living organism of this
nationality'.[84] Clearly, there was a complete reversal of ideological priorities
between Nazism and Italian fascism. Finally, there was a clear difference
of emphasis in terms of the significance accorded to the nation. Whereas
in German national socialism it was shrouded in a quasi-religious aura,
this was not present in Italian fascism.

One explanation for these differences is the idiosyncratic intellectual
heritage of Nazism. The most important elements of this were the racial
theories of Arthur de Gobineau and the British aristocrat and Germanophile
Houston Stewart Chamberlain and the German romantic *Volk* tradition,
as focused initially in the writings of figures like Paul de Lagarde, Julius
Langbehn and Moeller van den Bruck.[85] As Marx and Engels had seen the
motor of history in class struggle, Gobineau and Chamberlain saw the
motor in racial struggle. Gobineau's *Essay on the Inequality of the Human
Races* (1853–55) was an attack upon nineteenth-century liberalism and
socialism, in sum, on the radical legacy of the French Revolution. False
moralistic notions of human equality came up against the apparently
immovable scientific fact of unequal racial origin. For Gobineau, there

were three basic racial units arranged in a hierarchy, each with specific characteristics: the white, the yellow and the black. The lowest was the black and the highest was the white. Within the white there was a group — the Aryans — a form of super-elite who had to be kept free from admixture. Gobineau's message was not just one of racial typology. A great tragedy had befallen the human race, namely, the inevitable mixture or miscegenation of races. This spelt decay and entropy in civilization.

Little note was taken of Gobineau until the end of his life when he was befriended by the composer Richard Wagner in 1876. After both their deaths in 1882, Wagner's widow Cosima, with Ludwig Schemann, set up the Gobineau Society in 1894, with its own racial archive. A noted member of this group was Houston Stewart Chamberlain whose *Foundation of the Nineteenth Century* (1899) carried on the theme of racial speculation. Drawing upon Gobineau, he noted the immense significance of race. Unlike Gobineau, however, anti-Semitism appears as a dominant motif, combined with the superiority of the Teutonic Aryan. Again unlike Gobineau, Chamberlain looked more optimistically to the role of the Germans in maintaining purity and preventing miscegenation or *Volk*-chaos in Europe. Chamberlain joined the Nazi Party shortly before his death in 1927. Hitler and the Nazi ideologist Alfred Rosenberg remained profound admirers of his work.

The above pseudo-scientific racial ideas were linked by Nazi writers with the much older romantic *Volk* traditions of the early 1800s. Romanticism had glorified in the importance of intuition, emotion, and feeling. This was subtly integrated into the nationalist perspective. As Pois comments: 'What Fichte seemed to be establishing philosophically . . . the poets Arndt and Körner and the somewhat cruder patriot, Father Jahn, established on an intellectual level: the heroic, self-sacrificing individuality of *Volk*'.[86] By the early 1900s this heady concoction had combined with long-standing traditions of European anti-Semitism, philosophical vitalism and crude social Darwinist speculation about the fittest races. These formed a backcloth to national socialist speculations of the 1920s.

Given the above context, it was hardly surprising that national socialism developed an idiosyncratic vision of nationalism. The components of this vision can be summarized as follows: first, nationalism was *Volk*-orientated. The notion of the *Volk*, as Mosse noted, 'signified the union of a group of people with a transcendental "essence". This "essence" might be called "nature" or "cosmos" or "mythos", but in each instance it was fused to man's innermost nature.'[87] Mosse and other writers have charted the immense influence of *Volk* ideas across German culture. The *Volk* culture was contrasted to bourgeois culture. Alfred Rosenberg, particularly, focused on the centrality of the *Volk*, as expressed through Nordic peoples, in *The Myth of the Twentieth Century* (1930). The task, as laid down by Rosenberg, was clear:

defence against the infiltrating hordes of Africa; closing frontiers on the basis of anthropological characteristics; and the establishment of a Nordic European coalition in order to cleanse the European motherland of the ever-expanding disease-centres of Africa and Syria.[88]

Suspect history, classical studies, anthropology, phrenology, philology, the religious mysticism of Meister Eckhart, and even the mythology of the Niebelung and *Edda*, were all summarily roped in to support the case of the Nordic *Herrenvolk* (master race). The same bogus racial history was used by Hitler to justify his *Lebensraum* doctrine. The preservation of the Aryan entailed the growth of both numbers and soil to meet this expansion. Thus, as Hitler commented, 'Only an adequately large space on this earth assures a nation freedom of existence.'[89] As might be expected, this Nordic perspective was imbued with an occult pagan religious significance, often used as a contrast to Christianity. Hitler, and many of his compatriots like Rosenberg and Himmler, were deeply attracted by the occult.

The necessity of racial cleanliness encouraged positive support for eugenics programmes. National socialism, early on, set its face against mixed marriage and later legally prohibited Aryan marriage to Jews. Medical science, for Hitler, had to be devoted to such racial goals.[90] One of the systematic Nazi writers on this theme was a trained agronomist. Richard Walter Darré, in works like *The Peasantry as the Life-Source of the Nordic Race* (1928) and *A New Aristocracy out of the Blood and Soil* (1930), proposed a comprehensive eugenics programme in Germany comparable to animal husbandry, one of his actual specialisms.[91]

Because of its rural naturalism and worship of landscape, the Nordic *Volk* perspective tended to idolize the peasantry and farming community. Urban life was seen to be dominated by the bourgeoisie and Jews.[92] The true *Volk* was in the countryside. Darré saw the peasantry as the ideal eugenic breeding stock for sustaining the Nordic *Volk*. This led to preferential and positive policies being adopted towards the farming communities by the national socialists, providing tax incentives and subsidies. How successful such policies were in encouraging people to stay on the land and reproduce is highly questionable.

The other major aspect of this Germanic nationalism was its anti-Semitism. In fact, some would see it as the defining feature. Anti-Semitism, as stated, had been part not only of a European tradition, but was also integral to most of the German *Volk* writers throughout the nineteenth century. It had different manifestations in the Nazi Party. Some saw Jewishness as a spiritual or cultural problem, others saw it as a racial one. Jewishness was also associated with Bolshevism, urban and bourgeois life. Undoubtedly, though, under Hitler's obsessive and manic racial tutelage, the Jews became a central focus of nationalistic hatred and radical depersonalization. Their fate in the death camps in the Second World War is too well-known to dwell upon and well illustrates the terrifying power and immense responsibility that can become attached to ideas. Yet it should still be noted that such awful events virtually surpass our comprehension. The Nazi death camps stand like appalling monoliths before our moral and spiritual understanding in the twentieth century. Given some of the very recent attempts to dismiss the holocaust, it is worth reminding ourselves continually of the horrors which so many innocent human beings suffered.[93]

STATES AND LEADERS

The question of nationalism leads to a consideration of the question of the state in fascism. There was a common negative background to fascist views of the state. These expressed contempt for the liberal democratic state and particularly for the notion of multi-party systems. Parties signified compromise and coalition-making which stultified the national interest. As Primo de Rivera noted: 'It is essential to put a stop to political parties. Political parties are the result of a wrong political system, the parliamentary system ... What need have the people of these political intermediaries?'[94]

One German academic theorist, Carl Schmitt, who later joined the national socialists, encapsulated some of the initial anti-parliamentarianism in his book *The Crisis of Parliamentary Democracy* (1923), although such ideas had already been explored by the Italian theorist Pareto in the 1890s. The problem for Schmitt was that parliamentary government was premised on openness and discussion. These were the two essential principles of constitutional thought. Yet the reality of parliamentary life was far removed from this. The crisis of parliamentary government was that it was a façade. For Schmitt, 'small and exclusive committees of parties or of party coalition make their decisions behind closed doors' usually in cahoots with large business interests.[95] Political parties were simply power-brokers attempting to manoeuvre themselves into influential positions through numerical majorities.

Mass democracy was subject to a different, but mutually aggravating, crisis. Public discussion (which Schmitt defined as 'an exchange of opinion that is governed by the purpose of persuading one's opponent through argument') was an empty formality. The masses were won by propaganda, not by discussion.[96] The people had no say and yet, paradoxically, liberal democracy assumed that there was some kind of unity of interests of governors and governed. Once liberal parties gained power they jettisoned democracy and pursued their own interests. As Schmitt remarked: 'Against the will of the people especially an institution based on discussion by independent representatives has no autonomous justification for its existence, even less so because the belief in discussion is not democratic but originally liberal'.[97] Liberal parliamentary parties asserted this very autonomy. Mass democracy was therefore a façade.

There was also a view shared by fascists that liberal parliamentary states had not only fostered the social and economic crises of the 1920s out of greed and self-interest, but were unwilling to solve the problems. Some, like Oswald Mosley, after the 1914–18 war, were aware of just what could be done by states in times of crisis. States could act decisively and collectivize in war whereas, in peacetime, liberal democracy lacked the will, though not the means, to do something positive.[98]

The fascist conception of the state had a number of features which are highly inconsistent. Many fascists, like Mussolini, Gentile and Primo de Rivera, happily admitted that their vision of the state was 'totalitarian', although the meaning of the term, even in the 1920s and 1930s, was far from clear.[99] Gentile's explanation of totalitarianism was, in essence, that there was no separation between the individual and the state. Those who separate the individual from the state have not moved beyond abstract thinking. Concrete thought demonstrates that 'There is nothing really private . . . and there are no limits to State action'. The state 'comes to birth in the transcendental rhythm of self-consciousness'.[100] Since the state is the only foundation of the individual's rights and freedoms, it therefore 'limits him and determines his manner of existence'.[101]

The fascist state was often linked with the notion of force. 'Force' was opposed to 'right' and 'organicism' to 'mechanism'. Crude social Darwinist ideas lay behind these concepts. Thus, the state was the result of a 'struggle for existence'. As Alfredo Rocco wrote: 'The stronger and more powerful a state, the higher and richer the life of its inhabitants'. It is in fact the state's duty to be strong. Rocco continued, in a somewhat piqued tone, 'This idea of the state as a force (which as a result of the current general state of ignorance is seen as a German Prussian idea) is plainly a Latin and Italian one. It is directly linked with the intellectual tradition of Rome and was refurbished by Machiavelli's political philosophy.'[102]

The fascist understanding of freedom should be noted here. Freedom for most fascists coincided with the purposes of some wider entity like the nation, state or *Volk*. Freedom was never a purely individualistic notion. It had a definite social dimension. Freedom could never conflict with the state or nation. The stronger the state or nation, the richer the freedom of its citizens. This inner notion was contrasted with the external liberal freedom, defined as 'an unlimited natural right of the individual'.[103] As Rosenberg noted, this selfish liberal individualist dogma of liberty should be 'excluded from serious consideration'.[104] Freedom was seen as a spiritual idea, contrasted to the 'grubby materialism' of liberal freedom. The bearing of this argument upon economic freedom should also be noted. Economic freedom was tolerated only so long as it coalesced with the national interest. True freedom was therefore an inner condition of the individual, willing a higher national purpose.

There were, once again, different perceptions of the notion of 'inner'. In Italian fascism, as Mussolini argued, 'the only liberty which can be a real thing, the liberty of the State and of the individual within the State. Therefore, for the Fascist, everything is in the State, and nothing human or spiritual exists, ... outside the State.'[105] Freedom is for the individual to will the ends of the state, an idea which was further elaborated in the concept of the 'ethical state'. For national socialists, like Rosenberg, the case was different. The essence of the individual was the *Volkstum*. Thus, as Rosenberg commented, 'Freedom in the German sense consists of an inner independence ... Today, everybody indiscriminately speaks of an external "freedom", one which can only deliver us to race chaos. Freedom means fellowship of race.'[106] Freedom was therefore identified with the objectives of the race unit.

Despite sharing similar ideas on rights, organicism and force, the Italian fascist, often more Hegelian, vision of the *Totaler Staat* was rejected by national socialists. First, Hegel was repudiated as being too closely associated with the liberal *Rechtsstaat* tradition. Second, as previously emphasized, the state emphatically was not primary for national socialists. The nation and the *Volk* took absolute priority. As Rosenberg argued:

> The National Socialist movement is ... moulded for the security of the collective German *Volk* and of its blood and character. The state, as a most powerful and virile instrument, is placed at the disposal of the movement ... Only in this connection does the National Socialist state-concept become truly alive.[107]

It followed from this, for Rosenberg, that 'it behoves National Socialists not to speak any more of the total state, but of the National Socialist *Weltanschauung*, of the NSDAP as the embodiment of the *Weltanschauung*'.[108] Finally, following the establishment of the priority of the *Führerprinzep*, the state could not be primary or total for the Nazis. The *Führer* embodied the sovereign authority of the *Reich*. State authority was really *Führer* authority. Minimally, this might be called a Caesarist or Bonapartist notion. The idea of an independent state authority in this context was meaningless. As the notion of the *Duce* developed in the 1930s, an obvious but subtle contradiction began to emerge within Italian fascism over the importance of the state. How could both the *Duce* and the national state be supreme?

It is worth remarking here on the supposed organizational efficiency and coherence of the Nazi state. As suggested earlier, there is now a widely accepted view that the Nazi state was internally chaotic. In reality there was no clear top-down governance. The Nazis worked *with* an existing state bureaucracy, many of whom, despite pressure, had not joined the Nazi Party even by 1939. The Nazi-based SS, and other militarized elements, worked in tandem with the state police and army, not always communicating. Most of the concentration camps functioned on the edge of the official state framework. The power of the *Führer* jostled with shifting alliances within the confused structure of the national socialist party, a career civil service, a powerful military and large-scale industrialists. Martin Broszat has thus described the Nazi regime as an 'organizational jungle' where 'to suggest that the development of National Socialist policy consisted in steering towards and carrying out prefabricated long-term ideological aims in small doses is an over-simplification'.[109]

The above points throw some light on the notion of the leader – *Führer* or *Duce* – within fascism. There were a number of theoretical and historical precedents for the idea of the leader. Solon, Pericles, Alexander, Caesar and Bonaparte appeared as role models for some fascists. As Gentile put it, 'It is always the few who represent the self-consciousness and the will of an epoch'.[110] Mosley once defined fascism as 'collective Caesarism'.[111] The notion was also given a vague theoretical warrant in the political philosophies of Hegel and Rousseau, amongst others. In Italy and Germany, at the close of the nineteenth century, it received a sociological *imprimatur* in the elite theories of Mosca, Pareto and Michels, in the crowd psychology of Gustav Le Bon and in the notion of charismatic authority developed by Max Weber. The dynamism, realism and focus of effective decision-making by the leader were contrasted with the time-wasting of parliamentary coalition politics. The leader became the locus of the national interest. There was no need for elaborate democracy.

There are many problems with the leader concept. It did not appear to be essential for all the ideologists of national socialism in the early 1920s. In Italy it was comparatively late in developing. Elite theory, although accepted by many fascists, was often interpreted to mean collective leadership. Hitler and Mussolini, in the early 1920s, were not always revered. They were regarded as key figures in collective groupings but the realities of leadership were different from the theories. As Hans Mommsen has noted, in both Germany and Italy traditional entrenched institutional interests and shifting alliances within the fascist parties forced repeated concessions and circumscribed both Hitler's and Mussolini's rule.[112] Over-concentration on the leaders gives a false impression of the order and coherence of the regimes and implies that responsibility rested primarily with these men. It also neglects the empty theatricality, delusions of grandeur and burlesque quality of Mussolini's leadership in particular.[113]

Finally, the fascist state vision had an odd, immensely complex and tangled relationship with the ideas of 'syndicalism' and 'corporatism'. Both doctrines were far more characteristic of Italian fascism than of German national socialism. In the main, especially after 1933, the national socialists showed little concern for corporatism, either in theory or in practice. Hitler himself was only temporarily interested in the ideas, and then simply as a propaganda device. This does not mean that corporatist theory did not appear in Germany. National socialists such as Gottfried Feder, Gregor Strasser, Walther Darré and to some extent Rosenberg, were overwhelmingly in favour of some form of corporate organization. The emphasis of the Nazi writers was far more towards a neo-medievalist reading of corporations.[114] Corporations were part of the ancient *Volk*. This tradition went back to more romantic conservative theorists like Moeller van den Bruck and, later, Otto Gierke. The Italian fascists, on the other hand, explicitly repudiated the neo-medievalist reading of corporatism. They took a more rationalist and modernist approach to corporations, seeing them as a 'new way' forward which superseded both liberal and socialist conceptions of social organization, rather than as a means of recovery from the past.[115]

In Italian fascism, the corporatist idea related closely to the syndicalist tradition, which was not the case with national socialism. In addition, it is worth pointing out that the Catholic tradition in Italy has always had strong organicist and corporatist leanings. It therefore provided a receptive intellectual climate for corporatism. Syndicalism emerged in Italy in the early 1900s, at roughly the same time as in France, Spain and Britain. It was as much a reaction to Marxism and reformist socialism as to liberalism and capitalism. Gentile noted particularly the influence of Sorel on Italian syndicalism.[116] Most of the Italian fascists were qualified admirers of syndicalism for its anti-parliamentary and anti-democratic rhetoric, its highly moralistic tone on violence and its repudiation of compromise or collaboration with the bourgeoisie.[117] For Italian fascists, syndicalism represented a natural and important phenomenon of social development. It had played an important role in resisting liberalism, capitalism and individualism. Yet, as Alfredo Rocco argued, the time had come for the state to nationalize the syndicates. He contended that 'They must be placed firmly beneath the control of the state, which must lay down their precise functions'.[118] State-controlled national syndicalism incorporated associations within the body politic. The state directed the associations for the ends of the nation. Syndicates would then provide expertise to the state, professional training, public assistance, arbitrate disputes and prevent strikes and lockouts. As Rocco commented: 'Through these reconstituted syndicates the state would at last possess the technical bodies to enable it properly to fulfil the various functions in the economy which necessity forced upon it'.[119]

It is at this point that we can see the direct connection between syndicalism and corporatism. The state was the association of associations, or the corporation of corporations. As Gentile put it:

Fascism has ... taken over from syndicalism the idea of syndicates as an educative moral force, but since the antithesis between state and syndicate must be overcome, it has endeavoured to develop a system whereby this function should be attributed to syndicates grouped together into corporations subject to state discipline and indeed reflecting within themselves the same organization as the state.[120]

In fascism we see the corporation of syndicates governed for the national interest. If any form of parliamentary structure remained it would be an economic or social parliament of economic producers without the encumbrance of time-wasting parties. Employers' and workers' syndicates or associations would be linked together in the same corporate association. They would then change from being aggressive and defensive bodies into collaborative groups. There were attempts to establish such a structure in Italy, particularly between 1929 and 1932 under Guiseppe Bottai. The results, though, were profoundly flawed. In March 1930, a National Council of Corporations was set up with three levels, incorporating employers' and workers' organizations, a representative assembly of economic and social associations and the state bureaucracy, and finally, the Central Corporative Committee, comprising government ministers, presidents of workers' and employers' confederations, and top civil servants. All of these were under the watchful direction of Mussolini.[121]

Nothing of comparable interest developed in Germany. Furthermore, not all fascists were as enthusiastic about corporatism. Primo de Rivera, in a speech to Spanish fascists in April 1935, remarked: 'This stuff about the corporative state is another piece of windbaggery.' In his writings he was not always so unsympathetic to aspects of corporatism.[122] The other important issue concerning corporatism was its illusory aspect. Most scholars, on Italy particularly, admit that corporatism was a façade and never really succeeded in practice. As one writer commented, corporatism was 'a cloak for ruthless exploitation of labour and a reservoir of jobs for party hacks'.[123] It served an excellent propaganda function and also helped to integrate and emasculate intellectuals.

THE ECONOMY

In the fascist understanding of the economy we encounter many of the themes already discussed. There are four points to emphasize: first, politics took priority over economics; second, the focus of politics was on the nation and *Volk*, therefore economics was essentially determined by national objectives; third, the economic practices which were adopted were a mixture of socialist and liberal policies; and finally, there was, as in other areas of fascist ideology, a tension between prescription and reality in fascist economics.

In typically Hegelian fashion, Gentile wrote: 'The State is concrete universal will, whereas economics is concerned with the subhuman life of man — the corporeal ... It follows that there is an economic element in the will, and hence in the State; but it has been transcended, transfigured by the light of freedom.'[124] In essence, for Gentile, politics was the realm of will and freedom and was a higher form of life than the mechanism of economics. It therefore followed that politics, as expressed in the nation-state, was spiritually and morally superior to economics. In the case of national socialism, race and the *Volk* occupied this position.

Corporatism and autarky were typical of this priority of politics over economics. The former has already been touched upon. The corporate state integrated employers and employees. Each association regulated its membership and the nature of production. Industrial strife would be minimized in the interests of the nation. This was the 'third way' between capitalism and socialism. Organic and economic representation in a pro-ducers' parliament, guided by national ends, would replace geographical democratic political representation. As Alfredo Rocco argued:

> a Fascist economy is not an economy of association nor merely directed or controlled economy, it is above all an organized one. It is organized by the efforts of the producers themselves, with the state to direct and control them from above.[125]

Some of the most significant ideas utilized by fascism appear in this area. Mosley, pursuing these corporative notions in Britain, was the first politician who seriously attempted to understand and apply the ideas of Keynesian economics in his book *Greater Britain*.[126]

In the case of autarky, which was officially inaugurated by Mussolini on 23 March 1936, and was largely being pursued in Germany from the same period, the idea was for a self-sufficient economy marshalling its economic resources for national ends. The idea had been present in the writings of J. G. Fichte and Friedrich List in the previous century. In the case of both Germany and Italy it was tied to the war-footing of these countries in the later 1930s. In Germany, from 1936 onwards, the aim was economic self-sufficiency in preparation for international conflict.[127]

The puzzling question concerning fascist economics is its precise orien-tation. Given the early Marxist critique of fascism as the tool of mon-opoly capitalism it is strange to find such vigorous anti-capitalist rhetoric throughout the whole corpus of fascist writings. If one looks at the work of Nazis such as Gottfried Feder, Dietrich Eckhart and Gregor Strasser particularly, the NSDAP Twenty-Five Points, Primo de Rivera's *Guidelines of the Falange*, Mosley's *Greater Britain*, Drieu de Rochelle's writings or the various national syndicalist and corporatist proposals of some Italian fascists, the overwhelming impression is one of anti-capitalist argument.[128]

Primo de Rivera stated in his 1935 *Guidelines*, 'We reject the capitalist system, which disregards the needs of the people, dehumanizes private property and transforms the workers into shapeless masses prone to misery and despair.' Equally the Nazi writer Gregor Strasser argued in his 'Thoughts about the Tasks of the Future': '*We are Socialists*, are enemies, mortal enemies of the present capitalist economic system with its exploitation of the economically weak, with its injustices in wages, with its immoral evaluation of individuals according to wealth and money ... and we are determined under all circumstances to abolish this system!'[129] Strasser goes on to advocate an economy premised upon human 'need' as against 'profit'. The definition of 'humanity', however, was crucial. Strasser saw human beings as members of a nation or *Volk* and not of a class. Therefore it was the needs of the national, and not class, members which were really primary. Thus Strasser referred to fascist economics as 'national economics'. He noted that 'We have to learn that the ideas "world trade" − "balance of trade" − "export surplus" are ideas of a declining epoch ... and were *born out of speculation, not out of necessity*, not out of the soil!'[130] The programmes of these fascist groups and individuals encompassed wide-ranging economic and welfare proposals for altering the whole character of the economic system in line with national purposes, including employment programmes, nationalization, profit-sharing, expropriation of excessive profits, abolition of unearned income, and interference in loan capital and interest.

The socialist conception of economics, which was not tied to national ends, fared no better in the fascist framework. Marxist and bourgeois socialism were declared spiritually bankrupt, rooted in the same form of thinking as capitalism itself, i.e., not rising above the material categories of money and profit, as ends in themselves, and therefore unable to fulfil the higher spiritual objectives of the nation. However, not all fascists supported this argument. It was claimed by many that as long as personal self-interest, private property and capital accumulation did not undermine or interfere with national ends, then liberal capital economics was to be tolerated. In fact, it should be encouraged.[131] As Hitler declared:

> We must ... not dismiss a business man if he is a good business man, even if he is not yet a National Socialist; and especially not if the National Socialist who is to take his place knows nothing about business. In business, ability must be the only authoritative standard ... In the long run our political power will be all the more secure, the more we succeed in underpinning it economically.[132]

Overall, the central ambiguity of both the German and Italian fascist regimes was that they employed 'a battery of economic controls to which left-wing governments, outside the Soviet Union, could still only aspire to'. Yet the beneficiaries of these proposals were groups which usually 'supported more right-wing parties'.[133]

The final issue for discussion concerns the illusion and reality of fascist economics. We have already noted the well-established view of the illusion of the corporate state. Equally, the notion of autarky was very much a pipe-dream, particularly in Italy. It is difficult to make clear comparisons between Germany and Italy on the question of economics, since they were at very different stages of economic development in the earlier part of this century. In the early 1920s Italy had 21 per cent of its economically active population employed in industry; in Germany the percentage was 42.2. In addition, the proportional levels of GNP achieved by the industrial sector in Italy in 1920 had already been reached by Germany in 1870.[134] Further, despite the propaganda, it is questionable as to how far national socialists and Italian fascists consciously achieved any improvement in their economies. Massive rearmament, economic luck in terms of an upturn after the depression of the 1920s, punitive and disciplinary state work-programmes, wide-scale statistical juggling and massive propaganda, created the impression of an economic miracle. Many have argued that, in fact, in neither economy did fascism have any really distinctive effect. Certainly Hitler and Mussolini appeared to have little interest in, or commitment to, economic theories, as long as their nationalist and imperialist ambitions could be financially underpinned. As Mosse noted on national socialism: 'It nationalized when it wanted to nationalize ... It allied itself with big business when it wanted such an alliance.' Overall, it lacked a specific economic commitment.[135]

CONCLUSION

As already indicated, there are major difficulties in dealing with fascism. Because of the experiences of the Second World War there is considerable and justifiable moral censure attached to the ideology. Fascism has also had an ambiguous relation to the concept of ideology itself. Not only did fascists cultivate an irrationalist and anti-ideological stance, which makes it difficult to deal with the doctrine on the same level as other ideologies, but it is also questionable as to how far the ideology actually informed the conduct of fascists in power. In addition, the ideology includes some quite strange, crude and bizarre components. A charitable view might regard these as the eclectic, slightly mad and over-extended fragments of recognizable European traditions of thought about race, the state, or human nature. A less charitable view would dismiss them as pathological ravings. The difficulty that scholars have had with the ideology has led many to seek alternative non-ideological accounts of the character of the movement within the disciplines of psychology, economics and sociology, which were outlined in the earlier part of this chapter.

This latter tendency is one way of ignoring the uncomfortable fact that a closer look at some of the ideas of fascism and national socialism reveal affinities and overlaps with more acceptable ideologies, like liberalism, conservatism, syndicalism and socialism. The notions of an interventionist welfare-orientated state; corporatism and a more social-market economy; a social parliament of economic producers; ecological concerns about the destruction of nature; the problem of the unconscious, emotive and violent side of human nature; and a concern over the sense of alienation and spiritual emptiness of modern bourgeois civilization, are not exactly alien ideas to other ideological traditions. This affinity should alert us to possible misinterpretation. The above ideas were combined with highly emotive, xenophobic and vicious nationalisms; fuzzy pseudo-scientific racism; unstructured, messy and unexplained uses of academic theories like elitism, vitalism, pragmatism and social Darwinism; and the bizarre and over-optimistic claims of leaders.

In fact, in fascism we see many contradictory strands. There is a fundamental dichotomy between the particular and insular character of the nationalisms it promotes and the claims it makes to universal appeal. There are deep unresolved tensions between the notions of race, nation and state in both fascism and national socialism. There is also a paradox concerning their mixture of enthusiastic populism, on the one hand, looking to a new fascist individual, and extreme elitism and vitriolic contempt for the masses on the other. Fascism, as such, is not a particularly convincing ideology, in intellectual terms, but this does not mean that we should dismiss its ideological content out of hand. However, its intellectual confusions, lack of coherence and horrific conduct whilst in power need to be continually highlighted.

7
FEMINISM

—

The volume of literature on feminism has expanded at a phenomenal rate in the last three decades. With ecologism, it is probably one of the fastest growing of all ideologies. Unlike certain other ideologies, for example, conservatism or liberalism, the word itself causes few etymological problems since its *prima facie* meaning is fairly transparent. At its simplest, the word denotes the investigation of the oppression of women and an understanding and promotion of women in all spheres. Even this idea might still cause considerable debate and criticism. However, a different set of problems attach themselves to feminism — tied to the self-conscious identity of the movement itself. These problems, which will be touched upon in the following pages, may in part be due to the fact that feminism is still in the stage of intellectual and political formation by comparison with ideologies like liberalism.

An additional problem with articulating and studying the ideology of feminism is that it is subject to intense debate at this very moment. It is also a profoundly active/practical-orientated ideology and movement. This active/practical, or immanent, critique offered by feminism is almost unique, since its challenge is not only at the academic or political level but is also directed at certain deeply held beliefs about the very character of our society, our thought patterns and our personal and most intimate relations. Not all those who have previously studied or written about ideologies look particularly comfortable with feminist ideology. This immanent critique has permeated into every field: all dimensions of artistic creation, the social sciences, humanities and, more recently, into the natural sciences. In fact, some would claim that it subverts the very foundations of Western culture. The extent of the growth of feminist commentary has been breathtaking and surpasses the reading capacities of all but the most persistent scholar.

A problem that adds to the intensity of the debate is the occasionally insular character of many of the theoretical contributions. Many feminist writers, journals, presses and academic courses seem to be solely addressing other feminists, women who read feminist writings or just women in general. There is, though, a perfectly consistent argument at work within this apparent insularity. In short, if men are the *problem*, and it is in their interest to suppress women, why address anything to men or pay anything but hostile attention to their writings? They will either not understand or they will try to subvert women, whether consciously or unconsciously. If our present language (including the technical languages of the various academic disciplines) embodies subtle forms of sexual power and domination, how can men be addressed? If the feminist tries to express her point of view in such language, she has already subscribed to her own subordination and has lost the argument from the first syllable.[1] This view parallels the position of many anarcho-syndicalists, anarchists and Gramscian organic intellectuals. The more general argument from these latter groups was that workers or peasants needed to develop their own educational programmes and forms of thought. As soon as regular patterns of bourgeois thought were adopted, the argument and revolution were near to being lost. Rather, as Gramsci argued, proletarians must look for hegemonic power within even the canons of language and common sense. In the same way, women must resist the hegemonic patriarchal themes within language and common sense. There are also grounds for developing a new form of feminine discourse, a point that will be returned to. A related issue here for some feminists is the fact that many of the problems, traumas and difficulties experienced by women, like menstruation, remain women's issues. They cannot be fully grasped by men and have, indeed, often been made taboos by them. They are part of the unique experience of women and can only be experienced *by* other women. However, behind these arguments is a contention that women are both unique and possess an essential and universal nature. More recent feminist writers have in fact contested this point, pointing out differences *between* women.

Another difficulty of the essentialist claim concerning women (particularly of radical feminism) is that it often seems that feminism is being discussed without any broader historical, political or philosophical context. The world, it is suggested, has been waiting for feminism, which is now being fully realized, and the future 'truth' of history lies in its domain. Radical feminism is not alone in this: most radical ideologies have experienced such a sense of their messianic purpose. Also, given that men, until comparatively recently, have tended to write the bulk of history and philosophy, such thought has often been regarded by radical feminists as deeply suspect. Although it is quite easy to see the reasoning behind this position, it sounds like the vulgar Marxist claim from the Second International period: that all non-Marxist thought is bourgeois ideology and 'false-consciousness' and can be ignored with impunity. Despite the influence of such judgements, one suspects that it will go the same way as the vulgar Marxist view.

Beyond the rather generalized description of feminism offered above – a concern for the investigation of oppression and an understanding and promotion of women – it becomes immediately very difficult to suggest a more substantive definition of the term. It should be pointed out here that certain feminists would immediately question the search for any such definition, specifically those who have questioned the very character of rationalistic language, whether from a deconstructionist or poststructuralist viewpoint, or alternatively, because other dimensions of knowledge more closely represent the female pattern of thought than rational concept formation. Many postmodernist-inspired feminists would argue that even the binary opposition of terms like 'feminine' and 'masculine' are questionable, in so far as they offer a grand narrative of supposedly universal notions, which are in reality highly specific cultural and linguistic constructs. Following Foucault's attack on the categories of Enlightenment thought, as one writer has put it: 'Feminist analysis tends to regard the Western antinomies of subject and object, mind and body, reason and emotion . . . all in their gendered meaning and suspicious correspondence with the hierarchical division of Male and Female . . . these are the instrumentalities of power'.[2]

If we put this issue to one side for the moment, it is still clear that if the history of feminism as a movement is examined, then feminism has stood for many different and, at times, totally opposed ideas. Forms of feminism have been linked both with the promotion of chastity and the opening-up of free sexual relations, supported by freely available contraception. Some feminisms have stood for more open and freer heterosexual relations and others for political lesbianism. Some have celebrated the difference of women and their uniqueness, while others have gone so far as to advocate androgyny (almost an evolutionary hermaphroditism). Given the accounts that have been offered of other ideologies so far, these diverse doctrines should come as no great surprise to the reader. Feminism partakes of the same overlap and ambivalence on its substantive values as most ideologies.

This uncertainty is reflected in the attempted definitions which are formulated by some writers. The broadest notion would be that feminism is pursued by 'any group that have tried to *change* the position of women or ideas about women'.[3] This draws the net far too wide for some, since it could also include anti-feminists. Others focus more precisely, speaking of the essence of feminism being for women to attain 'equal worth with men in respect to their common nature as a free person'.[4] This definition is close to the idea that feminism is ultimately about sexual justice. Feminism exists, in this reading, to rectify the systematic injustices that women experience because of their sex.[5] Some would see this as narrowing the focus too much to a formal legalistic notion. Feminism is, for others, 'a general critique of social relationships of sexual domination and sub-ordination' or an 'opposition to any form of social, personal or economic discrimination which women suffer because of their sex'.[6] These definitions would widen the terms of the critique. For many feminists, much of the most insidious exploitation and domination of women takes place in areas underneath the surface of formal political and economic relationships in society. More recent poststructuralist and postmodernist feminists, however, would resist this whole effort of definition as another flawed attempt at metanarrative, namely, trying to fix and close a system of thought. One definite aspect of postmodernism and poststructuralism is, in Toril Moi's words, that it 'sees all metanarratives, including feminism, as repressive enactments of metaphysical authority'.[7] Thus all doctrine is seen to be fiction. There are no absolutes or solid grounds for definition.

Many of the above definitions in fact represent quite distinct strands of the overall movement. Despite the fact that there is a more general impetus behind feminism, concerned to improve the condition of women and resist oppression, there are diverse schools of feminist thought which give very different analyses of this process.

ORIGINS OF FEMINIST THOUGHT

Debates over the origins of feminism tie in with the substantive debates about the ideology itself. There is considerable sensitivity about the question of the historical origins of the movement. First, because men have tended to dominate historical writing until recently, there has been criticism of the exclusion of women or the marginalization of women's history. It is contended, in this context, that women have been written about by men, and men will tend to be, consciously or not, systematically gender-biased. Therefore the history of women has to be rediscovered by women for women. Second, this sensitivity to historical origins, coupled with the fact that the discipline of history itself can be part of a patriarchal male order, makes women much more sensitive to the account of the feminist move-ment. Dale Spender, commenting on the exclusion of certain important females from more general historical writing, remarks that this 'constitutes an example of almost every technique men have used to abuse, devolve and erase women'.[8] It makes male writing on the history of women look suspect from the start. Minimally, if a male is writing, the woman reader will be sceptical and wary, as, presumably, at this moment.

Another difficulty which occurs in this area is the question as to whether a concern with women's issues is the same as a feminist ideology. This might seem a small point but it is significant up to the present day. There are many women and men who are, or have been, concerned about the treatment of women in the family, education and at work, who would support full equalization in these spheres, yet who would, none the less, find it odd to be called feminists. The matter is not as clear-cut as this, but it is still important for any judgement on the history of women. There have been a number of women who have advocated certain changes in attitudes to women and argued for practical reforms, for example, later-nineteenth- and early-twentieth-century reformers like Mrs Humphrey Ward, Octavia Hill or Beatrice Webb. Whether one would proceed to the conclusion that these figures were necessarily feminist appears dangerously anachronistic. The latter two were even antipathetic to female suffrage.

Broadly, the debate concerning the origins of feminist thought and practice breaks down into four categories. The first three assume that the concept precedes the word. The first argues, in effect, that feminism dates from the dawn of human consciousness. The 'woman question' has always been with us. The female psyche is unique, unchanging, and wholly different to the male. In fact some would say that it is superior to the male in its innate ecological capacities and that the history of the human species has gone disastrously astray due to the dominance of males. Susan Griffin contends, from an eco-feminist standpoint, that women are closer to nature than men. She identifies the key voices of her book *Women and Nature* as 'the great chorus of woman and nature, which will swell with time'.[9] This more ahistorical notion, which derives from the realms of biological conjecture, psychoanalysis, religious speculation and Jungian archetypes, need not detain us for the moment.[10] The present interest is more concerned with direct political self-awareness. The psychology theme will be touched upon later.

Despite the fact that some have looked back to Plato's feminism, the more usual second point of origin is the early 1400s. The figure of Christina de Pizan is usually picked out here. We might, though, take note of Dale Spender's caution that 'virtually any woman chosen as a "beginning" would have predecessors'.[11] Christina de Pizan produced a work, *Book of the City of the Ladies* (1405), on which a great deal has been written by feminist scholars. There is an unresolved debate here as to whether de Pizan was concerned with something that could genuinely be called feminism. In other words, is it anachronistic to try to impose our present configuration of thought on the past?[12] A similar question could also be asked about the figure most frequently cited from the 1600s as the third point of origin – Aphra Behn (1640–1680). She was a dynamic personality by all accounts, whose comparatively short life spanned some spectacular experiences. She was involved in a rebellion in the West Indies, spied for the Court of Charles II against the Dutch and was a prolific author, writing seventeen plays and thirteen novels. She also appears to have actively promoted the idea of equality for women.[13]

Finally, the most popular – and probably correct – starting-point for considering feminism is the very late 1700s, particularly the immediate aftermath of the French Revolution. Western feminism, like most other ideologies, finds its origins here, although certain strands of thought pre-date the revolution. The actual definitive political movement is of course a much later product. The most significant event for the history of feminist thought in the revolution phase was the publication, in 1792, of Mary Wollstonecraft's *A Vindication of the Rights of Woman*. Miriam Kramnick has observed that 'Mary Wollstonecraft was the first major feminist, and *A Vindication of the Rights of Woman* ... is the feminist declaration of independence'.[14] This primacy of Mary Wollstonecraft – providing the first systematic statement of a feminist perspective – is widely recognized in twentieth-century feminist thought.

If we focus our attention on this last period, which saw the most prolific output in feminist writing, political agitation and self-consciousness, then a number of subdivisions must be noted. The most conventional division is between two waves: the first wave spanning the period 1830–1920 and the second wave 1960 to the present. This periodization usually contends that the interval 1920–60 was one of stagnation. Not all feminist writers follow this periodization precisely. The second wave has been subdivided again into two, and up to five, phases. Some recent writers have even contended that postmodernist feminism is a third wave.[15]

If we follow the more conventional two-waves account, the background for the first wave lies in the classical liberal rights perspective and the widespread utilization of Lockian language in the early nineteenth century. This perspective had its most immediate impact in America. Its more general format was the vigorous push for female enfranchisement and the extension of the normal civil and political rights to women. In the USA the background for such programmes lay in powerful, often middle-class, non-conformist religious movements, which encouraged women to become socially active in campaigns on such issues as temperance and the control of prostitution. Such women inevitably developed their own positive intel-lectual contributions to certain social debates. At the same time the growth of industrialization and modernization were already bringing more women into the workforce. This alone gave some women greater independence.

Most important in the American setting was the involvement of women in the anti-slavery and suffrage movements of the nineteenth century. The discourse of such movements argued against the 'rights-based' constitutional background of the American Declaration of Independence. The language of such complaint was readily available in the American constitutional documents. This debate was first raised in a public setting in the famous American Seneca Falls Convention of 1848, organized by Elizabeth Cady Stanton and Lucretia Mott. They issued an alternative Declaration of Independence paraphrasing the first Declaration line by line, but incor-porating women into the document. The upshot was a series of demands for equalization of property, educational opportunities, and an opening-up of the professions, all expressed through the language of natural rights.[16] After the vast conflagration of the American Civil War, black males gained suffrage rights in 1866. It struck many women activists who had worked against slavery and for black suffrage before, during and after the Civil War, as utterly incongruous that they should have struggled, successfully, for the basic political rights of black men, which were apparently then totally denied to women. The contradiction was starkly obvious to many. From 1878 onwards, the Nineteenth 'Anthony Amendment' was introduced into the US Congress every year until its acceptance in 1920.[17] The process of achieving enfranchisement was aided by organizations like the National American Women's Suffrage Association, formed in 1890 to campaign for the vote on a federal level.

In Britain and France, from the 1830s, utopian socialists in the Saint-Simonian and Owenite schools raised the question of complete female equality. The idea had, of course, already been argued by Mary Wollstone-craft. Harriet Taylor and J. S. Mill continually raised the issue in public debate.[18] There had been women's involvement in movements like the Anti-Corn Law League, agitation for the reform of property law, and campaigning for professional, educational and employment opportunities. There was also, as in America, a strong involvement in charity, social work and moral reform campaigns over the nineteenth century. Apart from the mid-nineteenth-century efforts of Harriet Taylor and J. S. Mill, the first politically effective pursuit of suffrage reform was in Mrs Pankhurst's Women's Social and Political Union, set up in 1903.

Yet with the achievement of the vote for women in the 1920s, many writers on feminism assumed a period of relative doldrums, apart from campaigns on pacifism. The Great Depression and the war periods absorbed much of women's attention and energy. The issues that were fought over in this period were practical and immediate welfare concerns, namely, to uphold and support the family unit. Ideas on family endowments, adequate health-care, school meals and maternity benefits, were pursued vigorously over the 1930s and eventually became part of regular public policy in post-1945 Britain, at least until the 1980s. The post-war era, particularly the 1950s, also saw a relatively fast growth in the economies of Britain and America. Large proportions of the populations of both countries experienced an increase in affluence. Convergence politics, consensus on the values of a pragmatic liberalism, the 'end of ideology' debate and concern about political apathy were characteristic of the decade. Women's issues were submerged for a time in a range of welfare concerns and material aspirations.

The second wave, in most estimates, began in the 1960s. A number of reasons have been offered for this rise of interest in feminism. There had been a widespread growth in women's education across Europe and

America, particularly from the 1940s. Women were increasingly gaining the qualifications to enter fully into the various professions previously dominated by men. In addition, a number of measures in the 1960s — legislation on abortion, equal pay and civil rights, the introduction of widely available birth control, particularly the contraceptive pill — facilitated women's greater freedom of choice in both public and private spheres.

Literature focusing on women's issues was slowly beginning to expand during this period. Simone de Beauvoir's *The Second Sex* (originally published in 1952, this became a popular paperback in 1961) and Betty Friedan's *The Feminine Mystique* (1965) were only the inauguration of this process. In Britain the work of Germaine Greer and Juliet Mitchell (particularly the former) made feminism a household term.[19] In addition, there were changing social attitudes to marriage, divorce and work. Women were now becoming gradually more independent, financially, socially and morally, of institutions like the family. Finally, a number of women's groups began to capitalize on these developments. In America particularly, apart from the better-known and more institutional associations like the National Organization for Women, there was a veritable explosion of women's groups in the late 1960s and early 1970s.[20]

Apart from the more usual liberal-rights-orientated claims, the early 1970s had other important components. In parallel with the radical anti-slavery experience of women in the nineteenth century, a number of women who had worked in civil rights campaigns, anti-Vietnam and peace movements in the 1960s, began to shift their interests, for a variety of reasons, into feminist issues. The primary reason for this change of focus was a disenchantment with the 'sexism' of the Marxist-socialist groups. Women often felt demeaned by the males in these groups and relegated to supportive roles and so took their Marxist-socialist and radical libertarian beliefs into feminism. In America, the radical libertarian element adopted a much more exuberant form. In Europe, the socialist component has had a much higher profile.

In the last two decades not only has the feminist movement grown enormously, but the literature has swelled exponentially. A number of journals and women's presses have come into being to market this material. Despite the fact that there has been considerable intellectual and practical consolidation, the 1980s were a difficult time for feminism. The literature in all fields went on growing, courses in women's studies flourished in higher education, and consciousness-raising on women's issues continued. Yet the 1980s also saw the predominance in Europe and America of the New Right, the reassertion of the importance of the traditional patriarchal family, attacks on abortion legislation and civil rights, plus the increasing stresses introduced by the attacks on the welfare state. In addition, unemployment grew during the decade. This tended to affect women in the family much harder than it did men. The New Right has not been particularly sympathetic to the feminist movement. There is the possibility of some formal sympathy in the market-orientated wing of the New Right, but this is rejected by the more predominantly socialist and Left libertarian tendencies of much of the feminist movement. Finally, the very late 1980s and early 1990s have seen a definite shift of intellectual interests in the feminist movement away from political and economic issues and towards cultural, psychological and linguistic preoccupations. This latter theorizing has burgeoned enormously in the last few years, particularly with the surge of interest in French feminist writing, post-structuralism and deconstruction theory. But such a vast amount of academic theory has paradoxically coincided, in the early 1990s with an increase in the social and economic problems for the many poor, for ethnic minorities and for Third World women.

THE NATURE OF FEMINISM

Feminism, like all of the ideologies we have been considering, has been influenced by certain historical traditions and has interacted and overlapped with a number of other ideologies. The Enlightenment emphasis on the language of reason, attacking superstitions, taboos and prejudices, has been one influential theme. The experience of the French Revolution and the powerful discourse on democratic rights was also crucial for the early stages of feminist argument. The impact of a more evangelical Protestantism was important for encouraging many women into active social work and involvement in social and political issues. The unitarians were especially noted for their belief in the role of women. The impact of the early utopian socialists was also significant, particularly the disciples of Saint-Simon, Charles Fourier and Robert Owen, all of whom, in their various ways, attacked the institution of marriage, the bourgeois nuclear family, promoted female equality, and advocated much freer sexual relations and communal child-care arrangements.

In terms of the movement of feminism, it is difficult to identify a consistent body of concerns, except in a very formal sense. Many of the equivocal and often contradictory principles we can observe in ideologies like socialism can also be seen in feminism. Feminism has fragmented into a number of different schools of thought, which quite often reflect very different emphases and doctrines. Some feminists have expressed discontent with this fragmentation, although it seems a forlorn protest. Rosalind Delmar, for example, comments that it 'signals a sclerosis of the movement'.[21] Such sclerosis, if indeed it is sclerosis, is part of every nineteenth and twentieth-century ideology.

The main schools within feminism have acquired something of an orthodox status. Liberal feminism, Marxist-socialist feminism and radical feminism are the three substantive schools most often cited. It is now advisable to include the more recent views of postmodernist feminists as a separate category, partly because these have generated such intense interest over the last decade.

Despite the predominance of these schools, it is strongly argued on the periphery of the movement that there should be a recognition of other elements. Black feminists claim a critical independence from these other schools, arguing in effect that they are all 'race-blind'. Anarchist feminists have also maintained their unique difference, premised upon some of the recognizable anti-authoritarian arguments of anarchism. A closely related element to anarchism is eco-feminism, particularly in America in the work of writers like Carolyn Merchant and Dolores LaChapelle.[22] Patriarchy is coupled with global destruction and pollution, while women are linked with a concern for nature and the earth. Finally, there are some comparatively recent debates on 'maternal thinking' and the 'ethic of care' which are difficult to categorize. There are also those who contrast 'civic feminism' with 'maternal feminism'. Some aspects of maternal feminism have acquired the title 'conservative pro-family feminism'. These latter debates will be examined briefly at the end of this section.

We will now consider the various schools in a little more detail. Liberal feminism is the most practically effective and (on the surface) most reasonably argued form of feminism, although one immediate criticism here is that there has not been enough attention within this school to the diversity of liberal thought itself. There is often an assumed consensus of beliefs around liberalism.

The language of liberalism has a perennial attraction for feminists, particularly the language of contract and rights, which is a potent weapon to use against patriarchal traditions. Liberals adhere formally to the values of rationalism, equality, freedom, individualism, including certain robust beliefs on the value of individual property ownership, the power of education, representative democracy, and the possibility of rational legal reform. Also, if one takes another belief central to much classical liberal thought, the free economy, it is clear that *all* (regardless of sex) should have equal access to compete in the market. Monopolies, whether private, public or sexual, are intrinsically suspect. Unjustified male monopoly, like any economic cartel, is implicitly frowned upon by the logic of market theory. Free markets imply free individuals, including women, who can compete on equal terms. The theme of overt feminist capitalism has not really been developed within the ideology, certainly not to the same extent as that of conservative capitalism, market socialism or green capitalism in the last decade. This is partly due to the fact that many feminists have associated the market qualities of competition, individualism and self-interest with masculinity.

Socialist and radical feminist writers are less sanguine about the future of liberal feminism and complain that liberalism has been, in fact, so deeply assimilated into our culture that it has virtually become invisible. Liberalism is seen, by such writers, as a 'specific ideology seeking to protect and reinforce the relations of patriarchal and capitalist society'.[23]

The liberal tradition, depending on when you date its inception, provides a number of openings for feminist criticism and argument, particularly in its social contract format.[24] The social contract tradition in Hobbes, for example, begins by stripping humans down to their basic motivations, in order to build a picture of the commonwealth. The image of decon-structed humans is intrinsically 'sexless' or genderless. The later inclusion by Hobbes of families, fatherly authority and male rulers, is for some feminist commentators an unjustified addition to the argument. Social contract argument, unless customs are incorporated within it, provides a medium for talking about human equality. Social contract writers, like Locke, also attacked divine right and patriarchal theory. There is, potentially, a logical extension from criticizing patriarchalism in political sovereignty to criticizing it within the family.[25] This step was never taken by Locke, although it is an implication of his argument. The arguments for social contract turn on the idea of separate free and equal individuals, *not* males or females. Finally, the politics of contract theory is built upon the foundations of reason, not of custom or tradition. Again this represents a potential challenge to the supposed 'natural order' of patriarchy. With some exceptions, most liberal theorists did not initially take these poten-tialities very seriously.[26]

Dale Spender, in *Women of Ideas*, cites a number of female writers who were exploring the liberal terrain in the nineteenth century, if not so systematically as Mary Wollstonecraft.[27] Among those who stand out as liberal feminists are Harriet Taylor, J. S. Mill, Margaret Fuller, Harriet Martineau – plus a large American contingent with activists like Lucretia Mott and Elizabeth Cady Stanton. In the post-1945 decades one of the books to have generated most interest in the liberal standpoint, during the early stage of the second wave, was Betty Friedan's *The Feminine Mystique*.

Before moving on to the other schools of feminism it is important to draw attention to the fact that there have been significant variations within the liberal argument. The most important of these for early liberal feminism was that between the natural rights and utility-based arguments, which are virtually irreconcilable in some formats. This separates out the liberal arguments of J. S. Mill and Mary Wollstonecraft. In addition, the relation of feminism to subsequent developments of liberalism into the twentieth century, as examined in chapter 2, has not as yet been explored by feminist writers. The more Rawlsian-inspired social liberalism that we find in recent liberal feminists like Janet Radcliffe Richards and Susan Moller Okin is potentially as much at odds with both the natural rights and utilitarian liberalism of Wollstonecraft and J. S. Mill as it is with the liberalism of Hayek.[28]

The second major school to be considered is socialist feminism. Despite the separation sometimes made in the literature between socialist and Marxist feminism, Marxism will be regarded as a species within the genus socialism. As argued in chapter 4, Marxism is emphatically *not* the summation or fruition of socialism. There are strong feminist themes running through many of the early socialist writers, for example, Fourier, the Saint-Simonians (rather than Saint-Simon directly), Robert Owen, William Thompson and Ann Wheeler. In the latter part of the nineteenth, and into the twentieth, century some of the more important theoretical contributions came from Friedrich Engels, August Bebel, Alexander Kollontai and Clara Zetkin.

Both Fourier and the Saint-Simonians premised the achievement of socialism on the equality and freedom of women. Progress was measured by the improvement in the condition of women. In the case of the Saint-Simonians it was also linked with their cult of the Great Mother, who was seen as a messianic saviour for humanity.[29] In Fourier, women were to have as full and equally fulfilling lives in the *Phalanstery* as men. Both Fourier and the Saint-Simonians also regarded marriage as outmoded. In Fourier, specifically, free love, bisexuality, lesbianism and polygamy were to be encouraged in the utopian community. He also advocated communal kitchens, housework and communal child-rearing.

Although not interested in the amorous experimentation of Fourier, Owen, in the course of his critique of property relations and religion in *New Moral World*, called for the abolition of marriage. For Owen, marriage was an artificial restraint on natural feeling and a cause of vice and misery, creating social inequalities and poverty. In fact, all three misfortunes were linked in his mind. *Religion* sustains *marriage* and this, in turn, encourages a *competitive economy* which generates poverty. Owen, in fact, believed in the natural superiority of women to men in terms of their capacities for sympathy and compassion. He also believed, like Fourier, in communal education, production, eating and child-care within the utopian structure.

An admirer of Owen, William Thompson (1785–1835), was stimulated to write directly on the question of women after reading one paragraph of James Mill's *Essay on Government*. In discussing the franchise, Mill had incorporated women's interests into those of men. Thompson tried to show in works like *An Appeal of One Half of the Human Race, Women, against the Pretensions of the Other Half, Men* (1825), that women should have equality of rights with men. All humans were equally capable of happiness in a future cooperative socialist society. He also challenged the monogamous family and existing divisions of labour. Similar themes were developed in Ann Wheeler's writings, although she was more directly influenced by the Saint-Simonians.[30]

Marx and Engels, in their early years, said very little on the question of women. Marx seemed to assume that women would be liberated under socialism. The human emancipation he anticipated in his essay 'On the

Jewish Question' incorporates the liberation of women. Many of Marx's and Engels' ideas on women were in fact derived from the utopians. In Engels, particularly, there is the added dimension of the materialist conception of history, and the placing of the human essence into labour. Engels also suggests that the family as a social unit, domestic labour and the position of women were not essentially part of nature but were rather due to mutable, historical and material circumstances, labour and the nature of property. The central contention was that the oppression of women was rooted in the impersonal logic of capitalism and private property, although Engels still made the fatal assumption, for many later feminists, of assuming some natural division of labour. Engels, unlike Marx, developed these ideas in his well-known work *The Origin of the Family, Private Property and the State.*

August Bebel (1840–1913), a leading figure and co-founder of the German SPD, followed roughly the same track as Engels, but his work *Women under Socialism* was, at the time of its publication, more overtly popular.[31] Bebel, despite some sympathy with J. S. Mill and Mary Wollstonecraft, argued that bourgeois liberal reform was in the end ineffective.[32] Bebel tried to show the economic factors underpinning social and legal inequality. In bourgeois marriage, private property is fundamental. For Bebel, women needed liberation from both bourgeois property and its concomitant, domestic slavery. Moreover, to gain true liberation, they needed to join the historic struggle of the proletariat as a whole. As a number of commentators have noted, the end product of Bebel's reflections is more imaginative than Engels'. In Bebel we have Fourier without the eroticism. He was deeply impressed by the 1892 Chicago Exhibition, specifically the time-saving electrical gadgets for the kitchen and household. His vision was of an administered society, with a great deal of leisure, art and science, low-cost food, air travel, and masses of electrical devices. Children would become a public responsibility. Monogamous relationships, however, if freely chosen on the basis of love, would still be present.

Alexandra Kollontai, Clara Zetkin and Charlotte Perkins Gillman extended the Marxian framework into the twentieth century, particularly Kollontai in the context of the Russian Revolution. By and large, most orthodox socialist interpretations of the role of women, from 1920 until the late 1950s, were embodied within a utopian or Marx–Engels format. The late 1960s and early 1970s saw some qualified rejection of this older framework, particularly of Engels, and an attempt to forge a new socialist feminism. The older Marx and Engels position was seen to be 'sex-blind'. As yet this movement has not moved very far from the stage of negative appraisal of traditional Marxism. Alison Jaggar comments on this: 'Socialist feminism is a very recent political tendency and it is still undeveloped, both practically and theoretically. For this reason, one cannot turn to an existing body of systematic theory ... Instead, one must attempt to extrapolate a systematic theory from the existing fragments.'[33]

The school of radical feminism is undoubtedly more than anything an American development. It has made few inroads into European feminism, although some still try to identify it as the major component of the 'second wave'. Radical feminism began in the late 1960s and early 1970s. The word itself has had a shifting meaning. Some have seen it as the great hope of feminism; others, like Betty Friedan, view it as the Achilles heel. The apparent extremes of radicalism have been seen as a reaction to the rightward move of politics in the 1980s, although the roots of radicalism in fact pre-date the emergence of the phenomenon of the New Right.

Radical feminism is a somewhat elitist movement sparked, as Alison Jaggar remarked, from 'the special experiences of a relatively small group of predominantly white, middle-class, college-educated American women'.[34] This elitism and occasional intellectual strangeness has had an alienating effect on many women encountering the ideas of radical feminism. Initially, radicalism derived from an acerbic critical relation to Marxism in the late 1960s. In one sense it represented a rejection of the Marxist New Left. Radicals argued, far more vigorously than the socialist feminists of the 1970s, that Marxism was 'sex-blind'. Yet their own arguments utilized both radicalized Freudian psychoanalysis and forms of social theory that bear the imprint of some New Left writers, like Wilhelm Reich and Herbert Marcuse.[35]

It is difficult to say whether there is an explicit theory at work within the radical perspective. Jaggar comments that radical feminists 'are not identified by adherence to an explicit and systematic political theory'.[36] Readers of the radical literature over the last two decades can encounter everything from Zen Buddhism to astrology. In this context it is difficult to find consistency in the ideas. There are two substantive reasons for this. Rational consistency itself is subject to critical debate within radical feminist thinking. It is contended that Cartesian rationality may be another aspect of male domination.[37] It is doubtful whether we will be able to identify the central values of radical feminism; there are too many different and often profoundly incommensurable views expressed within it.

Despite this ambiguity certain characteristics do stand out for both observers, protagonists and critics of radical feminism. Unlike the socialist feminists, many radicals formulate their ideas in an ahistorical, universalistic manner. This is partly due to the fact that many of their ideas are rooted in an emphasis on biologism and psychologism. They often contend that there are 'essential' universal characteristics to all women. Further, radicals do not suffer any of the anguish of socialist feminists on notions of sex and class. This is virtually absent from their writings. Despite the comparatively small size of the radical group, because of their outspoken commitment to certain ideas, they have probably acquired more of a reputation than other schools. Certain over-arching, often contradictory ideas have characterized the movement: for example, a concern to attack all forms of patriarchy and sexism, a belief in both androgyny and difference, the sex and gender debate, political lesbianism, mothering, studies on the character of rape and radical views on the future of the family.

Another more recent development, which has been a subject of debate in the late 1970s and early 1980s, is the relation between socialist and radical feminism. There are claims that a new self-critical socialist feminism (distinct from the older Marxist forms) has the possibility of forming a single systematic theory with radicalism. Others see a 'dual system' developing between the two. Yet others deny that there should be any relation at all between radicalism and socialism.

The late 1980s has also seen a steady growth of feminist interest in poststructuralism, deconstruction theory and postmodernism, initially from the areas of literary and cultural criticism. Derrida, Lyotard, Foucault and Rorty are the key influences on these strands. One of the first to develop this form of theorizing was the French-based strand of poststructuralist psychoanalytic feminism, particularly the writings of Julia Kristeva, Hélène Cixous and Luce Irigaray.[38] There has also been an enthusiastic American following for these writers.

The central issue is that language embodies our reality. The idea derives from Ferdinand Saussure. Speech as a collection of signs is underpinned by language which is understood as a formal system of underlying conventions. The laws of language form a deep structure to speech and such underlying structures can be studied scientifically. This structuralist idea influenced a number of theorists like Claude Lévi-Strauss and Roland Barthes. The common theme was that buried structures had to be uncovered to reveal meanings. These deep meanings were constituted by certain basic binary oppositions, like raw/cooked or man/woman. Signs do not work on their own but rather in the context of a network of contrasts, oppositions or differences, which constitute a language. The idea that we are constituted by the underlying structures of language was also developed by the French psychoanalytic theorist, Jacques Lacan. The parallel between, on the one hand, the surface of speech and the underlying deep structure of conventions, and, on the other hand, the psychoanalytic notion of conscious and unconscious, is fundamental to Lacan's thinking. For Lacan, the unconscious structures constitute our identity. The uncovering of language through language is the nub of Lacanian psychotherapy. This is one of the keys to understanding the character of the French feminist theories.

However, Foucault's poststructuralism and Derrida's deconstruction challenged the basic foundational binary oppositions uncovered by structuralists. Foucault deconstructed in order to show the 'power' underlying our knowledge and language. All the apparent intellectual assumptions of Western thought are divested of their epistemic privilege, and that includes notions of rationality and human agency. Foucault uses the Nietzschean notion of *genealogy* here to unpack these oppositions. Genealogy exposes the motives, pressures and power underlying our supposed rationality. All the sciences and disciplines (what Foucault calls our 'discursive formations') are shown to be congealed sets of preconceptual, unrationalized elements which constitute a society's regime of truth.

As suggested by the title of his work, *Margins of Philosophy*, Derrida's deconstruction idea works in a less overtly political manner. He is not concerned to 'show' the power underlying knowledge or discursive formations. Rather he tries, with an immensely close and sensitive reading, to examine the basic, often unconscious conventions, beliefs and oppositions within texts, in order to exhibit their arbitrariness or ambiguity. For Derrida it is the casual metaphors, footnotes, or margins of the text which are most revealing on these underlying assumptions. As one writer observes:

> Deconstruction, at its simplest, consists of reading a text so closely that the conceptual distinctions, on which the text relies, are shown to fail on account of the inconsistent and paradoxial employment of these very concepts within the text as a whole. Thus the text is seen to fall by its own criteria.[39]

Meaning, for Derrida, becomes immensely difficult to establish. It is never simply present in any text. Meaning remains deferred and difficult to pin down, playing endlessly within the complex web of language and experience. There is no pure meaning marking something objective in the world. There is also nothing outside 'the sign' and no definitive one meaning to a sign. This is the substance to Derrida's neologism *différance*. The meaning of a sign is dispersed throughout the whole body of signifiers. Thus final meaning is always withheld and deconstruction represents a permanent withholding operation. We remain suspended between alternatives. The attempt to fix upon a certain meaning, which Derrida terms 'logocentrism', is doomed to failure.

Postmodernism is immensely difficult to grasp or pin down. It represents many different things. Its primary influence has been in areas like architecture and fine art. In the art world it usually denotes a mixing of traditional styles and a celebration and play on their differences. In this sense, some see it as a reaction to the confining style of modernism (although it is interpreted by others as an extension of modernism). Literature and social and political theory are harder to explain in postmodern terms. For example, are James Joyce's *Ulysses*, T. S. Eliot's *Wasteland* or Ezra Pound's *Cantos* modernist or postmodern? They have been seen as the crowning achievement of modernism, although they also embody multiple traditional styles and 'rhetorics' in the characteristic postmodern vein.

In social and political theory, postmodernism represents a caricature of poststructuralism and deconstruction. Baudrillard and Lyotard are better described as postmodernist than are Derrida or Foucault. Postmodernists generally contend that there are no privileged authorities and that post-modernism itself is *not* a new style. Lyotard, for example, speaks of the postmodern condition as 'incredulity to metanarrative'.[40] All we have are multiple socially constructed fictional discourses. Postmodern theorists play and ironize among these fictions, refusing to synthesize or reify any of them. They thus oppose all closure, totalizing discourse and erasure of difference. They do not believe in truth, rationality, knowledge, subject-centred inquiry or the search for a coherent epistemology. The human self becomes a series of surface signifiers with no depth. Contradiction, difference and incoherence are welcomed. Therefore the task of the post-modernist is to disorder, debunk all attempts at certainty, closure or (to misuse Derrida's term slightly) 'logocentrism'. There is no objective account of reality, no certainty but uncertainty.

The French feminists have adopted some of these elements, reading Lacan's psychoanalytic structuralism through poststructuralist eyes. They contend that there is nothing outside language — no *hors texte*. As Cixous states, 'Everything is word, everything is only word ... we must grab culture by the word, as it seizes us in its words, in its language'.[41] The world is a text, or series of texts, embodying symbolic systems based upon certain basic binary oppositions of subject and object, reason and emotion, truth and falsity. Using, but changing, the more Foucaultian poststructuralism, the French feminists try to show the *male* power under-lying these oppositions in language. As Mary Hawkesworth notes:

> the locus of the individual's acquisition of language and the origin of all culture and social life, is characterized as unidimensional, structured in accordance with 'l'hom(m)o sexualité' ... Because it is language that structures sexuality around the male terms within systems of consciousness, the problematic of language and the problematic of sexuality become coterminous for women.[42]

Following Derrida's description of closure as 'logocentrism', Luce Irigaray suggests that this underlying male closure in language is 'phallocentrism', which represents a form of deep linguistic patriarchy. This is a form of oppression not previously perceived. What we think we perceive as the real is in fact the symbolic order constructed by men.

There are a number of things that can be done here. First, Irigaray advocates disrupting or deconstructing this male discourse, to resist all male attempts at systematization and to 'interrogate *the conditions under which systematicity is possible*' and consequently to concentrate, in good deconstructionist style, on the metaphors, margins and codes of male discourse.[43] Like Lacan's linguistically orientated psychotherapy, the French feminists see language as an area for therapeutic renewal. In this context, a second strategy is suggested, namely, to construct a woman's language and writing. Women must write and speak themselves into existence. Thus Irigaray uses the term *le parler femme* (women's speech) and Cixous *écriture feminine* (women's writing). These will allow them to express their unique character or 'sex-embodiness', which will liberate them from linguistic phallocentric patriarchy.

The above ideas do not totally correspond with postmodernism, although there are many overlaps. Many who regard themselves as postmodernist feminists are in fact followers of the French theorists. Full-blown postmodernism resists *all* closure. Having let the (non-Derridean) deconstruction genii out of the bottle, every discourse is disrupted, not just male discourse. Namely, reason is completely disordered and all certainty or privilege, including *écriture feminine*, is lost in the fictional play of language. Those, like Jane Flax or Christine Sylvester, who see themselves as postmodern feminists create more problems than they solve. Surely feminism itself, in this context, becomes another suspect certainty which needs disrupting. Thus Toril Moi asks: 'Is "postmodern feminism" simply another oxymoron, a new quagmire of contradictions for feminists to sink in?'[44]

It is not surprising that the French feminists (with one eye on deconstruction) are suspicious of the title 'feminist', because of its more overtly reformist and 'grand narrative' implications. There are enormous problems with French feminism which will be touched upon later, not least, in many feminist eyes, because once again it draws attention to women's difference, essentializing womanhood. It is also profoundly intellectually elitist and theorizes about language at the expense of social, economic and political concerns. The notion of full feminist postmodernism remains vague. It is difficult to use it as a marker (not that postmodernists appear to like markers, except as fictions). Some critics even regard it as a totally frivolous nihilism, an opiate for privileged intellectuals. In addition, the relation of poststructuralism and deconstruction to postmodernism is a matter of intense debate. Some theorists crush them into the same postmodern entity, others, with some justification, separate out poststructuralism, deconstruction *and* postmodernism into different endeavours. These, and other points, make the notion of postmodern feminism difficult to handle.

Finally, a number of recent debates in feminism have circled around the question of maternal thinking and caring. The psychoanalytic work of Nancy Chodorow and then Carol Gilligan, in the early 1980s, on the distinctive qualities of the female personality, gave rise to the supposition that because women are brought up in a society structured by gender (where women care for children), in consequence they have a different moral view on the world. For Gilligan, especially, women have a 'caring' approach: they are more altruistic, nurturing and self-sacrificing. Gilligan links this disposition with an 'ethic of care' which she contrasts to a more

male-orientated 'ethic of justice'.[45] Morality for women is therefore more
concerned with a caring disposition, attending to responsibilities and
relationships, than with finding the right or best principle, following rules
and focusing on rights and fairness, which are characteristic of the ethic
of justice. Other writers, like Sara Ruddick and J. B. Elshtain, also argue
that women are primarily involved in nurturing and preserving the lives of
children; unlike Gilligan, however, they think that such an idea could
have an immense impact on restructuring the public sphere. Ruddick and
Elshtain in particular think that 'maternal thinkers who make responsibility
to children and families their central commitment could radically reform
public values, could even create an "ethical polity" devoted to a politics
of compassion'.[46] They believe that this could have a dramatic impact
on politics in general.

This particular debate has given rise to two further developments. First,
the 'maternal thinking' argument has been vigorously contested from
a 'civic feminist' perspective. Mary Dietz's work is probably the most
systematic to date. She adopts a more traditional, virtually liberal feminist
stance, arguing that women and men, as citizens, 'can collectively and
inclusively relate to one another ... as equals who render judgements on
matters of shared importance, deliberate over issues of common concern,
and act in concert with one another'.[47] Dietz puts forward a reinvigorated
social liberal feminist case for equality and consequently denies the relevance of male and female difference. The second development is the
maternal thinking position taken by Elshtain and Ruddick (although not
necessarily Gilligan), which is now sometimes called 'conservative pro-
family feminism'.[48] This latter group has not been well received by other
sections of the feminist movement. It is regarded as a move backwards
into the older stereotyping of women's difference into gender roles.[49]

Given the diversity of feminist thought it is difficult to identify clear
motifs within the feminist movement. However, it is possible to discern
certain broad formal themes which have been the common core of much
feminist reflection. The response to these themes is in itself quite diverse.
Those that will be dealt with in the remainder of this chapter are: sex and
gender, the nature of oppression and subordination, the issue of equality
and difference, and the personal as the political.

SEX AND GENDER

This section touches upon the more traditional issue of human nature.
In the case of feminism, human nature is tied to one of the key issues
of ideological discussion and therefore must be approached in a rather
oblique manner. It is sometimes contended that feminism 'does not entail
any particular view of human nature'.[50] Despite this point, accounts of

human nature are given by some feminist writers, accounts which overlap with other ideologies like liberalism. Others are more concerned to question the relation of sexuality and gender to human nature. In this context the issue of human nature is not absent but is slightly more complex and difficult to articulate.

The problem of sex and gender has parallels with the debates on nature and nurture. The central issue here is whether the nature of women is biologically determined or socially constructed. The usual response to this is to argue that gender is a socially constructed artifice, whereas sex is biological. Women have been slotted into certain roles 'as if' they were natural or biologically determined for them. Such roles in fact have nothing natural about them. The psychology of women has been defined by men. The task of feminism is therefore to make women aware of this fact.

This particular argument can be found in a different format in the early liberal feminists like Mary Wollstonecraft. One of her primary claims was that women should not be identified as sexual beings, but rather as human beings. The terminology here is slightly different to the sex and gender debate, but close enough for some comparisons. Wollstonecraft was using the notion of 'sex' as virtually equivalent to gender, although she was also contending that even the biological aspect of women was not really an important point of difference. As she argued: 'The first object of laudable ambitions is to obtain a character as a human being, regardless of the distinction of sex'.[51] The important point was that the distinguishing mark of humans, as opposed to 'brute creation', was human reason. Sexuality, as such, was not very significant. Reason was understood as 'the simple power of improvement; or, more properly speaking, of discerning truth'.[52] As Wollstonecraft argued: 'The perfection of our nature and capability of happiness must be estimated by the degree of reason'.[53] A woman's first duty was therefore to reason. In fact, any duty she might be required to perform required reason, for 'how can a woman be expected to cooperate unless she knows why she ought to be virtuous?'.[54] The target for much of Wollstonecraft's argument was in fact Rousseau. She returned to him frequently during the course of the text. Rousseau, in works like *Emile*, had emphasized the sexual nature of women. He dwelt upon their submissiveness, dependence, voluptuousness and amusement for males. Furthermore, Rousseau had contrasted civic equality with the natural order of the family, predicated on the difference of the sexes. Women, because of their nature, appeared unsuited to the public, autonomous role of citizens. For Wollstonecraft, this idea of sexual difference in Rousseau was a destructive and dangerous artifice.

Wollstonecraft also uses arguments based upon the existence of a rational God to support her thesis concerning human nature. In short, she contends that a rational God would not create one half of the human race virtually mindless. Her religious mentor, Richard Price, had argued that all humans were equal and responsible before God. How, therefore, could women be excluded? As Wollstonecraft argued: 'Why should the gracious fountain of life give us passions, the power of reflecting, only to imbitter our days and inspire us with mistaken notions of dignity?'[55]

Apart from the theological theme, this argument is echoed in a different context by J. S. Mill. Women's sexual nature is again seen to be a socialized artifice. 'I deny,' says Mill, 'that anyone knows, or can know, the nature of the two sexes . . . What is now called the nature of woman is an eminently artificial thing — the result of forced repression.'[56] For Mill, we are clearly ignorant of the conditions in which character is formed; in fact, the majority of men appear to be plainly ignorant about women.[57] According to Mill, it cannot be said that women accept their servitude as natural. They campaign for suffrage, education and the like. Most often it is unreasoning male habits which keep women in such servitude. If women can develop and grow, then there are no grounds for seeing them as inferior. The liberation of women, for Mill, is thus only a matter of time. In the same way as slaves, vassals and black people have been liberated, so also will women. As he put it: 'The social subordination of women thus stands out as an isolated fact in modern social institutions'.[58]

In the early Marxist accounts, the natures of women and men are formed by historical and economic circumstances, although those specific circumstances can dictate markedly different roles for the sexes. As Marx and Engels stated in *The German Ideology*, 'The first division of labour is that between man and woman for child breeding'.[59] This thesis was developed by Engels in later writings. Women and the family are rooted, at least by Engels, in the economic conditions of life. Monogamous marriage leaves most women in the position of domestic slaves. Man earns the family wage (at least in propertied classes) and his wife works at home. As Engels remarked: 'In the family, he is the bourgeois; the wife represents the proletariat'.[60]

The difficulty of speaking about human nature in Marxism is its mutability. It would be hard to make out a clear case for the universality or unchangeable qualities of human nature within this argument. The apparent nature of humans is not fixed, but changes through historical circumstances. Thus the Marxist feminist finds some firm theoretical backing for the claim that much of the sexual/gendered nature of women is a product of particular historical and economic conditions of life. This lends more credence to the claim that artifice is at work. In the final analysis, this might lead to the conclusion that there are no significant differences between men and women. Nearly every role can be performed by both sexes.

Despite the above theoretical conclusion, many early male Marxist writers still appeared to accept the more domestic role of women. This latter tendency has been thoroughly criticized by socialist feminists since the late 1960s. They have, in consequence, pushed their analysis of the division of labour into the realm of the family. They have accepted certain aspects of the radicals' analysis, namely, that in addition to historical and economic conditions there are also biological and psychic aspects to the exploitation of women. As one writer has argued, traditional Marxism has come to be viewed as a halfway house where 'unspecified biological differences between men and women would mean that there could never be a complete abolition of the sexual division of labour'.[61]

The future of human nature in this more recent form of socialist feminism is more or less genderless and sexless. This would in fact appear to be the logical implication of the original Marxist argument. The ideal of many of the recent socialist feminists is therefore 'that woman (and man) will disappear as socially constituted categories'.[62] This process would be advanced if technologies developed to such a point where women could be relieved from both pregnancy and childbirth.

Many of the diverse elements of radicalism, which have used the sex/gender argument most robustly, are none the less deeply critical of both the socialist-Marxist and liberal perspectives. As one radical writer, Catherine Mackinnon, has commented, radicalism

> stands to marxism as marxism does to classical political economy: its final conclusion and its ultimate critique. Compared with marxism, the place of thought and things in method and reality are reversed in a seizure of power that penetrates subject and object and theory with practice. In dual motion, feminism turns marxism inside out and on its head.[63]

Marxist socialism, in this interpretation, always denotes a certain type of method, which Mackinnon identifies as dialectical materialism. Genuine feminism (by which Mackinnon means radical feminism) is alternatively concerned with the very different method of consciousness-raising, which she describes as 'the collective critical reconstitution of the meaning of woman's social experience'.[64] Thus, she contends that the two methods are fundamentally irreconcilable.

For all the confidence of much of the radicals' analysis there is little consistency on the question of human nature and the sex/gender issue. The earliest statements on the question arise in Simone de Beauvoir's writings.[65] She rejected many of the biological and historical materialist accounts. For Beauvoir, women have essentially the same nature as man, but they have been hampered and enslaved by one important fact — their bodies. The body does not determine the true nature of women, but it does explain much about their history. Despite some lack of intellectual sympathy with the feminist movement, she did envisage the future of women in fairly optimistic terms. With the greater availability of abortion, effective birth control and the redundancy of monogamy, women might finally begin to gain control of their bodies and join men in their cultural projects. Maternity would cease to rule the destiny of women. As Beauvoir put it: 'The fact that we are human beings is infinitely more important than all the peculiarities that distinguish human beings from one another'.[66] Some more recent radicals find Beauvoir's analysis lacking in awareness of the depth of patriarchy and the nature of women's oppression.

Beauvoir's position, which has parallels with some of the early liberal arguments (although set in a totally different philosophical framework, namely, her commitment to Sartrean existential philosophy), is worth comparison with another of the early radicals, Shulamith Firestone. Firestone's work *The Dialectic of Sex*, like Beauvoir's, argued that men and women are not really very different. For Firestone, as with Beauvoir but stated in much stronger terminology, it is the biology of women which determines their 'sex class' (a novel term introduced by Firestone to integrate Marxism into the analysis).[67] The sex class is embedded in the family, where women and children are at the mercy of men. Biologically reproductive differences lead to sexual divisions of labour. Firestone looks to new technologies for liberation. These technologies are far more extensive than anything anticipated by Beauvoir. Artificial insemination, test-tube babies, and domestic cybernetics will emancipate women (and children) from their biology. Firestone contends that with advances in medical science there is the possibility of males carrying the foetus in implanted wombs and possibly eventually lactating. Gender and sex will thus become redundant in an androgynous or unisex future.[68]

These early phases have been superseded by other attitudes and theories within radicalism. An androgynous aim may be a valuable ideal to strive for, but gender is the source of many problems which must be addressed, particularly male patriarchal exploitation. In addition, there are aspects of the masculine nature which radicals find abhorrent, for example, sexism, aggression and the potentiality for rape. Rape is, in fact, seen by some radicals as the defining aspect of masculinity and patriarchy.[69] As Robin Morgan put it, 'The violation of an individual woman is the *metaphor* for man's forcing himself on whole nations'.[70] Women, it was argued, would not wish to combine with any such masculine features in an androgynous future.

Radical feminists thus moved away from androgyny towards criticism of the 'male nature' and the way in which men tried to define femininity. This criticism had both a negative and a positive side. The negative side involves a critique of the masculine nature as the source of most social, political and international problems. For Andrea Dworkin masculinity *per se* represents death, violence and destructiveness.[71] Women, in this reading, are always the victims. Widely publicized information about rape, the nature and effects of pornography, and the abuse of women in marriage, have increased the profile of this point, although, again more recently, this kind of approach has been criticized for 'essentializing' the nature of women.[72] On the positive side, the nature and qualities of the female are held to be morally and spiritually superior and consequently lead to 'woman-centred analysis'.

Woman-centred analysis can take different forms. Some writers praise aspects of the feminine which were previously perceived as taboos or obstacles to women's lives, such as menstruation, motherhood and maternal thinking. More recently, 'maternal thinking' has taken on a high profile in the writings of Elshtain, Sara Ruddick and Carol Gilligan, although the latter theorist has not emphasized the impact of maternal thinking on the public realm. Ruddick's and Elshtain's views have been accused of promoting a conservative pro-family perspective which drives women back into the home. In this latter debate the argument on maternal thinking, as a way of criticizing the male mode of thought, loses some of its sting. Women's thought is accorded crucial importance, but not as a direct replacement for male thought. Elshtain claims, though, that these nurturing qualities should be manifest in the public sphere as well as in the family.

Other writers use this approach as a radical cultural device. As Jane Alpert comments:

> Feminine culture is based on what is best and strongest in women, and as we begin to define ourselves as women, the qualities coming to the fore are the same ones as a mother projects in the best kind of nurturing relationship to a child: empathy, intuitiveness, adaptability, awareness of growth as a process rather than as goal-ended, inventiveness, protective feeling towards others, and a capacity to respond emotionally as well as rationally.[73]

In Mary Daly, this cultural radical feminism emphasizes that women and their culture are both different and culturally superior to males. Such difference is expressed through the whole lifestyle and thought of women. Postmodernist feminists and poststructuralists would tend to oppose the fictional binary opposition of linguistic terms like masculine or feminism. The qualities which we associate with them could in fact be adopted by either sex. Thus this whole debate would be seen as a rhetorical fiction.

Other recent radicals, ignoring the postmodernists, have confidently suggested that 'feminine thinking' might be extended into a new form of superior epistemology and natural science. This aspect of radicalism has occasionally been singled out as a distinctive school called 'radical standpoint feminism'.[74] Standpoint theory, like postmodernism or post-structuralism, attacks notions of objectivity in science, rationality and logic in Western thought. This forms the basis to the question of whether 'the whole process of rational and scientific discourse might not be somehow inherently masculine'.[75] Masculine thought is seen to work in certain ways: for example, conceptually separating mind and matter, self and other, reason and emotion. Writers like Adrienne Rich, Catherine Mackinnon and Evelyn Fox Keller have consequently argued that the very notion of objectivity and rationality implies distance and separation which coincide with the male desire for autonomy – with all the problems accruing from such an attitude.[76] However, unlike postmodernism and poststructuralism, standpoint theory rejects relativism and present epistemology in the name of an as yet unspecified, but none the less superior objective feminine epistemology. In fact, some argue that Western culture is in desperate need of such a new way of thinking.[77]

THE NATURE OF OPPRESSION AND SUBORDINATION

The analysis of oppression follows the same contours of argument as in the previous section of this chapter. The liberal feminist perspective concentrates on justice, equality and rights. For Mary Wollstonecraft, the source of oppression was clear. As she commented:

> Women are everywhere in ... [a] deplorable state; for in order to preserve their innocence ... truth is hidden from them, and they are made to assume an artificial character before their faculties have acquired any strength. Taught from their early infancy that beauty is woman's sceptre, the mind shapes itself to the body, and roaming round its gilt cage only seeks to adore its prison.[78]

Women were denied the means to develop their reason. The gender and character of women were the result of their education. Men expected women to bring up children, act virtuously and manage a household, but this could not be done except by cultivating reason. Men, she complained, acted quite absurdly in this sphere. They wanted women to be noble beings, but tried to deny them the right to rational development. Men argued that women were naturally incapable of benefiting from education and also tried to deny it to them. Women in such an uneducated situation were equivalent to soldiers in a standing army where blind ignorance and obedience were the sole requirements. Such a mentality could only appeal to a despot.[79] Thus the source of oppression of women was the irrational denial of rights, particularly to education and the cultivation of reason. Ultimately such cultivation would lead some women to participate in employment and commerce. The purpose of Wollstonecraft's book was therefore to persuade men by reason to acknowledge and uphold the rights of women.

For J. S. Mill, the roots of oppression lay in a number of disreputable male motives. Like Bentham, Mill repudiated the natural rights perspective, although not the idea of legal rights for women. Men, in complete ignorance, claimed that women were naturally inferior. Yet, like Wollstonecraft, Mill contended that 'what women by nature cannot do, it is quite superfluous to forbid them doing'.[80] Men appeal to custom to uphold their oppression, but absolute monarchy and black slavery have appealed to the same idea. We should therefore be sceptical of such notions. Women could be educated and develop their own plans of life. Again Mill looked to the repudiation of certain legal and educational limitations on women for the sake of human progress. As he commented:

> the principle which regulates the existing social relations between the sexes – the legal subordination of one sex to the other – is wrong in itself, and now one of the chief hindrances to human improvement; and that it ought to be replaced by a principle of perfect equality, admitting no power or privilege on the one side, nor disability on the other.[81]

In one of his earliest essays, 'On the Jewish Question', Marx, like Mill, scorned the natural rights perspective. Marx, however, saw it as a cover for bourgeois property interests. Oppression is premised on the class and economic relations within capitalism. Women's oppression is rooted in the impersonal logic of capitalist expropriation. The family, private property, division of labour, domestic labour and the position of women are due to mutable historical and economic circumstances which underpin the legal and political injustices. As Engels remarked on the origin of monogamous marriage: 'It was the first form of the family based not in natural but in economic condition, namely, in the victory of private property over original, naturally developed, common ownership'.[82] For Engels, the first forms of exploitation can be observed in the family, namely, that the well-being of the man is maintained on the basis of the repression of the woman. The majority of women do not stay with men for love, but for economic support. It is thus that we have Engels' famous description of bourgeois marriage as legalized prostitution.[83]

The key to understanding oppression, in the view of many radical and socialist feminists, is encapsulated in the term *patriarchy*. Patriarchy is 'a political structure which favours man'.[84] The essence of this view is not to locate the oppression of women in legal and social rights or economic determinism, but rather in the deep psychic roots of masculine psychology, thought and language. Patriarchy lies in the masculine demeanour. The tendency is thus psychological, linguistic and biological. This masculine demeanour may be wholly identified with the male sex; alternatively it may be identified with certain qualities which could, in theory, be manifest in either sex.

The more recent socialist feminists find themselves in an uncomfortable situation here. In interpreting patriarchy they have tried to uphold, on the one hand, the historically mutable economic dimension and, on the other hand, the radicals' universalistic biological, linguistic, psychological and essentialist claims. For socialists, 'male supremacy and capitalism are defined as the core relations determining the oppression of women today'.[85]

Traditional Marxism is seen to be 'sex-blind', but the opposite error is committed by radicals who are accused of being 'history-blind', namely, ignoring the historical and material base to patriarchy.[86] Traditional Marxism failed to recognize the other forms of oppression suffered by women. This is the oppression which pre-dates and will post-date capitalism, and which results from reproduction and domesticity. By concentrating on large-scale industry, traditional Marxists failed to analyse women as workers in domestic settings (since the proletariat were viewed *within* industry). They also failed to note who benefits from such domestic labour.[87]

Socialist feminists are therefore attempting to widen our understanding of the division of labour and the oppression of women, to focus our attention on crucial links between reproduction and production, and thus on the role of the family within capitalism. In this sense, the understanding of women's alienation and oppression is deepened. Patriarchy is a combination of economic and sexual factors. Capitalism functions *with* patriarchy. The oppression of women is thus more deeply entrenched than suspected by traditional Marxism. Patriarchy has a material base.

The reaction of many radicals to this analysis is predictable. The oppression of women has its roots in the male biology and psychology. Some see this oppression in the very notion of masculinity, which is rooted in violence and aggression. For others, this violence and dominance is rooted in male language, thought and behaviour. French feminism has concentrated its attention on this latter area of language embodying 'phallocentric' concerns. The more psychoanalytic approach, in writers like Kate Millett, suggests that gender roles are socialized into children through the family and often reinforced by religion, myth and education. This at least provides some hope that males can be socialized into more acceptable attitudes in future. In the case of Irigaray, Cixous and Kristeva, therapy is premised upon women developing their own forms of language and writing.

EQUALITY AND DIFFERENCE

The idea of equality again highlights some of the central tensions within the feminist movement as a whole. Despite the fact that equality takes a very high profile within the liberal feminist perspective, it is regarded by Marxist feminists as suspect. Some radicals also have their suspicions about equality as a way of assimilating females into male norms. It is, of course, possible to be different but still equal. Yet in some cases feminists have argued that they simply do not want equality with men, since females are by nature superior, something the American liberal feminist Betty Friedan has called 'female chauvinism'. The central problem of the equality-and-difference argument is therefore focused on the question: should the aim of feminism be civil, political and social equality or, alternatively, should women repudiate equality and celebrate their difference? In recent years, a number of problems have arisen concerning the ambiguity of the notion of 'difference' and whether there is any 'essential' masculine or feminine gender. This latter issue ties in with the postmodernist refusal to reify any categories (such as gender).

The equality argument has had its most vigorous support in the more liberal wing of feminism. Equality is measured by Wollstonecraft in terms of legal rights to basic civil freedoms. Wollstonecraft's target was as much aristocratic as male privileges, namely the Burkean heritage which denied such equal rights and insisted on legal and political hierarchies. She was thinking here primarily of rights to life, liberty, economic independence, education, and access to the professions.[88] For Wollstonecraft, God 'impressed' such rights equally on all human souls. Apart from overt physical strength there is, according to Wollstonecraft, very little difference between men and women. In fact, women in the future should be able to strengthen both their bodies and their minds.

In the later nineteenth century, liberal equality arguments focused on the demand for the extension of political rights of suffrage. Mill, in his writings, contended that liberty is the great want of human nature. Without the chance to form one's own plan of life the individual remains stunted.[89] Maximizing liberty entailed maximizing utility. Liberty, for Mill, necessarily leads to a presumption in favour of equality. For Mill, contracts, marriage law, property law, education and suffrage should all be equalized.[90]

In the twentieth century, the liberal feminists have concentrated their attention on acquiring equality across a range of social welfare rights. In some cases the demand has been for increasing support and benefits for families and children; in others, for totally equal opportunities in terms of education, employment, pay, marriage, property, political participation and citizenship.[91] Such demands have had some marked successes in Britain and America over the 1960s and 1970s.

Despite the fact that egalitarian themes have punctuated the history of socialism, equality was viewed as just another bourgeois illusion when Marxism dominated the movement. Like justice and rights, it was regarded as part of the liberal capitalist ethos. For Marxists, inequalities undoubtedly exist and will be rectified by communism; inequality *per se* is not an evil, rather it is the symptom of a deeper malaise. Inequality is a feature of a society riven by class conflict. The position of women under capitalism is not due to their unequal treatment. Unequal treatment is a consequence of capitalism itself. Legal, political or social reforms would only be placebos. They would solve no problems. As such, the theme of equality has not made much headway within traditional Marxism and recent socialist feminism.

In the case of the radicals, the theme of equality and difference is pivotal. Initially, there were some egalitarian themes within radical feminism. For example, the early arguments for androgyny were based on a form of egalitarianism. It was a somewhat strange egalitarianism, in some cases premised on technological advances in biology. The later rejection of androgyny, as previously mentioned, led to a critical attitude towards equality both as a value and as a political goal. This is the phase which celebrated women's difference from men. The divide between males and females became known in radical literature as the 'gender gap'.[92]

The arguments surrounding difference theory are quite diverse and the history of its development since the 1960s has been immensely tangled. The earliest ideas on difference go back to theorists like Kate Millett who saw the masculine/feminine distinction as part of patriarchal exploitation. To a large extent the differences were viewed as social artifacts constructed to keep women within certain roles. Difference was then attacked by writers like Shulamith Firestone. In arguing for androgynous equality she wanted to destroy the political uses of difference. In the 1970s, however, difference began to reappear as a virtue. Initially, in the radical cultural feminists, it encompassed notions of female supremicism, the moral superiority of women, the value of sisterhood, political lesbianism, and separatism from men. It was also contended that women have a very different attitude to their bodies from men. The physical capacity to bear children gives the female a highly positive life-affirming attitude, whereas the male is more easily caught up in negative life-denying aggression, ambition and destructiveness. This particular theme has been taken up again by the eco-feminists who will often locate the environmental crisis in negative male values and attitudes to nature.

In the 1980s the tendency to cultural separatism gave way to a number of new developments. First, because of the importance of women's different culture and experience, the academic study of women's distinctive knowledge developed, acquiring the title 'woman-centred analysis'. The differences of women constituted a distinct way of life and thought. This led to the growth of women's studies courses and literature on women. Second, the experience rather than the patriarchal institution of motherhood was again taken seriously, particularly in the writings of Adrienne Rich. Third, the different but unique values of maternal thinking were highlighted. Women's distinct personalities and psyches were explored in the writings of Nancy Chodorow. Others argued that women, unlike men, embodied values of truthfulness, sensitivity to emotion, altruism, cooperation, nurturance and pacifism. Carol Gilligan developed her ideas on women's 'ethic of care' as against the masculinist 'ethic of justice'. Ruddick and Elshtain, also mentioned earlier, suggested that such maternal value and thought could be of immense benefit if brought into the public realm of politics. This has led to the contentious idea of 'pro-family feminism'.

The late 1980s saw the growing influence of French feminism, which also celebrated women's difference. It was suspicious of notions of equality and even of the term feminism as an assimilation into bourgeois reformism.

Although influenced by deconstruction themes and suspicious of the biological conceptions of difference, French feminists none the less repudiated
the masculine 'phallocentric' domination of language and called for a
uniquely different *écriture feminine* – a recoding of language. In this
argument, difference settled upon language. This latter issue overlaps with
'radical standpoint theory', which also contends the necessity for a new
and discrete feminine epistemology and science.

More recently, French feminists and difference theory in general has
been criticized from three perspectives. First, more rigorous feminist postmodernist and poststructuralist critics have drawn attention to the binary
opposition of gender (male and female) which essentializes womanhood,
establishes closure, and favours certain metanarratives.[93] In other words,
the difference arguments rely on certain basic oppositions which themselves
require deconstruction. The meaning of 'male' and 'female' must be deferred.
Simple-minded essentialism of the female obscures a multiplicity of possible
interpretations. Second, a related but more practical criticism of difference
theory contends that the danger of essentializing women is that they will
once again be forced into a 'natural' place in the family, or motherhood.
In this sense, difference, the 'gender gap' and essentialism can be viewed
as devices in the patriarchal toolkit.[94] Third, the supposed difference
between men and women ignores the differences between women themselves, in terms of age, race, class, culture, ethnicity, nationality, sexual
preference and marital status. These differences can, in fact, be far broader
than any supposed and fictive gender difference. To try to crush all women
into one category and all men into another is a form of totalizing and
repressive discourse. In this context, it is also suggested that there are *no*
universal or essential features to women. Gender essences are reified social
constructs. In fact, qualities which we associate with masculinity and
feminity can be practised by both sexes. Men, for example, can also be
cooperative and nurturant.

THE PERSONAL AS THE POLITICAL

In one sense the heading of this section has become the key slogan of the
feminist movement. The idea is fairly simple, although the ramifications
are multiple. The contention is that what have been previously regarded as
the discrete realms of the private and public are in fact deeply ideological
and manipulative devices, reflecting male patriarchal interests. Thus the
time-honoured distinction of 'public' and 'private' is in reality flawed and
obscures some highly political issues.

The origins of the 'personal as political' critique lie in the liberal feminist
position. Liberals have traditionally identified the personal life of individuals, the family, and the economy as private. It is particularly towards

the former two areas that liberal feminists have addressed their criticism. In the case of the early liberal feminists, like Wollstonecraft, the idea that women have their natural place in, and primary duty to, the home is an illusion. Women's first duty is to reason. In fact, this reasoning is a necessary logical preliminary to the performance of any duty, even within the family. As Wollstonecraft argued: 'The mind naturally weakened by depending on authority, never exerts its own powers, and thus the obedient wife is thus rendered a weak indolent mother'.[95] The idea of woman's sexual nature being a natural and private realm, or the notion of the family as a private realm, were seen as absurd propositions to Wollstonecraft. Her own favoured ideal was a civic republican model of the family, as a training ground for the public-spirited citizen and not as a realm of private passions. Marriage should be companionate and friendly in character rather than passionate.[96] Passion disturbs the minds of individuals and undermines the fabric of society.

Mill, and many of the liberal feminist tradition, have shared most of the above sentiments. In the 1960s this issue came to the fore in Betty Friedan's work *The Feminine Mystique*. She coined the phrase, 'the problem which has no name', to describe the fact that many women find themselves in a family context which is private and personal and also supposed to satisfy them, and yet experience deep frustration and discontent, something they cannot quite put a name to. Friedan's contention, in essence, is that all women share a fundamental problem of inequality – in status, rights and opportunities – with men. The private family structure obscures the patriarchal interests of men in maintaining this inequality. Overall, the liberal critique of the personal/political issue is to identify certain rights which are being denied to women. These rights can, in the main, be rectified by legal, social, political and educational reform. Such rectification will not destroy the family. In fact, liberals would still envisage women playing an active role in family life, although men would be expected to take an equal part in domestic work and the rearing of children. The family therefore still has an important traditional role to play, as Wollstonecraft also believed. To some extent this more egalitarian conception of the family would be endorsed by the proponents of 'maternal thinking' and the 'ethic of care', particularly the 'pro-family' feminists. The novel idea of the pro-family feminists is their suggestion that such maternal thinking (from either sex), which has previously been consigned to the family, should in future enter into the public realm. This breaks up the older continuities of the public/private division, in a distinct and original manner.

Marxist and socialist feminists address the problem of the 'personal and political' in the economic sphere although Marxism is predisposed to reject any separation of public and private from the outset. The distinction is regarded as an obscurantist device of liberal capitalist ideology, where the notion 'private' focuses on 'private property'. In Engels, the family is seen to be a historically changing institution. Previous societies have manifested different marital arrangements, like polygamy, according to different modes of production and ownership. The modern patriarchal monogamous family has nothing to do with loving relations; rather 'It was the first form of the family based not on natural but on economic conditions, namely, on the victory of private property over original, naturally developed, common ownership'.[97] The first class antagonisms arise within the family since it is always a situation where 'the well-being and development of the one group are attained by the misery and repression of the other'.[98] The permanent addenda to bourgeois marriage, for Engels, are prostitution and cuckoldry.

Although Engels looked forward to emancipation, easily dissoluble marriages, the destruction of men's dominance and equal employment for women, he still appeared to envisage both the continuance of monogamous marriage and the possibility that it was more natural for women to be involved in the bringing-up of children. Thus a Marxist blessing was put upon a sexual division of labour in the family. Alexander Kollontai did not share this particular idea. Marxism was also criticized by later socialist feminists. Such critics have contended that traditional Marxism did not explain why it was more natural for women to adopt this role.[99] Furthermore, it ignored the deeper roots of patriarchal dominance. There are forms of oppression other than private property and class. Such oppression pre-dates and post-dates capitalism. Marxism therefore needs to become involved in an analysis of women's labour in the family. It needs to ask who benefits from domestic labour. Patriarchal dominance is thus seen to have much deeper, if still material and historical, roots than previously anticipated. Women within this sexual division of labour service both men and capitalism. The subordination of women in the family is part of the economic foundation of society. In this reading, the private and public overlap and interpenetrate. The 'personal as political' is seen to be a deep-rooted biological, psychological, historical and fundamentally economic fact.[100] This focus on the family has led to a number of debates spilling over into New Left circles on the question of the Marxist interpretation of such things as housework and domestic labour.[101]

In the case of the radicals, the tendency has been to extend the critique of patriarchy within personal life to include biological, psychological and linguistic perspectives. Radical feminists have in fact made the most use of this 'personal as political' critique. They have tried to tackle the problem of patriarchy head on. They tend to relocate the whole issue of power in the personal realm and totally deny the private/public divide. For some radicals, male power in the personal realm is identified universally and ahistorically across cultures in practices like suttee, foot-binding, rape, pornography, genital mutilation, witch-burning and even male-dominated gynaecology. Mary Daly, for example, sees these as universal male sadomasochistic rituals designed to discipline and subdue women.[102] For some radicals the present culture of Western, and other, societies embodies a form of what has been called 'sexual fascism'. The personal and political in this case radically intersect. Radical standpoint theorists have also argued that even male language, rationality, science and philosophy embody subtle, deep-rooted forms of patriarchal domination. Thus, if a women believes that she is free from political manipulation when she is thinking in a private and personal manner, she is fundamentally mistaken. Male patriarchal epistemology can dominate even her most personal thoughts. The standpoint argument overlaps again with the French feminists, who contend that masculine themes (especially binary oppositions like public and private) dominate language and the construction of the self. It is less certain what the postmodern feminists would make of this argument except to deny – again – the opposition between public and private. If rigorous, they would also deny any counter-narrative which saw the public or private interpenetrated by political themes. In addition, postmodern critiques would see the universalizing and essentializing of women across cultures as completely illegitimate.

Such beliefs on the 'personal as political' have led many radical feminists to suggest extreme policies like separatism (separate living from men) and to formulate distinct feminine modes of thought. This in turn has led to some very damning indictments of the family and, in many cases, to a recommendation for its abandonment and suggestions for new forms of communal living.

CONCLUSION

The primary objective of liberal feminists is to bring women into the full rights of democratic citizenship. They envisage a future where legal, political, social and economic rights will have been achieved for all women. They will be on an equal footing with men in all spheres. This will be brought about by reason, persuasion and constitutional reform. The reformed family will remain, but men will have an equal role in domestic duties, and women's careers and lives will in no way be artificially hampered by the rearing of children. The institution of the family is thus seen to have a continuing and important role but it will be supported financially and socially in order to prevent inequalities occurring. Heterosexuality in established relationships is still seen as the social norm. Liberal feminism thus anticipates a future of total sexual justice. This would appear to be the aim of 'civic feminism'.[103] Maternal thinkers like Elshtain would most likely endorse the liberal picture, but would contend that the values and dispositions of women should carry over equally into the public realm.

Traditional Marxism envisaged women entering more fully into the workforce in large-scale industry. As Engels argued, 'The emancipation of women becomes possible when women are enabled to take part in production on a large, social scale, and when domestic duties require their attention only to a minor degree'.[104] Engels also favoured more easily dissoluble marriages, as well as economic independence. Kollontai, during the early stages of the Russian Revolution, was responsible for the intro- duction of a number of proposals and laws on women's issues, later stifled by Stalin. She managed, for example, to arrange for centralized domestic cleaning services, nurseries and child-care, and public kitchens, and worked towards the possibility of communal households in the future, mass free education and abortion on demand. She also believed (like Wollstonecraft) that intense monogamous relations should be discouraged since these made women vulnerable to men, and (unlike Wollstonecraft) that frequent changes of partner were far healthier. This gave rise to a remark, which is often quoted out of context, that sex is like thirst and needs simply to be satisfied. In Kollontai's view, sex should not be taken so seriously; in fact, she suggested that jealousy and sexual possessiveness should be discouraged by the state as the last vestiges of an outworn private property mentality.[105]

More recent socialist feminists, in widening their vision of exploitation, have, like Kollontai, suggested the expansion of free birth control, abortion, health care for women, child-care centres, and state recognition of domestc labour. There is an ambivalence about the role of the family in this setting, however. Men would obviously have to play a significant part in child- rearing, although there is some suggestion (a point that shows the influ- ence of the radicals) that heterosexuality would not necessarily be the norm. For recent socialist feminists, 'Normative heterosexuality must be replaced by a situation in which the sex of one's lover is a matter of social indifference'.[106]

Radical feminism embodies a diversity of proposals. Beauvoir argued for freely available birth control, abortion and less significance accorded to monogamy in order to facilitate the entrance of women into the cultural world with men. In Firestone, we enter a world of cybernetic communism, peopled by androgynes, where all humans participate in child-bearing and child-rearing. With the rejection of this androgynous future, other radicals identified the main problems as patriarchal culture. If males are the major problem, what strategy can be adopted? At its most extreme and most rare, a male pogrom has been suggested. At a less extreme level, lesbianism or separatism have been advocated. Mary Daly suggested a totally different and separate women's utopian culture. The use of the term lesbianism has parallels here. Lesbian usually denotes 'one who has withdrawn herself from the conventional definitions of feminity'.[107] Although some have advocated sexual lesbianism, most radicals who have argued for this strategy have envisaged it in a more political and philosophical light. If women consciously focus on their own culture and experience, then they begin to achieve some autonomy from patriarchy. This point has been expanded by radical standpoint theory into the conception of a feminist epistemology. It is also contended by some radicals that only women allow each other a sense of self. Women are sensitive to emotion and respect one another. They do not try to define each other. The suggestion of political lesbianism and separatism has led to the practice of 'sisterhood communities', where only women are allowed to live. Radicals have not resisted the notion of heterosexual relationships or even of the family. But heterosexuality should not be the norm and the family would have to be totally transformed so that women would no longer carry the burden of child-rearing or domestic work.

Postmodern and poststructuralist feminism concentrates on the paradigm of language. Its concern is primarily to deconstruct existing language and texts. Language is seen to be a potent weapon to undercut and expose patriarchy across the whole domain of culture and literature. In addition, French feminism is concerned to emphasize the unique manner in which women have contributed and can, in future, contribute to literary and imaginative culture. The most optimistic of such commentators would contend that if language can be decoded to expose the basic oppositions and unargued assumptions, then eventually our cultural symbols can be subtly recoded, thus effectively transforming, via language, our perceptual and cognitive worlds. The less optimistic have denied the essential character of femininity and masculinity, viewing them as social constructions which require deconstruction. It is difficult to know whether feminism means anything any more in this latter context.

The majority of informed criticism of feminism arises at the present moment from within the feminist movement itself. The liberal feminists, for example, have been attacked by both socialist and radical schools. Liberals, it is argued, appear content with the existing family structure and accept a weak and ineffective policy of formal equality. In so doing they neglect both the material and deep-rooted inequalities of capitalism and patriarchy and most of the deeper needs of women. Marxist feminists, on the other hand, are accused of sex-blindness, even by the more recent socialist feminists, and condemned for continuing to adhere to an uncritical view of the natural place of women and the family. Even the socialist feminists are accused by their radical critics of being sex-blind and caught in an unnecessary historical and materialist framework. Liberals have taken the more normal tack against the Marxists, criticizing their dogmatic materialism and abandonment of important values like individual liberty.

In the case of the radicals, the most distinctive criticism is the outlandish proposals they present. Liberals would contend that feminism will not be taken seriously while radicals are advocating political lesbianism, androgyny and separatism. Marxist and socialist critics of radicalism have accused them of ignoring the historical, economic and material basis to patriarchy and thus becoming trapped in an ahistorical and suspect biologism or psychologism. Liberals would also accuse the radicals of many of the same failings as they would Marxism and socialism. The more extreme measures suggested by the radicals would entail quite drastic assaults on individual freedoms, which many would find completely unacceptable.

Postmodern critics have tended to deconstruct the phallocentric character of language in all ideological movements. Liberal, socialist and radical feminists alike are seen as engaging in flawed metanarratives. Postmodernists deny the notion of any privileged position. Words and things have become totally unstuck in this analysis. The French feminists do not, in fact, appear to have grasped the intrinsic logic of their own position. There is no reason to stop at phallocentrism; 'feminocentrism' also needs deconstructing. As one observant critic sourly remarked, 'Although [feminists] support postmodernism's practice of universalizing suspicion, they don't seem to regard *their* cause as suspect. They know *their* credential to be intact'.[108] What we are left with is another series of fictions. As another recent critic observed, what can, at most, be hoped for from feminism is another moderately successful 'metafiction, or at least a fiction that will buy us time'.[109] A number of recent feminist writers have sensed that the postmodernist and poststructuralist roads will ultimately destroy any case for feminism itself. As one has said, 'Feminist postmodernism might be described as an oxymoron — two completely incompatible terms'.[110] It is difficult in this sense not to see the postmodernist path as a dead end.

In examining the feminist movement, one central problem strikes the observer. Many of the arguments of feminism revolve around the question of sameness and equality or difference. Those who reject the argument for difference between male and female, rather like those who reject payment for housework, argue that in effect such moves can stereotype women as inferior, or fix them irretrievably into certain roles. But the claim that all difference is socially or linguistically constructed can also lead to the proposition that there is no real difference between men and women. This latter proposition is deeply puzzling to ordinary men and women. It is even more puzzling when one considers the recent feminist point that there are many differences *between* women (and also between men, for that matter). In fact, many have suggested that there is no essence to either man or woman. However, if the notion of difference is defended it becomes difficult, other than by denigrating men or masculinity, not to see some difference in roles for both men and women — not necessarily unequal roles, but unquestionably different. The emphasis placed by some feminists (both radical and conservative) on childbirth, mothering and nurturing reflects this point. It is hard to know how these various views, which characterize the whole feminist movement and ideology, can be reconciled.

8
ECOLOGISM
—

Ecology has soared into the forum of public discussion in the last twenty years although, like all the ideologies examined, it has its claimants for ancient lineage. There are, however, serious debates concerning the origins of the movement which have repercussions on how we view it at the present moment. These debates will be considered in the next section.

There are immediate problems with the word 'ecologism' itself, which again have implications for the identity of the ecology movement. First, as Jonathan Porritt notes, the word 'ecologism' is somewhat 'daunting', still carrying much of the scientific, specialized character of its initial and continuing usage.[1] Further, the more empirical scientific aspect of the term limits its ability to convey its often deeply personal and political connotations for those working in the movement. In consequence, many of those who write on the ideology will refer to it, with some justification, as 'Green thought'. Even the term 'Green' is not without its own difficulties.[2] This particular debate, with all its circuitous arguments, is reflected in the change in name of the British Green Party (previously Ecology). Despite my strong sympathy for the title 'Green', I have not adopted it for the reason (apart from the side-issue of the awkward nature of 'Greenism') that it does not incorporate all that I would wish to see there. The title 'Green' has been linked so strongly in some discussions with a specific political stance (and certain accompanying values) that it does not really serve my purpose. In this sense the present chapter might be said to be taking a slightly unorthodox view of the movement.

The ecology movement has developed in the public domain since the 1970s. The movement appears in this sense to be historically very specific to the last decades of the twentieth century. The human race has, of course, been intervening in nature for a long time. However, the growth of industrialization in the last two hundred years has accelerated this process of intervention to worrying levels. The post-1945 era of industrial growth has been particularly staggering. As one of the environmental reports of the 1970s commented, 'In the last twenty-five [years], the power, extent and depth of man's interventions in the natural order seem to presage the most revolutionary [change] which the mind can conceive'.[3] It is the very scale and speed of growth in the the last forty years which many have found alarming.

Ecology as a scientific perspective has drawn attention to one very simple but important detail from which a great deal follows, namely, that the ecosphere is an interrelated system. What we call the environment is 'a system which includes all living things and the air, water and soil which is their habitat'.[4] In other words, the human species is part of an immensely complex, variegated and interrelated structure. What we sow in terms of industrial pollution, we will reap from the instability of the ecosphere. We cannot divorce ourselves from the ecosystem. This point constitutes the unique potency of ecologism. Before moving on from this it is worth noting immediately that the basic impetus, significance and public awareness which has been accorded to ecology has derived from its scientific support and evidence, not primarily from its moral or political stance.[5] On the other hand, ecology claims have had a uniquely personal dimension, not always shared by other ideologies (apart from feminism). Many ecologists have linked what they do in their personal lives – in terms of anything from purchasing toilet paper to unleaded petrol – to a global or universal crisis that has ramifications minimally for the next few generations.[6] This global/individual perspective is, in one sense, quite unique among ideologies.

The word ecology is a compound of the Greek terms *oikos* (meaning household or habitat) and *logos* (meaning the argument or science of something). In this sense there is a close and early relation to the term 'economy', which in its original use, going back to Aristotle, meant management of the household. Ecology was initially designed as a science dealing with the systematic relation between plants and animals and their habitat or environment.[7] It has retained, to the present day, its character as a distinct scientific discipline, which has been of interest not only to biologists but also to physiologists, zoologists, biologically inclined mathematicians, physical scientists, geographers, economists and town planners. From its beginnings as a science it has had powerful and fruitful cross-disciplinary connotations. From its inception ecologism has been characterized by a strong and traditional scientific empiricism. The more normative usage of the word, in terms of morality, politics and economics, is a slightly later and subtle modulation. Even in the 1990s there is a tangled and uneasy relationship between those who perceive ecology as an established science and those who mesh the scientific findings with strong doses of normative theory.

THE ORIGINS OF ECOLOGICAL THOUGHT

As mentioned in the first section, the debate about the origins of ecologism is pertinent to the character of the movement in the present. This point is not always immediately apparent from the literature on ecologism. There are some skeletons in the ecological cupboard which many prefer to ignore or pass over with unease. Most of these skeletons, some of which are comparatively harmless, relate to the longer-term origins of ecological ideas. It is contended in this chapter that we should not pass over these longer-term roots in silence, since they reveal the ideological complexity and diversity within the ecological perspective, a complexity which cannot be shunned by simply renaming one's perspective 'green'.

There is little contention concerning the first usage of the word 'ecology'. It was employed by the German zoologist and philosopher Ernst Haeckel in the late 1860s.[8] Haeckel's use of the term in works like *General Morphology* (1866) denoted 'the science of relations between organisms and their environment'.[9] There is, however, some argument about the importance of Haeckel's ideas which will be dealt with shortly. To be brief, there are three basic positions (largely internal to the ecology movement) taken on the question of origins. There is also some recent growth in social scientific explanations of ecology movements which will be mentioned later in the chapter.

The first account of origins will not detain us long, since it is common to most ideologies. This is the attempt to trace ecological sentiments back to the dawn of the human species, at least to the palaeolithic or neolithic periods. Various groups, like the Celts, become *idées fixes* for ecological writers. The basic point that is often made, even in many contemporary debates concerning 'primal' or tribal peoples, is that they were, or are, 'naturally' more ecologically aware than us. Early humans (some would go so far as to say 'before industrialization') had a much more responsive and caring view of the world around them. The impression is that pre-industrial or primal peoples implicitly respected nature and only took from it what they needed; whether they were hunter-gatherers or market gardeners, their animistic perspective led them to care for nature. Some would place a heavy emphasis here on the pre-Christian, rather than pre-industrial peoples.[10] Primal peoples are thus often accorded a kind of natural ancient wisdom which we would do well to rediscover. Hence, ecological literature is often peppered with quotations from shamans, mystics, Indian chiefs and gurus of various types.

There is something misty-eyed and vague about this kind of thinking. Every ideology stakes a claim here, but the ecology movement, in its search for holistic roots, has referred to it more intensely than others. The claim is of course unverifiable, at least in neolithic terms. In the present day there is a danger that we will look with unseemly ardour (like some anarchists) for those very sentiments that we want to find in primal peoples, translating their mythologies into our social or environmental anxieties. We also ignore, at our cost, the fact that the 'slash and burn' mentality and the disregard for pollution and habitat destruction were as characteristic of early neolithic human beings as of those who are now destroying the Brazilian rainforest. Such practices are often tied initially to survival economics. The landscape of Europe has not simply been shaped by industrialization. In earlier periods humans were limited by population numbers, technology and their social and economic environment. However, if certain neolithic humans had invented a smooth-stone chain-saw they would doubtless have used it freely.[11]

The second account of origins, which is by far the most popular and widely utilized, dates the ecology movement from the 1960s and 1970s. Many see this process of ecological awareness beginning in the 1960s. As Brian Tokar notes: 'The real origin of the Green movement is in the great social and political upheavals that swept the United States and the entire Western world during the 1960s'.[12] Some focus on certain seminal writings from the same decade. The earliest of these was Rachel Carson's *Silent Spring* (1962). Nearer the end of the decade Paul Ehrlich's *The Population Bomb* (1968) and Garrett Hardin's 'Tragedy of the Commons' (1968) raised the spectre not only of environmental collapse but also of its relation to overpopulation.[13] Others find the early 1970s a more convincing period, particularly in view of the widespread public reaction to events like the oil crisis and deeply resonant reports like the US Carter administration's *Global 2000 Report*; the unofficial UN report *Only One Earth* (1972); the Club of Rome's *The Limits to Growth* (1972); the *Ecologist* journal volume *Blueprint for Survival* (1972); and much more recently, the Brundtland Report *Our Common Future* (1987).[14] A vigorous case has been made in these reports for our concerns to be focused on the wholesale depletion of the environment. The later 1970s also saw the newly developed Green Parties contending at times successfully for political office, most notably the West German Greens from 1979. It is undoubtedly true that there has been both a vast growth of ecologically sensitive literature and a multiplication of politicized Green organizations since the 1970s.

There is a great deal to be said for the second perspective, in that the ecology movement has unquestionably moved into the forefront of politics in the last two decades. It should, though, be allied to a third perspective. There are positive and negative aspects to this third view, which identifies the roots of ecological ideas in the nineteenth century, although there is still some debate as to precisely when. One point — which is acknowledged by many writers, even those who favour the 1970s account — is that ecologism, to some degree, incorporates a critical reaction to the European Enlightenment tradition.[15] Ecologism looks sceptically at the supreme value of reason. It also denies the central place of human beings and that nature is without value and can simply be manipulated by humans. In this reading, ecologism has been associated with part of the Romantic movement's reaction to the Enlightenment in the early nineteenth century. The weakness in this account is the crucial role that rationality and empirical science play in the presentation of the ecology movement. In addition, the beliefs concerning global or universal equality of humans and species, which are present in large areas of ecology, do not square with the traditionalist, localized and often more hierarchically orientated character of romanticism.

If we move later into the nineteenth century, and consider the impact of both Malthusianism and Darwinism, we find something very different. Philosophies developed which tried to integrate a strongly materialist and scientific perspective with an immanent and naturalistic understanding of religion and morality. In other words, nature and evolution were imbued with a spiritual significance. On the one hand, such a philosophy accepted the developments of evolutionary science and the decline of more orthodox religion. On the other hand, it looked with an extremely sceptical eye on philosophies of consciousness such as idealism. Humans were subject to the evolutionary laws of nature. Into this scenario, an underlying significance, or pattern, to evolution and nature was imported. We can see this attempt clearly in many writers, some already encountered in this book, like Peter Kropotkin, L. T. Hobhouse, J. A. Hobson and Herbert Spencer. With the loss of God or gods, 'nature' and its underlying onto-logical significance became of supreme importance. Sciences could uncover these underlying patterns and structures which, whether consciously or not, took on a sanctified aura. Evolution was spiritualized. One of the most overt, one might almost say caricatured, examples of this in the twentieth century is the work of Teilhard de Chardin, which has influenced sections of the contemporary ecology movement.[16]

What is interesting here is that the first writer to use the neologism 'ecology' was overwhelmingly part of the above perspective. Ernst Haeckel was an influential figure whose ideas affected not only the scientific, but also the literary and religious establishments before the First World War. He was the product of a wave of evolutionary materialism in Germany, influenced by Darwinism, in the last decades of the nineteenth century. He felt that Darwin had put evolution on a firm scientific base. In serious academic works and more popular texts, like *The Riddle of the Universe*, Haeckel tried to develop a philosophical monism (premised on vitalist, as opposed to mechanistic, biology) which would ultimately act as a valid substitute for religion. Like Herbert Spencer (whom he deeply admired) and later Henri Bergson, Haeckel posited an evolving force or substance within the material world of nature, governed by a basic law — what he called the 'law of substance'.[17] Also like Spencer, he did not see evolving nature as lifeless. Denying atheism, he referred to his view as 'pantheism'.[18] God, for Haeckel, was completely immanent in nature, or as Haeckel put it, 'God, as an *intramundane* being, is everywhere identical with nature itself'.[19] With the death of the old gods, Haeckel proclaimed optimistically that 'the new sun of our realistic monism . . . reveals to us the wonderful temple of nature in all its beauty'. A nature religion thus replaced 'the anthropistic ideals of "God, freedom, and immortality" '.[20] Haeckel saw nature as a unified, balanced organism of which humans were a part, an organism which had religious significance. This monistic, natural and harmonious organism had lessons to teach us in terms of the organization of society as well as our relations with nature.

From its beginnings in the 1870s, ecologism has embodied scientific and evolutionary ideas. These were often meshed into a subtle pantheistic, holistic spiritualism. Nature itself was seen to have worth and moral standing and was tied integrally to our destiny as animals. Nature embodied a dynamic teleology which we ignored at our cost. Those now studying ecology who try to maintain the purity of the scientific motif, unsullied by religious input, need to pause for a few moments to study the history of their discipline. From Haeckel onwards, ecology has had moral and religious import for humanity. The manner in which we organized our societies, economies, and personal lives had bearing on the same naturalistic logic and teleology of nature. Such a vision was also markedly not focused primarily on humans; it was, rather, non-anthropocentric. In addition, nature and the 'natural' became the ultimate commendation. Living a natural life was the best life. This has had colossal implications for the twentieth century, stretching across our attitudes to the countryside, naturism, folk tradition, folk music, wholefood, vegetable growing, Eastern religions, nature reserves, health and homeopathic medicine and so forth – a vast litany of beliefs which cannot be examined here, but all of which existed well before the First World War.[21]

The disturbing aspect of the above claim for many in the ecology movement is twofold. First, it is clear that from its inception the ecological perspective incorporated, occasionally, some much more conservative (aesthetics-in-nature) and nationalist components, particularly the 'folkish' movements across Europe in the 1920s and 1930s. It is fortuitous that dissatisfied socialist and anarchist clientele have formed the staple membership of the ecology movement since the 1970s. Their powerful conjunction of pacifist and anti-statist attitudes has obscured this more diverse ancestry. A related problem here is that most of those who have written on the history of ecology over the last twenty years have been the believers in anarchist or socialist Green radicalism.

A second worry is the manner in which some of these ecological ideas developed, particularly the strong ecological perspectives of many fascist and Nazi movements. The Third Reich was keenly exploring wind technology, methane gas and other sources of alternative soft-energy. The Germans were the first to set up nature reserves in Europe and to plant deciduous woodlands in expansive planned programmes of reforestation. In addition, they were experimenting broadly on bio-dynamic and organic farming. Many, like Hitler, were keen vegetarians and Himmler, the head of the SS, was an ardent anti-vivisectionist.[22] This detail is the unspoken text underlying the recent heated debates within ecologism over potential 'eco-fascism' in some areas of the movement.

Outside of the above views there have been attempts in sociological and economic literature to deal with the history of the ecology movement, some of which link with a longer-term, nineteenth-century perspective. Lowe and Goyder, for example, in their study of environmental groups in politics, identify 'waves' of concern with ecological problems: the 1880s up to 1900; 1918 to 1939; and the 1950s and 1970s.[23] The authors argue that 'It is perhaps no coincidence that each of the periods of sudden growth of new environmental groups in the 1890s, the late 1920s, and the late 1950s and early 1970, occurred as similar phases in the world business cycle – towards the end of periods of sustained expansion'.[24] Once material needs have been satisfied for a certain sector of society, through economic prosperity, people begin to express concern about the 'costs' of prosperity, and also about the 'natural' surroundings which they now have the leisure and time to enjoy. They have the time, education, and financial security to be able to be alarmed about the environment.[25]

Other social investigators have contended that those who express ecological anxieties are often members of social classes on the periphery of industrialization, usually in the professional service sector of the community (academics, teachers, artists, actors, clergy, social workers and so on).[26] Advanced industrial economies show a marked growth of such service-sector occupations. Thus value-shifts towards ecology are tied to the changing occupational patterns of advanced industrial economies. The central ironic paradox here, of course, is that economic growth, with its consequent environmental effects (which are deplored by ecologists), has facilitated the expansion of an affluent, educated service sector which has in turn developed the capacity to enjoy the environment which is being disrupted by such growth. Interesting as these sociological and economic views are, they express little concern for the ideology per se. From the sociological and economic perspective, value-shifts and ideology tell us very little in themselves; it is the economic, class and occupational changes in advanced industrialization which reveal the real nature of ecology.

In conclusion, it has been contended that the attitudes we associate with ecology are not new. They did not suddenly spring upon us in the 1970s with pure radical credentials. Rather, they relate to a subtle and immensely potent conjunction of attitudes to nature which have been present in European thought since the late nineteenth century. Despite their widespread promotion by many different and politically diverse groups throughout the twentieth century, it is the accidental conjunction of circumstances, individuals and events in the 1970s which has provided a dynamic refocus for the ecological vocabulary. This act of refocusing has led to some attempts to define out earlier proponents. Despite the fact that this chapter will deal mainly with the 1970s phenomenon, the net of ecology is purposely widened to incorporate a broader array of political attitudes. Ecology may be a new form of ideological awareness but it is also a complex form which incorporates, like all ideologies, a variety of often contradictory tendencies.

THE NATURE OF ECOLOGY

There are a number of problems in dealing with ecology as a political ideology which are tied to the comparative newness of the movement. It is still in the process of formation. First, there is the problem that many in the movement believe that ecology is not an ideology. Ecology is seen to transcend ideology. Second, there is the troublesome relationship between contemporary eco-philosophy and the political ideology and practical movement of ecology. Finally, there is the issue of diversity within the movement, which raises the difficulty of classifying ecological schools of thought. This section will look at these three questions and then offer a working classification of schools of ecology.

One of the oft-cited slogans of the British and German Greens has been 'Neither left nor right, but forwards'. What is really implied by this comment is not a new ideology, but something which goes beyond ideologies altogether. For many, ideologies are part of a package of ideas and values which characterize an age or epoch, in the case of ecology a package which has been the root cause of the environmental crisis. As one writer puts it: 'Politics as we know it can no longer deal with these [environmental] issues because it shares the very mentality out of which they arose' – a view which is shared by many in the contemporary movement.[27] Ideologies of all persuasions are simply 'abstract systems, sets of logically consistent ideals ... governing our conduct, pronouncing truth about society'. As such, the author continues, 'They are more lethal than any physical danger the world holds, because their logic would enslave us'.[28] Thus the task is to go beyond ideology altogether.

This above view obviously inspires many in the movement. It can also be seen in most ideologies. It is, though, unacceptable. It is an obviously convenient lever to establish truthfulness – namely, 'I speak from the realm of objective truth, you are an ideologist'. Without rehearsing the arguments again, much of what we expect to find in an ideology is clearly present in ecology. There are metaphysical accounts of the nature of reality, human nature and the role of humans in the world, evaluations and assessments of the constituents of the best political, economic and social life, and recommendations and persuasive arguments concerning what ought to be done in these spheres. In fact, most of ecology's component parts have been with us in various guises for more than a century. Thus, as will be obvious from its inclusion in this book, ecology *is* an ideology.

Another awkward problem concerns the relation of eco-philosophy to the ideology and political practice of ecology. Andrew Dobson focuses on this point, noting that 'The politics of ecology does not follow the same ground rules as its philosophy'.[29] If one examines the ecology literature over the last two decades there appear to be several different discrete sets of activity going on, which often appear to be only vaguely aware of each other. This is unusual in terms of the previous ideologies that we have examined, where there is a much closer 'fit' between the more sophisticated philosophical thought and the ideological and practical sentiments. There is a growing amount of eco-philosophy, with sophisticated journals like *Environmental Ethics*, immensely learned and well-argued books on environmental ethics, and, on the other hand, a conglomeration of ideological, economic, New Age, practical pamphlets, books, communities and experimentation. Neither tendency appears to show much interest in the other. With the philosophers, this is due to a combination of professional rigour and academic compartmentalization; with the other tendency, it stems from a mixture of motives most likely focusing on general sentiments like 'fine words don't butter parsnips' – namely, that the philosophers are little concerned with practice. This lack of contact is none the less disconcerting.[30] An additional problem with the more practice-orientated ecology is a contradiction in itself. On the one hand, there is a tendency in much recent 'practical' literature to identify explicitly (on a fairly superficial level) with one of the rather more controversial wings of eco-philosophy – deep ecology.[31] On the other hand, in the same literature, and in actual practice, the key arguments deployed by many ecologists are often 'human prudential' arguments, which pay scant attention, in fact blatantly contradict, the thrust of deep ecology and even milder forms of eco-philosophy. Ecology, in other words, occasionally justifies itself simply on grounds of human survival. This point will be returned to later.

The third problem is diversity. Whereas many ecologists have recognized the value of diversity in the ecosphere, they are not so happy about its appearance within the ideology itself. There is a powerful desire in the movement for ideological purity and newness, unsullied by contact with other worn-out schemes. Yet it is clear that 'just as there are many socialisms and many liberalisms, so there are many ecologisms'.[32] In addition, these ecologisms derive from, and overlap with, many other established schemes of thought. The most tempting strategy is to simplify what is to count as ecology and to rule out stipulatively certain categories. My own categorization will incorporate much that has been ruled out by other commentators.[33]

The ecology movement, both politically and philosophically, has two broad tendencies with a large intermediate component. Let us take the philosophical typology first: at one end of the spectrum we can identify what might be called a 'light anthropocentrist' wing where the main body of arguments stresses that human beings are the sole criterion both of what is valuable and of what can value.[34] The value of nature in this component is usually instrumental in character, namely, that the natural world (including animals) functions or has value only *for* humans or in so far as humans give it value. Nature can still have considerable value here: it can be an early-warning system for us in terms of impending ecological disaster; it supports and nourishes us; we can do valuable experiments on it; we can exercise in it; and we can admire, relax in, be psychologically refreshed and aesthetically moved by its beauty.[35] All of these assets, however, are anthropocentric and instrumentally orientated. Nature without humans is valueless.

The other end of the philosophical spectrum is the deep ecology wing. This wing is closest to what is sometimes called the 'holistic' perspective. The primary locus of value is not the human individual but the ecosphere as a whole. It is therefore ecocentric as opposed to anthropocentric. Value here is intrinsic usually to the whole ecosphere; it is not given to it by humans and therefore the ecosphere cannot be used instrumentally for human ends. This is the most controversial eco-philosophy wing, whose inspiration came initially from the North American writer Aldo Leopold's *A Sand County Almanac* and later from the philosopher Arne Naess.[36] In spite of the fact that it is still in the process of forming, it already contains a number of tendencies: J. R. Rodman's emphasis on ecological sensibility; those following the early Naess writings who concentrate on intrinsic value and deep questioning; those who see profound religious (usually Buddhist) implications in deep ecology; and finally those – most notably Warwick Fox – who try to offer a profound new metaphysical philosophy focusing on the need for a fundamental change in human ecological consciousness and self-realization.[37] However, in all these tendencies, humans are viewed as one aspect of the ecosphere.

In between these two components is a broad intermediate category which can be usefully subdivided into two further tendencies. The basic position of the intermediate view is not to accept either pure anthropocentrism or ecocentrism. The bulk of contemporary ethical eco-philosophy subsists in this category. The two subtendencies of the intermediate position can be called 'moral extensionism' and 'reluctant holism'.[38] A rough-and-ready distinction between these subtendencies is that the former is more inclined towards anthropocentrism whereas the latter is far less so.

Under the 'moral extensionist' category, the best examples are the various animal liberation and rights arguments of figures like Peter Singer or Tom Regan – often called 'ethical sentientism'. Singer argues that 'sentience' is the locus of value. Animals are sentient, therefore animals are of value.[39] It follows that non-sentient life does not possess value. We extend value to creatures because we can reasonably see that they possess the faculty of sentience. Thus plants, rocks or rivers are ruled out. As Singer puts it: 'There is a genuine difficulty in understanding how chopping down a tree can matter *to the tree* if the tree can feel nothing'.[40]

The 'reluctant holism' wing extends arguments concerning value beyond sentience to a variety of notions: the intrinsic value of nature or the value of the total biosphere including plants. Most reluctant holists are, in other words, prepared to go much further than the moral extensionists in locating value well beyond humans and animals. This is the defining aspect of reluctant holism. Some would also contend that 'wholes' like the biotic community have value.[41] Yet such wholes do not usually include mountains or rivers. Many of the arguments within reluctant holism employ some form of intrinsic value claim, but most writers here, including J. Baird Callicott, Holmes Rolston III and Paul Taylor, would still want to keep a critical distance from the more absolute holism of deep ecology thinkers like Arne Naess and Warwick Fox.[42]

One final point of clarification, before moving to the political typology, concerns the notion of intrinsic value. It has been implied in some studies that what marks out deep ecology from other types of eco-philosophy is the former's commitment to intrinsic value. Intrinsic value can be formally defined as belonging to something which is valuable in itself, rather than belonging instrumentally.[33] There are two points to be made here in passing. First, there is no one single straightforward intrinsic value argument or claim. There are in fact mutually hostile intrinsic value claims. There are philosophers who see intrinsic value in objects in the world.[44] Others identify intrinsic value with the states and activities of objects, particularly those 'states of affairs' which contribute towards the flourishing of something.[45] Second, intrinsic value arguments are used across the eco-philosophical spectrum. They do not just inhabit the realm of deep ecology. In fact, deep ecologist philosophers, like Warwick Fox, appear to rest little reliance upon them in their more recent work.[46] On the other hand, intrinsic value theory can be used within anthropocentric ethics to speak of the intrinsic value of human persons as distinct from nature. Its most prevalent use is in the various elements of the intermediate eco-philosophical position, in very different formats, in the work of philosophers like Holmes Rolston III and Robin Attfield.

The question of the classificatory relation between the above philosophical views and the spectrum of political opinions must now be briefly explored. The same broad groupings can be identified as in the philosophical typology. One point that should be mentioned is that the political format in which these groups appear veers across pressure groups to political parties. There is no precise one-to-one correlation between any of these categories and political forms. Deep ecologists are therefore just as likely to be in parties or pressure groups. Thus, on the one hand, there is a 'light', more reformist wing within ecology. This wing is often divorced from the ecology perspective altogether.[47] Within this category we find some of the most traditional environmental groups, for example, conservation groups, preservation, single-issue and recreation groups. In fact, the large bulk of politically successful environmental groups tend to function in this category. Their major appeal is most usually premised on the importance of valuing and retaining some aspect of the environment for the benefit or survival of human beings. In other words, what underpins their appeal is the human prudential anthropocentric arguments. The reformist wing essentially works within existing institutional frameworks and political processes, although they might resort to some form of public demonstration to make a point.

At the other extreme is the deep ecology wing. Its appeal is to the Arcadian mentality, as Donald Worster calls it.[48] Deep ecologists usually want a total value-change in society — a new age to be constructed, where the whole perception of the world and nature changes. In this sense there are a number of what have been called 'ecotopias' lurking in the wings.[49] As argued in the philosophical typology above, there are a variety of tendencies here. There are those who believe in setting up alternative communities based on religious or secular principles and utilizing alternative techologies. They have a very distinctive social philosophy premised on concepts like 'bioregionalism', which we will come to. This area has also attracted support from a small but vociferous group of eco-feminists who see the deep society as the most likely to realize non-patriarchy. More controversially there is a somewhat forgotten nationalist and *völkisch* component which attracted many enthusiasts earlier in the century. Haeckel's philosophical monism (and those who utilized variants of it) conforms most closely to the deep model. The arguments of fascism and national socialism concerning the attachment of humans to land and place, which we examined in chapter 6, resonate within this perspective.[50]

Finally, and most controversially, we can clearly identify a violent and extremist wing within the deep ecologists. The Earth First! movement, originating in the USA, but also having affiliates in many other countries, takes some of the deep arguments to their logical but absurd conclusions. Nature becomes more important that human beings. Wilderness becomes an ultimate value. Industrialization is viewed as a foul corruption of the planet. Many Earth First! followers have consequently looked with benign tolerance on the mass spread of Aids, famine and the possible reintroduction of a reinvigorated smallpox virus, as the ecosphere reasserting a natural balance on the planet. Others have advocated policies of compulsory mass human sterilization. Some Earth First! followers have also engaged in direct action (what has become known colloquially as 'ecotage'), for example, spiking selected trees with long nails so as to mutilate loggers with chain saws (already with some success) and thus to deter future logging. Critics of this tendency, even within the ecology movement, have labelled it eco-fascism or eco-brutalism.

The intermediate position again attracts a diversity of political views. Also, the gap between the light reformist anthropocentric wing and the intermediate is very narrow. (Even the deep ecologists resort occasionally to anthropocentric human prudential arguments.) Another point to note here is that the intermediate position is differentiated from the reformist wing not so much by strategy as by a stronger overt ideological and philosophical commitment to moderate non-anthropocentrism. Furthermore, there is no precise 'fit' between the intermediate ideological/political views and the intermediate philosophical views, whereas there is a fairly close correlation between deep philosophers and deep practitioners.

The breakdown between views on the political dimension has led to the reappearance of some well-established ideological beliefs. There is, for example, a growing interest in what has become known as 'eco-capitalism' (another term might be 'eco-liberal capitalism'). This sees the market as the best device to control environmental problems. In addition, followng the work of Rudolf Bahro, there have been vigorous discussions of eco-socialism. The eco-socialists have two main views on ecology which parallel socialist attitudes to liberalism. On the one hand, eco-socialism comes to destroy bourgeois ecology (understood as a reformist middle-class and hopelessly utopian phenomenon).[51] The other view is that eco-socialism comes to fulfil, or bring to fruition, the radical materialist destiny of ecology. Eco-socialism also divides over the future of society, whether it moves towards an enlightened eco-socialist state or towards a non-state pluralist/commune socialism.

Another 'intermediate political position' is social ecologism, focusing on the work of the communist anarchist Murray Bookchin. As argued in chapter 5, this position tries to ally ecological concerns with traditional communist anarchism – a tradition which boasts Peter Kropotkin as an illustrious forebear. The ideal structure or 'affinity group' (for Bookchin) settles predictably upon the traditional democratic commune idea.

The social ecologist position appears to solve rather nicely many of the problems of 'actual' life and organization present within ecological thought, by feeding into a well-established tradition of thought. Thus it often provides the focus for discussions of what ecology actually implies in political terms. Ironically and puzzlingly, despite Bookchin's open and viciously expressed contempt for deep ecology (which he calls either eco-fascism or mystical 'eco-la-la'), the anarchistic democratic commune nestling within a bioregion appears also to form a model of organization within the deep category. In a slightly more authoritarian format (which was not unknown to anarchy) the commune is ironically a model for some more nationalistic ecologists.[52]

There are certain themes affirmed by philosophical and political ecologists of all types. Most assert, in some shape or form, the systematic inter-dependence of species and the environment. Although many have a very particular focus, they usually think in terms of the whole ecosystem. There is also a much less damaging and more positive attitude to nature than is found in all other ideologies. In addition there is a tendency to be, minimally, sceptical about the supreme position of human beings on the planet. Further, there is a shared general anxiety about what humans, via industrial civilization, are actually doing to the planet. As in previous chapters I will discuss many of these themes through the categories of human nature, politics and economics, trying to bring out the varying responses from the ecological schools.

NATURE AND HUMAN NATURE

The concept of human nature in ecologism cannot be easily discussed apart from the notion of nature in general, partly because of the philosophical centrality of the debate over anthropocentrism and non-anthropocentrism. The notion of nature in Western thought has oscillated between hero and villain. The idea of the villain is one which ecologists see characterizing pure anthropocentric thought. Nature in this reading is regarded as valueless, but still a potentially unruly and threatening entity, something which must be conquered, controlled, manipulated and exploited for human ends. This adversarial view of nature is one that most political ecologists see as the 'world-view' of the natural sciences up to this century. Bacon, Hobbes, Descartes and the Enlightenment make frequent appearances in ecological writings as the perpetrators of this attitude.

The hero, or at least the benign view of nature, which derives from the later nineteenth century, has two dimensions, extrinsic and intrinsic. The 'extrinsic view' would contend that nature is valuable for us, but that it is we who include nature in our moral constituency. Nature can be a valuable resource, but it is we who value it as such. It can even be judged to be intrinsically valuable, but only in relation to human beings. Thus nature becomes a hero because we value our survival and flourishing. In this reading, nature becomes valuable because of the value of human nature. This view is characteristic of many reformist and environmentalist groups.

The second or 'intrinsic view' (which can be found in the political inter-mediate and deep ecology wings) is that nature has an inner importance. For many political ecologists this intrinsic argument is indissolubly linked with the claim that humanity is tied to the totality of nature. Human nature is thus understood within the context of the totality of nature. Humans must therefore 'learn again to live with nature', not against it.[53] The most popular idea which encapsulates this linkage, for some political ecologists, is James Lovelock's Gaia hypothesis.[54] Lovelock, as a working scientist, put forward the hypothesis that the earth might be considered as a single self-regulating superorganism. For Lovelock, the existence of the atmosphere did not create living things; rather, living things, from bacteria onwards, created the atmosphere of the earth, merely by living. The fertility of the soil, the temperature of the atmosphere, the amount of oxygen we breathe, all are related to the complex interaction of organisms. Despite considerable scientific doubts concerning the hypothesis – in fact it might simply be interpreted, minimally, as a thesis concerning the demonstrable importance of organisms for the balanced ecosystems of the planet – it has none the less become a virtual talisman for sections of the political ecology movement.

Gaia has now, it even appears to Lovelock's consternation, been thoroughly spiritualized. Not only is the hypothesis seen to demonstrate our interdependence with the ecosphere (again this can still be read in anthropocentric and instrumentalist terms), but it shifts humans from the centre-stage, affirms our ecological equality with the totality of organisms, and could possibly change our attitude to nature. In more mundane terms, as one recent writer comments: 'The pragmatic strength of the Gaia hypothesis is that it offers to combine environmental science with morality. It thus seems to provide the kind of authority which ... a more routine dependence on science fails to deliver'.[55]

One reading of the latter intrinsic view sees certain values within nature itself. If humans are simply part of nature, then they are equal to other species. This doctrine takes on the garb of a central principle in deep ecology, namely 'biospherical egalitarianism'.[56] An additional confirmation of this point for some writers is that, apart from humans, nature embodies no authority hierarchies or stratification. A stable ecosphere tolerates and in fact fosters biological equality and diversity of species. This stable sustainable harmony, equality and tolerance of diversity of species is often viewed as a natural morality by some ecological writers. In other words, the qualities of harmony and tolerance are deciphered as natural values for the human species to cultivate. Some interpret primal societies as cultivating such a natural morality. As Brian Tokar notes: 'Modern civilizations have abandoned the life-affirming qualities of primitive cultures and created a way of life that is increasingly mobilized for death'.[57]

There are a number of complex problems with the intrinsic view and its linkage with the Gaia idea. Many eco-socialists have complained that the notions of nature, the environment and human nature are unduly narrow. As Michael Redclift comments: 'When we refer to "the environment" ... we are referring to something which has been produced by history through struggles and exploitation'.[58] Much of our environment and nature (including human nature) is causally related to poverty, ill-health, alienating work and simply the need to survive under an oppressive system. Certain ecologists are therefore seen to be in danger of romanticizing nature and relating all our problems to personal values. We are part of nature, but nature reflects the depredations of our social and economic arrangements. Environmental problems are therefore, as much as anything, political and economic problems spawned by capitalism.

Another problem relates to Lovelock's description of Gaia as a self-regulating organism. If humans pollute the atmosphere and poison themselves, then Gaia will adapt over millennia. It does not matter whether humans massively pollute the planet, die out as a species, or shepherd resources and survive, the superorganism is indifferent. In this sense the argument is neither serviceable for ecology to use against polluters nor for the importance of the survival of the human species. There is therefore no necessary ethical significance here; the Gaia theory is simply an observation of a natural process.

Most seriously of all, it is difficult to see what notion of human nature is derived from the intrinsic view and its linkage with the Gaia theory. If humans are simply part of nature, in the more 'indifferent' position of Gaia, then presumably we are free, like all other animals, to utilize the world around us. If it is in our nature to exploit and if we therefore destroy ourselves, the universe will not even blink. Yet not many political ecologists would accept this view. Usually a moral component is imported, most effectively our survival as a species, but more often the message is that as a species we can, via our self-consciousness, stand back and moderate our activities. As a species we are partially removed from the normal functioning of biological evolution.[59] We might be asked at this point in time to act in more ecologically caring ways and not to despoil our environment. The assumption behind this latter position is that qualitatively we are *not* quite part of nature. As a species we are uniquely distinct, although the Gaia view would still appear to want to deny this. Unless we imbue Gaia with a spiritual purpose and ontology, we appear caught in its indifference. If we step back from it, we either affirm directly the value of the survival of our own species, or we look for ways in which we can ensure an ethical response to nature. Both positions appear to assume that the human species is qualitatively distinct from nature. One of the many implications of this discussion is that there are potentially a number of different accounts of both nature and human nature present in ecology, the debates between which remain unresolved.

THE POLITICAL DIMENSION OF ECOLOGISM

One central difficulty of ecologism is the variety of political visions present in the movement. Again it is tempting to delimit the study and identify one particular tendency as the key, for example, the social ecologists' commune. There is also the problem of the public and private faces of ecology, namely, the private affirmation of beliefs and the coincidental public actions which appear to contradict them. Ecology is not alone in this, of course. The dilemma is partly a function of what Martin Seliger called the tension between the fundamental and operative dimensions of ideology.[60] In ecology, though, it is a sore point.

One of the problems which has affected the judgement of the political dimension of ecologism since the 1970s has been its close affiliation predominantly with socialism and, less significantly, with anarchism. This affiliation with both tendencies has muddied the waters concerning political beliefs. The problem is intensified by the fact that, particularly with socialism, we face a number of different schools, often with contradictory beliefs. In one of the socialist interpretations Bahro contends that Western industrialized, state-based societies are part of the environmental problem. Humanity, he insists, has reached the point where it has to 'find a new stable life-form'; he goes on to describe this as the '"reconstruction of God" – in other words, the kind of regulation which can only come from the recreation of spiritual equilibrium, within those levels of nature neglected by Marx'. Later he notes significantly that 'a solution to problems is best found in small groups', and mentions the Benedictine order of monks.[61] Other eco-socialists predictably find this an unsatisfactory and utopian notion. Thus, Martin Ryle draws a vigorous distinction between the decentralist anti-statism of 'Greens', as distinct from the enlightened statism of eco-socialists. To deal adequately with multinational companies, penalize polluters and the like, ecology *needs* an 'ecologically progressive "strong State" . . . to challenge the often remote and autocratic centres of power which now determine the economic fate of entire communities'.[62]

As mentioned already, Bookchin's nostrums rely heavily upon the traditions of communist anarchism. In *The Ecology of Freedom* (1982), Bookchin, like his intellectual forebear Kropotkin, finds his eco-anarchist promptings from within a more benign conception of nature. Nature is seen to be egalitarian and non-hierarchical. Bookchin links these ideas directly with the communist anarchist perspective which has close affinities with the pluralist/commune socialism of figures like Bahro.[63]

The upshot of these eco-socialist and eco-anarchist reflections is simply to add to the confusion of what ecologism presents as a political perspective. The picture is further clouded by mutual recriminations. Social ecologists attack the deep ecologists for engaging in mystical claptrap. Deep ecologists, amongst others, attack the eco-socialists as still at root being tied to industrial growth, therefore being part of the problem. Reformist environmentalists attack the social ecologists as redreaming the hopelessly nostalgic utopias of nineteenth-century anarchy. Before moving on to a more systematic presentation of the political visions within ecology, it is worth mentioning that there are still some formal common political concerns within the ecology movement, though responses to these differ markedly.

There is a strong sense in which many ecologists are probably as concerned about individual values and activities as they are with politics in general. Individuals are viewed as possessing varying levels of responsibility, but individual values are still seen to count in many significant ways. The stress on individual values and autonomy tends to make political ecology less likely to accept materialist accounts, although biology and evolutionary materialism do have a firm foothold in ecology (usually underpinned by some implicit moral pattern). The ecology perspective also tends to combine, uniquely, both respect for local autonomy in communities and a global message. In addition, all ecological schools are concerned to raise questions about the limits of economic growth in industrialized societies. This in turn leads to critical reflections on consumption patterns, production in industry and agriculture, energy use and the nature of technology, the concept of work, and finally, demographic patterns and population growth. These concerns are common to all ecologists. They all focus on the central theme of a *sustainable society*, one which will not damage, but will exist harmoniously with, the ecosystem. The responses to this theme vary widely.

It is difficult at this historical phase of the ecology movement to produce a definitive typology, yet there appear at present to be three distinct political visions working within the ideology. Adopting some of the terminology of William Ophuls, these can be called the maximum-sustainable society, the frugal-sustainable society, and the eco-anarchist commune.[64] The last vision is associated primarily with the work of Bookchin and communist anarchism. This will not be discussed since it would be duplicating what has been examined in chapter 5; also, many of the decentralist ideas of social ecologism appear within the second vision. The focus of the discussion will therefore be on the first two.

The maximum-sustainable vision for Ophuls denotes 'a society that aims to exist in equilibrium with its environment, but that is still based on such fundamental "modern" values as the dominance of man over nature, the primacy of material and other hedonistic wants and so on'.[65] My own use of this term differs from that of Ophuls in so far as the ideas of dominance over nature and hedonistic wants do not figure as either central or necessary elements. What I take this idea to cover is the conglomerate of ecological and environmental groups who subscribe to the belief that the present nation-state and its legal structure, modified to a greater or lesser degree by ecological consciousness, is adequate and in fact necessary to the task of meeting the requirements of ecological ideology. This is the most notable and most successful face of ecology, usually projected through pressure-group activity. It is characterized by a strong dose of realism and tends to soft-pedal on most issues, partly out of the need to gain agreement from electorates or institutions. One of the more hopeful signs here is a realization that ecological concerns are linked with political and constitutional questions.[66] In fact ecological reform might be dependent, more so than many have realized, on constitutional change within

contemporary states, a change involving not only the extension of account-
ability on limitations and the exercise of executive authority, but also
much closer and regularized scrutiny of the links between governments
and industry.

This vision encompasses both pressure groups and political parties.
It also encompasses, somewhat paradoxically, the various political and
philosophical dimensions of the ideology. It can, in other words, be found
in weak anthropocentrism and strong non-anthropocentrism. One would
not expect to find it among the social ecologists (eco-anarchists) although
it is clearly an important motif within reformist arguments and for some
eco-socialists. It also forms a background to eco-capitalism. It has, in other
words, a fairly wide appeal. Jonathan Porrritt, though in some writings
adhering closely to a deep ecological value position, criticizes the eco-
anarchists for their 'chronically unrealistic escapism'. He maintains that
the visions of such people 'have often been rather elitist and their reluctance
to dirty their hands in the muck and grime of contemporary politics is
regrettable'.[67] Despite still adhering to the deep ecological notion of a
sea-change in values, he contends that it is necessary to work within the
political system as it stands. Porritt is clearly committed to established
electoral politics. As he argues:

> I don't have a philosophical objection to the nature of the state as the ring-
> holder of the collective interests of all people in a country. I'm not an anarchic
> green or a fourth worlder; that approach to life is ludicrously nostalgic. It
> refers back to golden ages or ideas about human communities that have little
> relevance and are singularly unhelpful in terms of getting across to people
> the utterly unrealistic alternatives that we've got. I'm increasingly critical of
> what I call the manic minusculists ... I would see the state as exercizing its
> present functions but in a more sensitive way: in terms of basic services like
> education, health, and income distribution ... I would always uphold the
> need for some distributive mechanism to ensure basic fairness across regions.[68]

To dream of immediate small-scale non-state societies is thus to live in a
private comfortable dream world. Other writers, particularly some of the
eco-socialists like Martin Ryle, appear more confident than Porritt about a
progressive and strong eco-state. A state is needed to deal not only with
the massive problems of poverty and redistribution (which are intimately
related to the whole ecological problem for most eco-socialists) but also to
take on the vast powerful structures of multinational corporations.

One final group, and part of the above perspective, are the eco-capi-
talists.[69] Again this perspective sees the state forming a minimalist rule-of-
law background to the basic procedures of the market and consumer
choice to protect the environment. By definition this perspective views
the state as having an important but strictly limited role. Eco-capitalism
utilizes the more classical liberal vision of the state, as discussed in chapter 2.

The second political vision — of the frugal-sustainable society — is most characteristic of the deep ecologists. It is a society devoted to what Erich Fromm — in an influential little book on the ecology movement — called a 'being' as opposed to a 'having' society.[70] Those who propound this 'being' vision claim that it is based on a total value-shift, a new renaissance or paradigm change in the whole of humanity.[71]

Ophuls describes this as a relatively low-energy throughput society. It would be a more labour-intensive society, with little emphasis on material consumption, and encouragement of personal self-sufficiency and voluntary personal frugality. This vision most importantly places a heavy emphasis on the virtue or personal moral responsibilities of the individual.[72] Ophuls observes that it represents a return to a classical type of politics. He remarks that 'The picture of the frugal society that emerges resembles something like a return to the city-state form of civilization, but on a much higher and more sophisticated technological base'.[73] The difference from the classical *polis* is that Ophuls admits that a macroauthority would be needed to prevent conflict. Thus 'local politics would have to exist within a regional or global empire of some kind'.[74] It is not certain that deep ecologists would agree with the notion of an eco-empire. In fact, this clearly separates Ophuls from deep ecology. Some of the deep ecologists appear more enamoured of the idea of re-establishing fragmented tribal cultures. Thus, Brian Tokar, deploying the concept of bioregionalism, identifies one of its positive attributes as leading to the '"breakdown of nations" into self-sustaining, cooperatively-relating, ecologically-scaled entities'.[75]

The notions of frugality, self-reliance and voluntary simplicity carry a number of implications. In economics the call comes for Schumacher's vision of the Buddhist system, premised on meeting human need and caring for the environment.[76] This would be a society where energy would come from renewable sources like the sun and wind, and all non-renewable energy would be conserved and recycled. Technologies would be appropriate and not harmful. For many, this frugal society implies a strong spiritual dimension, usually of either a Buddhistic or a pantheistic form, which requires respect for the ecosphere. Again the principle of non-violence often figures as an adjunct to the Buddhist perspective.[77] It also implies a massive personal reassessment of our everyday activities. W. and D. Schwarz remark that 'Living simply is not just a question of keeping paper bags and making compost; it implies an awareness of what products we are using, what food we are eating, how it was produced and who was helped or exploited by our use'.[78] There is a changed concept of work, moving towards what James Robertson has referred to as an 'ownwork' society.[79]

There are a number of stipulations on size and geographical location laid down in this vision by writers like Edward Goldsmith and Kirkpatrick

Sale. To use the current vocabulary: a society needs to respect 'ecological carrying capacity', people need to 'dwell in place' and it needs to be 'human scale'. As Goldsmith argues: 'It is probable that only in the small community can a man or woman be an individual. In today's large agglomerations he is merely an isolate.' Goldsmith suggests neighbourhoods of no more than five hundred individuals, within communities of approximately five thousand and regions of five hundred thousand.[80]

On the question of geographical location, the most significant concept developed is that of the bioregion. Bioregions are not national, ethnic, administrative or overtly political units, but rather ecologically and biologically sustainable units. Tokar defines a bioregion as 'an area of land defined, not by political boundaries ... but by the natural, biological and geological features that cast the real identity of a place'. Mountain ranges, rivers, vegetation, weather patterns, soil, plants and fauna, characterize a bioregion and replace political/state boundaries.[81] Within such a bioregion there is a sustainable ecosystem where humans can 'live in place' without damaging their environment, as long as they 'strive to create self-supporting ways of life that fully complement the flows and cycles of nature that already exist there'.[82] Not only do bioregional ideas benefit the environment by linking our social, economic and political life with a natural self-sustaining entity; they also link the human being intimately with nature. Some writers, like Tokar, make further subdivisions between local watersheds and mountain ranges. Kirkpatrick Sale offers a more complex division, again comprised of ecoregions, georegions and morphoregions.[83] Such communities would, according to their proponents, encourage cultural diversity and autonomy.

A number of implications are seen to follow from the above idea. There is a strong suggestion that such small-scale communities would be characterized by grass-roots participatory, as opposed to representative, democracy.[84] The idea of decentralized public participatory assemblies meeting within bioregions to decide on policy appears as the central feature. There is also a strong implication that this will be a totally egalitarian 'post-patriarchal' society.[85]

Outside of this democratic vision there are other, somewhat darker aspects. One of the suggestions of bioregionalists is for economic autarky and regional self-sufficiency. This obviates the need for any trade except on absolute necessities. Trade encourages the satisfaction of unnecessary 'wants' or luxuries as opposed to needs, invites dependence on others outside one's bioregion, and is profoundly wasteful of time and fuel resources. On the question of wasted resources, some, like Bahro and Ophuls, suggest that we travel too much anyway. The bioregional society, for some exponents, is one which will not tolerate scarce resources being frittered away on pleasurable travel. Aeroplanes use vast amounts of non-renewable fuels to transport people often for no other purpose than personal hedonism. The frugal society will thus be a limited-mobility society, where people will spend their lives in one place, cultivating their own bioregional community loyalties.

One implication of the above is that the human population must be kept under strict control for the bioregional idea to work, and this has given rise to the title 'neo-Malthusianism' for those who pursue the idea. As Goldsmith remarks, 'Clearly we must go all out for the "unlikely event" of achieving the replacement-sized family (on average about two children per couple) *throughout the world by the end of the century.*'[86] He suggests there could be massive publicity and advertising campaigns concerning population levels, in relation to food and quality of life. This could be supplemented by free contraception, sterilization and abortion. Finally, research should be funded in all areas of demography and population control.[87] Others have made suggestions concerning the legal restriction on couples having more than the prescribed number of children, in the form of 'baby licences', and tax incentives for having less children.[88] The Earth First! group have their own particular solutions to these problems, as already mentioned. Finally, there are also some suggestions for immigration control, which Dobson in his recent study finds a worrying development.[89]

The above vision of the frugal society has a number of manifestations. One impression often given is that it is a democratic and egalitarian vision. This is where the strong affinity to communist anarchism can be observed. However, it is far from clear that all its proponents favour democracy and freedom. Goldsmith's ideas may be legitimately described as fostering an authoritarian, not a democratic, commune. The long transition to a genuine commune life will require the curtailment of many freedoms. Goldsmith notes that 'Legislation and the operation of police forces and the courts will be necessary to reinforce this restraint'.[90] In addition, the suggestions for controlling population from the neo-Malthusian wing would certainly be hard to reconcile with autonomy and equality. Goldsmith perhaps unknowingly feeds into a more traditional nationalistic ecology with roots earlier in the century.

Even within the more egalitarian perspective, the fostering of diversity would certainly not tolerate bioregions which opted, for example, for slavery, infanticide or cannibalism. In other words, despite the overt commitment to tolerant diversity, there appears to be a lurking demand for consensus underneath. There is therefore no demonstrable necessary connection within this vision between bioregionalism and decentralized communes, on the one hand, and democracy and equality, on the other. It is perfectly ecologically feasible to have authoritarian as well as more egalitarian communes.

One major unresolved difficulty of the frugal society which appears in all its formats is the question of an over-arching authority, like the state, to resolve potential conflict. Ophuls, as mentioned earlier, envisages an eco-empire. Others express deep disquiet at any over-arching structure. One writer comments that 'the direction of Green politics is local life – together, conversely, with the end of the Nation State as we know it'; he continues: 'The Nation State is the political expression of a dualistic cast of mind, and all its disjunctions are inimical to ecology'.[91] For Goldsmith, self-conscious individualism *per se* and centralized statism go hand in hand. Both undermine the ecological small-scale community. This point is also emphasized from an eco-socialist perspective in the writings of Bahro, and from a more radical deep egalitarian perspective in those of Tokar, Spretnak and Capra, and Robertson.[92] However, it is clear from other aspects of the eco-socialist wing, and also from writers like Porritt, that many would conversely like to tie a more frugal vision to an ecologically sensitive state.

This unresolved question of the state in ecological thought raises difficult questions concerning political and moral values. How is a socially responsible policy of egalitarianism, social justice and freedom to be guaranteed in a non-state situation?[93] Bioregional anti-statist ecologists appear to run into the same series of problems as many anarchists and, more recently, anarcho-capitalists: namely, how to guarantee important values without resorting to personal violence or threats. Some stress appears to be laid on changes in human nature or, alternatively, on persuasive reasoning. Surely, though, it might legitimately be argued that many necessary ecologically beneficial functions would be far better performed by a sensitive rule-of-law state, than haggled over by fragmented bioregional assemblies?

A NEW ECONOMICS?

One of the key economic themes of many in the ecology movement is the insistence that the major economic problem we face is neither capitalism nor the command economy but industrialism. As Porritt comments:

> By 'industrialism', I mean adherence to the belief that human needs can only be met through *permanent* expansion of the process of production and consumption – regardless of the damage done to the planet, to the rights of future generations ... The often unspoken values of industrialism are premised on the notion that material gain is quite simply more important to more people that anything else.[94]

The battle against industrialism is therefore one that is against a 'super-ideology', which subsumes all the other major ideologies. For Porritt, and many like him, the struggle against this super-ideology of industrialism takes place as much in the realm of values as in technical questions concerning economics. This form of analysis is severely qualified by eco-socialists, however, who deny, either from Bahro's commune position or from Ryle's statist position, that socialism is automatically committed to industrialism. Further, writers like Weston and Pepper argue that the real problem is capitalism, not industrialism, and that the talk about values is more or less irrelevant.[95]

Most ecological writers would be in moderate agreement that industrialism and capitalism are committed to the idea of economic growth. Growth is the panacea for social and economic problems. Yet for ecologists, growth is the root of the problems of destruction in the environment, loss of community and social alienation. Over the nineteenth century, in the industrializing economies, growth was possible and produced a cornucopia of rewards for certain societies. However, as Spretnak and Capra remark, because growth produced some worthwhile goods for an historically short period this does not mean that more growth is always desirable.[96] In the main, the systematic expression of 'growth' and the related ignorance concerning ecological problems, can be found in most orthodox classical economic theories.[97]

Industrialism and classical economic theories for many ecologists (although not all) are committed to a false and narrow conception of human beings – rational economic man – where money, the maximization of the satisfaction of interests, and profits, are the measures of all things. Cost and benefit in classical economic theory appear to have taken no account, until recently, of the benefits of clear water, a stable atmosphere, a predictable climate. These are accorded no economic value. As a recent book states: 'It does not appear to have occurred to economists that if our activities interfere too radically with the workings of Nature, then Nature might no longer be capable of providing the benefits we now take for granted and upon which our survival depends'.[98] The authors describe this as a 'cock-eyed view of the world'. Conversely, the 'New Economics', as it is often referred to in the ecology literature, is 'based upon a different perception of reality itself, it embodies a change in outlook as fundamental as, say, the Copernican revolution in astronomy'.[99]

One of the central arguments of this new economics is that classical economic theories assume that growth can go on infinitely. But in a world where resources, like non-renewable fuels, are finite, how *can* growth be infinite? Fossil fuels are ephemeral and will probably quite quickly be exhausted. As Pirages suggests, 'Most seem to agree that petroleum and natural gas will become scarce shortly after the year 2010'.[100] He contends that the majority of the industrialized world faces the ending of cheap non-renewable fuel. Yet, for Pirages, the modernization of all societies, especially the Third World countries, is still measured in terms of the faulty logic of economic growth. Instead of feeding their populations, these countries race, with International Monetary Fund encouragement, to expand exports. Local needs, a clean environment, healthy citizens, are simply ignored in the economic equation. These are not included as indicators of economic success.

In summary, growth-orientated economies cannot go on using finite resources. Technological innovations cannot solve the problems indefinitely, although appropriate small-scale technologies are seen as one aspect of the solution. Technological advances can only postpone the problems.[101] Governments and their bureaucracies are often seen in this context to be hand-in-glove with industry, effectively controlling information on environmental collapse through the multiple techniques of secrecy, scientific whitewashing, and public relations campaigns.[102] For many ecologists, a radical change is needed to our whole conception of the economic world. This is the root of the ongoing TOES (The Other Economic Summit), devoted to promulgating an alternative economic strategy. In sum, a sustainable economic order must replace a growth-orientated economic order.

The visions of what constitutes a sustainable order vary. These play upon two variations of a post-industrial society. They also cross-cut the various component elements of ecologism. One vision poses a decentralized, commune, agrarian and non-state order as the ideal. The other envisions a technologically sophisticated, affluent ecological state order.

The eco-socialist answer, as argued, varies according to the socialist affiliation. Bahro appears to put his faith in frugal decentralized commune life where needs and wants are reduced to the bare minimum. Martin Ryle, on the other hand, despite questioning growth in a fairly conventional manner, contends that the new economics of the TOES group does not go far enough in its attitude to large corporations. As Ryle notes, if we reject the ideas of the older economics, 'we must be prepared to confront the institutions which embody and enforce them'.[103] Ryle's views rely on an eco-state to perform this task. This also appears to be the view promulgated by writers like Weston and Pepper. Pepper and Weston, though, are far more vitriolic than Ryle in their criticism of more mainstream deep Greens, accusing them of putting up a 'smokescreen' around market capitalism.[104]

There are, in fact, mainstream converts to the view that capitalism has got the answers. Elkington and Burke, particularly, contend that although market capitalism may have been part of the problem, with the help of Green capitalists it can be part of the solution.[105] The authors predict that the 1990s will be the Green decade, when consumers will demand products that are environmentally friendly. The environment is thus becoming 'a major new competitive area for business'.[106] The authors argue that, instead of engaging in Luddite sentimentalism towards industry, we should carefully distinguish not between a sustainable economy and an industrial growth economy, but rather between sustainable and unsustainable growth. The former is one which, via the market, adjusts to recycling, cleaner technologies, infrastructural investment and alternative energy — all generated by the demands of the Green consumer. The Body Shop and supermarket chains like Tesco and Sainsburys are held up as typical of this new trend. The authors see this as a 'new age capitalism'.[107]

The response to such a view from the eco-socialists is predictably critical. But the eco-capitalist conviction also brings a stinging dismissal from Porritt and Winner. They comment that 'all that has happend is that some ... companies are making a lot of money causing pollution – and then making even more by cleaning up some of the mess'.[108] Eco-capitalism is thus seen as a classic case of double standards, offering no answers to the massive destruction of the environment by industry. Nevertheless, it should be noted again at this point that Porritt, a somewhat half-hearted deep ecology proponent, still does not want to do away with the state, seeing it potentially as a major actor in the ecological debate.

The other side of the post-industrial and economic vision is that of the decentralized commune – the more frugal society. James Robertson describes this as a SHE economy (Sane, Humane, Ecological) as opposed to a HE economy (Hyper-Expansionist).[109] This SHE vision has a number of component elements. It tries to redefine most of the major economic concepts like demand, supply, production, consumption, and economies of scale in ecological terms. Thus, whereas in much classical economic theory humans are regarded as consumers or producers, the new economics puts humans and their total physical, moral and spiritual welfare first.[110] Taking their cue from Schumacher's and Fromm's work, the new economists regard morality as integral to economics. The qualitative goals of a satisfying and meaningful life are seen as more important than quantitative values. Instead of economic growth, human development and the satisfaction of physical, social, economic and cultural needs are regarded as more significant. Needs are seen as being 'of absolutely central significance to the New Economics'.[111] Needs extend beyond those of physical survival and include cultural well-being.

Formal contractual relations are replaced by mutual ethical concerns between people. Intuitive sympathetic concern would supplant intellectual and rational distance. Highly specialized occupations would be displaced by the all-round competence and self-reliance of citizens. Large-scale and destructive technologies would be replaced by human-scale and relatively harmless ones.

The concept of work changes radically in this vision. New concepts of employment are fostered. Writers like James Robertson and Guy Dauncey suggest the development of informal 'ownwork' to replace the concept of formal employment, something that most exponents see as applicable as much to Third World as to industrialized societies.[112] We should not confuse, according to this argument, *work* with a *job*. Work needs to be rethought, localized, and linked with many other occupations, including housework, growing your own vegetables, sharing a job, or doing DIY. As Robertson comments: 'Ownwork means activity which is purposeful and important and which people organize and control for themselves. It may be either paid or unpaid.'[113] The vision here is of a total radical shake-up of the way our whole society views work. It is also a vision of self-reliance, self-help, and decentralization, labour-intensive, localized and small-scale in terms of technology.[114] For most writers on this theme it means the extension of workers' cooperatives.

One other strategy which pervades most of the formulations of the frugal vision is the replacement of welfare benefits with what is generally called a 'Basic Income Scheme', or at least some form of minimum income scheme. The idea in fact goes back to the 1920s and Major C. H. Douglas, although Henry George's theories also appear to be inspirational for some writers.[115] In the post-war era it has been considered by social policy analysts outside the ecology movement. Basic Income ideas suggest a national wage to replace welfare benefits − financed from administrative savings and higher taxation, particularly (for ecologists) from those who pollute or use non-renewable resources − to be paid to all citizens over a certain age, regardless of work. The Basic Income would create a sense of independence for the majority of citizens. Work would be 'socially' expected from citizens; however, with changes in the concept of work, this could be performed in any number of contexts. This point is also tied, in some writings, to schemes for localized banking (and occasionally currencies) and marked changes in taxation, usually entailing much greater redistribution of wealth.[116]

Wealth in this theory is measured not just by monetary values or capital interests but also by the health and well-being of people. As Robertson comments:

> The idea that the development of healthier people, and the creation of a social and physical environment which enables people to be healthy, might be treated as productive investment in a society's capital assets, as the development of its most important resources (its people), is alien to conventional economics. The New Economics, in contrast, redefines the creation of wealth to include the creation of health.[117]

Thus health and need replace monetary wealth and growth. In addition, new economic indicators are suggested. The old indicators are seen as 'inadequate and inappropriate'.[118] Ekins, and many like him in the TOES group, suggest that new indicators would include social justice; satisfaction of the whole range of human needs; achievement of aspirations by citizens; more equitable distribution of income and work; greater self-reliance and self-esteem; greater conservation and ecological enhancement and sustainability; and more efficient use of resources. All this entails the replacement of Gross National Product (GNP) with the Adjusted National Product (ANP). ANP, unlike GNP, takes full account of social and environmental costs. It incorporates health and social indicators and the informal economy with its new working patterns.[119]

The most systematic expression of this more frugal vision is the Steady-State Economy, which is closely associated with the work of Herman Daly.[120] The idea can be found stated in J. S. Mill's economic writings in the nineteenth century. The basic point for Daly is that industrial economies must change in the next few decades. He suggests, in a neo-Malthusian vein, that populations must be stabilized. As indicated in the previous section, this could be achieved by many different means. Wealth would be more evenly distributed. Further, the amount of stock produced should be stabilized to minimize throughput. Ideally, all raw materials would be recycled to slow down depletion of finite resources. As Daly states, in a now recognizable argument which he links to the law of entropy: 'in a finite world nothing physical can grow forever'.[121] Growth could still take place in such an economy, but it would be tied to knowledge and less harmful technology. Yet it would not be the aim of economic activity. Economies which simply maximize throughput and do not try to conserve energy, deplete the finite stock of our planet's energy and create pollution. This, in turn, requires more energy to cope with waste. Such wasteful economies measure GNP by a growing throughput, which contains a suicidal logic for Steady Staters.

Daly suggests an economy based on slowed-down throughput, stable population, energy conservation, use of renewable resources like solar power, insulation, wider use of public transport and bicycles. Daly not only believes this is necessary on an economic and scientific base, but also that there is a strong moral case for such changes. He claims that we need to develop the idea of stewardship and also greater humility towards our planet and its resources.[122]

There are several ambiguities with the above schemes. Apart from the worries expressed by many concerning the population controls of the neo-Malthusians (discussed in the previous section), it is also not particularly clear as to the intended role of public authorities and the state. There are a series of stipulations against social injustice and excessive inequalities of wealth and a strong dislike of commercial advertising. There are also suggestions for taxation changes, Basic Income Schemes, a denial of the necessity of trade and the promotion of protectionism and autarky in the economy. Yet these are all linked with an encouragement of local autonomy and a denial of the relevance of the state. It is difficult to see how any of these reforms could be achieved without some form of central authority.

Each of the above proposals has its own body of criticism. The Basic Income Scheme, for example, has come in for close and critical scrutiny. Would the scheme offer enough to provide a decent standard of living? Surely it would not tackle the question of wide-scale disparities in income; in fact, it could risk stigmatizing a new underclass. Further, what if people did not work at all? How could their behaviour be dealt with? Unless a

Steady-State frugal society was achieved quickly, the Basic Income would have to keep up with inflation, and this would entail more economic growth, which would appear to contradict the general thrust of the frugal argument.

CONCLUSION

One immediate conclusion to draw is that the ecology movement and its ideology are still in the process of formation. In this sense, this chapter represents a snapshot of a moving phenomenon. Ecology does, though, draw attention to our global responsibilities and indicates that we are interrelated with the ecosphere. However, it is worth pointing out a number of damaging internal disjunctions within the ideology. There has been little consciousness to date of the gulf which separates the philosophy from the political practice of ecologism. On one side, philosophers meander through the well-worn byways of environmental philosophy, recommending utilitarianism or ecocentrism, while, on the other side, the practitioners appear drawn to rather simple generalizations, the consequences of which they do not appear very certain about. In addition, the debate concerning anthropocentrism and non-anthropocentrism, which is now so central to philosophical discussions, appears to have no bearing whatsoever on the way environmental policies are justified in practice. This is, to say the least, strange.

Another odd disjunction in the movement is its attitude to the natural sciences and to the scientific discipline of ecology. As suggested at the beginning of this chapter, the strength of the political ecology movement derives to a large degree from the scientific standing of its analyses. However, this strength is combined with a continual moral and philosophical critique of the character of mechanistic natural science and its fatal link with industrialism. Although writers like Capra have insisted on the distinction between the outdated 'mechanistic' and the new 'systems' conception of natural science, the scientific community themselves do not appear to have taken the distinction seriously and express, at times, marked hostility to the political ecologists.[123] This tension remains perennially puzzling.

Further, the ideology of ecology has suffered, since its appearance in the political limelight two decades ago, from the tension between two streams of thought. The 1970s saw the upsurge of both environmental interests and the beginnings of disillusionment with socialism in many quarters. The ecology/Green movement provided an ideal haven for disillusioned socialists and anarchists. Yet it was also at this stage that attempts began to be made to popularize and systematize the ideas of the movement. In consequence, late-nineteenth and early twentieth-century socialist and anarchist vocabulary, with all its baggage of diverse and often contradictory meanings was fully employed.

At the same time, however, socialist and anarchistic affiliates found themselves bedfellows with another kind of vocabulary, which concentrated on the terminology of deeply held values, spiritual reverence of nature, metaphysical world-views, frugality, simplicity, the wisdom of ancient primal peoples, living in harmony with the land and its folk memories. Socialist writers, quite logically, often react violently to this form of vocabulary, accusing it of mysticism, racism, dangerous and simple-minded religiosity, genuflecting to capitalism, and affluent middle-class utopianism with no grasp of political and economic realities.

The socialist anxiety and criticism is understandable since the roots of ecology are in fact as faithfully reflected by the deep ecology, frugal and spiritual movement. The ancestry of such views can be found in the changing philosophical beliefs concerning nature and social existence in the latter half of the nineteenth century. Such beliefs were expressed in terms that are still recognizable today within the ecology movement. As we now know only too well, many of these ideas were utilized by political movements, like folkish nationalism and national socialism, in the early twentieth century. We regard such movements with suspicion and anxiety. However, it is worth pointing out that such vocabulary is not the exclusive property of such movements. There is no reason why it should not be re-explored in a sensitive and open manner. Yet the ancestry of this vocabulary is often denied by many who use it. There are two reasons for this. First, they wish to distance themselves, understandably, from any association with eco-fascism. Second, there is a rather bland belief that we have reached or are about to reach, a new age, paradigm, or renaissance where all ideologies will appear antiquated. This latter millennialist belief appears misguided.

9
ICONS AND ICONOCLASM
—

What has been achieved in this book? Certain facets of ideologies have been examined. First, ideologies are more complex internally than we are often aware. This problem is usually dealt with within ideologies by denunciation or determined silence. The book has been based on this internal complexity. We are faced by doctrines which look, *prima facie*, moderately coherent. Yet closer analysis often reveals profound internal disagreement. Second, each ideology has certain central questions, values or ideas. However, these elements are formal and can only be considered as general signposts. They gain supplementation within the various schools. This is where major internal differences of interpretation arise. Third, ideologies are not just internally complex; they also overlap with each other and use common modes of argument. In fact there are, on occasions, more affinities between schools of differing ideologies than there are similarities between schools within an ideology. This has given rise to the many compounds like liberal conservatism, social liberalism, socialist feminism or anarchist communism. This might be called the external complexity, although 'internal' and 'external' begin to look rather meaningless in such a context. We are confronted by a vast web of interlinked concepts.

Each and every skein of ideological concepts and values has its own iconography. Most skeins of concepts with ambitions to explain or understand usually claim that their iconography is not just another 'ism', but rather is the actual ontological nature of reality. History has ended on a number of occasions in the last few centuries without apparent success, leaving successive generations of iconographers and hagiographers with the additional problem not only of explaining the icon, but also why it has not yet instantiated itself successfully in reality. Some icons have also had second and third comings, rising miraculously, but always appearing frayed at the edges and tawdry after comparatively short historical periods.

I have taken as my task the unpacking of a collection of icons which have markedly affected human life over the last two centuries. The fact that I have unpacked them in this manner might be regarded by many as a form of iconoclasm. Some might consider the manner of my unpacking and the emphasis on overlapping as destructive of the pristine purity of a particular favoured icon. Perhaps my discussion has either sullied a position or marginalized it. Others may regard my analysis as trivial, drawing lessons from the obvious, in that ideologies do plainly contain diverse components and often conceptually intermingle. In this sense it is a flawed iconoclasm. Even if this is true, there is a residual therapeutic function in such analysis. Others still may regard my argument as an attempt at being 'positionless' or to step beyond ideological beliefs and deny the reality of all icons. What, after all, it might be said, is *my* ideology or my iconography? Are not all iconoclasts secret iconographers? This has been a prevailing aspect of much ideological work. As one writer perceptively remarks, 'To have a *theory* of ideology therefore is, paradoxically, a slippery slope to having "an ideology"'.[1] What else can I do here except to plead guilty? The only mitigating circumstance is that I have tried to understand.

Each of the ideologies that has been examined could potentially perform a running commentary on all the others. In fact the book, in its totality, could have been written from each distinct ideological perspective. I have tried, however, to avoid this particular path, as far as possible. Rather I have unpacked and examined the passion of the arguments from within each perspective, concentrating on their internal complexity.

Given the quotation from Umberto Eco with which this book opens, it might be considered that I am engaging, mildly, in a covert postmodernist exercise of some kind, namely, presenting the multiple styles of political rhetoric; there does not appear to be any ultimate truth or foundation to the ideologies, rather they might be said to emerge as a series of metaphors or fictions. Reality is constructed from within such ideological skeins, none of which appear to be privileged above others. We are faced therefore with a necessary diversity of fictions. Despite that fact that I am persuaded that reality does lie in our conceptual and linguistic appraisals, I have not unpacked, as far as I know, any binary oppositions. I have no interest in endlessly deconstructing the conceptual world with reflexive argument. I do not wish to look into the remote margins or footnotes of ideologies or to reinscribe their signifiers. I am firmly ensconced in the 'logocentric' world, and the notion of some vague power underlying such systems does not strike me as very persuasive. I am also firmly of the belief that ideologies usually constitute, and seek, a metaphysics of real presence. They want their positions to be considered as *the* ontology. They are not therefore fictions. This appears to me to be the human condition. We believe in systems and real absolutes, and have doubts, occasionally quite paralysing reflexive doubts. But we cannot live by reflexive doubt. That is both a burden and a blessing of the negative side of our reasoning capacity.

This book might be better considered as a rather complex conversation about conceptions of the absolute and real, which many wish to live by, even though accompanied by the inevitable doubts. The reader will also have gathered that I consider certain ideologies easier to live by than others.

However, if the study of ideology is considered as a conversation, then that implies listening. It also implies doubt, self-doubt, mutual respect, and some humility in understanding. This could have the effect of undermining, partially, the absolutes of particular ideologies, which would be no bad thing.

NOTES

1: The Nature of Ideology

1. See Kennedy, 'Ideology'; Head, 'Origins of "idéologue" and "idéologie"' and *Ideology and Social Science.*
2. Head, *Ideology and Social Science*, p. 28.
3. Ibid., p. 4.
4. See Kennedy, 'Ideology', p. 356; Head, *Ideology and Social Science*, pp. 114ff.
5. See Kennedy, 'Ideology', p. 358.
6. See Stein, 'Beginnings of "Ideology"', p. 169.
7. Quoted in Kennedy, 'Ideology', p. 362.
8. As Engels stated in one letter: 'Men make their history, only they do so in a given environment, which conditions it, and on the basis of actual relations already existing, among which the economic relations, however much they may be influenced by the other — the political and ideological relations — are still ultimately the decisive ones, forming the keynote which runs through them'; quoted in McLellan, *Ideology*, p. 22.
9. See the various contradictory discussions of this point as to whether Marx did or did not employ the term false consciousness, as well as Engels own odd usage of the term; see Plamenatz, *Ideology*, p. 25; Seliger, *Marxist Conception of Ideology*, pp. 28ff; Parekh, *Marx's Theory of Ideology*, pp. 12ff; McLellan, *Ideology*, pp. 18ff; Adams, *Logic of Political Belief*, pp. 9ff.
10. Ricoeur, *Lectures on Ideology and Utopia*, p. 8.
11. Mannheim, *Ideology and Utopia*, p. 69.
12. See n. 11 above.
13. See, for example, Williams, *Concepts of Ideology*, pp. 27–8; Ricoeur, *Lectures on Ideology and Utopia*, p. 167.
14. Mannheim, *Ideology and Utopia*, pp. 70ff.
15. Ibid., pp. 137ff.
16. 'The rather bleak passages at the end of *Ideology and Utopia* foreshadow the debate on the "end of ideology" in the United States'; see McLellan, *Ideology*, p. 49.
17. Fukuyama, 'End of History?'

18. This point is discussed again in the chapter on conservatism.
19. Writers like W. H. Greenleaf, Noël O'Sullivan, R. N. Berki, Ken Minogue and David Manning were very influenced by Oakeshott. In the volume edited by Manning, *The Form of Ideology*, many of the MA group, run by Manning in the 1970s at Durham University, contribute essays. Michael Oakeshott was the external examiner for ten years, suggesting in his preface to the above volume, that the seminars of the course enjoyed 'an unusual intellectual continuity' (p. vii). Other recent authors, like Gordon Graham in *Politics in its Place* and Ian Adams in *The Logic of Political Belief*, express their great intellectual debt to Manning's Oakeshottian stance, but appear to want to force a critical distance. However, both otherwise fairly reasonable books are marred by the slightly obsessive attempt to exorcize sprites which might not be familar to the average reader. For a very readable recent discussion of this group in relation to Oakeshott's thought, see Williams, *Concepts of Ideology*, ch. 3.
20. Lipset, *Political Man*, p. 406; see also Daniel Bell's classic statement of the case in the book with the resounding title *The End of Ideology: On the Exhaustion of Political Ideas in the 1950s*; Shils, 'The End of Ideology' and 'Concept and Function of Ideology'; and Waxman (ed.), *End of Ideology Debate*.
21. Lipset, *Political Man*, p. 408
22. See Duncan, 'Understanding Ideology', p. 649.
23. Butler and Stokes, *Political Change in Britain*.
24. See Goldie, in Ball, Farr and Hanson (eds), *Political Innovation*, p. 268.
25. Shils 'Concept and Function of Ideology', p. 74.
26. MacIntyre, *Against the Self-Images of the Age*, p. 5.
27. Hamilton, 'Elements of Ideology', p. 22.
28. Kuhn, *Structure of Scientific Revolutions*; Feyerabend, *Against Method*; Lakatos and Musgrave, *Criticism and the Growth of Knowledge*; Hesse, *Revolutions and Reconstructions*.
29. See Adams, *Logic of Political Belief*, pp. xiii, 3. The same spirit pervades the work of Corbett, *Ideologies* and Plamenatz, *Ideology*. In fact it has been, with varying degrees of self-consciousness, a supposition of much analytical political theory to the present.
30. This resonates with Martin Seliger's central distinction between 'restrictive' and 'inclusive' notions of ideology; see *Ideology and Politics*.
31. For a recent account of some of the diversity and complexity of recent views on ideology, see Thompson, *Studies in the Theory of Ideology*.
32. Seliger, *Ideology and Politics*, p. 120.
33. Ibid., pp. 192–3.
34. Ball, *Transforming Political Discourse*, p. 4.
35. Farr in Ball, Farr and Hanson, *Political Innovation*, pp. 24–5.
36. For Ricoeur, 'the capacity for distanciation is always a part of theory'; see *Lectures on Ideology and Utopia*, p. 233.

2: Liberalism

1. See Collins, *Liberalism in 19th-Century Europe*, p. 3.
2. Eccleshall, *British Liberalism*, p. 4.
3. See Hayek, *Philosophy, Politics, Economics and the History of Ideas*, p. 119; Gray, *Liberalism*, p. x.

4. Arblaster, *Western Liberalism*, p. 7.
5. See Laski, *Rise of European Liberalism*; Macpherson, *Political Theory of Possessive Individualism*; Arblaster, *Western Liberalism*.
6. For critical comment on this point, see Hall, *Liberalism*, pp. 1–3.
7. I have discussed these in detail in my *Theories of the State* (ch. 3).
8. See Constant, *Political Writings*.
9. Talmon, *Origins of Totalitarian Democracy*.
10. In fact, the situation in France was far more complex than this. The more constitutionally orientated liberals were also divided over various issues.
11. See Sheehan, *German Liberalism*.
12. Figgis, *Political Thought from Gerson to Grotius*, p. 118.
13. For the positive view of Spencer, see Greenleaf, *British Political Tradition*, p. 48, and Gray, *Liberalism*, p. 31. The 'maverick' interpretation can be found in Eccleshall, *British Liberalism*, p. 31.
14. If one reviews the literature on liberalism, a number of attempts have been made to clarify such schools. For example: integral as against formal liberalism, Hallowell, *Decline of Liberalism*, p. 20; rationalist Gallican liberalism as against British sceptical liberalism, Hayek, *Constitution of Liberty*, pp. 55–6; minimum function *laissez-faire* liberalism as against pluralist interventionary liberalism, McCloskey 'Problem of Liberalism', pp. 250ff; rationalist transcendental liberalism as against mechanistic reductive liberalism, Dunn, *Western Political Theory*, p. 34; collectivist as against libertarian liberalism, Greenleaf, *British Political Tradition*; classical versus modern liberalism, Gaus, *Modern Liberal Theory*; classical versus revisionary liberalism, Gray, *Liberalism*; Kantian versus utilitarian liberalism, Sandel (ed.), *Liberalism and its Critics*. Other commentators see liberalism as a complex series of traditions with a symbolic unity around certain strategies; see Manning, *Liberalism*, or Eccleshall, *British Liberalism*.
15. See Giesey and Salmon in Hotman, *Francogallia*, p. 124.
16. As Pocock remarks: 'Though Locke supplied a theoretical background to the constitution, he did not write or think within the changing framework of commonly accepted ideas about the constitution, and it is arguable that in the eighteenth century he was a writer largely for those who were situated somewhat outside the established order'; see Pocock, *Language and Time*, p. 144.
17. As Eccleshall remarks: 'Both liberals and socialists ... have dipped into a shared stream of radical beliefs which flowed from the civil war of the seventeenth century'; see Eccleshall, *British Liberalism*, p. 44.
18. Dangerfield, *Strange Death of Liberal England*, p. 20.
19. This was the title for a book; see Graham and Clarke, *New Enlightenment*.
20. This applies mainly in Britain and to some degree in Germany before the First World War. However, the new liberal ideas also developed slightly later in other European countries, for example in Italy, in the writings of Guido de Ruggiero; see Bellamy, 'Idealism and Liberalism'.
21. See Vincent, 'New Liberalism in Britain', for a detailed outline of the scholarly interpretations of the new liberalism in Britain.
22. Keynes and Beveridge in Britain were 'New Liberals' but of a different type to Hobson and Hobhouse. Certainly they were less concerned with the moral case for liberalism. For discussion of this, see Freeden, *Liberalism Divided*.
23. Hallowell, *Decline of Liberalism*, p. 20.

24. See Vincent, 'Classical Liberalism', pp. 143—4.
25. See Bernstein, *Liberalism in Edwardian England.*
26. In the sense that it could be argued, via a traditional contractarian liberalism, that individuals are actually prior to society and possess fundamental rights. However, this could be interpreted as not so much indicating any actual or natural priority as a hypothetical moral priority of the individual to society.
27. Dewey, *Individualism.*
28. In Hayek, *New Studies on Philosophy.*
29. Gaus, *Modern Liberal Theory*, p. 2; Eccleshall, *British Liberalism*, pp. 6—7.
30. See Parekh in Berki and Parekh (eds), *Morality of Politics*, p. 81.
31. Rothbard's ideas are discussed in ch. 5, 'Anarchism'.
32. Ritchie, *Principles of State Interference*, p. 57, n. 1.
33. Herbert, *Right and Wrong of Compulsion by the State*, p. 14.
34. Barry, *Classical Liberalism*, p. 106.
35. Rand calls this 'objectivist ethics'. As she states: 'The Objectivist ethics proudly advocates and upholds *rational selfishness* — which means: the values required for man's survival *qua* man — which means: the values required for *human* survival ... The Objectivist ethics holds that *human* good does not require human sacrifices and cannot be achieved by the sacrifice of anyone to anyone'; see Rand, *Virtue of Selfishness*, p. 31.
36. Quoted in Tame, 'The Moral Case for Private Enterprise', in Turner (ed.), *Case for Private Enterprise*, p. 17.
37. Humboldt, *Limits of State Action*, p. 37.
38. Ibid., p. 18.
39. Ibid., p. 16; Mill, *Utilitarianism.* Kant's liberalism was close to Humboldt's. Kant was primarily interested in moral and philosophical argumentation concerning the moral respect for individuals as ends-in-themselves. However, the upshot of Kant's liberalism is far from clear in political practice. See Howard Williams's discussion of this point, *Kant's Political Philosophy*, p. 128.
40. Sidgwick, *Elements of Politics*, p. 58.
41. Wiltshire, *Herbert Spencer*, p. 154.
42. Dicey, *Law and Public Opinion in England*, p. xxx.
43. See Spencer, *Man Versus State*, essay 4; Nozick, *Anarchy State and Utopia*, pp. 32—3; see also Arblaster, *Western Liberalism*, pp. 350—2 and Pearson and Williams, *Political Thought and Public Policy.*
44. Hayek, *Constitution of Liberty*, pp. 38, 57 and 61. John Gray follows Hayek in scolding Mill. In an essay he remarks that 'The dominant Millian paradigm of contemporary liberalism is radically defective and ought to be abandoned. We are wise, I believe, if we return to the classical liberals'; see Gray 'Mill's and Other Liberalisms' in Haakonssen (ed.), *Traditions of Liberalism*, p. 137.
45. See Gray, *Hayek on Liberty*, pp. 42—3.
46. Green, *Prolegomena to Ethics*, s. 234. For an outline of Green's contribution, see Vincent and Plant, *Philosophy, Politics and Citizenship.*
47. Hobhouse, *Liberalism*, p. 128. For J. A. Hobson's views on this point, see Allett, *New Liberalism*, p. 204.
48. See Hobhouse, *Metaphysical Theory of the State*, p. 60, and Collini, *Liberalism and Sociology*, pp. 10, 97.
49. Freeden, *Liberalism Divided*, p. 108.

50. As Eccleshall remarks on this theme, for liberals 'political stability pre-supposes a moral community of individuals who cooperate in the pursuit of common objectives'; see Eccleshall, *British Liberalism*, p. 6.
51. Freeden, *Liberalism Divided*, p. 266.
52. See, for example, Berlin in Sandel (ed.), *Liberalism and its Critics*. There have been attempts to reformulate this whole idea, for example, Mac-Callum, 'Negative and Positive Freedom'. However, these will not concern the present discussion directly.
53. Hayek, *Philosophy, Politics, Economics and the History of Ideas*, p. 134.
54. Hayek, *Constitution of Liberty*, pp. 16—17.
55. Gray, *Liberalism*, p. 62. As Hayek put it, 'Law, liberty and property are an inseparable trinity'; see Hayek, *Law, Legislation and Liberty*, Vol. I, p. 107.
56. See quote in Eccleshall, *British Liberalism*, p. 21.
57. Ritchie, *Natural Rights*, pp. 11—12.
58. For Nozick there are certain areas where freedom can be restricted, for example, if the genuine entitlement to property is interfered with or where the Lockean provisos are infringed; see Nozick, *Anarchy State and Utopia*, pp. 85, 178—82.
59. Macpherson redefines negative liberty as 'counter-extractive liberty', which implies 'immunity from the extractive power of others'. For Macpherson, this 'moves away from the mechanical image of negative liberty as a "field (ideally) without obstacles"'. It also implies restraining market activity; see Macpherson, *Democratic Theory*, p. 118.
60. Green, *Works*, vol. 3, pp. 370—1.
61. Samuel, *Memoirs*, p. 25. J. A. Hobson also commented that 'Free land, free travel, free power, free credit, security, justice and education, no man is "free" for the full purposes of civilized life today unless he has all these liberties'; see Hobson, *Crisis of Liberalism*, p. 113.
62. See Vincent and Plant, *Philosophy, Politics and Citizenship*, pp. 73—6.
63. See Hayek, *Constitution of Liberty*, p. 440, n. 10.
64. Hayek, *Philosophy, Politics, Economics and the History of Ideas*, p. 140.
65. Hayek, *Constitution of Liberty*, p. 93.
66. A less biological way of putting this is to argue that distributive justice creates dependency in certain groups in society. This dependent class, which survives on welfare benefits, is then incapable of engaging in competitive independent activity in the market. Hayek would not go to the same social lengths as Spencer.
67. Quoted in Greenleaf, *British Political Tradition*, p. 81.
68. See Acton, *Morals of Markets*, p. 71.
69. Gaus, *Modern Liberal Theory of Man*, p. 43.
70. Green, *Works*, p. 376.
71. For Rawls, 'All social primary goods — liberty and opportunity, income and wealth, and the bases of self-respect — are to be distributed equally unless an unequal distribution of any or all of these goods is to the advantage of the least favoured', Rawls, *Theory of Justice*, p. 303. Rawls' theory of justice is a uniquely clever argument given that he utilizes devices from classical liberalism, like contractualism and rational asocial individual-ism, to establish a social liberal position on distributive justice. In Rawls' account, rational self-interest ultimately achieves the same ends as benevol-ence and altruism.
72. Ritchie, *Natural Rights*, p. 16.

73. Gray, *Hayek on Liberty*, p. 77.
74. There are other liberal theorists, like John Rawls and Ronald Dworkin, who also adopt this Kantian approach but interpret the notion of a 'fair' or 'right' order in a much more generous way than Hayek or Nozick.
75. See Sandel, *Liberalism and the Limits of Justice*.
76. See Sandel, *Liberalism and its Critics*, pp. 5–6. There have been some very recent attempts in political theory to revive Green's arguments as another basis for social liberalism. For example, a recent essay notes that 'While classic individualist liberals have long eschewed political argument about collective ends, social liberals have insisted upon the indispensability of some common interpretations about ends for the achievement of key liberal commitments such as the ideal of self-determination. Social liberal thinkers thus anticipated many of the arguments of contemporary communitarians ... I have in mind thinkers such as T. H. Green and the New Liberals in Britain, Emile Durkheim and his school in France, and Josiah Royce, John Dewey, and George Herbert Mead in the United States'; see William M. Sullivan, 'Bringing the Good Back In', in Douglass, Mara and Richardson (eds), *Liberalism and the Good*, p. 149.
77. Hayek, *Constitution of Liberty*, p. 14.
78. Hirschman, *Passions and Interests*, p. 42.
79. See essay by Kenneth L. Schmitz, 'Is Liberalism Good Enough?', in Douglass, Mara and Richardson, *Liberalism and the Good*.
80. For example, Arblaster, *Western Liberalism*.
81. Greenleaf, *British Political Tradition*, p. 25.
82. See Gray, *Liberalism*, pp. 27–8.
83. Adam Smith had been committed to state education; Cobden wanted state regulation of railways and education; Mill always saw conspicuous exceptions to *laissez-faire*. Children and the insane, for example, must be looked after paternalistically; Sidgwick was also clear that defence and care of children, postal networks, regulation of canals and seaways, weights and measures, etc., must be looked after by the state.
84. Hobson, *Crisis of Liberalism*, pp. 92–3.
85. See Gray, *Liberalism*; Barry, *Classical Liberalism*.
86. Ruggiero, *History of European Liberalism*, p. 48.
87. Ibid., p. 157.
88. Laski, *Rise of European Liberalism*, p. 243.
89. Ibid., p. 248.
90. See, particularly, Freeden, *Liberalism Divided*.

3: Conservatism

1. Kirk, *Portable Conservative Reader*, p. xii.
2. Blake, *Conservative Party*, p. 7.
3. O'Sullivan, *Conservatism*, p. 9.
4. Scruton, *Meaning of Conservatism*, p. 21.
5. Allison, *Right Principles*, p. 2. Ted Honderich has given this claim a severe philosophical drubbing in his recent book on conservatism; see Honderich, *Conservatism*, ch. 2.
6. See Huntington, 'Conservatism'. A fairly recent essay by Arthur Aughey expresses great impatience with Huntington's thesis, arguing that it would be 'laughable were it not so influential'. Despite some sympathy with his

view, I cannot really see the reason for Aughey's objections to it, other than his vague thesis concerning conservatism's place in a 'wider tradition', which left me unconvinced and puzzled; see Aughey, in Eatwell and O'Sullivan (eds), *Nature of the Right*, p. 102.

7. Cecil, *Conservatism*, p. 9.
8. Kirk, *Portable Conservative Reader*, p. xii.
9. Schuettinger (ed), *Conservative Tradition*.
10. See Auerbach, *Conservative Illusion*, p. 5; see also Austern, *Edmund Burke and Joseph de Maistre*, p. 22.
11. Auerbach, *Conservative Illusion*, p. 26.
12. Stanlis, *Burke and the Natural Law*.
13. Smith, *Disraelian Conservatism*, pp. 8, 16.
14. Pocock, *Virtue, Commerce, and History*, p. 210, and O'Gorman (ed.), *British Conservatism*, p. 9.
15. Feiling, 'Coleridge'; Cecil, *Conservatism*; Quinton, *Politics of Imperfection*; Huntington, 'Conservatism'; and Eccleshall, 'English Conservatism as Ideology'.
16. Eccleshall, 'English Conservatism as Ideology', p. 71; see also Eccleshall, *English Conservatism since the Restoration*.
17. Eccleshall, 'English Conservatism as Ideology', p. 71.
18. O'Gorman, *British Conservatism*, p. 9.
19. Schochet, *Patriarchalism*, p. 120; Figgis, *Divine Right of Kings*, p. 176.
20. See Dickinson, *Liberty and Property*, p. 18.
21. O'Gorman, *British Conservation*, p. 9.
22. See Kirk, *Conservative Mind*, p. 4.
23. Pocock notes a peculiarity here, that 'If conservatism is the defence of the existing order, the conservatism of the eighteenth century was the defence of a revolution'; see Pocock, *Virtue, Commerce, and History*, p. 158.
24. Allison, *Right Principles*, p. 3.
25. Gilmour, *Inside Right*, p. 53. Ted Honderich also wishes to redeem Hume from the clutches of conservatism, but in this case for the sake of his philosophical reputation 'as no doubt the greatest of British philosophers'; see Honderich, *Conservatism*, p. 47.
26. Johnson and Boswell, *Western Islands of Scotland and Hebrides*, p. 342.
27. O'Sullivan, *Conservatism*, pp. 29–30; on the inception of conservative thought at the time of the French Revolution, see also Roger Eatwell in Eatwell and O'Sullivan, *Nature of the Right*, p. 63.
28. See Honderich, *Conservatism*, pp. 124ff.
29. Hampsher-Monk, *Edmund Burke*, p. 19; see also O'Gorman, *Edmund Burke*, p. 55, and Dickinson, *Liberty and Property*, p. 283.
30. This can be seen quite clearly in French conservatives, see selections from Maurras in McClelland (ed.) *The French Right*; Griffiths, 'Anti-capitalism'; T. S. Eliot's *Idea of a Christian Society* provides another anti-capitalist statement.
31. Smith, *Disraelian Conservatism*, p. 2; Blake, *Conservative Party*, pp. 24–5; Hoover and Plant, *Conservative Capitalism*.
32. Mannheim, *Conservatism*, p. 47.
33. O'Sullivan, *Conservatism*, pp. 28, 82–3.
34. Hartz, *Liberal Tradition in America*; for more recent critical discussion on this theme; see Aughey's essay in Eatwell and O'Sullivan, *Nature of the Right*, pp. 108–12.

35. See Noble, 'Conservatism in USA', p. 635. In the last decade American writers like Nathan Glazer, Irving Kristol and Daniel Bell have been called 'neo-conservatives'. Although bewailing the existence of 'big government', the growth of welfare budgets and the weakening of individual self-reliance, they have not been concerned to further or defend the economic interests of unregulated capitalism. Rather, unregulated markets are seen to undermine potentially the political values of American society; see Kristol, 'When virtue loses all her loveliness'; O'Sullivan, *Conservatism*, p. 145.
36. See Hans-Jürgen Puhle, 'Conservatism in Modern German History'.
37. On the question of classification, see Allison, *Right Principles*, p. 7. On the pure doctrine, see Quinton, *Politics of Imperfection*, and G. Graham, *Politics in its Place*, p. 172.
38. Greenleaf, *British Political Tradition*; Hampsher-Monk, *Edmund Burke*.
39. Epstein, *German Conservatism*; Schuettinger, *Conservative Tradition*.
40. See Norton and Aughey, *Conservatives and Conservatism*, and the much more sophisticated and perceptive account by Roger Eatwell of 'styles of thought' in the right, namely, the reactionary, moderate, radical, extreme and new rights; see Eatwell in Eatwell and O'Sullivan, *Nature of the Right*, pp. 63ff.
41. O'Sullivan criticizes Roger Scruton on this count. He contends that 'Scruton ... has in fact committed the greatest of political errors'; he has 'asked too much of politics. Ironically, the result is that he threatens to submerge civil in social philosophy'; see O'Sullivan in Eatwell and O'Sullivan, *Nature of the Right*, p. 180.
42. See selections from the work in Buck (ed.), *How Conservatives Think*, pp. 56–8.
43. Gilmour, *Britain Can Work*; see also Macmillan, *Middle Way*.
44. For the history of these early groups, see Bristow, 'Liberty and Property Defence League'.
45. See, for example, Bosanquet, *After the New Right*; Hall and Jacques (eds), *Politics of Thatcherism*; Levitas (ed.), *Ideology of the New Right*; N. P. Barry, *The New Right*; and D. King, *The New Right*; Eatwell and O'Sullivan *Nature of the Right*, ch. 1; Hoover and Plant, *Conservative Capitalism*.
46. D. Green, *The New Right*.
47. In Hall and Jacques, *Politics of Thatcherism*, and Levitas, *Ideology of the New Right*, the neo-authoritarian or neo-conservative element is included in the surveys of the new right.
48. See Cowling (ed.), *Conservative Essays*; Scruton, *Meaning of Conservatism*.
49. See Cowling, *Conservative Essays*.
50. Maistre, *Considerations on France*, p. 97.
51. Scruton, *Meaning of Conservatism*, p. 34.
52. The classic case is Burke's notion of a 'natural aristocracy'. Conservative thinkers have given different reasons and accounts of such natural leadership.
53. Viereck, *Conservatism Revisited*, pp. 44–5.
54. Maistre, *Considerations on France*, p. 23.
55. Honderich, however, is keen still to associate Burke's position with strong religious themes. He notes that 'Burke chooses to refer only to *the invisible world*. Elsewhere he is more plain-spoken: "God willed the state". We had better not interfere with it then'; see Honderich, *Conservatism*, p. 159.
56. For a twentieth-century religious reading, see Hogg, *Case for Conservatism*.
57. Interestingly certain recent classical liberal writers, like Hayek, also try to

utilize the imperfection thesis in a limited format. Hayek, for example, contends that we have limited stocks of knowledge at our disposal which necessarily inhibit our judgements in politics and economics.

58. Kirk, *Conservative Mind*, p. 6.
59. Scruton, *Meaning of Conservatism*, p. 11.
60. Maistre, *Considerations on France*, pp. 88, 95, 103.
61. See Mannheim, *Conservatism*, pp. 139–40; and Aris, *Political Thought in Germany*, p. 224.
62. See Kirk, *Portable Conservative Reader*, p. xv.
63. Burke selections in Hampsher-Monk, *Edmund Burke*, pp. 188–9; also Burke, *Political Writings and Speeches*, pp. 294–5.
64. Quoted in Epstein, *German Conservatism*.
65. See Oakeshott, *Rationalism in Politics*.
66. See Coleridge's explanation of the 'Idea' in the opening sections of his *On the Constitution of the Church and State* which expounds this theme, pp. 12–13; for discussion of this, see Muirhead, *Coleridge as Philosopher*, pp. 65ff; also Calleo, *Coleridge and the Modern State*, pp. 63 ff.
67. Maistre, *Considerations on France*, p. 95.
68. Quoted in Mannheim, *Conservatism*, p. 132.
69. There are parallels with the cities of Brasilia or even Canberra for some residents!
70. Oakeshott, *Rationalism in Politics*; see also Greenleaf, *Oakeshott's Philosophical Politics*, pp. 47ff.
71. See Wolin, 'Hume and Conservatism', p. 1001.
72. See Allison, *Right Principles*, p. 36.
73. Scruton, *Meaning of Conservatism*, p. 42.
74. Hampsher-Monk, *Edmund Burke*, p. 36.
75. The *makroanthropos* or large man. See selections from Novalis's and Müller's writings in Reiss (ed.), *Political Thought of the German Romantics*.
76. Cobban, *Edmund Burke*, p. 88.
77. Maistre, *Considerations on France*, p. 80.
78. Nisbet asserts confidently that 'Conservatism is unique among major political ideologies in its emphasis upon ... the Judaeo-Christian morality', see Nisbet, *Conservatism*, p. 68; see also Cecil, *Conservatism*, p. 75; Rossiter, *Conservatism in America*, p. 44; Hogg, *Case for Conservatism*, ch. 2.
79. See Quinton, *Politics of Imperfection*, p. 90; Scruton, *Meaning of Conservatism*, p. 171; Allison, *Right Principles*, p. 18; Tännsjö, *Conservatism*, p. 30.
80. Nisbet, *Sociological Tradition*, p. 48, and *Conservatism*, p. 77.
81. Allison, *Right Principles*, p. 32.
82. For the discussion of the 'national clerisy' idea, see Coleridge, *Constitution of Church and State*, pp. 77ff; Eliot's notion of the 'Community of Christians' can be found in Eliot, *Christian Society*, pp. 42–3.
83. Mallock, *Aristocracy and Evolution*. As he states in his preface, his use of the word *aristocracy* refers to 'the exceptionally gifted and efficient minority, no matter what position in which its members may have been born' (p. v); he later notes that 'the civilization of the entire community depends alike for its advance and for its maintenance on a struggle which is confined within the limits of an exceptional class' (p. 151).
84. Viereck, *Conservatism Revisited*, p. 30. One academic commentator on this elite theme maintains that the elites of conservatism in Britain have changed

markedly since 1688. They shifted from aristocratic landed groups, to commercial and industrial groups, and finally to the middle classes in the twentieth century; see Eccleshall, 'English Conservatism as Ideology'; see also Allison's criticl comments on this argument, *Right Principles*, p. 63.

85. See Scruton, *Meaning of Conservatism*, p. 48, and Covell, *Redefinition of Conservatism*, p. 63.
86. Maistre, *Considerations on France*, p. 92.
87. Nisbet, *Conservatism*, p. 40.
88. Waldegrave, *Binding of Leviathan*, p. 90.
89. Quintin Hogg remarks that 'The basis of the justification for the right to own private property is ultimately the belief in the infinite value of human personality, but this value can only be seen in its true light in a world assumed to be theocentric – God-centred'; see Hogg, *Case for Conservatism*, pp. 98–9; see also Nisbet, *Conservatism*, p. 56.
90. Hogg, *Case for Conservatism*, p. 99.
91. See Scruton, *Meaning of Conservatism*, pp. 72–3.
92. See Dickinson, *Liberty and Property*, p. 285.
93. See Ortega y Gasset, *Revolt of the Masses*.
94. See selections from Maurras's writings in McClelland (ed.), *The French Right*. For discussion of Dawson's criticism of democracy in relation to Maurras and T. S. Eliot, see O'Sullivan, *Conservatism*, pp. 135ff.
95. Pugh, *Making of Modern British Politics*, p. 3.
96. See Smith, *Salisbury on Politics*.
97. Scruton, *Meaning of Conservatism*, p. 59.
98. Worsthorne in Cowling, *Conservative Essays*, p. 149.
99. Eccleshall in Eccleshall *et al.* (eds), *Political Ideologies*, p. 102; see also Nisbet, *Conservatism*, p. 37; Auerbach, *Conservative Illusion*, p. 37; Macpherson, *Burke*.
100. Gilmour, *Britain Can Work*, pp. 65–6.
101. Hampsher-Monk, *Edmund Burke*, p. 20.
102. Despite the fact that liberal conservatives are keen to maximize market freedom, they feel definite qualms concerning how far such freedoms should extend. When social and moral issues of, for example, sexual, family and private morality or censorship of published material arise, then many liberal conservatives appear far less keen to extend freedom. However, there are libertarian aspects of the New Right spectrum who do wish to extend freedom into these areas and well beyond. The New Right libertarians (or anarcho-capitalists) are so keen to extend freedom, and are consequently so anti-statist, that they will be explored in chapter 5 under the rubric of anarchy.
103. Eliot, *Christian Society*, pp. 97–8.
104. See Schuettinger, *Conservative Tradition*, p. 17.
105. See Calleo, *Coleridge and the Modern State*, p. 3.
106. Nisbet, *Conservatism*, p. 65.
107. Discussing parsons, stock-jobbers, naval and military officers, Cobbett notes: 'Here are thousands upon thousands of pairs of this Dead Weight, all busily engaged in breeding gentlemen and ladies; and all, while Malthus is wanting to put a check upon the breeding of the labouring classes; all receiving a *premium for breeding*! Where is Malthus? Where is the check-population parson?'; see Cobbett, *Rural Rides*, p. 161.
108. See Calleo, *Coleridge and the Modern State*, pp. 13, 20.

109. See Griffiths, 'Anti-Capitalism', pp. 723, 735.
110. This is partly what Sir Henry Maine had in mind in his idea of the movement of societies from status to contract.
111. See Waldegrave, *Binding of Leviathan*, pp. 58ff; Scruton, *Meaning of Conservatism*, pp. 94ff; Gilmour, *Britain Can Work*; Covell, *Redefinition of Conservatism*, pp. 56–7.
112. Gilmour, *Britain Can Work*, p. 2; see also Cowling, *Conservative Essays*, pp. 1ff.
113. Gilmour, *Britain Can Work*, p. 12.
114. Ibid., p. 101.
115. Graham sees it as a strength, *Politics in its Place*, p. 185. More recently Honderich sees it as a manifest weakness, *Conservatism*, ch. 2.

Chapter 4: Socialism

1. This notion of contract is used predominantly within the liberal contractarian tradition (from Locke to Rawls), to explain the character of our obligations and the nature of authority. However, it has also been utilized by some anarchists, particularly Proudhon, who favoured it as a device to oppose the state. Proudhon's view will be explored in ch. 5.
2. Marx's interpretation has admittedly a lot more to it. He also saw 1789 and 1848 as necessary political events in the historical movement towards a social revolution of the proletariat.
3. See Claeys, *Citizens and Saints*, p. 323.
4. Lichtheim, *Origins of Socialism*, p. 219; see also Beer, *History of British Socialism*.
5. See C. H. Johnson, *Utopian Communism France*.
6. 'The inner organization of this primitive Communistic society was laid bare, in its typical form, by Morgan's crowning discovery of the true nature of the *gens* and its relation to the *tribe*', Marx and Engels, *Communist Manifesto*, p. 79.
7. In the preface to the 1888 English edition, Engels writes of the *Manifesto* as 'the most international production of all Socialist literature', ibid., p. 61.
8. The SPD name and form was adopted in 1890.
9. See Miller and Potthoff, *German Social Democracy*; see also Bernstein's work *Evolutionary Socialism*, Tudor and Tudor (eds), *Marxism and Social Democracy*. It is not quite so certain though that the actual political activity of the SPD always bore out the rigid theoretical commitments.
10. See Dennis and Halsey, *English Ethical Socialism*.
11. For More and the Levellers as part of the origin of socialism, see Greenleaf, *British Political Tradition*, p. 351.
12. Hill in Winstanley, *Law of Freedom*, p. 9. The socialist revisionist writer Eduard Bernstein also wrote his first Marxist-inspired work on the English Civil War. Other contemporaries to Winstanley, like James Harrington, are sometimes singled out too. A number of scholars have explored the dynamics of this claim. One of the first was C. B. Macpherson's *The Political Theory of Possessive Individualism*. It is worth noting briefly though that George Woodcock sees Winstanley as an original libertarian anarchist. He comments that 'the efforts of Winstanley and his friends to follow out its principles on St George's Hill stand(s) at the beginning of the anarchist tradition of direct action'; see Woodcock, *Anarchism*, p. 46.

13. Hobsbawm, *Age of Revolution*.
14. Lichtheim, *Origins of Socialism*, p. viii.
15. Schwartz, *Chinese Communism*, pp. 73ff; Fanon, *Wretched of the Earth*.
16. Greenleaf, *British Political Tradition*, pp. 350ff.
17. Berki, *Socialism*.
18. See Manuel, *New World of Saint-Simon* and *Prophets of Paris*; also, for a more general study of utopianism, Goodwin, *Social Science and Utopia*.
19. On Fourier, see Riasanovsky, *Charles Fourier*.
20. On Saint-Simon, see Saint-Simon, *Social Organization*; Manuel, *New World of Saint-Simon*; Ionescu (ed.), *Political Thought of Saint-Simon*. On Owen, see Morton, *Robert Owen*.
21. See Dennis and Halsey, *British Ethical Socialism*.
22. See Marx and Engels, *Selected Writings*.
23. See Landauer, *For Socialism*. Proudhon is discussed in ch. 5.
24. D. Miller, 'Marx, Communism and Markets', pp. 182ff; see also A. Nove's study, *Economics of Feasible Socialism*. This perspective has affected socialist parties (including communist parties) throughout Western Europe in the last decade.
25. See Estrin and Le Grand (eds), *Market Socialism*; Forbes (ed.), *Market Socialism*; and the most systematic study to date by Miller, *Market, State and Community*.
26. As George Orwell put it: 'leading back through Utopian dreamers like William Morris and mystical democrats like Walt Whitman, through Rousseau, through the English Diggers and Levellers, through the peasant revolts of the Middle Ages, and back to the early Christians ... Underneath it lies the belief that human nature is fairly decent to start with, and is capable of indefinite development. This belief has been the main driving force of the Socialist movement'; quoted in Crick, *Orwell*, p. 507.
27. See Penty, *Restoration of the Guild System*, or Landauer, *For Socialism*.
28. 'Finely graded passions had to be correctly combined in groups and series so they could obtain free expressions and satisfaction', Riasanovsky, *Fourier*, p. 42. Fourier believed that there were twelve basic human passions, subject to eight hundred and ten subtle nuances. If one allowed a doubling of these nuances, in order to accommodate mutual passions between individuals, then one could calculate the ideal population size for a *phalanstery*, which was approximately 1620.
29. See Claeys, *Citizens and Saints*, p. 16.
30. See McLellan, *Engels*, p. 73.
31. Engels, 'Speech at the Graveside of Karl Marx', Marx and Engels, *Selected Writings*. Engels' work 'came to be accepted as the authoritative frame of reference through which Marx's work was to be viewed', Wright, *Socialisms*, p. 43.
32. Lenin's own particular position was not wholly consistent. He blended, paradoxically, a voluntaristic stance with a rigid materialism. It is difficult to reconcile the activism of his work *What Is to Be Done?* with the crude determinism of his philosophical work *Materialism and Empirio-Criticism*. It is difficult not to see Lenin as something of a revolutionary opportunist.
33. See Miller and Potthoff, *German Social Democracy*, pp. 240–2.
34. Anthony Arblaster in Parekh (ed.), *Concept of Socialism*, p. 148.
35. Beatrice Webb, for example, admired Herbert Spencer whom she knew personally, noting that 'he taught me to look on all social institutions exactly

as if they were plants or animals – things that could be observed, classified and explained, and the actions of which could to some extent be foretold if one knew enough about them', B. Webb, *My Apprenticeship*, p. 38.

36. See Crosland, *Future of Socialism*, p. 84.
37. S. Webb, *Facts for Socialists*, Tract no. 5., quoted in M. Cole, *Story of Fabian Socialism*, p. 18.
38. Greenleaf, *British Political Tradition*, p. 371.
39. Selections from *The New Christianity* can be found in Saint-Simon, *Social Organization*, pp. 81ff.
40. Fourier remarked that 'Truth and commerce are as incompatible as Jesus and Satan'; merchants were no better than highway robbers; see Riasanovsky, *Fourier*, pp. 161–2.
41. See Marx, *Early Texts*.
42. See Jay, *Dialectical Imagination*.
43. See, particularly, the final chapter of Bernstein's *Evolutionary Socialism* entitled 'Kant not Cant'. See, also, Gay, *Dilemma of Democratic Socialism*, pp. 145ff.
44. See Olivier's essay in Shaw (ed.), *Fabian Essays in Socialism*, pp. 96ff; also Ball, 'Moral Aspect of Socialism'.
45. Dennis and Halsey, *English Ethical Socialism*, pp. 125–26. Beatrice Webb also speaks of the development over the nineteenth century of a 'class consciousness of sin among men of intellect and men of property'; see B. Webb, *My Apprenticeship*, pp. 179–80.
46. Callaghan, *Socialism in Britain*, p. 55.
47. Wright, *British Socialism*, p. 2.
48. Tawney, *Acquisitive Society*; Dennis and Halsey, *English Ethical Socialism*, p. 151; Greenleaf, *British Political Tradition*, p. 414; Wright, *British Socialism* and *Socialisms*; Terrill, *Tawney and His Times*.
49. I am taking these as more or less equivalent in this case, although with the advent of feminist criticism of socialism, it is wise to be very cautious about the value of 'fraternity'. The majority of nineteenth-century socialists, trade unions and the like were literally talking in terms of brotherhood. Many contemporary socialists would *not* relish this gender-biased description and would find it a very limited understanding of community, which undoubtedly must include all women as equal citizens. For discussion of this point, see Anne Phillips essay 'Fraternity' in Pimlott (ed.), *Fabian Essays*.
50. For early-nineteenth-century uses, see Claeys, *Citizens and Saints*, p. 299; on William's use of the notion of community, see R. Williams, *Long Revolution*.
51. See Crick, *Orwell*, p. 507.
52. On aspects of this theme, see David Miller's essay 'In what sense must Socialism be Communitarian?' in Paul, Miller, and Paul (eds), *Socialism*; also Plant, *Equality, Markets and the State*.
53. See Plant, *Community and Ideology*.
54. Wood, 'Marx on Rights and Justice', p. 281.
55. See, Crick in Pimlott, (ed.), *Fabian Essays*, p. 157.
56. For example, are needs absolute or relative to particular circumstances? If needs are absolute, what is to be included under such rubric? What is the relation between needs and wants? Can there be a clear hard-and-fast distinction between such notions? These and many other questions plague the discussion of need.
57. As Beatrice Webb commented 'We do not have faith in the "average sensual

man", we do not believe that he can do much more than describe his grievances, we do not think that he can prescribe the remedies ... We wish to introduce the professional expert'; see B. Webb, *Our Partnership*, p. 120. On Fabian elitism, see Callaghan, *Socialism in Britain*, pp. 34–5.

58. Tawney, *Equality*.

59. On the Kantian rational will argument, see Bernstein, *Evolutionary Socialism*. Mill's later reflections, 'Chapters on Socialism', figure in the utilitarian guise; see Mill, *On Liberty*.

60. See discussion in Plant, 'Socialism, Markets and End-States', in Estrin and Le Grand, *Market Socialism*.

61. Cole, *Self-Government in Industry* and *Guild Socialism Restated*.

62. I have discussed this issue in more detail in my *Theories of the State* (ch. 5). See also Bobbio, *Which Socialism?* and Markovic's comment, from a very different angle, that 'For Marx, the question is how to strive for the general goals of the community consciously and freely, and in the most rational and most human way possible. For that, the State is no longer necessary', Markovic, *Democratic Socialism*, p. 19.

63. Barker, 'Fabianism and the State' in Pimlott, *Fabian Essays*, p. 28. Barker notes in this essay the 'The whole conception of the Fabian state as depicted by the Webbs is a massive and high-minded self-denying ordinance' (p. 34).

64. See Hirst, 'Democracy: Socialism's best reply to the right', in Hindess (ed.), *Reactions to the Right*.

65. The change in name to PDS (Partito Democratico della Sinistra) indicates symbolically some marked ideological shifts.

66. The best selected collection of Gramsci's writings is *Selections from Prison Notebooks*; see also the studies by Femia, *Gramsci's Political Thought*, and Simon, *Gramsci's Political Thought*.

67. For the medieval wing of the Guild, see Penty, *Restoration of the Guild System*, and for the national guilds see S. G. Hobson, *National Guilds and the State*, and Cole, *Guild Socialism Restated*.

68. Tawney, *Acquisitive Society*.

69. See Plant, *Equality, Markets and the State*, p. 5.

70. See Gorz, *Farewell to the Working Class*; Kitching, *Rethinking Socialism*, pp. 62–3.

71. Beatrice Webb described the rank and file socialists as 'unusually silly folk (for the most part feather-headed failures) and heaped together in one hall ... they approached raving imbecility'; see B. Webb, *Our Partnership*, p. 134.

72. This is part of the essential message of recent advocates of market socialism; see Estrin and Le Grand, *Market Socialism*.

73. See Penty, *Restoration of the Guild System*, and Cole, *Guild Socialism Restated*; also, for the best detailed study of Cole, see Wright, *G. D. H. Cole*.

74. See Plant, 'Socialism Markets and End States' in Estrin and Le Grand, *Market Socialism*, p. 71.

75. Estrin and Le Grand, *Market Socialism*, p. 23.

Chapter 5: Anarchism

1. The notion of doing without the state or government, in a more positive sense, can be taken in two senses. It can either imply a harmless, antiquated, but unworkable utopianism, something to be grown out of, or it can betoken a contemporary, workable alternative to the state. The capacity to

live in such a stateless society stands in precise ratio to personal and political maturity.

2. As one writer comments, 'Anarchism, encompassing as it does such a broad spectrum of ideas, cannot be as precisely defined in ideological terms as Marxism'; see Cahm, *Kropotkin* p. ix; see also discussion in D. Miller, *Anarchism*, p. 2; Gaus and Chapman, in Pennock and Chapman (eds), *Anarchism*, p. xvii; also Ritter, *Anarchism*.

3. Proudhon, *Selected Writings*, pp. 88−9. It is worth noting here in passing that Proudhon did accept a distinction, in these remarks, between the sovereign state and government.

4. Marx's criticisms of Proudhon in *The Poverty of Philosophy* were regarded favourably by Bakunin.

5. For a detailed account of the debates over this period, see Cahm, *Kropotkin*, pp. 36−43.

6. See Clark, 'Master Lao and the Anarchist Prince', in Clark, *Anarchist Moment*, p. 163. David Miller, amongst other commentators, mentions this point in passing; see Miller, *Anarchism*. p. 3. James Joll speaks of Zeno and the Stoics in the same vein, *Anarchists*, p. 13.

7. Taylor, *Community, Anarchy and Liberty*, p. 33.

8. He also contends that peasant communities, village communities, Kibbutzim and utopian communes within developed states have an anarchist character; ibid., pp. 35−7.

9. Ibid., p. 38.

10. To be fair, Taylor partially recognizes this latter claim, although he still tends to treat it in a sanitized ahistorical conceptual manner.

11. Pilgrim, *'Anarchism and Stateless Societies'*, p. 367.

12. See P. Thomas, *Karl Marx and the Anarchists*, pp. 7−8; also Cahm, *Kropotkin*, pp. 7. For a good study of Godwin as an anarchist, see Clark, *Philosophical Anarchism of William Godwin*.

13. Rocker, *Anarcho-Syndicalism*, p. 21. David Apter also put the same point quite neatly, namely, that anarchism combines a socialist critique of capitalism with a liberal critique of socialism; see 'The Old Anarchism and the New' in Apter and Joll (eds), *Anarchism Today*, pp. 1−2. See also, for roughly the same idea, D. Miller, *Anarchism*, p. 3.

14. For the classic study of the Spanish experience, see Brenan, *Spanish Labyrinth*.

15. See Avrich, *Russian Anarchists*, pp. 209–22; Guérin, *Anarchism*, pp. 98−101; Arshinov, *Makhnovist Movement*.

16. See, for example, Bookchin, *Ecology of Freedom, Post-Scarcity Anarchism*, or *Towards an Ecological Society*; or Ward, *Anarchy in Action*.

17. For more detail on this publishing activity, plus information concerning a new Anarchist Research Group founded in Britain in 1984−5, see Goodway (ed.), *For Anarchism*, pp. 1−16.

18. On the question of the debates on violence and pacifism, see Friedrich, 'Anarchist Controversy'.

19. In one of his more recent works he describes himself as both an eco-anarchist and later an anarcho-communist; see Bookchin, *Toward an Ecological Society*, pp. 92, 251n.

20. Kropotkin, *Mutual Aid*, pp. 217ff.

21. See Bookchin, *Ecology of Freedom* and *Toward an Ecological Society*.

22. For an excellent study of French syndicalism, see Jennings, *Syndicalism in France*.

23. See Holton, *British Syndicalism 1900–1914*; Morgan, 'Socialism and Syndicalism'.
24. Rocker, *Anarcho-Syndicalism*, p. 134.
25. D. Miller, *Anarchism*, pp. 125, 132.
26. J. Carroll's introduction to Stirner, *The Ego and His Own*, p. 33.
27. Ibid., p. 34. See also, for a more rigorous separation of Stirner from anarchism, Patterson, *Max Stirner*; also D. McIntosh, 'Dimensions of Anarchy' in Pennock and Chapman, *Anarchism*, pp. 240ff.
28. Clark, *Max Stirner's Egoism*, p. 89.
29. Gaus and Chapman, and Wieck, in Pennock and Chapman, *Anarchism*, pp. xxv, 215.
30. See R. Graham, 'The Role of Contract in Anarchist Ideology', in Goodway, *For Anarchism*, p. 163.
31. See V. Richards, 'Notes for a Biography', in *Malatesta: Life and Ideas*, p. 209; Guérin, 'Marxism and Anarchism' in Goodway, *For Anarchism*, p. 118.
32. The best study of Marx's relation to anarchy is Paul Thomas's *Karl Marx and the Anarchists*. The relation of anarchy to liberalism is mentioned in a number of studies, although it remains to be systematically dealt with.
33. Rothbard in Pennock and Chapman, *Anarchism*, p. 193.
34. He remarked: 'We do not believe in the infallibility nor even the general goodness of the masses', V. Richards (ed.), *Malatesta: His Life and Ideas*, p. 109.
35. Kropotkin, *Mutual Aid*, p. ix.
36. Ibid., p. 14. Hobbes' individualism is linked by Kropotkin with the views of T. H. Huxley and competitive evolution. In fact Huxley, in his essay 'The Struggle for Existence in Human Society', which stimulated Kropotkin to draft *Mutual Aid*, uses Hobbes to elucidate his notion of competitive evolution. Huxley's essay appeared in *The Nineteenth Century* in February 1888.
37. As Kropotkin notes: 'Sociability and need of mutual aid and support are inherent parts of human nature that at no time of history can we discover men living in small isolated families, fighting each other for the means of subsistence', *Mutual Aid*, p. 153.
38. Ibid., p. 112.
39. On Kropotkin's faith in the 'good sense' of the masses, see Kropotkin, *Conquest of Bread*, p. 109. On the judgement of Kropotkin's naivety, see Malatesta, *Anarchy*, pp. 34–5.
40. Bookchin, *Toward an Ecological Society*, pp. 59–60.
41. Berkman, *ABC of Anarchism*, p. 27.
42. The instinctive, destructive and unsystematic image of Bakunin's ideas, which he liked to foster, can be overdone. For a correction to this view, see the study by Kelly, *Mikhael Bakunin*. On Bakunin's legacy, see Avrich, 'Legacy of Bakunin.'
43. Bakunin, *Statism and Anarchy*, p. 205. For a discussion of Bakunin's disapproval of Kropotkin's conception of evolution and progress, see Thomas, *Karl Marx and the Anarchists*, pp. 286–8; Avrich, *Russian Anarchists*, pp. 92ff; and Avrich's introduction to Bakunin's, *God and the State*, p. vi.
44. See Sorel, *Reflections on Violence*. For one of the best recent studies, see Jennings, *George Sorel*. On Bergson's general influence, see also Scott, *Syndicalism and Philosophical Realism*, or Pilkington, *Bergson and His Influence*.
45. Sorel spoke of an epic state of mind in the vein of Homeric heroes or

Nietzschean supermen – a new age of chivalry and chasteness; see Sorel, *Reflections on Violence*, pp. 230ff. As T. E. Hulme, his translator, commented 'It is difficult ... to understand a revolutionary who is anti-democratic, an absolutist in ethics, rejecting all rationalism and relativism, who values the mystical element in religion ... who speaks contemptuously of modernism and *progress*, and uses a concept like *honour* with no sense of unreality'; see Hulme, *Speculations*, p. 250.

46. Godwin, *Enquiry Concerning Political Justice*, p. 758.
47. Ibid., p. 761.
48. Stirner, *The Ego and His Own*.
49. The best-known Christian defence of anarchy is by Leo Tolstoy, though it could hardly be called an orthodox interpretation of Christian belief; see Tolstoy, *Kingdom of God and Peace Essays*.
50. For the psychological disposition argument, see the idiosyncratic work of Gustav Landauer, *For Socialism*.
51. Proudhon, *Revolution in the 19th Century*, p. 292. It is clear, though, that Proudhon did not use the notion of the state, sovereignty or law in a very consistent fashion; see Vernon, *Citizenship and Order*, pp. 82ff.
52. Nock, *Our Enemy the State*.
53. Rothbard in Pennock and Chapman, *Anarchism*, p. 195.
54. Bakunin, *Statism and Anarchy*, p. 3.
55. The term 'spook' is Stirner's.
56. Rothbard, *For A New Liberty*, p. 35
57. See Bakunin, *Statism and Anarchy*, pp. 14, 26.
58. Kropotkin, *Mutual Aid*, n., p. 165.
59. Ibid., p. 294.
60. There are some ambiguities here, for example, Bakunin's and Proudhon's interest in American federalism, or Proudhon's dalliance with parliamentary politics and later interest in the state. As one recent commentator notes, Proudhon 'uses the term "state" without embarrassment and, what is more to the point, ascribes to the state enormous importance; it is "prime mover and general director" ... On the question of jurisdiction, however, what Proudhon proposes, fairly abstractly viewed, is more like a federal state than a confederation'; see Vernon, *Citizenship and Order*, pp. 82–3.
61. Bookchin puts the point in a similar way, suggesting that 'Marxism may well be the ideology of capitalism *par excellence* precisely because the essentials of its critique have focused on capitalist production without challenging the underlying cultural sensibilities that sustain it', see Bookchin, *Toward an Ecological Society*, 29.
62. Kropotkin, *The State*, p. 41.
63. Berkman, *ABC of Anarchism*, p. 9.
64. Rocker, *Anarcho-Syndicalism*, p. 31.
65. I am leaving aside the recurring problem of the diverse moral grounds on which anarchists have accounted for the value of liberty.
66. Stirner, *The Ego and His Own*, p. 118.
67. Clark, *Max Stirner's Egoism*, pp. 61ff.
68. There is some interesting discussion of this in Fowler, 'Anarchist Tradition of Political Thought'.
69. Rothbard in Pennock and Chapman, *Anarchism*, p. 193.
70. Rothbard, *For A New Liberty*, p. 23; see also Berkman, *ABC of Anarchism*.
71. On the issue of self-government, see Proudhon, *Selected Writings*, p. 94;

Bakunin, *God and the State*, p. 30; Clark, *Anarchist Moment*, p. 225; also see Wolff, *In Defence of Anarchism* and Carter, *Political Theory of Anarchism*. For some of the ripostes to Wolff, see essays by R. T. De George, G. Wall and P. Riley in Pennock and Chapman, *Anarchism*.

72. Leo Tolstoy argued that true liberty corresponded with the ethical code of the Sermon on the Mount, see Tolstoy, *Kingdom of God*; see also Malatesta on freedom necessarily being tied to moral goals, *Anarchy*, p. 24.

73. Rocker, *Anarcho-Syndicalism*, p. 32.

74. Bookchin makes a very strong point on this in his various writings; see discussion in Clark, *Anarchist Moment*, pp. 224ff. In some writers it involves assertions that rationality, authenticity and self-expression are also involved in liberty. Michael Taylor, in a discussion of this issue, argues that he could share such a view of self-expression and autonomy 'if it could be shown that the critical choosing activity central to this conception of autonomy does not itself have causal determinants'; however, he contends that this is unlikely to be done, see Taylor, *Community, Anarchy and Liberty*, p. 150. He also points to a problematic element on the linkage of positive liberty (autonomy) with community, namely that '*it is precisely those things which limit autonomy which also limit the degree to which these [anarchistic] utopias are truly communities*', ibid., p. 164.

75. Tolstoy, *Kingdom of God*.

76. There were exceptions to this. Rothbard for one tries to construct, in his various works, an anarcho-capitalist law code, redeemed from government or the state, and premised essentially on rights to self-ownership, non-aggression and homesteading. Other anarchists also try to redeem government from the state.

77. Proudhon, *Revolution in the 19th Century*, pp. 206–7.

78. Proudhon comments: 'The Social Contract is the supreme act by which each citizen pledges to society his love, his intelligence, his labour, his services, his products and his goods in return for the affection, ideas, works, products, services and goods of his fellow citizens'; ibid., p. 114.

79. Ibid., p. 112.

80. See D. Wieck, 'Anarchist Justice', in Pennock and Chapman, *Anarchism*, p. 217.

81. Kropotkin, *Mutual Aid*, pp. 58–9.

82. See discussion of this in Avrich, *Russian Anarchists*, p. 29.

83. Kropotkin, *Conquest of Bread*, p. 15.

84. Ibid., pp. 238, 241.

85. I am thinking here of ventures like A. S. Neill's Summerhill school.

86. D. MacIntosh in Pennock and Chapman, *Anarchism*, p. 268.

87. Quoted in Clark in Pennock and Chapman, *Anarchism*, p. 19.

88. Rothbard in Pennock and Chapman, *Anarchism*, pp. 191–2.

89. As Clark comments: 'The union of egoists is an association in which people work together, not for the common welfare, or greatest happiness, but because of each individual's desire that he or she should own as much as is possible'; see Clark, *Max Stirner's Egoism*, p. 79.

90. Stirner, *The Ego and His Own*, p. 142.

91. Bakunin has some remarks on his federated vision in *Statism and Anarchy*, pp. 13, 46, 198.

92. Bookchin, *Toward an Ecological Society*, pp. 47–9.

93. Kropotkin, *Conquest of Bread*, pp. 179–84.

94. Kropotkin has much more practical, down-to-earth advice to offer on such communes in his *Field, Factories and Workshops*.
95. Bookchin, *Toward an Ecological Society*, pp. 68–9. This point echoes both Gandhi and Schumacher.
96. Kropotkin, *Conquest of Bread*, pp. 161ff. Kropotkin shared this view with a number of others at the time, for example, the Marxist writer August Bebel; see Bebel, *Women and Socialism*. It would now be subject to a critique from within contemporary feminist ideology; see ch. 7.
97. Graham in Goodway, *For Anarchism*, p. 157.
98. Graham introduction to Proudhon, *Revolution in the 19th Century*, p. ix.
99. See Holton, *British Syndicalism 1900–1914*, p. 17.
100. On the attitudes of syndicalists in Wales, see Morgan, 'Socialism and Syndicalism'.
101. Holton, *British Syndicalism 1900–1914*, p. 35.
102. See Best (ed.), *Industrial Syndicalist*, p. 65. On the *Bourse du Travail*, see Joll, *Anarchists*, pp. 197–200.
103. Graham in Goodway, *For Anarchism* , p. 171.
104. Proudhon, *Revolution in the 19th Century*, pp. 146, 244.
105. Bakunin, *Statism and Anarchy*, p. 13.
106. See Alan Ritter in Pennock and Chapman, *Anarchism*, p. 131.

Chapter 6: Fascism

1. Nolte, *Three Faces of Fascism*, p. 17.
2. See Juan Linz's essay in Laqueur (ed.), *Fascism*, p. 14.
3. Mussolini mentions this ancestry; see 'Doctrine of Fascism', p. 168.
4. Mack Smith, *Mussolini*, p. 47.
5. See introduction by Miller Lane and Rupp (eds), *Nazi Ideology*, p. xxv.
6. Robert Skidelsky, *Oswald Mosley*, p. 299. On the complex relation of fascism to the right, see essays in Eatwell and O'Sullivan (eds), *Nature of the Right*.
7. Rocco, 'Political Doctrine of Fascism', pp. 42–4.
8. Sternhell in Laqueur, *Fascism*, p. 333. On fascism as the inheritor of a long-standing conservative tradition, see Weiss, *Fascist Tradition*.
9. It should be noted, though, that there are a number of subtly distinct views expressed by scholars. For example, nineteenth-century intellectual themes could be viewed as an innocuous backdrop, with a number of potentialities for later development. Alternatively, there could be said to be quite definite continuities of ideas. Nineteenth-century thinkers were thus fascist in all but name. Again there could be some formal intellectual continuities, but the fascists totally distorted the ideas for their own nefarious ends. Finally, the continuity of ideas existed but these would not have developed in the way they did without the catalyst of war, depression and social unrest.
10. Carsten, *Rise of Fascism*, p. 63.
11. Trevor-Roper, in Woolf (ed.), *European Fascism*, p. 18.
12. See n. 11 above.
13. One of the older, if still fairly sophisticated, accounts utilizing this general determinist line of argument was Franz L. Neumann, *Behemoth*. See also Kitchen, *Fascism*.
14. Marcuse, *Reason and Revolution*, p. 410.

15. Quoted in H. A. Turner (ed.), *Reappraisals of Fascism*, p. 119.
16. See Mosse, *Nazism*, p. 49. Further critical discussion of this point can be found in Hans Mommsen's essay in Laqueur, *Fascism*, p. 157.
17. See David Forjacs' essay in Forjacs, (ed.), *Rethinking Italian Fascism*, p. 43.
18. Erikson, *Young Man Luther*, p. 104; see also Binion, 'Hitler's Concept of Lebensraum'.
19. Koenigsberg, *Hitler's Ideology*, p. 85. The emphasis is Koenigsberg's.
20. Adorno, *Authoritarian Personality*.
21. O'Sullivan, *Fascism*, p. 25; see also Carsten in Laqueur, *Fascism*, pp. 465ff.
22. An aspect of this religious crisis was expressed by the psychoanalyst Carl Jung. He argued that Christian myths have died. In our present civilization 'myth has become mute, and gives no answers', thus, 'We stand perplexed and stupefied before the phenomenon of Nazism ... We stand face to face with the terrible question of evil and do not even know what is before us'; see Jung, *Memories, Dreams and Reflections*, pp. 363–4.
23. Quoted in Ruggiero, *European Liberalism*, p. 343.
24. Collingwood, 'Fascism and Nazism', pp. 170ff. This essay has been reprinted in Collingwood, *Essays in Political Philosophy*, ed. David Boucher. Boucher discusses the essay in the introduction to this volume and in his larger study of Collingwood; see Boucher, *Social and Political Thought of R. G. Collingwood*.
25. See Rauschning, *Revolution of Nihilism*.
26. Maritain's *Twilight of Civilization*, quoted in O'Sullivan, *Fascism*, p. 24.
27. Pois, *National Socialism*, p. 28.
28. Stern, *Politics of Cultural Despair*; Mosse, *Crisis of German Ideology*; Pulzer, *Political Anti-Semitism in Germany and Austria*.
29. See Gregor, *Interpretations of Fascism*, p. 45.
30. Barrington Moore Jnr, in *Social Origins of Dictatorship and Democracy*, uses the term 'conservative modernization' to describe the Italian fascist development. See also Organski, *Stages of Political Development*; Apter, *Politics of Modernization*; and G. E. Black, *Dynamics of Modernization*.
31. Sauer, in Turner, *Reappraisals of Fascism*, p. 132.
32. On the general dissatisfaction with the modernization thesis, especially in Germany, see Bracher in Laqueur, *Fascism*, p. 205.
33. I will only touch upon a few of the better-known political views. There are other notable and interesting views which could be reviewed, given space. For example, O'Sullivan in his work on fascism, speaks of fascism as a new 'activist style' of politics contrasted to 'limited' politics. This activist style is identified by certain features like a new theory of freedom, an exaggerated belief in the potency of the human will, a theory of popular sovereignty and a new theory of evil; see O'Sullivan, *Fascism*, ch. 1. For some positive discussion and use of this idea; see H. Williams, *Concepts of Ideology*, pp. 94–5.
34. Bullock, *Hitler*, p. 237; Mack Smith, *Mussolini*; Nolte, *Three Faces of Fascism*; Trevor-Roper, *Last Days of Hitler*. Also for some discussion of this interpretation, see Pois, *National Socialism*, pp. 15ff.
35. On national socialism on this point, see W. Carr in Laqueur, *Fascism*, pp. 122ff.
36. Arendt, *Origins of Totalitarianism*; Popper, *Open Society and its Enemies*; Talmon, *Origins of Totalitarian Democracy*; Friedrich and Brzezinski, *Totalitarian Dictatorship and Autocracy*.
37. The rootless and isolated quality of the masses is explored by theorists of

the mass society, For discussion of this view in relation to fascism, see Gregor, *Interpretations of Fascism*, pp. 118ff.

38. This point will be explored in the section on the state within this chapter.
39. On classes and fascism, see Carsten in Laqueur, *Fascism*, p. 460.
40. Linz, in Laqueur, *Fascism*, p. 16.
41. Ibid., p. 17.
42. Ibid. p. 18.
43. For excellent material on French fascism, see Soucy, *Fascism in France*, *Fascist Intellectual* and *French Fascism*.
44. See Weber, *Varieties of Fascism*. There is considerable debate on this whole issue; see Eatwell and O'Sullivan (eds), *Nature of the Right*.
45. See Stanley Payne in Turner, *Reappraisals of Fascism*, p. 151.
46. See Wood in Eatwell and O'Sullivan *Nature of the Right*, pp. 141–3. Primo de Rivera, the leading light of the Spanish Falange, also attempted to differentiate fascism from the right, although he claimed (in a characteristic move by fascists) that they were neither left nor right; see 'Foundation of the Spanish Falange' in Primo de Rivera, *Selected Writings*, pp. 53–4. It should also be pointed out again here that fascism has an equally problematic relation to socialism, often being seen in Italy during the 1920s, for example, as the organic, natural successor to socialism; see Adrian Lyttelton in Laqueur, *Fascism*, p. 83.
47. See discussion of this question by Cassels in Turner, *Reappraisals in Fascism*.
48. Zev Sternhell remarks that 'Nazism cannot ... be treated as a mere variant of fascism: its emphasis on biological determinism rules out all efforts to deal with it as such'; Sternhell in Laqueur, *Fascism*, p. 328.
49. For the general response of European fascists to Germany, see Mosse, *Crisis of German Ideology*, pp. 314ff. On Mussolini's quite ripe remarks, see Mack Smith, *Mussolini*, p. 216. Mussolini noted to his colleagues that when Hitler spoke on these issues he was like a 'gramophone with just seven tunes and once he had finished playing them he started all over again'. Admittedly, Hitler had also stated in conversations with Mussolini that Italians, presumably because of their darker complexion, might have traces of Negroid blood and therefore were inferior to the Aryans, which certainly would not have endeared him to Mussolini; see Mack Smith, *Mussolini*, p. 214–5.
50. On the issue of violence, see Klaus Epstein in Turner, *Reappraisals of Fascism*, p. 17.
51. Nolte, *Three Faces of Fascism*, p. 574; de Grand, *Italian Fascism*, ch. 10.
52. See, for example, Mussolini's article 'Which Way is the World Going?' from the party journal *Gerarchia*, February 1922; also Lyttelton (ed.), *Italian Fascisms*.
53. Roberts, *Syndicalist Tradition and Italian Fascism*, p. 318. Roberts continues that 'The problems that bothered ... non-Marxist critics of liberalism, from Proudhon and Mazzini to Durkheim and Duguit, were very much involved in the crisis of liberal Italy ... Had it implemented the corporativist revolution, left fascism would have brought to fruition a major strand in the tradition of anti-Marxist criticism of liberalism and capitalism'; ibid., pp. 319–20.
54. The Twenty-Five Points can be found in Miller Lane and Rupp, *Nazi Ideology*, and Oakeshott (ed.), *Social and Political Doctrines*. The programme was committed to provide: full employment (7); the abolition of unearned income and the emancipation from interest charges (11); confiscation of all war profits (12); nationalization of all business combines (13);

profit-sharing in industry (14); communalization of department stores and aid to small traders (16); confiscation of land without compensation for communal purposes (17); usury and profiteering punishable by death (18); nationalized education (20); abolition of child labour, etc.

55. See Bellamy's useful discussion of Gentile in *Modern Italian Social Theory*, Ch. 6.

56. Quoted in Mack Smith, *Mussolini*, p. 200. Interestingly, this squares with Bullock's assessment of Hitler's early ideas as wholly unoriginal: 'They were the cliches of radical and Pan-German gutter politics', Bullock, *Hitler*, p. 44.

57. Schmitt's contribution tends rather to substantiate some of the more negative criticisms employed by national socialism; see Schmitt, *Crisis of Parliamentary Democracy*. Heidegger's role is more ambiguous. Although initially fairly enthusiastic about national socialism he appears to have become disenchanted.

58. Linz in Laqueur, *Fascism*, p. 15.

59. See A. Hamilton, *Appeal of Fascism*.

60. Marinetti, 'Futurist Manifesto' in Lyttelton, *Italian Fascisms*, p. 211.

61. Papini also noted 'Mourning over the dead, wasting one's time in sentimentality, humanitarian moaning, drawing back in the face of all the platitudes on the sacredness of human life, would be to deny the force of life that is throbbing and growing and glowing all around us. And life is not worth living unless it is full and intense: sacrificing the heroic intensity of such a life in favour of life that is merely ephemeral would deprive the world of its greatest value'; see Papini in Lyttelton, *Italian Fascisms*, pp. 106–7. For similar views on the spiritual necessity of war, see Gentile, 'Philosophic Basis of Fascism', p. 290.

62. Primo de Rivera, *Selected Writings*, p. 56; Papini in Lyttelton, *Italian Fascisms*, p. 100. See also Gentile, 'Philosophic Basis of Fascism', p. 292; Mussolini, 'Doctrine of Fascism', pp. 170–1.

63. Gentile, 'Philosophic Basis of Fascism', p. 301.

64. Ibid., pp. 300–1. I have only given a very thin summary of Gentile's answer here. Gentile in fact situates the argument on intellectualism in his doctrine of immanent idealism. Whether or not immanent idealism really ties into the fascist case (which I doubt), Gentile's account is probably the most sophisticated response from any fascist to this issue.

65. Bullock, *Hitler*, p. 37.

66. Mack Smith, *Mussolini* p. 145. Compare these remarks on the masses with Hitler's, quoted in Bullock, *Hitler*, p. 37.

67. Rocco, 'Political Doctrine of Fascism', p. 33. See also Mussolini, 'Doctrine of Fascism', p. 166. Sternhell comments on this that 'Fascist ideology was born of a political tradition that considered the individual as a function of group life'; see Sternhell in Laqueur, *Fascism*, p. 364.

68. Gentile, 'Philosophic Basis of Fascism', p. 301.

69. Gentile, *Genesis and Structure of Society*, p. 82.

70. Ibid., p. 131. See also Gentile in Lyttelton, *Italian Fascisms*, p. 307; Mussolini, 'Doctrine of Fascism', pp. 167–8.

71. See Mosse, *Crisis of German Ideology*, p. 15; Sternhell in Laqueur, *Fascism*, p. 337.

72. As Robert Pois comments: 'The wish to live in close harmony with nature (to live authentically) and revulsion against the admittedly often alienating life-patterns of urban existence-these are phenomena extant throughout a

Western World increasingly uncomfortable with the problems attendant upon first mechanized, and now automated, societies. Taken but slightly out of context, many of the statements of Nazis ... would be applauded by the average, somewhat unreflective, environmentalist'; see Pois, *National Socialism*, p. 122. Hitler's well-known love of animals and enthusiastic vegetarianism are not unrelated to this perspective.

73. Hitler, *Mein Kampf*, p. 313.
74. One scholar notes that Mussolini 'liked to think of himself as man excluded from communion with others as if by some divine law'; however, much of the time Mussolini appeared to feel simply socially inadequate and ill-at-ease. It is contended that one of the reasons for his introduction of the Roman salute instead of the handshake was his personal revulsion against physical contact; see Mack Smith, *Mussolini*, p. 127.
75. Quoted in Pois, *National Socialism*, p. 70.
76. See also, for wonderful accounts of Marinetti's fascist cookbook, O'Sullivan, *Fascism*, p. 143.
77. See Mack Smith, *Mussolini*, p. 174.
78. Papini in Lyttelton, *Italian Fascisms*, pp.. 101–3. See also de Grand, *Italian Fascism*, p. xii.
79. Charter of Labour, 21 April 1927; see Oakeshott, *Social and Political Doctrines*.
80. Primo de Rivera, *Selected Writings*, p. 60.
81. E. Corradini in Lyttelton, *Italian Fascisms*, p. 139. See also J. Goebbels, 'National Socialism or Bolshevism', and A. Rosenberg, 'The Folkish Idea of the State', in Miller Lane and Rupp, *Nazi Ideology*, pp. 70, 78. Goebbels, in the above, argues that national socialism is anti-capitalist, anti-semitic and anti-bourgeois.
82. See Papini in Lyttelton, *Italian Fascisms*, p. 104.
83. Mussolini, 'Doctrine of Fascism', p. 167. See also Gentile's clear statement of the same point in *Genesis and Structure of Society*, p. 121.
84. Hitler, *Mein Kampf*, pp. 357–8.
85. See the comprehensive study of these now rather obscure figures, Stern, *Politics of Cultural Despair*.
86. Pois introduction to Rosenberg, *Selected Writings*, p. 19.
87. Mosse, *Crisis of German Ideology*, p. 4.
88. Rosenberg, *Selected Writings*, p. 80.
89. Hitler, *Mein Kampf*, p. 587.
90. Hitler, *Mein Kampf*, pp. 365–7.
91. Darré comments thus: 'He who leaves the plants in a garden to themselves will soon find to his surprise that the garden is overgrown by weeds and that even the basic character of the plants has changed. If therefore the garden is to remain the breeding ground for the plants, if, in other words, it is to lift above the harsh rule of natural forces, then the forming will of a gardener is necessary ... Exactly thus, speaking now of the folk, was the old German legal order intended, whose weeding and tending (which no doubt arose out of the blood consciousness of the Germanic peoples, based on an ideological foundation) created the conditions of existence needed for life and growth'; quoted in Miller Lane and Rupp, *Nazi Ideology*, p. 115.
92. The human soul was closely linked to landscape in this tradition. Late-nineteenth-century German writers like Ratzel and Riehl were concerned to elucidate this point in their writings. As Mosse comments, Riehl 'analysed

the various population groupings of Germany in terms of the landscape they inhabited'; see Mosse, *Crisis of German Ideology*, pp. 19ff.

93. See the essay by R. Eatwell, 'The Holocaust Denial: A Study in Propaganda Technique', in Cheles, Ferguson and Vaughan (eds), *Neo-fascism in Europe*.

94. Primo de Rivera, *Selected Writings*, pp. 61–2. See also Hitler, *Mein Kampf*, p. 416, and Mussolini, 'Doctrine of Fascism', p. 166.

95. Schmitt, *Crisis of Parliamentary Democracy*, p. 50.

96. Ibid., p. 5.

97. Ibid., p. 15.

98. See Skidelsky, *Oswald Mosley*, p. 72. Gentile also defines fascism in one passage as 'a conception of the state, with the purpose of solving the political problems that had reached exasperation as a result of the unbridled passions of the uninformed masses after the war', Gentile in Lyttelton, *Italian Fascisms*, p. 306.

99. See Mack Smith, *Mussolini*, p. 173; Gentile in Lyttelton, *Italian Fascisms*, p. 301; Primo de Rivera, 'Guidelines of the Falange: The Twenty-Six Points', November 1934, Point VI, *Selected Writings*. For the various ambiguous senses of totalitarianism, see Forjacs, *Rethinking Italian Fascism*, pp. 2–3.

100. Gentile, *Genesis and Structure of Society*, pp. 179, 183

101. See Gentile, 'Philosophic Basis of Fascism', p. 301. Mussolini, who expressed little interest in individual liberty, described it as a 'decomposing corpse'; quoted in Mack Smith, *Mussolini*, p. 162.

102. Rocco in Lyttelton, *Italian Fascisms*, p. 262.

103. Rocco in Lyttelton, *Italian Fascisms*, p. 260. Gentile commented on this theme that 'The absurdities inherent in the liberal concept of freedom were apparent to liberals themselves early in the nineteeth century. It is no merit of fascism to have again indicated them'; see Gentile, 'Philosophic Basis of Fascism', p. 304. The context of the Germanic understanding of freedom has been well documented; see discussion in Stern, *Politics of Cultural Despair*, p. xxix.

104. Rosenberg, *Selected Writings*, p. 93.

105. Mussolini, 'Doctrine of Fascism', p. 166; see also Papini, Rocco and Gentile in Lyttelton, *Italian Fascisms*, pp. 110, 260, 313–4; Gentile, 'Philosophic Basis of Fascism', p. 303; and for the concept of freedom developed in the most systematic manner, see Gentile, *Genesis and Structure of Society*, pp. 122–3.

106. Rosenberg, *Selected Writings*, p. 98; see also his later remarks on freedom in a speech made in June 1935, 'Weltanschauung und Kunst', p. 162.

107. Rosenberg, *Selected Writings*, p. 192. Hitler makes exactly the same point when he remarks, 'We, as Aryans, can conceive of the state only as the living organism of a nationality which not only assures the preservation of this nationality, but ... leads it to the highest freedom'; see Hitler, *Mein Kampf*, p. 358.

108. Rosenberg, *Selected Writings*, p. 192. Pois remarks that the Nazis 'generally did not accept the notion of the total or "totalitarian state"'; see Pois, *National Socialism*, p. 67.

109. Broszat, *The Hitler State*, p. 358.

110. Gentile, 'Philosophic Basis of Fascism', p. 291.

111. Quoted in Skidelsky, *Oswald Mosley*, p. 313. Mussolini appeared to admire Lenin for his dynamic leadership. He also liked to encourage the comparison of his achievements with great figures of the past. The monthly fascist

periodical *Gerarchia* likened Mussolini to Socrates, Plato, Machiavelli and Napoleon; see Mack Smith, *Mussolini*, p. 194.

112. See Mommsen and Bracher essays in Laqueur, *Fascism*.
113. The best study of this is Mack Smith, *Mussolini*.
114. Gottfried Feder provides a typical example of the national socialist attempt to outline a corporate state idea. He called for a new type of state to replace the liberal Weimar Republic: 'It must especially break with parliamentary parties and parliamentary cliques, and above all, it must not mix political and economic types of popular representation in a *single* parliament ... The *House of the People* (as the first chamber) represents the political interests of the whole people, while the *Central Council* must represent the *economic* interests of the working population'; see 'The Social State' reprinted in Miller Lane and Rupp, *Nazi Ideology*, p. 34.
115. On Moeller van den Bruck, see Mosse, *Crisis of German Ideology*, p. 283. On the repudiation of medieval corporatism, see Rocco in Lyttelton, *Italian Fascisms*, p. 296; also Cassel's essay in Turner, *Reappraisals of Fascism*, p. 75.
116. See Gentile, 'Philosophic Basis of Fascism', p. 296. On the odd relation of Sorel to Mussolini, see Jennings, *George Sorel*, pp. 159–60. For a detailed study of syndicalism in relation to Italian fascism, see Roberts, *Syndicalist Tradition and Italian Fascism*.
117. For deeply supportive remarks on syndicalism on these themes, see A. Lanzillo's essay in Lyttelton, *Italian Fascisms*, pp. 202–3.
118. Rocco in Lyttelton, *Italian Fascisms*, p. 280.
119. Ibid., p. 281.
120. Gentile in Lyttelton, *Italian Fascisms*, p. 312; Rocco also speaks of 'syndicalism or corporativism'; presumably the two ideas had been perceived as one and the same tendency; see Rocco in Lyttelton, *Italian Fascisms*, p. 276.
121. See the excellent discussion of this whole area in Lyttelton, *Seizure of Power*, ch. 9.
122. Primo de Rivera, *Selected Writings*, p. 172.
123. Cassels in Turner, *Reappraisals of Fascism*, p. 70; see de Grand, *Italian Fascism*, pp. 88, 163.
124. Gentile, *Genesis and Structure of Society*, p. 147.
125. Rocco in Lyttelton, *Italian Fascisms*, p. 295.
126. Skidelsky remarks that 'In terms of economic understanding, the programme expounded by Mosley in *Greater Britain* was far in advance of anything produced by continental fascism'; see Skidelsky, *Mosley*, p. 302.
127. Bullock, *Hitler*, pp. 358–9.
128. Despite the fact that many Italian fascists were committed in practice to the idea of the free market from the early 1920s.
129. Primo de Rivera, *Selected Writings*, p. 134. Strasser in Miller Lane and Rupp, *Nazi Ideology*, p. 89. The stress is Strasser's.
130. Strasser in Miller Lane and Rupp, *Nazi Idelogy*, p. 89. The stress is Strasser's.
131. See Rocco in Lyttelton, *Italian Fascisms*, p. 294.
132. Hitler quoted in Bullock, *Hitler*, pp. 281–2.
133. Milward in Laqueur, *Fascism*, p. 409.
134. See Milward in Laqueur, *Fascism*, p. 411.
135. Mosse, *Nazism*, p. 48.

Chapter 7: Feminism

1. See, for example, Dale Spender, *Man-Made Language*. This particular idea of language embodying patriarchal or 'phallocentric' themes has been developed by French feminists like Irigaray, Cixous and Kristeva, as well as their American followers.
2. Aladjem, 'Philosopher's Prism', p. 278.
3. Banks, *Faces of Feminism*, p. 3.
4. Charvet, *Feminism*, p.1.
5. Radcliffe-Richards, *Sceptical Feminist*, pp. 13–14.
6. Carole Pateman, 'Democracy and Feminism' in Pateman, *Disorder of Women*; Bouchier, *Feminist Challenge*, p. 2; Randall, 'Feminism and Political Analysis', p. 514.
7. Toril Moi's essay in Lovell (ed.), *British Feminist Thought*, p. 368.
8. Spender, *Women of Ideas*, p. 34.
9. See Griffin, *Women and Nature*, p. xvii. Griffin also states that: 'The fact that man does not consider himself a part of nature, but indeed considers himself superior to matter, seemed to me to gain significance when placed against man's attitude that woman is both inferior to him and closer to nature' (p. xv). The work of Mary Daly is also linked with this perspective; see Daly, *Gyn-Ecology* and *Pure Lust*.
10. On Daly's use of Jungian themes see, for example, Daly, *Pure Lust*, ch. 2.
11. Spender, *Women of Ideas*, p. 33.
12. See, for example, Mary Hawkesworth, 'Feminist Rhetoric', pp. 452–3 and n. 30.
13. Virginia Woolf comments very favourably on the founding role of Aphra Behn in *A Room of One's Own* (1929).
14. Kramnick in Wollstonecraft, *Vindication of the Rights of Women*, p. 7; see also Tomalin, *Life and Death of Mary Wollstonecraft*.
15. See Dietz on the phases internal to the second wave 'Citizenship with a Feminist Face', p. 19; and H. Eisenstein on four waves or phases, *Contemporary Feminist Thought*. On postmodernist feminism being a 'third wave', see discussion of C. Sylvester in Zalewski, 'Debauching of Feminist Theory', p. 33.
16. Olive Banks notes 'They therefore specifically applied the language of natural rights to the relationships between men and women and laid claims to the equality of the sexes'; see Banks, *Faces of Feminism*, p. 29.
17. Named after Susan B. Anthony, a veteran campaigner who introduced the proposition.
18. The utopians and liberal writers will be examined in more detail in later sections of the chapter.
19. Greer, *Female Eunuch*; Mitchell moved more decisively towards psychoanalytic interests in *Psychoanalysis and Feminism*. For discussion and examples of British feminism (Greer and Mitchell onward), see the recent study and reader, Lovell, *British Feminist Thought*.
20. See Bouchier, *Feminist Challenge*, pp. 44ff.
21. Delmar in Mitchell and Oakley (ed.), *What is Feminism?*, p. 3.
22. See 'Feminism and Ecology' and 'Ritual is Essential', appendices B and F in Devall and Sessions, *Deep Ecology*, pp. 229–31 and 247–50.
23. Z. Eisenstein, *Liberal Feminism*, p. 5.
24. See Pateman, *Sexual Contract*.

25. Okin, *Women in Western Political Thought*, p. 200.
26. For the exceptions – Condorcet, Helvetius, Von Hippel and Wollstonecraft, see the excellent and detailed essay on these and other theorists by Ursula Vogel in Evans *et al.* (eds), *Women and Political Theory*.
27. Aphra Behn, Mary Astell, Catherine Macauley, and Olympe de Gouges; see Spender, *Women of Ideas*, pp. 44–50.
28. Radcliffe-Richards, *Sceptical Feminist*. Okin comments that all feminists 'acknowledge the vast debts of feminism to liberalism. They know that without the liberal tradition, feminism would have had a much more difficult time emerging', Okin, *Justice, Gender, and the Family*, p. 61. However, both Okin and Radcliffe-Richards want Rawlsian liberalism and theories of justice to be extended fully to the family and women. Child-rearing, domestic work and the like must be included in any discussion of justice. Okin regards this as a logical progression of Rawlsian arguments.
29. See introduction by Felix Markham to Saint-Simon, *Social Organization*, pp. xxxvii–xxxix.
30. See B. Taylor, *Eve and the New Jerusalem*, p. 22, on the relation of Wheeler to Bentham. Wheeler is also said to have introduced Fourier and Owen, although the two men did not seem to like one another.
31. Bebel's *Women under Socialism* was an immensely popular work, a fact which appeared to irritate Engels. It was originally published in 1878, revised 1883, and 1891. The 50th German edition appeared in 1910.
32. See Diana Coole's excellent study, *Women in Political Theory*, pp. 208ff.
33. Jaggar, *Feminist Politics*, p. 304; see also Z. Eisenstein (ed.), *Capitalist Patriarchy*, p. 1, and Tong, *Feminist Thought*.
34. Jaggar, *Feminist Politics*, p. 83.
35. See, for example, Greer, *Female Eunuch*; Firestone, *Dialectic of Sex*; Millett, *Sexual Politics*.
36. Jaggar, *Feminist Politics*, p. 84.
37. As one feminist writer has argued, women-centred theory 'demands the dethroning of logic and reason, and an acceptance of the postulate of woman's especial ties to nature; of those who do not share it, it requires a Kuhnian-style non-rational conversion to a new paradigm'; see J. Evans, 'Overview of the Problem for Feminist Political Theorists', in Evans *et al.*, *Women and Political Theory*, p. 4. She suggests that Thomas Kuhn, the philosopher of science, is closest to such a women-centred account.
38. See Moi (ed.), *French Feminist Thought*.
39. Lawson, *Reflexivity*, p. 93.
40. Lyotard, *Postmodern Condition*, p. xxiv.
41. Quoted in D. C. Stanton's essay in Eisenstein and Jardine (eds), *Future of Difference*, p. 73.
42. Hawkesworth, 'Feminist Rhetoric', p. 449.
43. Irigaray, *The Sex which is Not One*, p. 74.
44. Moi in Lovell, *British Feminist Thought*, p. 368.
45. See Chodorow, *Mothering*; Gilligan, *In a Different voice*.
46. Boling, 'Democratic Potential of Mothering', p. 608.
47. Dietz, 'Citizenship with a Feminist Face', p. 28.
48. Elshtain, *Public Man, Private Woman* and 'Reflections on War and Political Discourse'; Ruddick, *Maternal Thinking*. For critical discussion and further bibliography on this, see Dietz 'Citizenship with Feminist Face'; see also

J. Stacey 'Are Feminists Afraid to Leave Home? The Challenge of Pro-Family Feminism' in Mitchell and Oakley, *What is Feminism?*

49. See J. Stacey in Mitchell and Oakley, *What is Feminism?* Also Boling, 'Democratic Potential of Mothering', pp. 608ff.
50. Ruth Levitas in Forbes and Smith (eds), *Politics and Human Nature*, p. 116.
51. Wollstonecraft, *Vindication of the Rights of Woman*, p. 82.
52. Ibid., p. 142.
53. Ibid., p. 91.
54. Ibid., p. 86; see also p. 156.
55. Ibid., p. 94.
56. Mill in Collini (ed.), *On Liberty*, p. 138; although in Mill, and also Engels, there are clearly quite strong residual beliefs about the 'natural' place of women.
57. Although Mill did look to the possibility of such a future science of human character — ethology.
58. Mill in Collini, *On Liberty*, p. 137.
59. Quoted by Engels in Marx and Engels (eds), *Selected Writings*, p. 503.
60. Engels in 'Origin of the Family', ibid., p. 510.
61. Jaggar, *Feminist Politics*, p. 69.
62. Ibid., p. 132.
63. Mackinnon, 'Feminism, Marxism, Method and the State: An Agenda for Theory' in Keohane, Rosaldo and Gelpi (eds), *Feminist Theory*, p. 30.
64. Ibid., p. 29.
65. Simone de Beauvoir, *Second Sex*.
66. Ibid., p. 684.
67. Firestone, *Dialectic of Sex*. Jaggar sees this work as the first 'sustained and systematic work by a contemporary radical feminist'; see Jaggar, *Feminist Politics*, p. 85.
68. Kate Millett preferred the term unisex to androgynous in *Sexual Politics*.
69. Speaking of the German extermination camps of the Second World War, a contemporary feminist writer claims that 'in creating a female degraded beyond human recognition, the Nazis set a new standard of masculinity, honoured especially in the benumbed conscience that does not even notice sadism against women because that sadism is so ordinary', Dworkin, *Pornography*, p. 145. The various writings of Dworkin pursue such themes; see Dworkin's *Women Hating* or *Intercourse*.
70. Quoted in Jaggar, *Feminist Politics*, p. 264.
71. See Dworkin, *Pornography*, pp. 52–3.
72. See Randall, 'Feminism and Political Analysis', p. 522.
73. Quoted in Jaggar, *Feminist Politics*, p. 97.
74. See Randall, 'Feminism and Political Analysis', p. 521.
75. See Coole, *Women in Political Theory*, p. 266; also Lloyd, *Man of Reason*; Macmillan, *Women, Reason and Philosophy*; and Radcliffe-Richards, *Sceptical Feminist*.
76. See Rich, *Of Woman Born*, and Keller, *Reflections on Science and Gender*.
77. See H. Eisenstein, *Contemporary Feminist Thought*, p. 66; or articles by Oakley, Rose and Ruzek in Mitchell and Oakley, *What is Feminism?* Not all agree on the positive view of standpoint theory. Vicky Randall contends that it is over-ambitious; see Randall, 'Feminism and Political Analysis', p. 523.
78. Wollstonecraft, *Vindication of the Rights of Woman*, p. 131.
79. Ibid., pp. 124–5.

80. Mill in Collini, *On Liberty*, p. 143.
81. Ibid., p. 119.
82. Engels in Marx and Engels, *Selected Writings*, p. 502.
83. Ibid., p. 504.
84. Z. Eisenstein, *Radical Future of Liberal Feminism*, p. 8.
85. Z. Eisenstein (ed.), *Capitalist Patriarchy*, p. 5.
86. As Heidi Hartmann put it: 'While Marxist analysis provides essential insight into the laws of historical development, and those of capital in particular, the categories of Marxism are sex-blind. Only a specifically feminist analysis reveals the systematic character of relations betwen men and women. Yet feminist analysis by itself is inadequate because it has been blind to history and insufficiently materialist. Both Marxist analysis, particularly its historical and materialist method, and feminist analysis, especially the identification of patriarchy as a social and historical structure, must be drawn upon if we are to understand the development of Western capitalist societies and the predicament of women within them', Hartmann in Sargent (ed.), *Unhappy Marriage of Marxism and Feminism*, pp. 2–3; see also Rowbotham, *Women, Resistance and Revolution*; Z. Eisenstein, *Capitalist Patriarchy*; and A. Kuhn and A. M. Wolpe (eds), *Feminism and Materialism*, for more detail and bibliography on these debates.
87. Hartmann in Sargent, *Unhappy Marriage of Marxism and Feminism*, p. 9. There has been considerable debate about this point in more recent years within New Left circles.
88. Wollstonecraft mentions, very tentatively, at the end of her book, the equal rights of suffrage, but it is only a passing remark; see Wollstonecraft, *Vindication of the Rights of Woman*, p. 260.
89. As Mill argued: 'The principle which regulates the existing social relations between the sexes − the legal subordination of one sex to the other − is wrong in itself, and now one of the chief hindrances to human improvement; and that it ought to be replaced by a principle of perfect equality'; see Mill in Collini, *On Liberty*, p. 119. Charvet complains that Mill does not bring out the full justification for the presumption in favour of equality. He simply assumes equality to be just; see Charvet, *Feminism*, p. 36.
90. Diana Coole sees Mill's marital ideas as 'perhaps the most progressive aspect of his thought', Coole, *Women in Political Theory*, p. 144.
91. For example, Radcliffe-Richards, *Sceptical Feminist*; Dietz, 'Citizenship with a Feminist Face'; Okin, *Justice, Gender and the Family*.
92. See Hawksworth, 'Feminist Rhetoric', p. 464, n. 16.
93. See Flax, 'Gender and Feminist Theory' and *Thinking Fragments*.
94. To 'posit woman's difference, whether as a function of biology, morphology, psychology, sexuality, or specific life experiences is to raise the specter of essentialism. Any such projection of "male" and "female" ... as un-questioned essences is dangerous for feminism, for any essential difference identified can provide a foundation for an argument to keep "woman" in her "natural" place, a ploy all too familiar in the patriarchal repertoire'; see Hawkesworth, 'Feminist Rhetoric', p. 451.
95. Wollstonecraft, *Vindication of the Rights of Woman*, p. 166.
96. As she observed: 'A master and mistress of a family ought not to continue to love each other with passion', ibid., p. 113.
97. Engels in Marx and Engels, *Selected Writings*, p. 502.
98. Ibid., p. 503.

99. See Jaggar, *Feminist Politics*, pp. 67–9; Hartmann in Sargent, *Unhappy Marriage of Marxism and Feminism*, p. 9.
100. See Rosalind Petchesky's remarks on production and reproduction in 'Dissolving the Hyphen: A Report on Marxist-Feminist Groups 1–5' in Z. Eisenstein, *Capitalist Patriarchy*, pp. 376–7.
101. See article 'The "Family Wage": Some Problems for Socialists and Feminists' by M. Barrett and M. MacIntosh in Lovell, *British Feminist Thought*.
102. Daly, *Gyn-Ecology*.
103. For example, Dietz, 'Citizenship with a Feminist Face'.
104. Engels in Marx and Engels, *Selected Writings*, p. 579.
105. See Kollontai, *Selected Writings*.
106. Jaggar, *Feminist Politics*, p. 132.
107. H. Eisenstein, *Contemporary Feminist Thought*, p. 51.
108. See Kariel, 'Feminist Subject Spinning in the Postmodern Project', p. 255.
109. O'Neill essay in Silverman (ed.), *Postmodernism*, pp. 78–9.
110. Zalewski 'Debauching of Feminist Theory', p. 34. Toril Moi also comments that 'If postmodernism, at least in Lyotard's sense of the term, sees all metanarratives, including feminism, as repressive enactments of metaphysical authority, what then can it mean to declare oneself a feminist postmodernist or, perhaps more accurately, a postmodern feminist? Does it mean anything at all'; see Moi essay in Lovell, *British Feminist Thought*, p. 368. Vicky Randall also notes on postmodernism that to 'feminists seriously committed to exposing and relieving the oppression of women, such a "solution" is altogether too drastic since it undermines the credibility of feminist claims along with everybody else's'; see Randall, 'Feminism and Political Analysis', p. 523; see also Aladjem on the self-destructive logic implicit in Foucault's arguments when applied to feminism, in 'Philosopher's Prism', pp. 279–80.

Chapter 8: Ecologism

1. Porritt, *Seeing Green*, p. 3. The term 'ecology' is, of course, still the name of an established science.
2. See n. 1 above. Thus Porritt entitles his initial book *Seeing Green* and Andrew Dobson his excellent recent book *Green Political Thought*.
3. Ward and Dubos, *Only One Earth*, p. 37.
4. Goldsmith (ed.), *Blueprint for Survival*, p. 69.
5. Witness the media and political attention concerning scientific claims on holes in the ozone layer. For discussion of this point, see Yearley, *The Green Case*, p. 45. However, there are ambiguities concerning the problematic relation of science and the more normative concerns. These will be taken up in the ensuing discussion.
6. Green politics starts with the recognition 'that we find ourselves in a multifaceted, global crisis that touches every aspect of our lives', Spretnak and Capra, *Green Politics*, p. xv.
7. According to Anna Bramwell, the early use of 'ecology' had strong etymological relations to other terms like 'ethology' and 'economics'; see Bramwell, *Ecology in 20th Century*, pp. 14–15; one might also add here 'ethnology' (the study of races).
8. Haeckel was Professor of Zoology for many years at the University of Jena.
9. Quoted in Bramwell, *Ecology in 20th Century*, p. 40. I have found Bramwell's research in this area both stimulating and immensely helpful. I cannot say

that I share the sentiments behind her book, which in my view tend to mar the text.

10. The significance of Christianity here is that some have traced the ecological crisis back to the very character of Christianity. The classic article to first introduce this idea was Lynn White Jnr, 'Historical Roots of Ecological Crisis'. However, it is disputed by a number of writers. Much of the debate turns on the interpretation of the concept of 'Christian Stewardship'. One of the clearest and most balanced counter-arguments to Lynn White's is Robin Attfield, *Ethics of Environmental Concern*.

11. Max Oelschlaeger's recent work *The Idea of the Wilderness* argues, in fact, that things began to go wrong in the Neolithic period; before this time hunter-gatherers had not unduly affected the environment.

12. Tokar, *Green Alternative*, p. 34.

13. For discussion of the origins of the movement here, see Pepper, *Roots of Modern Environmentalism*, and more generally Worster, *Nature's Economy*.

14. See, for example, Spretnak and Capra, *Green Politics*, pp. 157ff; Porritt, *Seeing Green*, pp. 26ff; Weston (ed.), *Red and Green*, pp. 15ff.

15. See Dobson, *Green Political Thought*, pp. 8–9.

16. See Russell, *Awakening Earth*.

17. See Haeckel, *Riddle of the Universe*, pp. 224, 310.

18. Contemporary ecologial theologicans, particularly those who self-consciously adopt the title 'creation spirituality' distinguish their position from pantheism. They call themselves 'panentheists', arguing in effect that God should not be understood as totally immanent or totally identified with nature. God is both immanent and transcendent. This is therefore distinct from Haeckel; see, for example, M. Fox, *Original Blessing*, ch. 1.

19. Haeckel, *Riddle of the Universe*, p. 236. Haeckel's views have strong parallels with Spinoza's monistic philosophy. It is therefore not completely fortuitous that more recent eco-philosophers like Naess, Devall, Sessions and Warwick Fox are clearly fascinated with Spinoza's philosphy.

20. Ibid., p. 311. The peculiar term 'anthropistic' appears to be Haeckel's, or his translator's, neologism. There is a close term 'anthropic' (meaning 'of or belonging to a human') which the *Oxford English Dictionary* records as 'rare' and dating from 1859.

21. There is a study to be written on 'nature' and its normative impact on twentieth-century thought and values. Bramwell's work is a reasonable starting-point for such research; see Bramwell, *Ecology in 20th Century*.

22. Aspects of this particular history have been explored by Bramwell, ibid.

23. Lowe and Goyder (eds), *Environmental Groups in Politics*, pp. 15ff. Tim O'Riordan has also spoken of three waves: the first dating back to the early romantic period, approximately 150 years ago, incorporating figures like Wordsworth, Emerson and Thoreau; the second phase between 1900 to 1920, incorporating the age of the environmental technocrat and thus programmes of reforestation, soil conservation, etc.; and the third phase, from the mid-1960s, when environmental concerns became part of vigorous public debate, well-informed pressure groups were formed and environmental regulations were developed and institutionalized; see Porritt and Winner, *Coming of the Greens*, p. 20.

24. Lowe and Goyder, *Environmental Groups in Politics*, p. 25.

25. Another way of approaching this is in terms of Anthony Downs' idea of 'issue attention cycles', where the public become alarmed about a particular

issue (like environmental pollution); enthused about trying to solve it; then become entrapped in spiralling costs and cynicism; and finally abandon it in favour of another 'issue' which alarms them. Although this appears, possibly, too cynical a view; see Downs, 'Up and Down with Ecology'.

26.   See the work of Stephen Cotgrove and Andrew Duff summarized in Lowe and Goyder, *Environmental Groups in Politics*, pp. 26–7.

27.   Ash, *New Renaissance*, pp. 15–16. Porritt, in 1984, contended that 'Having written the last two general election manifestoes for the Ecology Party, I would be hard put even to say what our ideology is. Our politics seems to be a fairly simple mixture of pragmatism and idealism, common sense and vision. If that's an ideology, it's of a rather different sort from those that dominate our lives today'; however, he goes on later to attack both socialism and conservatism, contending that 'there must be something with which we can replace [them]; not another super-ideology (for ideologies are themselves part of the problem) *but a different world view*'; see Porritt, *Seeing Green*, pp. 43–4. See also Porritt and Winner, *Coming of the Greens*, p. 11, and W. and D. Schwarz, *Breaking Through*, ch. 1.

28.   Ash, *New Renaissance*, pp. 27–8.

29.   Dobson, *Green Political Thought*, p. 69.

30.   There are attempts to bridge this gap, although comparatively few as yet. Dobson has drawn attention to the problem in a number of places; see Dobson, 'Deep Ecology' and *Green Political Thought*; in a response to Dobson, Robin Attfield has claimed that his recent work with Katherine Dell, *Values, Conflict and the Environment*, 'is the most developed attempt to carry through Dobson's project of relating ecophilosophy to social practice' (Attfield 'Deep Ecology', p. 65). They deploy a sophisticated form of cost-benefit analysis premised on 'an analysis of the value-impacts of actions and policies', which will in turn allow some judgements to be made concerning decisions on the environment (ibid., p. 65). It remains to be seen whether this tendency receives a receptive audience. Given the massive problems that public policy analysis has had with cost-benefit analysis on issues like airport or railway location over the last three decades omens do not bode well.

31.   See Spretnak and Capra, *Green Politics*, p. 29; Bunyard and Morgan-Grenville, *Green Alternative*, p. 281; W. and D. Schwarz, *Breaking Through*, pp. 126–7; Tokar, *Green Alternative*, ch. 1; Porritt and Winner, *Coming of the Greens*, p. 10; and for discussion of this point, Dobson, *Green Political Thought*, pp. 47–8.

32.   Dobson, *Green Political Thought*, p. 11.

33.   I should point out here that in my own categorization in the text, I will be simplifying and also avoiding the philosophical problems of the particular components, so as not to unduly complicate matters. However, the typology that I utilize is still more complicated than usual. The usual typology to be found in the literature (which I am *not* deploying and do *not* endorse) is to draw a distinction between 'shallow' and 'deep' ecologists, usually along the following lines:

Deep	*Shallow*
Ontological monism	Ontological divisions
Ethics derived from metaphysics	Ethics separate from metaphysics
Intrinsic value	Instrumental value

Voluntarist	Determinist
Systems science	Mechanistic science
Biosphere or ecosphere of value	Humans of primary value
Radical	Reformist
Advocates sustainable future	Endorses industrialism

34. Richard Sylvan calls this form of argument the 'Sole Value Assumption'; see his 'Critique of Deep Ecology'. A form of this argument can be found in an article by W. H. Murdy, 'Anthropocentrism: A Modern Version'. Murdy says, 'To be anthropocentric is to affirm that mankind is to be valued more highly than other things in nature – by man ... It is proper for man to be anthropocentric'; he later contends that our ecological problems do not stem from anthropocentrism *per se*, but rather from conceiving anthropocentrism too narrowly; see Murdy in Scherer and Attig (eds), *Ethics and the Environment*, pp. 13, 20.
35. For discussion of these, see W. Fox, *Toward a Transpersonal Ecology*, p. 160.
36. Leopold, *Sand County Almanac*; also Naess, 'Shallow and Deep Ecology Movement' and *Ecology, Community and Lifestyle*.
37. See Rodman in Scherer and Attig, *Ethics and the Environment*; the second tendency is best seen in the work of Arne Naess and also exemplified in Devall and Sessions, *Deep Ecology*; for the Buddhist interpretation, see Gary Snyder's essay 'Buddhism and the Possibilities of a Planetary Culture', appendix G in Devall and Sessions, *Deep Ecology*; Warwick Fox's work is best exemplified in the detailed reply to Sylvan's critique of deep ecology (see Sylvan, 'Critique of Deep Ecology'; W. Fox, *Approaching Deep Ecology*) and more recently in a very comprehensive study, *Toward a Transpersonal Ecology*. A recent summary of eco-philosophy literature describes Fox's 1986 piece as 'The best explanation and defence of the Deep ecology position'; see Katz, 'Environmental Ethics', p. 268. Fox's work is clearly inspired by Naess; however, the more recent 1990 book makes a number of subtle changes which, in my view, distances him from Naess.
38. I am employing, but altering, terminology used by J. R. Rodman and Robin Attfield.
39. See Singer, *Expanding Circle*, p. 123; see also Regan, *Case for Animal Rights*.
40. Singer, *Expanding Circle*, p. 123.
41. See, particularly, the work of Paul Taylor, *Respect for Nature*. He distinguishes vigorously between 'human centred' axiology and 'life centred' axiology, identifying himself with the latter. On the biocentric life-centred view, see Taylor, pp. 99–100.
42. Callicott in Scherer and Attig, *Ethics and the Environment*, and also Callicott, 'Non-anthropocentric Value Theory'; Holmes Rolston III, *Environmental Ethics*, and article 'Are Values in Nature Subjective or Objective?' in Elliot and Gare (eds), *Environmental Philosophy*; Taylor, *Respect for Nature*.
43. For an excellent discussion of intrinsic value with bibliographical references, see Attfield, *Theory of Value and Obligation*, ch. 2. See also the interchange in *Cogito*: Dobson, 'Deep Ecology', and Attfield, 'Deep Ecology and Intrinsic Value'.
44. For example, Holmes Rolston III, *Environmental Ethics*.
45. 'The kind of things which can be of intrinsic value are not objects, people or other creatures, but experiences, activities and the development of capacities ... talk about the intrinsic value of people, when it is not another way of

talking about their standing or their rights, should be taken to concern the intrinsic value of their living a worthwhile life', Attfield, *Theory of Value and Obligation*, p. 31.

46. See W. Fox, *Approaching Deep Ecology*, and, more particularly, *Toward a Transpersonal Ecology*.

47. For example, Murray Bookchin places a heavy emphasis on the distinction between social ecologism and environmentalism; see Bookchin, *Toward an Ecological Society*, p. 27. Even in balanced academic assessments, like Dobson's, the distinction still appears quite firmly; see Dobson, *Green Political Thought*, p. 3.

48. Worster, *Nature's Economy*.

49. In other words, the political equivalent of utopias.

50. One recent writer notes here: 'The green analysis of environmental and social issues is within the broad framework of right-wing ideology and philosophy. The belief in "natural" limits to human achievement, the denial of class divisions and the Romantic view of "nature" all have their roots in the conservative and liberal political traditions'; see Weston, *Red and Green*, p. 24.

51. As Weston remarks: 'To think that whooping cranes are important (possibly more so) than people one has to be free of the more pressing human problems like that of poverty', ibid., p. 3.

52. Apart from the *völkisch* tradition, I have in mind here the strange but consistent work of Edward Goldsmith, *A Blueprint for Survival*.

53. Ash, *New Renaissance*, p. 23. There is a conflation of two points here, namely: (a) the intrinsic value of nature and (b) the idea that humanity is intrinsically part of nature. I am suggesting that many in the political deep ecology wing (particularly) would contend that both claims are connected and both are correct.Humans *are* at one with nature and nature *is* intrinsically valuable. However, I am not saying here that these two points *are* necessarily linked. In fact I would contend that they are not. They can be treated quite separately.

54. Lovelock, *Gaia*. The word 'Gaia' in its original use was the 'earth goddess'. It should be noted, though, that the idea of the earth as a self-regulating organism – 'living earth' – had already been discussed by a number of scientists and philosophers at the end of the nineteenth century; see Bramwell, *Ecology in 20th Century*, pp. 61ff.

55. Yearley, *The Green Case*, p. 146. See also this section for a summary of some of the objections from the scientific community.

56. See W. Fox, *Toward a Transpersonal Ecology*, p. 118; Devall and Sessions, *Deep Ecology*, p. 67. Fox appears to be somewhat disenchanted with the idea in this later work.

57. Tokar, *Green Alternative*, pp. 9–10. This particular idea has been criticized in an earlier section. I also engage in some criticism of it within the chapter on anarchism.

58. Redclift in Weston, *Red and Green*, p. 86. Weston also notes that 'it is the social, political, economic and physical world in which we live. This means that environmentalists should be concerned with both the physical and social world', *Red and Geeen*, p. 2.

59. One way out of this impasse is to argue that our self-consciousness has evolved naturally and is therefore part of nature. Yet there is always something

puzzling and unresolved in such an argument. The theory of evolution is premised on our *being* self-conscious. The theory of evolution is a product of self-consciousness. Therefore self-consciousness is the premise upon which the theory of evolution develops. Yet the above argument, in asserting that self-consciousness has evolved naturally, implies that natural evolution is the premise to self-consciousness. This appears to conflict with the second argument. My own view of this is that self-consciousness implies some difference from the normal functioning of evolution, although I am not quite sure of the nature of that difference.

60. See ch. 1 for some discussion of this point.
61. Bahro, *From Red to Green*, pp. 221–2.
62. Ryle, *Ecology and Socialism*, p. 66. I should emphasize the point here that Ryle capitalizes the 'state'. On the other hand, Ryle does admit that such a state would still owe more of its values to William Morris's vision of socialism than to Marxism, see pp. 69–70.
63. See Bookchin, *Ecology of Freedom* and *Toward an Ecological Society*. However, one suspects that Bookchin would give Bahro's Benedictine proposal short shrift.
64. See Ophuls in Pirages (ed.), *Sustainable Society*; see also Ophuls' own work, *Ecology and the Politics of Scarcity*.
65. Ophuls in Pirages, *Sustainable Society*, pp. 162–3.
66. Goldsmith and Hildyard (eds), *Green Britain*, pp. 117–18.
67. Porritt, in Goldsmith and Hildyard (eds), *Green Britain*, p. 345.
68. Porritt quoted in W. and D. Schwarz, *Breaking Through*, pp. 259–60. See also Porritt, *Seeing Green*, pp. 10–11.
69. See Elkington and Burke, *Green Capitalists*; also the practically motivated book for Green consumers, Elkington and Hailes, *Green Consumer Guide*. This position, which relies on market methods to achieve environmental ends, will receive more discussion in the next section on the new economics.
70. See Fromm, *To Have or To Be?*
71. Robertson speaks of a fundamental movement from instrumental to 'inner directed expressive values' in *Future Work*, pp. 76–9; see also Spretnak and Capra, *Green Politics*, pp. xvi, 29; Ash, *New Renaissance*, pp. 24ff.
72. James Robertson remarks that the new society would move 'away from quantitative to qualitative values and goals; away from the impersonal towards the personal and interpersonal; and away from the earning and spending of money towards the meeting of real human needs', introduction to Spretnak and Capra, *Green Politics*, p. xx.
73. Ophuls in Pirages, *Sustainable Society*, p. 168. I should point out here that I am not suggesting that Ophuls is a deep ecologist, rather the vision he outlines here contains much that is attractive to the deep ecologists. Interestingly Bookchin in discussing his vision of a social ecological commune also focuses, in the steps of Kropotkin, on a reinvigorated understanding of the *polis*; see Bookchin, *Toward an Ecological Society*, p. 104.
74. Ophuls in Pirages, *Sustainable Society*, p. 168.
75. Tokar, *Green Alternative*, p. 31.
76. See Schumacher's amazingly popular work *Small is Beautiful*, ch. 4.
77. Non-violence figures as one of the *four* pillars of an ecological society, with ecology, social responsibility and grassroots democracy, in Spretnak and Capra, *Green Politics*, p. 41.

78. See also W. and D. Schwarz, *Breaking Through*, p. 207. On this question of the change in the whole 'lifestyle', see Porritt and Winner, *Coming of the Greens*, ch. 8.
79. Robertson, *Future Work*. This will be explored a little more in the next section.
80. Goldsmith, *Blueprint for Survival*, pp. 51, 53. Kirkpatrick Sale suggest neighbourhoods of 500–1000 and larger units of 5,000–10,000; see Sale, *Dwellers in the Land*, pp. 62–4.
81. Tokar, *Green Alternative*, p. 27.
82. See n. 81 above.
83. Ibid., p. 27, and Sale, *Dwellers in the Land*; see also Dobson's discussion here, *Green Political Thought*, pp. 117ff.
84. 'An organization structured with participatory democracy sets its basic policy according to the voting at large assemblies. It allows individuals access to all party officials, and it eschews hierarchical structure'; see Spretnak and Capra, *Green Politics*, p. 35; Bahro, *From Red to Green*, p. 222; Tokar, *Green Alternative*, p. 98. There are strong parallels, here between the deep ecologists and the social ecologists like Bookchin who make a great deal of participatory democracy as contrasted to representative democracy; see Bookchin, *Toward an Ecological Society*, p. 216.
85. See Spretnak and Capra, *Green Politics*, p. 47; Robertson, *Future Work*, pp. 79–80.
86. Goldsmith, *Blueprint for Survival*, p. 48.
87. Ibid, p. 49.
88. Andrew Dobson reminded me here of the well-established Chinese government policy of one child per family, which appears, in fact, to have the support of the people.
89. See Dobson, *Green Political Thought*, pp. 96–7.
90. Goldsmith, *Blueprint for Survival*, p. 50.
91. Ash, *New Renaissance*, pp. 53–4.
92. Goldsmith, *Blueprint for Survival*, p. 52; Tokar, *Green Alternative*, p. 31; Spretnak and Capra, *Green Politics*, pp. 45, 178–9; Robertson, *Future Work*, p. 141.
93. There is an additional problem here in that there is no consistent line of argument on what is meant by 'freedom' in an ecological context. There is usually some disparagement of liberal notions of negative freedom; see Pirages, *Sustainable Society*, p. 9; however, it is not clear what notion of freedom is being deployed in its place.
94. Also on the question of the 'super ideology', see Porritt in Goldsmith and Hildyard, *Green Britain*, pp. 344–5. For a very similar commentary on industrialism and growth, see Goldsmith, *Blueprint for Survival*, p. 26.
95. See Pepper's contemptuous remarks on this theme in *Roots of Modern Environmentalism*, p. 5.
96. Spretnak and Capra, *Green Politics*, p. 78.
97. 'Present day economists, whether neo-classical, Marxist, Keynesian, or the post-Keynesian schools (monetarist, supply-side, and others), generally lack an ecological perspective. Instead of recognizing the economy as one aspect of a whole ecological and social fabric, they tend to isolate it and to describe it in terms of highly unrealistic theoretical models . . . they disregard the social and environmental costs generated by all economic activity'; ibid., pp. 77–8.
98. Goldsmith and Hildyard, *Green Britain*, p. 25.

99. Ekins (ed.), *Living Economy*, p. xviii.
100. Pirages, *Sustainable Society*, p. 3.
101. See Spretnak and Capra, *Green Politics*, p. 88.
102. See Goldsmith and Hildyard, *Green Britain*, pp. 6–20.
103. Ryle, *Ecology and Socialism*, p. 46.
104. Weston in his introduction and Pepper's article in Weston, *Red and Green*, pp. 28, 119–21. See also Pepper's heated discussions in *Roots of Modern Environmentalism*, also Porritt and Winner's somewhat irate response to Pepper and Weston as 'the angry spluttering from worn-out ideologues who have long since lost touch with the real world' in *Coming of the Greens*, p. 256.
105. Elkington and Burke, *Green Capitalists*, p. 23; see also Pearce, Markandya and Barbier, *Blueprint for Green Economy*.
106. Elkington and Burke, *Green Capitalism*, p. 239.
107. Ibid., p. 252.
108. Porritt and Winner, *Coming of the Greens*, p. 151; see also Yearley's discussion, *The Green Case*, p. 106.
109. Robertson, *Future Work*, p. 5.
110. See Ekins, (ed.), *Living Economy*, pp. 44ff; part 2 of the book is entitled 'Putting People First'.
111. Ibid., p. 55.
112. Robertson, *Sane Alternative* and *Future Work*; Dauncey, *Unemployment Handbook* and *Nice Work*.
113. Robertson, *Future Work*, p. x.
114. Ibid., p. xii; Ekins, *Living Economy*, p. 169; Schwarz, *Breaking Through*, p. 22.
115. See Robertson, *Future Work*, p. 175.
116. See Ekins, *Living Economy*, pp. 241ff; Spretnak and Capra, *Green Politics*, pp. 97ff.
117. Robertson in Ekins, *Living Economy*, p. 114. This Ruskinian notion of 'health as wealth' is in fact one of the main points of Robertson's earlier book, *The Sane Alternative*.
118. Ekins, *Living Economy*, p. 128.
119. Ibid., pp. 139–65.
120. Daly (ed.), *Steady-State Economy*; see also his article 'The Steady-State Economy: What, Why and How' in Pirages, *Sustainable Society*.
121. Daly notes that in mining concentrated ores we convert usable energy into unusable energy. Entropy, as distinct from the conservation of energy, implies that in rearranging matter we continually reduce energy in the whole system. Usable energy is a finite resource; see Pirages, *Sustainable Society*, pp. 107–10.
122. Daly has recently produced, with John B. Cobb, another much more extended presentation of such arguments. Because their book came into my hands at the very last stage of writing this text I have not been able to integrate their arguments; see Daly and Cobb, *Common Good*.
123. On the systems view as opposed to the mechanistic view, see Capra, *Turning Point*. On the scientific ambivalence and opposition, see Yearley, *The Green Case*, ch. 4.

Chapter 9: Icons and Iconoclasm

1. Goldie in Ball, Farr and Hanson (eds), *Political Innovation*, p. 272.

BIBLIOGRAPHY

Acton, H. B. 1971 *The Morals of Markets: An Ethical Explanation*. London: Longman.

Adams, Ian 1989 *The Logic of Political Belief: A Philosophical Analysis*. London and New York: Harvester Wheatsheaf.

Adorno, Theodore W. 1950 *The Authoritarian Personality*. New York: Harper & Row.

Aladjem, Terry 1991 'The Philosopher's Prism: Foucault, Feminism, and Critique', *Political Theory*, 19, 2.

Allett, J. 1981 *The New Liberalism: The Political Economy of J. A. Hobson*. Toronto and London: University of Toronto Press.

Allison, L. 1984 *Right Principles: A Conservative Philosophy of Politics*. Oxford: Blackwell.

Apter, David 1965 *The Politics of Modernization*. Chicago: Chicago University Press.

Apter, D. E. and Joll, J. (eds) 1971 *Anarchism Today*. London: Macmillan.

Arblaster, A. 1984 *The Rise and Decline of Western Liberalism*. Oxford: Blackwell.

Arendt, Hannah 1951 *The Origins of Totalitarianism*. London: Allen & Unwin.

Aris, R. 1965 *History of Political Thought in Germany 1789–1815*. New York: Frank Cass.

Arshinov, P. 1974 *The History of the Makhnovist Movement 1918–21*. Chicago: Black and Red Detroit/Solidarity.

Ash, M. 1987 *New Renaissance: Essays in Search of Wholeness*. Bideford: Green Books.

Attfield, R. 1983 *The Ethics of Environmental Concern*. Oxford: Blackwell/New York: Columbia University Press.

Attfield, R. 1987 *A Theory of Value and Obligation*. London and New York: Croom Helm.

Attfield, R. 1990 'Deep Ecology and Intrinsic Value: A Reply to Andrew Dobson'. *Cogito*. 4/1.

Attfield, R. and Dell, K. (eds) 1989 *Values, Conflict and the Environment*. Oxford: Ian Ramsey Centre, and Cardiff Centre for Applied Ethics.

Auerbach, Morton M. 1959 *The Conservative Illusion*. New York: Columbia University Press.

Austern D. M. 1984 *The Political Theories of Edmund Burke and Joseph de Maistre as Representative of Conservative Libertarianism and Conservative Authoritarianism*. Ann Arbor: Michigan University Press.

Avrich, Paul 1967 *The Russian Anarchists*. Princeton, NJ: Princeton University Press.

Avrich, Paul 1970 'The Legacy of Bakunin'. *The Russian Review*, 29.

Bahro, R. 1984 *From Red to Green*. London: Verso and NLB.

Bahro, R. 1986 *Building the Green Movement*. London: GMP.

Bakunin, M. 1970 *God and the State*. New York: Dover.

Bakunin, M. 1990 *Statism and Anarchy*. Cambridge: Cambridge University Press.

Ball, Sidney 1896 'The Moral Aspect of Socialism'. *International Journal of Ethics*, VI.

Ball, Terence 1988 *Transforming Political Discourse: Political Theory and Critical Conceptual History*. Oxford: Blackwell.

Ball, Terence, Farr, James, and Hanson, Russell L. (eds) 1989 *Political Innovation and Conceptual Change*. Cambridge: Cambridge University Press.

Banks, Olive 1981 *Faces of Feminism*. Oxford: Martin Robertson.

Barr, John (ed) 1971 *The Environment Handbook*. London: Ballantine and Friends of the Earth.

Barrington Moore Jnr 1967 *Social Origins of Dictatorship and Democracy*. London: Allen Lane.

Barry, N. P. 1986 *Classical Liberalism and Libertarianism*. London: Macmillan.

Barry, N. P. 1987 *The New Right*. London: Croom Helm.

Beauvoir, Simone de 1954 *The Second Sex*. London: Jonathan Cape.

Bebel, A. 1971 *Women under Socialism*. New York: Schocken.

Beer, Max 1984 *A History of British Socialism*. Nottingham: Spokesman.

Bell, Daniel 1965 *The End of Ideology: On the Exhaustion of Political Ideas in the 1950s*. New York: Free Press.

Bellamy, R. 1987a *Modern Italian Social Theory*. Oxford: Polity Press.

Bellamy, R. 1987b 'Idealism and Liberalism in an Italian "New Liberal Theorist": Guido de Ruggiero's *History of European Liberalism*', *The Historical Journal*, 30, 1.

Berki, R. N. 1975 *Socialism*. London: Dent.

Berki, R. N. and Parekh, B. (eds) 1972 *The Morality of Politics*. New York: Crane, Russak & Co.

Berkman, A. 1977 *The ABC of Anarchism*. London: Freedom Press.

Bernstein, E. 1961 *Evolutionary Socialism*. New York: Schocken Books.

Bernstein, G. L. 1986 *Liberalism and Liberal Politics in Edwardian England*. London: Allen & Unwin.

Best. G. (ed.) 1974 *The Industrial Syndicalist: Documents in Social History*, 3. Nottingham: Spokesman Books.

Binion, Rudolph 1973 'Hitler's Concept of Lebensraum: The Psychological Basis'. *History of Childhood Quarterly*, 1.

Black A. 1984 *Guilds and Civil Society*. London: Methuen.

Black C. E. 1967 *The Dynamics of Modernization*. New York: Harper & Row.

Blake, R. 1985 *The Conservative Party from Peel to Thatcher*. London: Fontana, Collins.

Bobbio, N. 1987 *Which Socialism? Marxism, Socialism and Democracy*. Minneapolis: University of Minnesota Press.

Boling, P. 1991 'The Democratic Potential of Mothering'. *Political Theory*, 19, 4.

Bookchin, M. 1982 *The Ecology of Freedom*. Palo Alto: Cheshire Books.

Bookchin, M. 1986a *Post-Scarcity Anarchism*. Montreal and Buffalo: Black Rose Press.

Bookchin, M. 1986b *Toward an Ecological Society*. Montreal and Buffalo: Black Rose Press.

Bosanquet, N. 1983 *After the New Right*. London: Heinemann.

Boucher, David 1989 *The Social and Political Thought of R. G. Collingwood*. Cambridge: Cambridge University Press.

Bouchier, D. 1983 *The Feminist Challenge*. London: Macmillan.

Bramwell, Anna 1989 *Ecology in the 20th Century*. London and New Haven: Yale University Press.

Brenan, G. 1969 *The Spanish Labryinth*. Cambridge: Cambridge University Press.

Bristow, E. 1975 'The Liberty and Property Defence League and Individualism'. *The Historical Journal*, 18.

Broszat, Martin 1981, *The Hitler State: The Foundation and Development of the Internal Structure of the Third Reich*. London and New York: Longman.

Brundtland, Gro Harlem 1987 *Our Common Future*. Oxford: Oxford University Press.

Buck, P. W. (ed.) 1975 *How Conservatives Think*. Harmondsworth: Penguin.

Bullock, Alan 1962 *Hitler: A Study in Tyranny*. Harmondsworth: Penguin.

Bunyard, P. and Morgan-Grenville, F. (eds) 1987 *The Green Alternative*. London: Methuen.

Burke, E. (n.d.) *Edmund Burke: Selections from his Political Writings and Speeches*. London: T. Nelson & Sons.

Butler, D. and Stokes, D. 1974 *Political Change in Britain*. London: Macmillan.

Butterfield, H. 1950 *The Whig Theory of History*. London: George Bell.

Cahm, C. 1989 *Kropotkin and The Rise of Revolutionary Anarchism*. Cambridge: Cambridge University Press.

Callaghan, J. 1990 *Socialism in Britain*. Oxford: Blackwell.

Calleo, D. P. 1966 *Coleridge and the Idea of the Modern State*. New Haven, Conn.: Yale University Press.

Callicott, J. Baird 1984 'Non-anthropocentric Value Theory and Environmental Ethics'. *American Philosophical Quarterly*, 21.

Capra, F. 1982 *The Turning Point: Science, Society and the Rising Culture*. London: Fontana, Flamingo, Collins.

Carsten, F. L. 1980 *The Rise of Fascism*, 2nd edn. London: Batsford.

Carter, A. 1971 *The Political Theory of Anarchism*. London: Routledge & Kegan Paul.

Cecil, H. 1912 *Conservatism*. London: Thornton Butterworth.

Charvet, J. 1982 *Feminism*. London: Dent.

Cheles, L., Ferguson, R., and Vaughan M. (eds) 1991 *Neo-Fascism in Europe*. London and New York: Longman.

Chodorow, Nancy 1978 *Mothering: Psychoanalysis and the Sociology of Gender*. Berkeley and Los Angeles: University of California Press.

Claeys, G. 1989 *Citizens and Saints: Politics and Anti-Politics in Early British Socialism*. Cambridge: Cambridge University Press.

Clark, J. P. 1976 *Max Stirner's Egoism*. London: Freedom Press.

Clark J. P. 1977 *The Philosophical Anarchism of William Godwin*. Princeton, NJ: Princeton University Press.

Clark, J. P. 1986 *The Anarchist Moment: Reflections on Culture, Nature and Power*. Montreal and Buffalo: Black Rose Press.

Cobban, A. 1962 *Edmund Burke and the Revolt Against the Eighteenth Century*.

London: Allen & Unwin.

Cobbett, William 1985 *Rural Rides*, first published in 1830. Harmondsworth: Penguin.

Cole, G. D. H. 1917 *Self-Government in Industry*. London: George Bell.

Cole, G. D. H. 1953–60 *A History of Socialist Thought*, 7 vols. London: Macmillan.

Cole, G. D. H. 1980 *Guild Socialism Restated*. First published 1920. New Brunswick, NJ.: Transaction Books.

Cole M. 1961 *The Story of Fabian Socialism*. London: Heinemann.

Coleridge, S. T. 1976 *On the Constitution of the Church and State*. London: Routledge & Kegan Paul.

Collingwood, R. G. 1940 'Fascism and Nazism', *Philosophy*, 15.

Collingwood, R. G. 1989 *Essays in Political Philosophy*, ed. David Boucher. Oxford: Clarendon Press.

Collini, S. 1979 *Liberalism and Sociology: L. T. Hobhouse and Political Argument in England 1880–1915*. Cambridge: Cambridge University Press.

Collini, S. (ed.) 1989 *J. S. Mill, On Liberty and Other Writings*. Cambridge: Cambridge University Press.

Collins, I. 1957 *Liberalism in Nineteenth-Century Europe*. London: Historical Association, no. 34.

Constant, B. 1988 *Political Writings*. Cambridge: Cambridge University Press.

Coole, Diana 1988 *Women in Political Theory: from Ancient Misogyny to Contemporary Feminism*. Brighton: Harvester.

Corbett, P. 1965 *Ideologies*. London: Hutchinson.

Covell, C. 1986 *The Redefinition of Conservatism: Politics and Doctrine*. London: Macmillan.

Cowling, M. (ed.) 1978 *Conservative Essays*. London: Cassell.

Crick, B. 1982 *George Orwell: A Life*. Harmondsworth: Penguin.

Croce, B. 1946 *Politics and Morals*. London: Allen & Unwin.

Crosland, C. A. R. 1980 *The Future of Socialism*. London: Jonathan Cape.

Daly, Herman E. (ed.) 1973 *Towards a Steady-State Economy*. San Francisco: Freeman.

Daly, Herman E. and Cobb, John B. 1990 *For the Common Good*. London: Green Print.

Daly Mary 1979 *Gyn-Ecology: The Metaethics of Radical Feminism*. London: Women's Press.

Daly, Mary 1984 *Pure Lust: Elemental Feminist Philosophy*. London: Women's Press.

Dangerfield, G. 1966 *The Strange Death of Liberal England*. London: MacGibbon & Kee.

Dauncey, Guy 1981 *The Unemployment Handbook*. London: National Extension College.

Dauncey, Guy 1983 *Nice Work If You Can Get It*. London: National Extension College.

Dennis, N. and Halsey, A. H. 1988 *English Ethical Socialism*. Oxford: Clarendon Press.

Devall, Bill and Sessions, George 1985 *Deep Ecology: Living as if Nature Mattered*. Salt Lake City: Gibbs M. Smith Inc.

Dewey, John 1931 *Individualism: Old and New*. London: Allen & Unwin.

Dicey, A. V. 1905 *Lectures on the Relation between Law and Public Opinion in England during the Nineteenth Century*. London: Macmillan.

Dickinson, H. T. 1977 *Liberty and Property: Political Ideology in the Eighteenth*

Century. London: Methuen.

Dietz, Mary 1985 'Citizenship with a Feminist Face; The Problem of Maternal Thinking'. *Political Theory*, 13, 1.

Dobson, Andrew 1989, 'Deep Ecology'. *Cogito*, 3/1.

Dobson, Andrew 1990 *Green Political Thought*. London: Unwin Hyman.

Dolgoff, S. 1972 *Bakunin on Anarchy*. New York: Vintage Books.

Douglass, R. B., Mara, G. M., and Richardson, H. S. (eds) 1990 *Liberalism and the Good*. London: Routledge.

Downs, A. 1972 'Up and Down with Ecology – the issue attention cycle', *Public Interest*. 28.

Duncan, G. 1987 'Understanding Ideology'. *Political Studies*, XXXV.

Dunn, J. 1979 *Western Political Theory in the Face of the Future*. Cambridge: Cambridge University Press.

Durkheim, E. 1959 *Socialism and Saint-Simon*. London: Routledge & Kegan Paul.

Dworkin, Andrea 1974 *Women Hating*. New York: Dutton.

Dworkin, Andrea 1981 *Pornography: men possessing women*. London: Women's Press.

Dworkin, Andrea 1987 *Intercourse*. London: Arrow Books.

Eatwell, R. and O'Sullivan, N. (eds) 1989 *The Nature of the Right: European and American Politics and Political Thought since 1789*. London: Pinter.

Eccleshall, R. 1977 'English Conservatism as Ideology'. *Political Studies*, XXV.

Eccleshall, R. 1986 *British Liberalism: Liberal Thought from the 1640s to the 1980s*. London: Longman.

Eccleshall, R. 1990 *English Conservatism since the Restoration*. London: Unwin Hyman.

Eccleshall, R., Geoghegan, V., Jay, R., and Wilford, R. (eds) 1984 *Political Ideologies*. London: Hutchinson.

Ehrlich, P. 1968 *The Population Bomb*. London: Ballantine.

Eisenstein, Hestor 1984 *Contemporary Feminist Thought*. London: Unwin Hyman.

Eisenstein, Hestor and Jardine, Alice (eds) 1990 *The Future of Difference*. New Brunswick, NJ, and London: Rutger University Press.

Eisenstein, Zillah 1981 *The Radical Future of Liberal Feminism*. New York and London: Longman.

Eisenstein, Zillah (ed.) 1979 *Capitalist Patriarchy and the Case for Socialist Feminism*. New York and London: Monthly Review Press.

Ekins, Paul (ed.) 1986 *The Living Economy: A New Economics in the Making*. London: Routledge & Kegan Paul.

Eliot, T. S. 1939 *The Idea of a Christian Society*. London: Faber & Faber.

Elkington, J. and Hailes, Julia 1988 *The Green Consumer Guide*. London: Gollancz.

Elkington, J. and Burke, T. 1989 *The Green Capitalists*. London: Gollancz.

Elliot, R. and Gare, A. (eds) 1983 *Environmental Philosophy*. Milton Keynes: Open University Press.

Elshtain, J. B. 1981 *Public Man, Private Woman*. Princeton, NJ: Princeton University Press.

Elshtain, J. B. 1985 'Reflections on War and Political Discourse: Realism, Just War, and Feminism in a Nuclear Age'. *Political Theory*, 13, 1.

Elshtain, J. B. (ed.) 1982 *The Family in Political Thought*. Brighton: Harvester.

Engels, F. 1968 *The Origins of the Family, Private Property and the State*, in Karl Marx and Friedrich Engels, *Selected Writings*. London: Lawrence & Wishart.

Epstein, K. 1966 *The Genesis of German Conservatism*. Princeton, NJ: Princeton University Press.

Erikson, Erik H. 1958 *Young Man Luther: A Study in Psychoanalysis and History*. London: Faber & Faber.

Estrin, S. and Le Grand, J. (eds) 1989 *Market Socialism*. Oxford: Clarendon.

Evans, J. *et al.* (eds) 1986 *Women and Political Theory*. London: Sage.

Fanon, F. 1965 *The Wretched of the Earth*. Harmondsworth: Penguin.

Feiling, K. 1949 'Coleridge and the English Conservatives', in F. J. C. Hearnshaw (ed.), *Social and Political Ideas of Some Representative Thinkers of the Age of Reaction and Reconstruction*. Cambridge: W. Heffer.

Femia, J. 1981 *Gramsci's Political Thought*. Oxford: Clarendon Press.

Feuer, Lewis S. 1975 *Ideology and the Ideologists*. Oxford: Blackwell.

Feyerabend, P. 1975 *Against Method: Outline of an Anarchistic Theory of Knowledge*. London: NLB.

Figes, E. 1970 *Patriarchal Attitudes*. London: Macmillan.

Figgis, J. N. 1922 *The Divine Right of Kings*. Cambridge: Cambridge University Press.

Figgis, J. N. 1956 *Political Thought from Gerson to Grotius*. Cambridge: Cambridge University Press.

Firestone, Shulamith 1971 *The Dialectic of Sex*. New York: Bantam Books.

Flax, Jane 1986 'Gender as a Problem In and For Feminist Theory'. *American Studies*, 31.

Flax, Jane 1990 *Thinking Fragments*. Berkeley: University of California Press.

Forbes, I. (ed.) 1986 *Market Socialism: Whose Choice?* Fabian Tract 516. London: Fabian Society.

Forbes, I. and Smith, S. (eds) 1983 *Politics and Human Nature*. London: Pinter.

Forjacs, David (ed.) 1986 *Rethinking Italian Fascism: Capitalism, Populism and Culture*. London: Lawrence & Wishart.

Fowler, R. B. 1972 'The Anarchist Tradition of Political Thought'. *Western Political Quarterly*, 25.

Fox, Matthew 1983 *Original Blessing*. Santa Fe, New Mexico: Bear and Co.

Fox, Warwick 1984 'Deep Ecology: A New Philosophy for our Time?'. *The Ecologist*. 14.

Fox, Warwick 1986 *Approaching Deep Ecology: A Response to Richard Sylvan's Critique of Deep Ecology*. Hobart: University of Tasmania.

Fox, Warwick 1990 *Toward a Transpersonal Ecology: Developing a New Foundation for Environmentalism*. London and Boston: Shambala.

Freeden, M. 1978 *New Liberalism: An Ideology of Social Reform*. Oxford: Clarendon Press.

Freeden, M. 1986 *Liberalism Divided: A Study in British Political Thought 1914– 1939. Oxford: Clarendon Press*.

Friedan, Betty 1965 *The Feminine Mystique*. Harmondsworth: Penguin.

Friedrich C. J. 1972 'The Anarchist Controversy over Violence'. *Zeitschrift fur Politik*, 19.

Friedrich, C. J. and Brzezinski, Z. K. 1966 *Totalitarian Dictatorship and Autocracy*, 2nd edn. New York: Praeger.

Fromm, E. 1979 *To Have or To Be?* London: Abacus, Sphere Books.

Fukuyama, Francis 1989 'The End of History?' *National Interest*, Summer.

Gasset, Ortega y 1972 *The Revolt of the Masses*. London: Allen & Unwin.

Gaus, G. F. 1983 *The Modern Liberal Theory of Man*. London: Croom Helm.

Gay, P. 1952 *The Dilemma of Democratic Socialism*. New York: Columbia University Press.

Gentile, Giovanni 1928 'The Philosophic Basis of Fascism', *Foreign Affairs*, VI, 2.

Gentile, Giovanni 1946 *The Genesis and Structure of Society*, trans. H. S. Harris. Urbana and London: University of Illinois Press, 1960.

Gilligan, Carol 1982 *In a Different Voice*. Cambridge, Mass: Harvard University Press.

Giesey, R. E. and Salmon, J. H. M. 1972 Introduction to F. Hotman, *Francogallia* Cambridge: Cambridge University Press.

Gilmour, I. 1977 *Inside Right: A Study of Conservatism*. London: Quartet.

Gilmour, I. 1983 *Britain Can Work*. Oxford: Martin Robertson.

Godwin, W. 1976 *Enquiry Concerning Political Justice*. Harmondsworth: Penguin.

Goldsmith, E. (edited for *Ecologist*) 1972 *A Blueprint for Survival*. Harmondsworth: Penguin.

Goldsmith, E. and Hildyard, N. (eds) 1986 *Green Britain or Industrial Wasteland*. Oxford: Polity.

Goodway, D. (ed.) 1989 *For Anarchism: History, Theory and Practice*. London: Routledge.

Goodwin, B. 1978 *Social Science and Utopia*. Brighton: Harvester.

Gorz, A. 1982 *Farewell to the Working Class*. London: Pluto.

Graham, D. and Clarke, P. 1986 *The New Enlightenment: The Rebirth of Liberalism*. London: Macmillan.

Graham, G. 1986 *Politics in its Place*. Oxford: Clarendon Press.

Gramsci, A. 1986 *Selections from the Prison Notebooks*. London: Lawrence & Wishart.

Grand, Alexander de 1989 *Italian Fascism: Its Origin and Development*, 2nd edn. Lincoln and London: University of Nebraska Press.

Gray, J. N. 1986a *Liberalism*. Milton Keynes: Open University Press.

Gray, J. N. 1986b *Hayek on Liberty*, 2nd edn. Oxford: Blackwell.

Green, David 1987 *The New Right*. Brighton: Wheatsheaf.

Green, T. H. 1883 *The Prolegomena to Ethics*, ed. A. C. Bradley. Oxford: Clarendon Press.

Green T. H. 1888 *Works of T. H. Green*, vol. 3. London: Longmans.

Greenleaf, W. H. 1966 *Oakeshott's Philosophical Politics*. London: Longmans.

Greenleaf, W. H. 1983 *The British Political Tradition: The Ideological Heritage*, vol. 2. London: Methuen.

Greer, G. 1971 *The Female Eunuch*. London: Paladin.

Gregor, J. A. 1974 *Interpretations of Fascism*. New Jersey: General Learning Press.

Griffin, Susan 1978 *Woman and Nature: The Roaring Inside Her*. London: Women's Press.

Griffiths, R. 1978 'Anti-capitalism and the French Extra-Parliamentary Right, 1870–1940', *Journal of Contemporary History*, 13, 4.

Guérin, D. 1970 *Anarchism*. New York and London: Monthly Review Press.

Haakonssen, Knud (ed.) 1988 *Traditions of Liberalism*. Canberra: Centre for Independent Studies.

Haeckel, E. 1929 *The Riddle of the Universe*, trans. J. McCabe. London: Watts & Co.

Hall, J. A. 1988 *Liberalism*. London: Paladin, Grafton Books.

Hall, S. and Jacques, M. (eds) 1983 *The Politics of Thatcherism*. London: Lawrence & Wishart.

Hallowell, J. H. 1946 *The Decline of Liberalism as an Ideology*. London: Kegan Paul, Trench & Trubner.

Hamilton, Alistair 1971 *The Appeal of Fascism: A Study of Intellectuals and Fascism*. London: Blond.

Hamilton, Malcolm B. 1987 'The Elements of Ideology'. *Political Studies*. XXXV.

Hampsher-Monk, Iain 1987 *The Political Philosophy of Edmund Burke*. London: Longman.

Hardin, G. 1968 'The Tragedy of the Commons'. *Science*, 162.

Hartz, L. 1955 *The Liberal Tradition in America*. New York: Harcourt, Brace & World.

Hawkesworth, M. 1988 'Feminist Rhetoric'. *Political Theory*, 16, 3.

Hayek, F. A. 1944 *The Road to Serfdom*. London: George Routledge & Sons.

Hayek, F. A. 1960 *The Constitution of Liberty*. London: Routledge & Kegan Paul.

Hayek, F. A. 1978 *New Studies on Philosophy, Politics, Economics and the History of Ideas*. London: Routledge & Kegan Paul.

Hayek, F. A. 1982 *Law, Legislation and Liberty*. London: Routledge & Kegan Paul.

Head, B. W. 1980 'The origins of "idéologue" and "idéologie"'. *Studies on Voltaire and the Eighteenth Century*, 183.

Head, B. W. 1985 *Ideology and Social Science: Destutt de Tracy and French Liberalism*. Dordrecht: Martinus Nijhoff.

Hearnshaw, F. J. C. (ed.) 1949 *Social and Political Ideas of Some Representative Thinkers of the Age of Reaction and Reconstruction*. Cambridge: W. Heffer.

Herbert, A. 1978 *The Right and Wrong of Compulsion by the State*. Indianapolis: Liberty Classics.

Hesse M. 1980 *Revolutions and Reconstructions in the Philosophy of Science*. Brighton: Harvester.

Hill, C. 1973 Introduction to Gerard Winstanley's *The Law of Freedom and Other Writings*. Harmondsworth: Penguin.

Hindess, Barry (ed.) 1990 *Reactions to the Right*. London: Routledge.

Hirschman A. O. 1977 *The Passions and the Interests: Political Arguments for Capitalism before its Triumph*. Princeton, NJ: Princeton University Press.

Hitler, Adolf 1939 *Mein Kampf*. London: Hutchinson, 1969.

Hobhouse, L. T. 1911 *Liberalism*. London: Thornton Butterworth.

Hobhouse, L. T. 1918 *The Metaphysical Theory of the State*. London: Allen & Unwin.

Hobsbawm, E. J. 1977 *The Age of Revolution: Europe 1789–1848*. London: Abacus.

Hobson, J. A. 1909 *The Crisis of Liberalism: New Issues of Democracy*. London: P. S. King.

Hobson, S. G. 1920 *National Guilds and the State*. London: George Bell.

Hogg Q. 1947 *The Case for Conservatism*. Harmondsworth: Penguin.

Holton, B. 1976 *British Syndicalism 1900–1914: Myths and Realities*. London: Pluto Press.

Honderich, T. 1991 *Conservatism*. Harmondswroth, Penguin.

Hoover, K. and Plant, R. 1989 *Conservative Capitalism in Britain and the United States*. London and New York: Routledge.

Hulme, T. E. 1965 *Speculations*. London: Routledge & Kegan Paul.

Hülsberg, W. 1988 *The German Greens*. London and New York: Verso.

Humboldt, Wilhelm von 1969 *The Limits of State Action*, originally published in Germany, 1852. Cambridge: Cambridge University Press.

Huntington, S. P. 1957 'Conservatism as an Ideology'. *American Political Science Review*, 51.

Ionescu G. (ed.) 1976 *The Political Thought of Saint-Simon*. Oxford: Oxford University Press.

Irigaray, Luce 1985 *The Sex which is Not One*. New York: Cornell University Press.

Jaggar, Alison 1983 *Feminist Politics and Human Nature*. Brighton: Harvester.

Jay, Martin 1976 *The Dialectical Imagination: A History of the Frankfurt School and the Institute of Social Research 1923–50*. London: Heinemann.

Jennings, J. R. 1985 *George Sorel: The Character and Development of his Thought*. London: Macmillan.

Jennings, J. R. 1990 *Syndicalism in France*. London: Macmillan.

Johnson, C. H. 1974 *Utopian Communism in France: Cabet and the Icarians 1839–1851*. Ithaca, NY: Cornell University Press.

Johnson, S. and Boswell, J. 1978 *A Journey to the Western Islands of Scotland and The Journal of a Tour to the Hebrides*. Oxford: Oxford University Press.

Joll, James 1964 *The Anarchists*. Boston: Little, Brown & Co.

Jung, C. G. 1967 *Memories, Dreams and Reflections*. London: Collins.

Kariel, H. S. 1990 'The Feminist Subject Spinning in the Postmodern Project'. *Political Theory*, 18, 2.

Katz, Eric 1989 'Environmental Ethics: A Selected Annotated Bibliography 1983–1987'. *Research in Philosophy and Technology*, 9.

Keller, Evelyn Fox 1985 *Reflections on Science and Gender*. New Haven, Conn.: Yale University Press.

Kelly, A. 1982 *Mikhail Bakunin: A Study in the Psychology and Politics of Utopianism*. Oxford: Clarendon Press.

Kennedy, R. Emmet 1979 '"Ideology" from Destutt de Tracy to Marx', *Journal of the History of Ideas*, 40.

Keohane, Nannerl O., Rosaldo, M. Z. and Gelpi, B. C. (eds) 1982 *Feminist Theory: A Critique of Ideology*. Brighton: Harvester.

King, D. 1987 *The New Right*. London: Macmillan.

Kirk, R. 1967 *The Conservative Mind*. Chicago: Henry Regnery.

Kirk, R. 1982 *The Portable Conservative Reader*. Harmondsworth: Penguin.

Kitchen, Martin 1976 *Fascism*. London: Macmillan.

Kitching, G. 1983 *Rethinking Socialism*. London: Methuen.

Koenigsberg, Richard A. 1975 *Hitler's Ideology: A Study in Psychoanalytic Sociology*. New York: Library of Social Services.

Kolakowski, L. and Hampshire, S. (eds) 1974 *The Socialist Idea*. London: Weidenfeld & Nicolson.

Kollontai, Alexander 1977 *Selected Writings*. London: Allison & Busby.

Kramnick. M. B. 1985 Introduction to Mary Wollstonecraft, *A Vindication of the Rights of Woman*. Harmondsworth: Penguin.

Kristol, I. 1970 'When virtue loses all her loveliness'. *The Public Interest*. 21.

Kropotkin, P. 1903 *The State: Its Historic Mission*. London: Freedom Press.

Kropotkin, P. 1914 *Mutual Aid: A Factor in Evolution*. Boston: Porter Sargent.

Kropotkin, P. 1968 *The Conquest of Bread*. New York: Benjamin Blom.

Kropotkin, P. 1974 *Fields, Factories and Workshops Tomorrow*. London: Allen & Unwin.

Kuhn, T. S. 1970 *The Structure of Scientific Revolutions*, 2nd edn. Chicago: Chicago University Press.

Kuhn, A. and Wolpe, AnnMarie 1978 *Feminism and Materialism*. London: Routledge & Kegan Paul.

Lakatos, I. and Musgrave, A. 1970 *Criticism and the Growth of Knowledge*. Cambridge: Cambridge University Press.

Landauer, G. 1978 *For Socialism*. St Louis: Telos.

Laqueur, Walter (ed.) 1979 *Fascism: A Reader's Guide*. Harmondsworth: Penguin.

Larrain, Jorge 1979 *The Concept of Ideology*. London: Hutchinson.

Laski, H. J. 1936 *The Rise of European Liberalism*. London: Allen & Unwin.

Lawson, H. 1985 *Reflexivity*. London: Hutchinson.

Lebrun, R. A. 1965 *Throne and Altar*. Ottawa: University of Ottawa Press.

Lenin, V. I. 1988 *What is to be Done?* Harmondsworth: Penguin.

Leopold, Aldo 1968 *A Sand County Almanac*. New York: Oxford University Press.

Levitas, Ruth (ed.) 1986 *The Ideology of the New Right*. Oxford: Polity Press.

Lichtheim, G. 1969 *The Origins of Socialism*. London: Weidenfeld & Nicolson.

Lichtheim, G. 1975 *A Short History of Socialism*. London: Fontana, Collins.

Lipset S. M. 1969 *Political Man*. London: Heinemann.

Lloyd, G. 1984 *The Man of Reason*. London: Methuen.

Lovell, Terry (ed.) 1990 *British Feminist Thought: A Reader*. Oxford: Blackwell.

Lovelock, James 1979 *Gaia*. Oxford: Oxford University Press.

Lowe, P. and Goyder, J. (eds) 1983 *Environmental Groups in Politics*. London: George Allen & Unwin.

Lyotard, Jean-Francois 1984 *The Postmodern Condition*. Minneapolis: University of Minnesota Press.

Lyttelton, Adrian 1987 *The Seizure of Power: Fascism in Italy 1919–1929*, 2nd edn. London: Weidenfeld & Nicolson.

Lyttleton, Adrian (ed.) 1973 *Italian Fascisms: From Pareto to Gentile*. London: Jonathan Cape.

MacCallum, G. 1967 'Negative and Positive Freedom'. *The Philosophical Review*. LXXVI.

MacIntyre, A. 1971 *Against the Self-Images of the Age*. London: Duckworth.

Mack Smith, Dennis 1983 *Mussolini*. London: Paladin Books.

Macmillan, C. 1982 *Women, Reason and Philosophy*. Oxford: Blackwell.

Macmillan, Harold 1966 *The Middle Way*. London: Macmillan.

Macpherson, C. B. 1962 *The Political Theory of Possessive Individualism*. Oxford: Oxford University Press.

Macpherson, C. B. 1973 *Democratic Theory: Essays in Retrieval*. Oxford: Oxford University Press.

Macpherson, C. B. 1980 *Burke*. Oxford: Oxford University Press.

Maistre, Joseph de 1974 *Considerations on France*, originally published 1797. Montreal and London: McGill-Queens University Press.

Malatesta, E. 1980 *Anarchy*. London: Freedom Press.

Malatesta, E. 1984 *Malatesta: His Life and Ideas*. ed. V. Richards. London, Freedom Press.

Mallock. W. H. 1901 *Aristocracy and Evolution*. London: Macmillan.

Mannheim, Karl 1960 *Ideology and Utopia*. London: Routledge & Kegan Paul.

Mannheim, Karl 1986 *Conservatism: A Contribution to the Sociology of Knowledge*. London: Routledge & Kegan Paul.

Manning, D. 1976 *Liberalism*. London: Dent.

Manning, D. (ed.) 1980 *The Form of Ideology*. London: Allen & Unwin.

Manuel, F. E. 1956 *The New World of Henri Saint-Simon*. Cambridge, Mass.: Harvard University Press.

Manuel, F. E. 1962 *The Prophets of Paris*. Cambridge, Mass.: Harvard University Press.

Marcuse, Herbert 1973 *Reason and Revolution*, 2nd edn. London: Routledge & Kegan Paul.

Markham, F. 1964 Introduction to Henri de Saint-Simon, *Social Organization, The Science of Man and Other Writings*. New York: Harper & Row.

Markovic, M. 1982 *Democratic Socialism*. Brighton: Harvester.

Marx, K. 1972 *Early Texts*. Oxford: Blackwell.

Marx, K. and Engels, F. 1967 *The Communist Manifesto*. Harmondsworth: Penguin.

Marx, K. and Engels, F. (eds) 1968 *Selected Writings*. London: Lawrence & Wishart.

Marx, K. and Engels, F. 1970 *The German Ideology*, ed. C. J. Arthur. London: Lawrence & Wishart.

McBriar, A. M. 1962 *Fabian Socialism and English Politics 1884–1918*. Cambridge: Cambridge University Press.

McClelland, J. S. (ed.) 1971 *The French Right: From de Maistre to Maurras*. London: Jonathan Cape.

McCloskey, H. J. 1965–6 'The Problem of Liberalism'. *Review of Metaphysics*, 19.

McLellan, David 1977 *Engels*. London: Fontana, Collins.

McLellan, David 1986 *Ideology*. Milton Keynes: Open University Press.

Meadows, D. 1972 *The Limits to Growth*. London: Earth Island.

Mill, J. S. 1962 *Utilitarianism and Other Essays*. London: Dent.

Mill, J. S. 1989 'The Subjection of Women' and 'Chapters on Socialism', in *On Liberty and Other Writings*, ed. Stefan Collini. Cambridge: Cambridge University Press.

Miller, David 1984 *Anarchism*. London: Dent.

Miller, David 1990 *Market, State and Community: Theoretical Foundations to Market Socialism*. Oxford: Clarendon Press.

Miller, David 1987 'Marx, Communism and Markets'. *Political Theory*, 15, 2.

Miller, S. and Potthoff, H. 1986 *A History of German Social Democracy: From 1848 to the Present*. Leamington Spa and New York: Berg.

Miller Lane, Barbara and Rupp, L. J. (eds) 1978 *Nazi Ideology Before 1933: A Documentation*. Manchester: Manchester University Press.

Millett, K. 1970 *Sexual Politics*. London: Virago.

Minogue, K. 1985 *Alien Powers: The Pure Theory of Ideology*. London: Weidenfeld & Nicholson.

Mitchell, Juliet 1974 *Psychoanalysis and Feminism*. Harmondsworth: Penguin.

Mitchell, Juliet and Oakley, Ann (eds) 1986 *What is Feminism?* Oxford: Blackwell.

Moi, Toril (ed.) 1987 *French Feminist Thought: A Reader*. Oxford: Blackwell.

Morgan K. O. 1975 'Socialism and Syndicalism: The Welsh Miners Debate 1912'. *Bulletin of the Society for the Study of Labour History*, 30.

Morton, A. L. 1962 *The Life and Ideas of Robert Owen*. London: Lawrence & Wishart.

Mosse, G. L. 1966 *The Crisis of German Ideology: Intellectual Origins of the Third Reich*. London: Weidenfeld & Nicolson.

Mosse, G. L. 1978 *Nazism: A Historical and Comparative Analysis of National Socialism*. Oxford: Blackwell.

Muirhead, J. H. 1954 *Coleridge as Philosopher*. London: Allen & Unwin.

Mussolini, Benito 1932 'The Doctrine of Fascism' in *Enciclopedia Italiana*, reprinted in Michael Oakeshott (ed.) *The Social and Political Doctrines of Contemporary Europe*, originally published 1939. Cambridge: Cambridge University Press, 1953.

Naess, A. 1973 'The Shallow and the Deep, Long-range Ecology Movement. A. Summary'. *Inquiry*, 16.

Naess, A. 1989 *Ecology, Community and Lifestyle*. Cambridge: Cambridge University Press.

Neumann, F. L. 1942 *Behemoth: The Structure and Practice of National Socialism*. London: Gollancz.

Nisbet, R. A. 1970 *The Sociological Tradition*. London: Heinemann.

Nisbet, R. A. 1986 *Conservatism*. Milton Keynes: Open University Press.
Noble, D. 1978 'Conservatism in the USA'. *Journal of Contemporary History*, 13, 4.
Nock, Albert Jay 1946 *Our Enemy the State*. Caldwell, Idaho: Caxton.
Nolte, Ernst 1969 *Three Faces of Fascism: Action Française, Italian Fascism and National Socialism*. New York: Mentor Books.
Norton, P. and Aughey, A. 1981 *Conservatives and Conservatism*. London: Temple Smith.
Nove, A. 1983 *The Economics of Feasible Socialism*. London: Allen & Unwin.
Nozick, R. 1974 *Anarchy State and Utopia*. Oxford: Blackwell.
Nye, Andrea 1989 *Feminist Theory and the Philosophies of Man*. London and New York: Routledge.
O'Gorman, F. 1973 *Edmund Burke: His Political Philosophy*. London: Allen & Unwin.
O'Gorman, F. (ed.) 1986 *British Conservatism: Conservative Thought from Burke to Thatcher*. London: Longman.
O'Sullivan, N. 1976 *Conservatism*. London: Dent.
O'Sullivan, N. 1983 *Fascism*. London: Dent.
Oakeshott, Michael (ed.) 1953 *The Social and Political Doctrines of Contemporary Europe*. Cambridge: Cambridge University Press.
Oakeshott, Michael 1962 *Rationalism in Politics and Other Essays*. London and New York: Methuen.
Oelschlaeger, Max 1991 *The Idea of Wilderness*. New Haven, Conn.: Yale University Press.
Okin, S. M. 1979 *Women in Western Political Thought*. Princeton, NJ: Princeton University Press.
Okin, S. M. 1989 *Justice, Gender, and the Family*. New York: Basic Books.
Ophuls, William 1977 *Ecology and the Politics of Scarcity: Prologue to a Political Theory of the Steady State*. San Francisco: W. H. Freeman.
Organski, A. F. 1969 *The Stages of Political Development*. New York: Alfred A. Knopf.
Parekh, B. (ed.) 1975 *The Concept of Socialism*. London: Croom Helm.
Parekh, B. 1983 *Marx's Theory of Ideology*. London: Macmillan.
Parel, Anthony (ed.) 1983 *Ideology, Philosophy and Politics*. Waterloo, Ontario: Wilfrid Laurier Press.
Pateman, C. 1988 *The Sexual Contract*. Oxford: Polity Press.
Pateman, C. 1989 *The Disorder of Women*. Oxford: Polity Press.
Patterson, R. W. K. 1971 *The Nihilist Egoist: Max Stirner*. Oxford: Oxford University Press.
Paul, E. F., Miller, F. D., and Paul, J. (eds) 1989 *Socialism*. Oxford: Blackwell.
Pearce, D., Markandya, A., and Barbier, E. B. 1989 *Blueprint for a Green Economy*. London: Earthscan.
Pearson, R. and Williams, G. 1984 *Political Thought and Public Policy in the Nineteenth Century*. London: Longman.
Pennock, J. R. and Chapman, J. W. (eds) 1978 *Anarchism: Nomos XIX*. New York: New York University Press.
Penty, A. J. 1906 *The Restoration of the Guild System*. London: Swan Sonnenschein.
Pepper, David 1984 *The Roots of Modern Environmentalism*. London: Croom Helm.
Perlin, T. M. (ed.) 1979 *Contemporary Anarchism*. New Jersey: Transaction Books.
Pilgrim, J. 1965 'Anarchism and Stateless Societies'. *Anarchy*, 58.
Pilkington, A. E. 1976 *Bergson and His Influence: A Reassessment*. Cambridge:

Cambridge University Press.

Pimlott, B. (ed.) 1984 *Fabian Essays in Socialist Thought.* London: Heinemann.

Pirages, D. (ed.) 1977 *The Sustainable Society: Implications for Limited Growth.* New York and London: Praeger.

Plamenatz, J. 1971 *Ideology.* London: Macmillan.

Plant, R. 1974 *Community and Ideology.* London: Routledge & Kegan Paul.

Plant R. 1984 *Equality, Markets and the State,* Fabian Tract 494. London: Fabian Society.

Pocock, J. G. A. 1973 *Politics, Language and Time: Essays on Political Thought and History.* London: Methuen.

Pocock, J. G. A. 1985 *Virtue, Commerce, and History.* Cambridge: Cambridge University Press.

Pois Robert 1986 *National Socialism and the Religion of Nature.* London: Croom Helm.

Popper, Karl 1945 *The Open Society and its Enemies.* London: Routledge & Kegan Paul.

Porritt, J. 1984 *Seeing Green: The Politics of Ecology Explained.* Oxford: Blackwell.

Porritt, J. and Winner, D. 1988 *The Coming of the Greens.* London: Fontana, Collins.

Primo de Rivera, José Antonio 1972 *Selected Writings.* ed. Hugh Thomas. London: Jonathan Cape.

Proudhon, Pierre-Joseph 1970a *What is Property?* New York: Dover.

Proudhon, Pierre-Joseph 1970b *Selected Writings.* ed. Stewart Edwards. London: Macmillan.

Proudhon, Pierre-Joseph 1989 *General Idea of Revolution in the Nineteenth Century.* London: Pluto Press.

Pugh, M. 1982 *The Making of Modern British Politics.* Oxford: Blackwell.

Puhle, Hans-Jürgen 1978 'Conservatism in Modern German History'. *Journal of Contemporary History,* 13, 4.

Pulzer, P. G. J. 1964 *The Rise of Political Anti-Semitism in Germany and Austria.* New York: Wiley.

Quinton, A. 1978 *The Politics of Imperfection.* London: Faber & Faber.

Radcliffe-Richards, J. 1982 *The Sceptical Feminist: A Philosophical Enquiry.* Harmondsworth: Penguin.

Rand, Ayn 1964 *The Virtue of Selfishness: A New Concept of Egoism.* New York: Signet Books, New American Library.

Randall, Vicky 1991 'Feminism and Political Analysis'. *Political Studies,* XXXIX, 3.

Rauschning, H. 1939 *The Revolution of Nihilism: A Warning to the West.* New York: Longmans Green & Co.

Rawls, J. 1970 *A Theory of Justice.* Oxford: Oxford University Press.

Regan, T. 1983 *The Case for Animal Rights.* London: Routledge & Kegan Paul.

Reich, Wilhelm 1975 *The Mass Psychology of Fascism.* Harmondsworth: Penguin.

Reiss, H. (ed.) 1955 *The Political Thought of the German Romantics.* Oxford: Blackwell.

Riasanovsky, N. V. 1969 *The Teaching of Charles Fourier.* Berkeley: University of California Press.

Rich, A. 1976 *Of Woman Born.* New York: W. W. Norton.

Richards, Vernon (ed.) 1984 *Errico Malatesta: His Life and Ideas.* London: Freedom Press.

Ricoeur, Paul 1986 *Lectures on Ideology and Utopia,* ed. G. H. Taylor. New York: Columbia University Press.

Ritchie, D. G. 1902 *The Principles of State Interference*. London: Swan Sonnenschein.
Ritchie, D. G. 1903 *Natural Rights*. London: Swan Sonnenschein.
Ritter, Alan 1980 *Anarchism: A Theoretical Analysis*. Cambridge: Cambridge University Press.
Roberts David 1979, *The Syndicalist Tradition and Italian Fascism*. Manchester: Manchester University Press.
Robertson, James 1983 *The Sane Alternative*. Cholsey: Turning Point, The Old Bakehouse, private printing.
Robertson, James 1985 *Future Work*. Gower: Temple Smith.
Rocco, Alfredo (n.d.) 'The Political Doctrine of Fascism' in *Reading on Fascism and National Socialism* (selected by Members of the Philosophy Department of the University of Colorado). Denver: Alan Swallow.
Rocker, Rudolf 1989 *Anarcho-Syndicalism*. London: Pluto Press.
Rodman, J. R. 1983 'Four Forms of Ecological Consciousness Reconsidered' in Scherer and Attig (eds), *Ethics and the Environment*. New Jersey: Prentice Hall.
Rolston III, Holmes 1988 *Environmental Ethics: Duties to and Values in the Natural World*. Philadephia: Temple University Press.
Rosenberg, Alfred 1971 *Selected Writings*. ed. Robert Pois. London: Jonathan Cape.
Rossiter, C. 1982 *Conservatism in America*. Cambridge, Mass.: Harvard University Press.
Rothbard, Murray 1978 *For A New Liberty: The Libertarian Manifesto*. New York: Collier Macmillan.
Rowbotham, Sheila 1972 *Women, Resistance and Revolution: A History of Women and Revolution in the Modern World*. New York: Random House.
Ruddick, S. 1980 'Maternal Thinking'. *Feminist Studies*, 6, 2.
Ruggiero, Guido de 1927 *The History of European Liberalism*. Oxford: Oxford University Press.
Russell, Peter 1982 *The Awakening Earth: The Global Brain*. London: Ark.
Ryle, Martin 1988 *Ecology and Socialism*. London: Radius.
Saint-Simon, Henri de 1964 *Social Organization, The Science of Man and Other Writings*. New York and Evanston: Harper & Row.
Sale, Kirkpatrick 1985 *Dwellers in the Land: the Bioregional Vision*. San Francisco: Sierra Book Club.
Samuel, H. 1902 *Liberalism: An Attempt to State the Principles of Contemporary Liberalism*. London: Grant Richards.
Samuel, H. 1945 *Memoirs*. London: Cresset.
Sandel, M. 1982 *Liberalism and the Limits of Justice*. Cambridge: Cambridge University Press.
Sandel, M. (ed.) 1984 *Liberalism and its Critics*. Oxford: Blackwell.
Sargent, Lydia (ed.) 1986 *The Unhappy Marriage of Marxism and Feminism: A Debate on Class and Patriarchy*. London: Pluto Press.
Scherer, D. and Attig. T. (eds) 1983 *Ethics and the Environment*. New Jersey: Prentice Hall.
Schmitt, Carl 1985 *The Crisis of Parliamentary Democracy*. originally published 1923. Cambridge, Mass.: MIT Press.
Schochet, G. 1975 *Patriarchalism in Political Thought*. Oxford: Blackwell.
Schuettinger, R. L. (ed.) 1976 *The Conservative Tradition in European Thought*. New York: G. P. Putnam.
Schumacher, E. F. 1973 *Small is Beautiful*. London: Sphere Books.
Schwartz, B. 1951 *Chinese Communism and the Rise of Mao*. Cambridge, Mass.: Harvard University Press.

Schwarz, W. and D. 1987 *Breaking Through: The Theory and Practice of Wholistic Living*. Bideford: Green Books.

Scott, J. W. 1919 *Syndicalism and Philosophical Realism*. London: A. & C. Black.

Scruton, R. 1980 *The Meaning of Conservatism*. Harmondsworth: Penguin.

Seliger, Martin 1976 *Ideology and Politics*. London: Allen & Unwin.

Seliger, Martin 1979 *The Marxist Conception of Ideology*. Cambridge: Cambridge University Press.

Shaw, G. B. (ed.) 1931 *Fabian Essays in Socialism*. London: The Fabian Society and Allen & Unwin.

Sheehan, James 1978 *German Liberalism in the Nineteenth Century*. London: Methuen.

Shils, Edward 1955 'The End of Ideology'. *Encounter*, November.

Shils, Edward 1968 'The Concept and Function of Ideology'. *International Encylopaedia of the Social Sciences*, vol. VII.

Sidgwick, H. 1897 *The Elements of Politics*. London: Macmillan.

Silverman, H. J. (ed.) 1990 *Postmodernism – Philosophy and the Arts*. London: Routledge.

Simon, R. 1991 *Gramsci's Political Thought*, rev. edn. London: Lawrence & Wishart.

Singer, Peter 1983 *The Expanding Circle: Ethics and Sociobiology*. Oxford: Oxford University Press.

Skidelsky, Robert 1975 *Oswald Mosley*. London: Macmillan.

Skinner, Q. 1978 *The Foundations of Modern Political Thought*, in 2 vols. Cambridge: Cambridge University Press.

Smith, Paul 1967 *Disraelian Conservatism and Social Reform*. London: Routledge & Kegan Paul.

Smith, Paul 1972 *Lord Salisbury on Politics*. Cambridge: Cambridge University Press.

Sorel, G. 1975 *Reflections on Violence*. London and New York: Collier Macmillan.

Soucy, Robert 1972 *Fascism in France: The Case of Maurice Barrès*. Berkeley and London: University of California Press.

Soucy, Robert 1979 *Fascist Intellectual: Drieu de Rochelle*. Berkeley and London: University of California Press.

Soucy, Robert 1986 *French Fascism: The First Wave (1924–1933)*. New Haven, Conn. and London: Yale University Press.

Spencer, H. 1884 *The Man Versus the State*, republished in 1940. London: Watts & Co.

Spender, Dale 1980 *Man-Made Language*. London: Routledge.

Spender, Dale 1983 *Women of Ideas and what Men have done to Them*. London: Routledge.

Spretnak, C. and Capra, F. 1986 *Green Politics: The Global Promise*. London: Paladin, Collins.

Stanlis, P. 1958 *Edmund Burke and the Natural Law*. Ann Arbor: Michigan University Press.

Stein, J. W. 1956 'Beginnings of "Ideology"'. *South Atlantic Quarterly*, 55.

Stern, Fritz 1974 *The Politics of Cultural Despair: A Study in the Rise of Germanic Ideology*. Berkeley: University of California Press.

Stirner, Max 1971 *The Ego and His Own*, ed. John Carroll. London: Jonathan Cape.

Sylvan, R. 1984/5 'A Critique of Deep Ecology'. *Radical Philosophy*, in two parts, 40 and 41.

Sylvester, C. 1990 'The Emperor's Theories and Transformations: Looking at the Field through Feminist Lenses' in C. Sylvester and D. Pirages (eds), *Transformations in the Global Economy*. London: Macmillan.

Talmon, J. L. 1952 *The Origins of Totalitarian Democracy*. London: Secker & Warburg.

Tännsjö, Torbjörn 1990 *Conservatism for our Time*. London and New York: Routledge.

Tawney, R. H. 1921 *The Acquisitive Society*. London: George Bell.

Tawney, R. H. 1964 *Equality*. London: Allen & Unwin.

Taylor, B. 1983 *Eve and the New Jerusalem: Socialism and Feminism in the Nineteenth Century*. New York: Pantheon Books.

Taylor, M. 1982 *Community, Anarchy and Liberty*. Cambridge: Cambridge University Press.

Taylor, Paul W. 1986 *Respect for Nature: A Theory of Environmental Ethics*. Princeton, NJ: Princeton University Press.

Terrill, Ross 1974 *R. H. Tawney and His Times: Socialism as Fellowship*. London: André Deutsch.

Thomas, Paul 1980 *Karl Marx and the Anarchists*. London: Routledge & Kegan Paul.

Thompson, J. B. 1984 *Studies in the Theory of Ideology*. Oxford: Polity Press.

Thompson, W. 1824 *An Inquiry into the Principles of the Distribution of Wealth most conducive to Human Happiness*, republished 1963. New York: Augustus M. Kelley.

Tokar, B. 1987 *The Green Alternative: Creating an Ecological Future*. San Pedro: R. & E. Miles.

Tolstoy, Leo 1974 *The Kingdom of God and Peace Essays*. Oxford: Oxford University Press.

Tomalin, C. 1974 *The Life and Death of Mary Wollstonecraft*. London: Weidenfeld & Nicolson.

Tong, R. 1989 *Feminist Thought*. London: Unwin Hyman.

Trevor Roper, Hugh 1947 *The Last Days of Hitler*. London: Macmillan.

Tudor, H. and Tudor, J. M. (eds) 1988 *Marxism and Social Democracy*. Cambridge: Cambridge University Press.

Turner, C. (ed.) 1979 *The Case for Private Enterprise*. London: Bachman & Turner.

Turner, H. A. (ed.) 1975 *Reappraisals of Fascism*. New York: New Viewpoints.

Vernon, R. 1986 *Citizenship and Order: Studies in French Political Thought*. Toronto: Toronto University Press.

Viereck, Peter 1950 *Conservatism Revisited: The Revolt against Revolt 1815–1949*. London: John Lehmann.

Vincent, Andrew (ed.) 1986 *The Philosophy of T. H. Green*. Aldershot: Gower.

Vincent, Andrew 1987 *Theories of the State*. Oxford: Blackwell.

Vincent, Andrew 1990a 'Classical Liberalism and Its Crisis of Identity'. *History of Political Thought*, XI, 1.

Vincent, Andrew 1990b 'The New Liberalism in Britain 1880–1914'. *Australian Journal of Politics and History*, 36, 3.

Vincent, Andrew and Plant, R. 1984 *Philosophy, Politics and Citizenship: The Life and Thought of the British Idealists*. Oxford: Blackwell.

Waldegrave, W. 1978 *The Binding of Leviathan: Conservatism and the Future*. London: Hamish Hamilton.

Ward, Colin 1973 *Anarchy in Action*. London: Allen & Unwin.

Ward, B. and Dubos, R. 1972 *Only One Earth: The Care and Maintenance of a Small Planet*. Harmondsworth: Penguin.

Waxman, Chaim (ed.) 1968 *The End of Ideology Debate*. New York: Funk & Wagnells.

Webb, B. 1926 *My Apprenticeship*. London: Longmans.

Webb, B. 1948 *Our Partnership* London: Longmans.

Weber, Eugene 1964 *Varieties of Fascism*. London: Van Nostrand.

Weiss, H. J. 1967 *The Fascist Tradition: Radical Right-Wing Extremism in Modern Europe*. New York: Harper & Row.

Weston, Joe (ed.) 1986 *Red and Green: A New Politics of the Environment*. London: Pluto Press.

White Jnr, Lynn 1971 'The Historical Roots of our Ecological Crisis', originally published 1967, reprinted in John Barr (ed.) *The Environment Handbook*. London: Ballantine and Friends of the Earth.

Williams, H. 1983 *Kant's Political Philosophy*. Oxford: Blackwell.

Williams, H. 1988 *Concepts of Ideology*. Sussex: Wheatsheaf Books.

Williams, Raymond 1961 *The Long Revolution*. London: Chatto & Windus.

Wiltshire, D. 1978 *The Social and Political Thought of Herbert Spencer*. Oxford: Clarendon Press.

Wolfe, W. 1975 *From Radicalism to Socialism*. New Haven, Conn.: Yale University Press.

Wolff, R. P. 1970 *In Defense of Anarchism*. New York: Harper & Row.

Wolin, S. 1954 'Hume and Conservatism'. *American Political Science Review*, 48, 4.

Wollstonecraft, M. 1985 *A Vindication of the Rights of Woman*, originally published 1792. Harmondsworth: Penguin.

Wood, Allan 1979 'Marx on Rights and Justice'. *Philosophy and Public Affairs*, 8, 3.

Woodcock, G. 1972 *Pierre-Joseph Proudhon: His Life and Work*. New York: Schocken Books.

Woodcock, G. 1975 *Anarchism*. Harmondsworth: Penguin.

Woolf, S. J. (ed.) 1968 *European Fascism*. London: Weidenfeld & Nicolson.

Woolf, Virginia 1929 *A Room of One's Own*. London: Hogarth Press.

Worster, D. 1977 *Nature's Economy: The Roots of Ecology*. San Francisco: Sierra Book Club.

Wright, A. W. 1979 *G. D. H. Cole and Socialist Democracy*. Oxford: Clarendon Press.

Wright, A. W. 1983 *British Socialism*. London: Longman.

Wright, A. W. 1987 *Socialisms*. Oxford and New York: Oxford University Press.

Yearley, S. 1991 *The Green Case: A Sociology of Environmental Issues, Arguments and Politics*. London: Harper Collins Academic.

Zalewski, M. 1991 'The Debauching of Feminist Theory/The Penetration of the Postmodern'. *Politics*, 11, 1.

INDEX

—

Wright, A. W., 99, 253, 254

Yearley, S., 270, 274, 277

Zalewski, M., 266, 270
Zetkin, Clara, 183, 184
Zola, E., 114